# MISADVENTURES OF THE MOST FAVORED NATIONS

ALSO BY PAUL BLUSTEIN

*The Chastening*

*And the Money Kept Rolling In (And Out)*

# MISADVENTURES OF THE MOST FAVORED NATIONS

Clashing Egos,
Inflated Ambitions,
and the Great Shambles
of the World Trade System

## PAUL BLUSTEIN

**PUBLIC**AFFAIRS
New York

PublicAffairs books are available at special discounts for bulk purchases in the
U.S. by corporations, institutions, and other organizations. For more information,
please contact the Special Markets Department at the Perseus Books Group, 2300
Chestnut Street, Suite 200, Philadelphia, PA 19103, call (800) 810–4145, ext.
5000, or e-mail special.markets@perseusbooks.com.

Designed by Brent Wilcox
Text set in 10.75 point Simoncini Garamond

Library of Congress Cataloging-in-Publication Data
Blustein, Paul.
    Misadventures of the most favored nations / Paul Blustein.—1st ed.
        p.    cm.
    Includes bibliographical references and index.
    ISBN 978–1-58648–718–8 (hbk. : alk. paper)
    1. World Trade Organization.   2. International trade.   3. Commercial treaties.
4. International economic relations.   I. Title.
HF1385.B58 2009
382'.92—dc22

                                                                    2009014881

First Edition

10 9 8 7 6 5 4 3 2 1

*To Yoshie*

# CONTENTS

AUTHOR'S NOTE AND ACKNOWLEDGMENTS  ix

1 | Paging Mr. Black  1

2 | The Intergalactic Trade Organization  17

3 | The WTO and Its Discontents  41

4 | Clueless in Seattle  57

5 | "There Are Only A-Pluses"  83

6 | Removing the Stain  109

7 | The Uprising of the Rest  131

8 | Jewels and Pirates  157

9 | His Holiness, Pope Bob  173

10 | One Chicken McNugget  199

11 | When Peter Met Susan  223

12 | Even the Loopholes Have Got Loopholes  247

13 | Losing It  261

14 | If Only There Were a Better Way  277

NOTES  297
INDEX  327

# AUTHOR'S NOTE AND ACKNOWLEDGMENTS

Having written two books about the International Monetary Fund, and now this one about the World Trade Organization, I suppose I can lay claim to being the world's foremost author of behind-the-scenes accounts about vaguely sinister international economic institutions with three initials. This specialty, I'll admit, is an acquired taste. But in the process of covering trade as part of my beat at the *Washington Post*, I became increasingly convinced that the WTO, like the IMF, is a tremendously important institution deserving of thorough journalistic dissection, and that behind the Doha Round's ups and downs lay many dramas of both individual and collective significance. In addition, I realized that the WTO offers an ideal prism through which to illuminate many of the pluses and minuses of globalization, as the trade body is arguably the most essential element in the glue that holds the globalized economy together. So when the *Post* offered a generous buyout in 2006 to senior staff members, I accepted and began work on this book as journalist in residence in the Global Economy and Development Program at the Brookings Institution, at the gracious invitation of Lael Brainard, the program's director.

Except for Antarctica, which has yet to emerge as a major power in the WTO, I traveled to all the world's continents in the process of gathering material for the book. Along the way, I benefited enormously from the kindness of friends, strangers, and sources who helped make my journeys both productive and memorable.

A few examples: In my efforts to gain the perspective of French farmers, I stayed with my old friend Blair Pethel, who has chucked journalism to start a new and amazing life as a vintner in Burgundy. Not only did Blair put me up at his wondrous seventeenth-century home in the town of Beaune, but he also arranged interviews with his farmer neighbors and interpreted for me as well.

To glean insight into the background of Kamal Nath, the Indian trade minister, I hitched a ride on Nath's private jet on a weekend visit to the impoverished district that he represents in Parliament, where we flew around to villages on his helicopter and where—in perhaps the most unforgettable experience related to my research—I was nearly squished several times amid mobs of his frenzied constituents. In Livingstone, Zambia, where I ventured in search of an example of how developing-country businesses are often frustrated by logistical problems in global markets, Ron Parbhoo sacrificed his usual Sunday golf outing to meet me for an interview on the banks of the Zambezi River, with clouds of mist from Victoria Falls rising nearby. And Anastasia Carayanides and Chelsey Martin of the Australian embassy in Washington arranged my inclusion in Australia's International Media Visitors' Program, a tour of the country for groups of journalists, which enabled me to meet Australian policymakers whom I needed to interview as well as some Asia-Pacific trade officials at a meeting in Cairns. As a rule I don't accept such government-financed trips, but I felt comfortable making an exception for the Aussies. Although centrally involved in key WTO negotiations, Australian officials did not figure to be prominent targets of either praise or blame in this book.

When I embarked on the project, I already had some material in my files from my coverage of a few WTO meetings and from stories I had written about various trade-related controversies. But gathering the information that constitutes the core of the book required interviews with more than 150 people, including current and former officials of the WTO Secretariat, current and former trade negotiators from numerous WTO member governments, business lobbyists, congressional staffers, and representatives of nongovernmental organizations. I also interviewed dozens of farmers, workers, and businesspeople in various countries to help illustrate abstract concepts and complex trade issues with real-life examples.

My profound thanks go to all those who took the time to help make my book as accurate and comprehensive as possible, especially the substantial number of people who endured multiple interviews and follow-up questions. In this regard I owe special acknowledgement to Keith Rockwell, the WTO's spokesman, for facilitating interviews with many of his colleagues in Geneva and encouraging them to be open with me. During the course of this project, Keith became a great friend.

With a few exceptions, "deep background" rules applied to the interviews conducted with policymakers, negotiators, and other sources knowledgeable about key events, which meant I could use the information but could not quote interviewees or cite them as sources unless granted permission to do so. Many sources were understandably reluctant to be quoted on sensitive matters, in part because some of the top policymakers involved continue to hold important jobs. To the greatest extent possible, I have attributed quotes by name, but I trust readers will understand that in certain cases this proved infeasible, and I hope they can accept my assurances that unattributed material has been carefully researched and checked. I obviously had to remain vigilant against accepting self-serving accounts of events, and I sought to cross-check information with as many sources as possible.

A list of interviewees appears in the "Notes" section at the end of the book, including those who were quoted on the record plus those who were interviewed on deep background and who later granted permission to be listed as sources for the book.

A number of interviewees shared notes of key meetings in which they had participated—sometimes by letting me sift through their notes myself, sometimes by laboriously reading through their scribblings that they knew only they could decipher. I am immensely grateful to these people, who for obvious reasons shall not be named, for enabling me to write a much more authoritative narrative. They recognized that, given a decent interval between the publication of the book and the events in question, little harm would result from their disclosure of this information, and that the cause of historical accuracy would be well served by my being able to rely on contemporaneous records rather than the hazy and sometimes selective memories of interested parties. For the most part, when people are quoted as saying things in closed-door meetings, their words come directly from notes taken by participants, unless otherwise specified in the narrative or in the "Notes" section. On a couple of occasions, I have simply quoted people as having said things based on information gleaned from interviews, because the memories of those who were present are so vivid and the information has been corroborated by other sources. But in general, when I didn't have notes, transcripts, memos, or other contemporaneous sources of information, I paraphrased what people said rather than put their remarks in quotes.

Being a U.S. citizen based in Washington, I wanted to make sure I got a fair and balanced picture of the events I was chronicling from sources other than the American trade negotiators who were close at hand. That was the main reason for my extensive travels, which in addition to France, India, Zambia, and Australia included Brazil, South Africa, Beijing, Tokyo, Brussels, Amsterdam, London—and, of course, several visits to Geneva. Although space limitations prevent me from providing details, I wish also to thank the following people for skilled assistance and assorted acts of warmheartedness concerning the international portion of my research: Sukhmani Singh, Inderjit Singh Jaijee, Karuna Javaji, Mitra Kalita, Ch. Sathyam, Ameet Nivsarkar, Sudhanva Sundararaman, Col. S. V. Ramachandran, Ed Luce, Bart Fisher, Cora Wong, Brian Wu, Joe Nkole, Tim Carrington, Bob Liebenthal, John Fynn, Paulo Sotero, Cristiano Romero, Gabriela Antunes, Alessandro Prieto, Pedro de Camargo Neto, Andréa Ferrari, Elza Sapucaia, George Firmeza, Ron Sandrey, Nick Vink, Mohammad Karaan, Jayne Ferguson, Jane Smith, Neil Smail, and Darrell Morris.

My decision to join Brookings' Global Economy and Development Program was a stroke of good fortune. Lael Brainard made generous provisions for my accommodation at Brookings and also offered wise counsel about how I should approach the book. Her staff, including Raji Jagadeesan, Anne Smith, Ann DeFabio Doyle, Sun Kordel, Amy Wong, and Yamillett Fuentes provided extremely helpful support in their varied areas of expertise. My colleagues in "Global" have been a pleasure to work with, and Brookings has been a terrifically stimulating and nurturing environment.

Friends in journalism often ask how I'm financially able to do books on these sorts of topics, given that my prospects of hitting the best-seller lists or garnering a movie contract are, shall we say, tenuous. The answer is that I couldn't possibly manage without the beneficence of foundations whose aims include informing the public debate on issues of global import. The Smith Richardson Foundation, which provided funding for both my previous books, bestowed hugely welcome support on this one too, as did the William and Flora Hewlett Foundation. I want to express my profound gratitude to both these foundations, especially to Allan Song at Smith Richardson and to Ann Tutwiler, who shepherded my project at Hewlett before moving on to join the Obama administration. Al once again came through with incisive advice when I was drawing up my proposal, which greatly aided in focusing my approach to the whole subject. Ann, who is an expert in trade, agriculture, and development, provided very helpful guidance throughout the project on issues large and small. In the final months, I was obliged to solicit extra funding because the Doha Round negotiations were dragging on much longer than I had expected at the outset, and at that point Hewlett provided a supplemental grant, together with the German Marshall Fund (GMF) of the United States, making it possible for me to finish the book properly. To Joe Guinan, Nicola Lightner, and their colleagues at GMF, I am also deeply appreciative, not only for the grant but for many insights that helped me get my arms around the material.

I. M. "Mac" Destler, whose *American Trade Politics* sets an impossibly high bar for anyone else seeking to write on the history of trade, read several of my early chapters and helped me avoid making embarrassing goofs in print. Having said that, I am of course responsible for any errors and omissions that remain. A number of other academics and trade lawyers with whom I consulted are included in the list of interviewees. I would be remiss in failing also to mention several people who assisted me in other ways at various points, including Eric Schnapper, Jason Sykes, Daniel Pruzin, Philippe Ries, Jerry Hagstrom, Ann Hornaday, and Laine Kaplowitz.

Is there a book editor in the entire world who has a more pleasant way than Clive Priddle does of inducing an author to make major improvements in a manuscript that has been slaved over? I can't imagine that there is. Clive, who edited one of my previous books, was the main reason I once again sought out PublicAffairs as my publisher; I'm very glad I did, because I need editing that is both strong and congenial, and from Clive that's exactly what I got. Kathy Delfosse did a masterful job of copyediting, coming up with elegant wording that I hadn't been able to generate on my own for many difficult passages. And Tom Wells meticulously produced the index. It has been an honor to have my work included in the "good books about things that matter" that PublicAffairs publishes, and for that I salute all my friends at PublicAffairs, who also include publisher Susan Weinberg, founder and editor-at-large Peter Osnos, managing editor Melissa Raymond, publicist Tessa Shanks, and assistant editor Niki Papadopoulos.

Finally, family matters: I thank my daughter, Nina, for going on her junior year abroad to Bologna, and my son, Nathan, for doing the same in Vienna, because that gave me extra incentive to fly to Geneva for research, happy in the knowledge that I could combine my trips with visits to my sorely missed offspring. I also thank sons Dan and Jack, now eight and six, respectively, for taking good care of their mother during my travels. Which, of course, brings me to the subject of my wife, Yoshie: When one works as hard and as long on something as I have on this book, especially given the extended absences it entailed, one obviously builds up a substantial amount of debt to one's partner in life. Dedicating this book to Yoshie is a small token of recognition for that, and of my appreciation for many other things besides. As she well knows, though, her support and sacrifices are just a part of why she means so much to me.

# 1 | PAGING MR. BLACK

THE POSSIBILITY OF DYING AT THE HANDS OF TERRORISTS WAS WEIGHING heavily on the three dozen passengers from the U.S. government who were flying to Doha, Qatar, on November 7, 2001, for a meeting of the World Trade Organization (WTO). Less than two months had passed since the September 11 attacks on New York and Washington, D.C., and nerves were also jangling as a result of the anthrax spores sent by mail that had killed U.S. postal workers a few weeks earlier. Most of the passengers were employees of the Office of the U.S. Trade Representative, and they were unaccustomed to traveling in such luxury—the plane bearing them to Qatar was a government jet usually reserved for VIPs such as the secretary of state or secretary of defense, with plush seats and a special private area for a cabinet officer, who in this case was Robert Zoellick, the trade representative. But these were extraordinary circumstances; Zoellick and his team were flying into a war zone, which is what the Middle East had suddenly become, because combat in Afghanistan had recently gotten under way.

Many of their colleagues, offered the chance beforehand to stay home if they wished, had decided against attending the WTO meeting. The WTO had leaped to prominence two years earlier when its previous major meeting, in Seattle, Washington, was disrupted by fierce antiglobalization protests; fears abounded that the Doha meeting would offer an irresistible target for Muslim fanatics. Confidential briefings that U.S. trade officials received in Washington, D.C., about the potential threats in Qatar caused some to become so frightened that they walked out of the briefings in tears. Security experts conducting the briefings told the participants that although every possible precaution would be taken to protect the meeting, information received from intelligence sources indicated that a skilled al Qaeda truck bomber was at large in Qatar. The security officers also warned that they were worried about shoulder-fired missiles being used to down the planes carrying trade negotiators to the Persian Gulf emirate. Many of the U.S. trade officials who decided to go to Doha adopted a fatalistic attitude. "I remember thinking, in the days before leaving home, maybe this would be it. Maybe I'd be killed," says Joseph Papovich, who was an assistant trade representative.

Looking out the plane's windows as they neared Qatar, the officials were unnerved to see U.S. military fighters flying alongside, and that was nothing compared to the scare they got upon landing. Only about half an hour before they touched down, a gunman with an AK-47 and body armor had attacked the Qatari military base where they were arriving, which was used by U.S. warplanes. Although the gunman had been killed—and Qatari authorities would later dismiss him as a mentally unstable loner—the security forces on the ground were unsure at the time whether he had been acting in concert with others or whether additional attacks were imminent. So the plane's passengers were quickly herded into buses. There, they were informed of the incident by blustery, drill-sergeant-like security officers, who instructed them about what would happen if the buses came under assault on the way to the hotel: Another bus would pull alongside, and the passengers would crawl on the floor to the door, leaving all briefcases behind, and board the second bus as quickly as possible.

"If I say 'down,' you will get down!" bellowed a security man to the dazed trade officials in one of the buses. "Everyone tight with that?"

"Yeah," one of the passengers was heard to mutter. "Sphincter tight." On the long ride to the hotel in the capital city of Doha, recalls Jeffrey Bader, another of the trade officials, "there was dead silence, the entire drive in. Just dead silence."

Besides the group from the U.S. government, many of the other participants in the WTO meeting—2,600 official delegates, 800 journalists, and 400 representatives of business and nongovernmental organizations (NGOs)—were also girding for danger in Doha. Japan was sending a medical team for its trade negotiators, and Taiwan was providing its thirty-three-member delegation with gas masks and antibiotics to combat anthrax. As for the bureaucrats at the WTO's headquarters in Geneva, a number had declined to go. Of those who did go, some insisted upon—and the WTO provided—a special life insurance policy, so that at least their families would be taken care of in the event of their deaths. Indeed, much consideration had been given in the weeks prior to the meeting about moving it to Singapore or some other seemingly safer venue. That idea had been quashed by Vice President Richard Cheney after he received a phone call from the emir of Qatar, an important U.S. ally, who was adamant about hosting the meeting as planned.

So just getting to Doha was no small achievement. And now the delegates, representing the WTO's 142 member countries, faced an immense and difficult task as they settled in for the meeting, which was scheduled to last five days. Their mission was to decide whether, and under what terms, to launch a "round"—that is, a series of negotiations, which would take place over several years—aimed at reaching an agreement to lower trade barriers and to reform the rules of the global trading system. The system had undergone eight of these during the post–World War II era; the most recent, the Uruguay Round, lasted from 1986 to 1994, and the one prior to that, the Tokyo Round, lasted from 1973 to 1979.

There was broad concurrence in Doha that the top priority of any new negotiations must be to bestow more of the benefits of globalization on developing countries, and especially on the 2.8 billion people in the developing world who were still scraping by on less than two dollars a day. The main question before the meeting—and it was contentious—was what specific subjects and goals the talks ought to address.

During the weeks and months prior to the meeting, exhortations had abounded about the importance of reaching agreement to launch a round. In part, that reflected the need to show international solidarity in the wake of 9/11; a trade round, the *Financial Times* observed, "is increasingly considered essential for symbolic and psychological reasons as much as for economic ones," because it "would send a powerful political signal of countries' determination to make common cause in the face of adversity." Others said an accord at Doha could help ward off global recession. No less an authority than Federal Reserve Board chairman Alan Greenspan told a Senate committee that a successful round would "significantly enhance world economic growth."

But the main emphasis was on the need to start work on a substantively meaningful pact so that the countries the global system had left behind would have greater opportunities to share in the gains. Mike Moore, the WTO's director-general, had underlined the significance of the challenge in a speech on October 9: "Trade is a key engine for growth, but currently developing country products face many obstacles in rich country markets," Moore said. "By opening these markets, we can help lift millions of people out of poverty. And the most effective way to achieve these market openings is by launching a new round." Expressing similar sentiments was the antipoverty group Oxfam, which—while offering a different vision from Moore's of how the round should proceed—said in a briefing paper: "Improved access to northern markets would help to create employment opportunities in developing countries and achieve a fairer distribution of global wealth. Trade is far more important than aid in this respect."

Spreading globalization's bounty to the world's least fortunate, many world leaders argued, was no longer merely a moral imperative. The 9/11 attacks had added a crucial international-security dimension, making it all the more urgent to succeed at Doha. "Terrorism and hatred grow their strongest roots in poor soil," Pierre Pettigrew, Canada's trade minister, wrote in an op-ed calling for a new round. "Economic and social development in the world's poorest nations will help to erode the hopelessness that can breed hate." Zoellick delivered speeches and wrote op-eds making a similar argument. Often cited, by both officials and commentators, were projections by the World Bank of the degree to which the poor stood to benefit. "The World Bank estimates, over the next decade and a half, that further trade liberalization could lift 320 million people out of poverty," editorialized the *Chicago Tribune*. "That's a worthy goal for Qatar—and a potent weapon in the war against terrorism."

Yet launching a round was hardly simple. Two years earlier, WTO members had failed, in spectacular fashion, to do so at their ministerial meeting in Seattle. That meeting had broken up, with no agreement, amid discord over many of the same issues that divided nations in Doha, notably farm-trade rules and proposals to expand the WTO's jurisdiction into such new areas as government purchases. Furthermore, the WTO operates by consensus; in theory, at least, any member country has the right to block a text from being approved, a negotiating agenda from being agreed, or a pact from going into effect. This means that in any agreement the organization reaches, each country needs to gain more in concessions from others than it gives up in concessions it makes. So the process is often likened, aptly, to a giant multidimensional chess game.

Security issues were an ever-present distraction as the meeting got under way amid fierce debate. Machine-gun-toting Qatari police and military personnel in purple camouflage protected miles of roads surrounding the Sheraton Resort and Convention Hotel, where the meeting was taking place, and at every point of entry, credentials were checked and bags were thoroughly searched. In hotels, security officials wearing traditional kaffiyeh headdresses and *thobes* (traditional white robes) manned metal detectors and patrolled halls at all hours. Providing special protection for the U.S. delegation were about fifteen agents from the Naval Criminal Investigative Service (NCIS, which later gained fame in a TV series about its exploits) and a platoon of marines from the Fleet Antiterrorism Security Teams (FAST, the commandos trained for rapid deployment in case of security crises at U.S. government installations abroad). They were dressed in civilian clothing—some in suits, some in polo shirts and slacks—to avoid creating too intrusive a presence, and they declined to say what agency of the U.S. government they came from. (I was able to find out only long afterward.) Nonetheless, it was obvious from the marines' youth, demeanor, and buzz cuts who they were, and nobody cared to press the matter, especially given the brusque manner in which they scrutinized all items carried by reporters, even pads of paper and packs of gum, before they permitted entry into press conferences conducted by U.S. officials.

American citizens attending the meeting, including journalists like me, were quietly given a password—"Paging Mr. Black"—which, if broadcast over the hotel public address system, would mean that some type of terrorist threat was materializing. We were to gather at the hotel pool for evacuation by helicopter to U.S. Navy ships patrolling some distance offshore. In one heart-stopping episode, the hotel PA system at the Ritz-Carlton, where the American delegation was staying, broadcast the words "We have an announcement . . ." and then said nothing. Many Americans were also issued special cell phones for use in an emergency. The SUVs that transported Zoellick and other U.S. officials between the Ritz and the Sheraton—about a ten-minute drive—were themselves accompanied by other bodyguard-filled SUVs that wove back and forth across the road in winding patterns around the vehicle they were protecting. Gallows humor helped ease stress; after one commotion in the halls of the convention center, Zoellick told an aide, "Just remember what [veteran Middle East negotiator] Dennis Ross told me—if you hear '*Allah-o-akhbar*,' hit the deck."

Tension ran especially high when delegates saw the news on November 12 that an American Airlines plane had plunged nose-first into a New York neighborhood shortly after taking off from Kennedy International Airport. Walking down the hall with the sizable security detail that followed him everywhere, Zoellick was besieged by reporters asking whether the crash was terrorist related. (It turned out to be an accident.) One particularly aggressive journalist, a woman from China, tried to push her way through the security detail; finding her way blocked by a Qatari guard, she kicked him in the shin—causing his pistol to fall from under his *thobe* and skitter across the floor. Thinking that the gun belonged to the woman and that she might be attacking Zoellick, security personnel grabbed him and hustled him into a nearby elevator for safety while others pounced on the gun. "Your job sucks," Zoellick said wryly to one of the guards, NCIS special agent Ed Winslow, after he had regained his composure. "No, sir," Winslow bantered back. "Yours does."

Sometime early in the conference, Zoellick was informed by a security aide of intelligence indicating that the man responsible for the bombing of the U.S.S. *Cole* in 2000 was heading for Doha by air. Zoellick ordered his aide to make sure the man was arrested at the airport, and over the next couple of days he queried his aide several times about what had happened to the bomber. "Finally he told me they traced him to Beirut, and didn't think he had come," Zoellick recalls. "And the last part of the story that I heard was, they broke into the guy's apartment—but it turned out to be the wrong guy."

Battling over the terms of the WTO declaration was so intense that on November 13, the fifth and supposedly final day, the official deadline of midnight came and went without a decision about whether to launch a round, as Zoellick and his counterparts from twenty-two other countries spent the entire night in negotiations chaired by Director-General Moore. Even after that all-nighter broke up, more high-stakes haggling ensued on the fourteenth because of a serious threat by the Indian government, which had never liked the idea of a round, to withhold its support from the consensus.

At last, twenty hours into overtime, came the official announcement that the WTO was launching the "Doha Development Agenda"—or, as it would commonly be known, the Doha Round. The member nations pledged to finish a far-reaching accord by the end of 2004 that would broadly liberalize trade, with a central focus on revamping rules that had been tilted against developing countries for years. In particular, the final deal would be expected to establish new rules in agriculture, which had been largely left out of global trade negotiations even though most poor people in developing nations make their livings in rural areas. The declaration issued by the WTO envisioned that the deal would achieve "substantial improvement in market access" for farm products, and it also promised "substantial reductions" in the subsidies that rich nations pay their farmers, because the lavish government support those farmers enjoy gives them an unfair competitive advantage in global markets against their poor-country brethren.

The news drew jubilant responses from prominent leaders and commentators. Hailing the round's potential importance in the war against terror, the *Los Angeles Times*, in an editorial titled "Trade's Peacemaking Role," opined: "Freer trade will be a boost for poor nations like newfound U.S. ally Pakistan, which depends heavily on exports. There is ample evidence that nations that increase trade create new jobs and reduce poverty. When there is more money to build schools and provide medical care, offering the hope that life will get better, the temptations to violence and terror lessen." Equally effusive was a statement issued by President George W. Bush, who, although welcoming the potential benefits for American workers and farmers, said, "Today's decision offers fresh hope for the world's developing countries. . . . It reflects our common understanding that a new trade round can give developing countries greater access to world markets, and lift the lives of millions now living in poverty."

| * |

Globalization moves in fits and starts, sometimes three steps forward, sometimes two steps back; sometimes at a gallop, sometimes at a crawl. It took a calamitous tumble in the autumn of 2008, as the problems stemming from irresponsible housing loans in the United States sent financial markets crashing not only on Wall Street but in Europe, Asia, and Latin America. That implosion reflected massive malfunctions in the financial side of globalization—the transnational movement of money in the form of loans, stock and bond purchases, derivative transactions, and various other flows, which has burgeoned to previously unimaginable levels in the past two decades. Rapid financial globalization has long been a subject of skepticism and a source of worry among economists. Well before the crash, many experts were pointing with alarm at the titanic sums of money traversing borders, continents, and oceans, because of the heightened risk of bubbles and panics; and they were expressing lack of confidence in the ability of international institutions to govern the global financial system effectively. Readers of my previous work are well aware that I am in sympathy with these skeptics, worriers, and confidence-lackers. My books on the financial crises of the late 1990s and the Argentine crisis at the turn of the twenty-first century took a dim view of the way financial globalization has developed.

The subject of this book is a different facet of globalization—the trading system, which involves the international movement of goods and services rather than of financial instruments. The benefits of globalized trade command a much broader consensus among economists than do the benefits of globalized finance. To be sure, disagreements may rage about the size of the gains from trade, the impact of trade on inequality, and the speed with which developing countries should liberalize, among other controversies. And the system has many wrongs that need righting; that was the rationale for the Doha Round in the first place. But among sensible and knowledgeable people, nobody disputes that, overall, the expansion of trade has been a force for growth and higher living standards. Agreement is universal that disaster would ensue from a substantial reversal in market-openness, especially if this were to take the form of an outbreak of protectionism like that of the 1930s, when the United States raised tariffs sharply under the infamous Smoot-Hawley Tariff Act, triggering a worldwide cycle of retaliation and counter-retaliation. Agreement is universal, too, that to govern the liberalization of trade and to settle disputes, a multilateral system is far superior to alternatives such as regional or bilateral arrangements among countries.

The trading system is at risk of joining the financial system in crisis. That is the central message of this book, and the story of how the system reached this parlous state will unfold in chapters to come.

Seven years of negotiations followed the WTO meeting in Doha, producing official agreement on nothing more than a skeletal outline of a final agreement. During that period, the lofty ambitions that were expressed in 2001 for a poverty-reducing trade accord became almost laughably implausible. At several junctures, gatherings of top negotiators broke up in such acrimony as to leave the viability of the Doha Round in serious doubt. The governments of major countries often bowed to the heavy influence of domestic interest groups that feared losing big, so the negotiations moved gradually in the direction of a watered-down deal that, despite some beneficial elements, could not be credibly claimed to work wonders for the poor. Although negotiators agreed to the principle that tariffs should be sharply reduced, they also insisted on so many loopholes and exceptions that, by 2008, the terms they were considering would have had a minimal impact on existing flows of goods—and even then, their efforts to cut a deal fell woefully short. The bickering dragged on for so long that in the meantime, several new trade controversies cropped up, leaving the round vulnerable to criticism that it was out of step with changes that had swept the global economy. As the round suffered flameout after flameout and as its shortcomings became more glaring, it became a target of mockery, with the stature of the WTO—global trade's referee—shriveling in the process.

The failure by WTO members to deliver on the Doha promise of instilling greater fairness into the rules of international trade is lamentable. After the financial market crash, the implications of their discord became much more dire.

The crash greatly magnified the danger that governments around the globe will resort to protectionism. Up until that point, it was easy to dismiss worries that countries would turn inward and engage in trade wars as they had in the thirties. As long as global growth was rising smartly, the idea that policymakers would repeat Depression-era mistakes by walling off their economies from foreign competition seemed ludicrous. After the crash, those fears look a lot less far-fetched as recessionary forces spread to every major region of the world. It is still unclear, as this book is being finished, how many millions will lose their jobs, how many companies will shut their doors, and how many communities will face ruin. But the impact is bound to intensify pressure on politicians to raise trade barriers. The groundswell of revulsion against unfettered capitalism, which has so far been aimed mainly at the system governing flows of money, is unlikely to spare the system governing the international flow of goods and services.

The evidence since late 2008 has been far from reassuring. A summit in Washington, D.C., of the Group of 20 (G-20) major economies issued a pledge on November 15, 2008, to refrain from protectionist measures for twelve months, but within weeks many among the twenty had taken actions that would restrict imports or discriminate against foreign goods by various means. Russia significantly increased tariffs on used cars, steel, pork, and poultry. India imposed higher levies on imported iron and steel and banned imports of Chinese toys. Argentina imposed licensing requirements on imported car parts, textiles, televisions, shoes, and other products. Indonesia issued regulations limiting imports of clothing, electronics, shoes, toys, and food by restricting shipments to five designated ports and requiring thorough inspection of all containers by the country's notoriously slow customs service. (The Indonesian government claimed that the measures were necessary to combat smuggling, but the moves came after intense lobbying by industry and labor unions, which called for responding to the economic downturn with policies aimed at self-reliance.)

Richer nations tended to favor more subtle approaches that didn't involve directly raising obstacles at the border. The giant economic stimulus package approved by the U.S. Congress in February 2009 included "Buy American" provisions ensuring that infrastructure projects funded by the bill would use mainly U.S.-made iron, steel, and manufactured goods. Other wealthy nations followed suit with their own "buy local" provisions in public spending programs, and the same happened after Washington began offering subsidized loans to rescue General Motors and Chrysler, which clearly discriminated against foreign automakers operating in the U.S. market. Governments in at least ten countries rushed aid to their own car manufacturers, with some (notably France) applying political pressure to keep the firms from shedding jobs at home or adding them overseas.

Policymakers understandably felt they had no choice but to adopt measures such as these, given the depths into which their economies were plunging and the anger among voters over the bailouts of huge financial institutions. Presumably, most of these policies can be terminated once economies recover. But their enactment creates the general impression that markets all over the world are now rigged in favor of domestic producers, which could further undermine support for free trade and lead to the erection of still more, higher, and long-lasting barriers.

So far, the protectionist and quasi-protectionist steps that nations have taken aren't egregious enough to be deemed an epidemic. It is entirely possible that the global economic downturn will be mild enough, and policymakers stiff-spined enough, that no such epidemic will erupt. President Barack Obama isn't antitrade, and neither are his economic advisers. But remember, it was President Bush, a supposedly ardent free trader, who succumbed to demands from the beleaguered steel industry for stiff tariffs in 2002. And if the slump worsens significantly in the months ahead, even well-intentioned politicians may buckle under similar pleas for relief from overseas competition.

By delaying and disagreeing time after time in the Doha talks, and by letting the prospective deal get so diluted, WTO members passed up the opportunity for meaningful insurance against protectionism. Had an ambitious Doha agreement been reached—especially if it had happened in, say, 2006—protectionist impulses would have been more containable, because an agreement's terms could have included substantial new restrictions on countries' ability to raise tariffs. Not that such a deal would have prevented all types of economic nationalism—it would not have stopped some of the policies that many countries have adopted since the fall of 2008, such as pressuring banks to lend at home instead of abroad or giving bailouts strictly to domestic auto manufacturers. But it could have reduced the danger arising from the traditional kind of protectionism that still threatens to inflict long-term damage on the trading system.

More important, the Doha Round's travails, combined with the current economic environment, have ominous ramifications for the long-run health of the multilateral trading system. Even if governments can beat back the forces of Smoot-Hawleyism, events to date cast disquieting doubt on the WTO's ability to maintain its status as the central rule-setter for international trade.

The WTO is a source of great perplexity even to well-informed laypeople; this book will hopefully help demystify it. In the fevered imaginations of antiglobalization militants, the trade body wields power in much the same way as the Trilateral Commission was believed to operate twenty years ago: a shadowy cabal of the ruling class, aided by technocrats, forcing the whims of multinational corporations down the collective throats of the global masses. More knowledgeable critics recognize that the WTO is, like the United Nations, a collection of the world's governments, setting rules by reaching agreements among its members. Still, critics excoriate the organization as a secretive, undemocratic institution that has the power, in the name of free trade, to intrude into laws and regulations that are normally the province of sovereign states (a notable example being the ruling by a WTO tribunal in 2006 against the European Union's restrictions on genetically engineered crops). Admirers of the WTO retort that it is the prime upholder of the principles of liberalization that have helped fuel global economic expansion over most of the past six decades.

As this book will show, there is some validity in the characterizations of both the WTO's critics and its defenders. But the main point to be kept in mind is this: For all its faults, the WTO is a crucial linchpin of stability in the global economy. Just shy of fifteen years old, it is the current embodiment of the multilateral system that was established after World War II to prevent a reversion to the trade policies of the thirties. The WTO's rules keep a lid on the import barriers of its member countries (which at last count numbered 153), and members take their trade disputes to WTO tribunals for adjudication rather than engaging in tit-for-tat trade wars. That arrangement keeps trade disputes from turning unnecessarily destructive, just as any rule-of-law system helps contain tendencies toward the law of the jungle. In addition, the WTO is the guardian of the "most favored nation" principle, under which member nations pledge to treat each other's products on a nondiscriminatory basis. This principle is a valuable bulwark against trade blocs of the sort that, during the thirties, stoked rivalries among the great powers. In sum, the WTO is the ultimate safekeeper of open world markets.

The WTO's ability to continue performing these functions is in peril because of disillusionment over the Doha Round, which has made the trade body appear increasingly irrelevant and ineffectual. Its dominance as a rule-setting institution has already been battered in recent years by an explosion of bilateral and regional trade deals. More than two hundred of these are currently in force, ranging from the big and well-known such as the North American Free Trade Agreement (NAFTA), to the small and obscure such as the Singapore-Jordan free-trade agreement. Governments are increasingly tempted to view these pacts as reasonable substitutes for multilateralism, especially as skepticism deepens over the possibility of forging substantive new deals in the WTO. Although the WTO is not about to fall to pieces overnight, the danger is that its authority will erode to the point that member nations will start to flout their commitments and ignore the rulings of WTO tribunals.

One all-too-plausible scenario is that the WTO's apparent incapacity to strike agreements will prompt countries to resort increasingly to litigation—filing cases against each other—rather than trying to negotiate. WTO tribunals would then be forced to render judgments on more and more politically explosive disputes. Climate change, for instance, is an issue that is particularly fraught with risk in this regard. Influential U.S. and European policymakers are proposing laws to control greenhouse gas emissions that would involve the use of tariffs on goods from foreign countries that aren't reducing their emissions—Chinese and Indian products being the most likely targets of such tariffs. It's far from clear that those sorts of tariffs are legal under WTO rules. So imagine the furor that would erupt if the WTO were to rule against them, in effect saying that trade has to take priority over saving the planet. Alternatively, imagine the furor if the WTO were to rule such tariffs to be legal, and the Chinese responded by imposing their own duties on American and European goods, based on the reasoning that Western countries are the ones most guilty of having created the climate change problem in the first place. That's just one example of the sorts of situations that could greatly increase the threat of trade wars and a breakdown in respect for the system that has helped keep protectionism at bay.

Americans may assume that they would be hurt less than citizens of other nations if the WTO were to disintegrate, and from a strictly commercial standpoint, they would be right. The size of the U.S. market means that America will always have big partners with whom it can trade on terms that suit it. The nations that would be affected most are the poorest, smallest, and most vulnerable, for whom the WTO affords protection against bullying by the wealthy. That is precisely why, from a longer-term perspective, undermining the WTO would badly damage U.S. interests. The 9/11 attacks showed the importance of taking all practical measures to bring poor nations into the economic mainstream. Impoverished countries pose an acute risk of becoming havens for terrorists and of presenting other threats to the United States, including the spread of weapons and disease, because their governments are often incapable of countering—or unwilling to counter—such problems. Preventing them from becoming more marginalized than they already are should be a top priority for Washington, and although a healthy WTO is hardly sufficient to achieve that aim, it is essential.

| * |

To show how and why the multilateral trading system has come to its current pretty pass, this book chronicles the major events in the system over the past decade. It is a dispiriting tale for anyone who believes in the power of globalization to raise living standards around the world. It includes a detailed recounting of the WTO's mortification at Seattle in 1999, because although that meeting was not part of the Doha Round, the story behind the "Battle of Seattle" is essential to understanding subsequent developments. The narrative encompasses the triumphant launch of the round at Doha in 2001 and the colorful collapse of the September 2003 ministerial in Cancún, Mexico, which exposed the depth of the rift between wealthy countries and developing ones. The action then moves to the 2004 meeting in Geneva, where WTO members appeared to impart the round with fresh momentum by thrashing out a "framework" agreement. From that point on, the story consists of one letdown after another: the Hong Kong ministerial in 2005, which barely managed to reach agreement on an extremely modest set of measures; breakdowns in Geneva in mid-2006 and in Potsdam, Germany, in June 2007; and, finally, the emotionally draining climax—the July 2008 meeting of ministers that collapsed after nine days, the longest such gathering in the trade body's history.

This series of ups and downs makes for a long saga. It involves complex economic issues as well as a large and frequently changing cast of main characters. Readers will encounter four U.S. trade representatives (Charlene Barshefsky, Bob Zoellick, Rob Portman, and Susan Schwab), three WTO directors-general (Mike Moore, Supachai Panitchpakdi, and Pascal Lamy), two top Brazilian negotiators with the same first name (Celso Lafer and Celso Amorim), and two other key players named Kamal (Yousef Hussain Kamal, the Qatari minister who chaired the Doha meeting, and Kamal Nath, who became India's commerce and industry minister in 2004). Along the way, various coalitions of countries will shoulder their way onto the stage—the Like Minded Group, the African Group, the G-20, the G-33, and so on.

As the narrative progresses, it is important to keep track of changes in who's in and who's out. In this case, "in" refers to the WTO's inner circle of power, the small group of countries that gets the first chance to decide on the main elements of a deal before submitting the terms to the wider WTO membership to see if consensus can be attained. For a sign of how power is shifting in the global economy, the variations in this group's composition are revealing. At one point in the narrative, the inner circle consists of the United States, the European Union, Japan, and Canada—the coterie of wealthy, industrialized nations known as the Quad. But later the membership of the inner circle changes to include some of the economic dynamos of the developing world, countries whose large size and rapid growth have enabled them to muscle their way to the table. At that point the group goes by the name of the Five Interested Parties—the United States, the European Union, Brazil, India, and Australia—followed by various permutations known as the G-6, the G-4, and the G-7, the last of which includes China.

Each major milestone covered in this book will have its own unique dynamic, its own bones of contention, its own dramas, its own set of protagonists, naysayers, tantrum-throwers, and goats. Trade wonks who are familiar with the prominent policymakers in question may delight in reading about their high-decibel confrontations, logistical cock-ups, late-night heroics, scathing put-downs, and tearful despondency. But beyond uncovering titillating tidbits, delving into the round's twists and turns serves an illuminating purpose. The ineluctable nature of multilateral trade rounds is that they *are* long, they are laden with issues that affect the lives of millions but are often dry and technical, and they are negotiated by myriad people whose job tenure tends to be shorter than the negotiations themselves. Only by going behind the scenes, examining the key turning points in all their gory splendor, is it possible to properly depict how chaotic, random, uncontrollable, and dysfunctional the process of a round can be. Only by laying bare the scrambling, floundering, blustering, threatening, and bluff-calling that goes on is it possible to elucidate the difficulty of successfully completing such an undertaking.

One reason why it is crucial to explore these events is to hold officials and their governments accountable for their roles. The Doha Round's woes stem to some extent from the failings of individuals. The pages of this book are replete with personality clashes, egotistical excesses, petty point-scoring, and strategic blunders—including some miscalculations by policymakers renowned for their brilliance, notably Bob Zoellick (currently the president of the World Bank) and Pascal Lamy (the former European trade commissioner, now the WTO's director-general). One of the worst mistakes, in retrospect, was to raise unrealistic expectations at the outset about the impact that trade policy alone could have in alleviating poverty.

But another key reason for closely scrutinizing how the round went awry is to expose deeper, more systemic problems at the root of the WTO's predicament. Could any set of policymakers, no matter how intelligent and well intentioned, have done any better, given the way the WTO works? Or has the system itself become fatally flawed? Is it capable of coping with the realities of the early twenty-first century?

Conceivably, the Doha Round marks the end of an era. Given the experience of the past seven years, the nations of the world may never again attempt a giant multilateral trade round. It is far from clear, however, that there are viable alternatives for resolving the numerous issues still facing the trading system. To take just two of those issues: The recent food crisis highlighted the problem of countries cutting off exports of grain to world markets, and climate change raises thorny questions about how to enforce an international regime for reducing carbon emissions without violating existing WTO rules. A round in which all WTO members make concessions in some areas to extract gains in others may be the only way to work out these issues satisfactorily. So here's a truly frightening thought: The fate of open global markets may depend on decades more of Doha Round–style chaos, uncontrollability, and dysfunctionality.

That prospect is all the more unsettling because of two fundamental trends that emerge clearly from the Doha epic. The first is what Fareed Zakaria has called "the rise of the rest," referring to the fast growth and rapidly increasing influence of Brazil, India, China, Egypt, South Africa, and other large developing countries. Their advancement has rendered the multilateral trading system much more difficult to manage. No longer are pretty much all the important decisions worked out among a handful of mostly rich countries, as was the case in decades past. Today, not only does the WTO have more members than ever, but it has many more members that matter, and more that want to play a much greater role in the increasingly free world of trade they have joined. The dispersion of global trade among a larger number of countries with vastly different levels of development is obviously welcome. But in an institution that operates by consensus, the forging of decisions has become immensely more complicated.

The second factor, which may be even more responsible for hamstringing the WTO, is a change in the globalization zeitgeist—a shift that preceded the recent crisis of confidence in global markets and was in some ways a harbinger of it.

In the mid-1990s, after the Uruguay Round concluded, economist Ernest Preeg titled his book about that round *Traders in a Brave New World*, reflecting prevailing attitudes during a period when capitalism was ascendant around the globe and countries were falling over each other to liberalize. An apt title for a book about the Doha Round might be "Traders in a Frightened New World." Sprinkled throughout the narrative of Doha is evidence that globalization has sped so far and so fast that its forward progress may be reaching some natural limit, at least for the medium term. Perhaps the most compelling sign is the unease about the pace of economic integration that has mounted with the emergence of China as an export powerhouse. As shall be seen in Chapter 11, the fear-of-China factor has had a marked impact on the round by making developing countries much more cautious about opening their economies further. At the same time, faith has eroded in the supposedly magical, growth-enhancing properties of tariff cuts and other moves that lower trade barriers. This erosion of faith is not entirely misplaced, as shall be seen in Chapter 10, which recounts the sharp downward revisions that have been made in the World Bank's estimates of the round's economic benefits. For all these reasons, plus more, many WTO members have held back from taking the steps needed to make a deal happen.

One way of viewing this change in the zeitgeist is to perceive the multilateral trading system as the victim of its own success. As many observers have noted, so much market opening has occurred during the past few decades that the low-hanging fruit is gone; the barriers that remain are the ones that are the most politically intractable. Furthermore, the achievements of past trade rounds have given multinational corporations most of the access to foreign markets that they want. As a result, they are not nearly as spirited as they used to be in pressing their governments to strike deals, so political forces opposed to liberalization gain the upper hand.

The system's past, including the creation of the WTO and the events leading up to it, is the subject of Chapter 2. No doubt the length of the strides taken during this period help account for the system's current tribulations. But that is cold comfort. Later chapters will show the stewards of global trade traipsing from one misadventure to another, and it should be all the more distressing to contemplate the magnitude of the progress that is now in jeopardy.

# 2 | THE INTERGALACTIC
## TRADE ORGANIZATION

ON A BRISK DECEMBER MORNING IN LATE 2006, A LINE OF DARK
sedans—mostly Mercedes-Benzes, with a smattering of BMWs, Volvos, and
Lexuses—snaked down a U-shaped driveway and pulled up to the front of the
WTO's headquarters, the Centre William Rappard, an Italianate villa, named for
a Swiss diplomat, on the shores of Lake Geneva. As on many sunny days in
Geneva, the snow-capped peaks of the Alps were resplendent in the distance for
anyone choosing to stroll to the lakeside park in the back of the building. But the
limousines' passengers—ambassadors to the WTO from its member countries—
did not linger to admire the scenery; security guards were occasionally barking at
chauffeurs to keep the line moving, because well over a hundred vehicles were arriving. So the diplomats alighted quickly and strode across a short bridge to a
modern building, through the doors and into a large semicircular chamber, the
Salle du Conseil (Council Room), which has a high ceiling with skylights allowing
natural light to stream through. Some chatted with colleagues as they took their
places at their countries' desks, each of which was equipped with a placard displaying the country's name, plus a microphone and earpieces for listening to simultaneous interpretation. Most of the ambassadors were men in dark suits,
though a fair number were women, and a few wore clothing of their native lands
or ethnic groups, such as the Indian ambassador's bright blue turban.

This is the General Council, the WTO's primary decision-making body,
which meets in formal session five times a year and is outranked only by ministerial conferences. Council meetings are normally closed to journalists (afterward, WTO spokespeople brief reporters on the proceedings, and minutes are

published). Desirable as it might be to open the sessions to public scrutiny, the Geneva press corps may consider it a mercy that they are closed, because the discussion tends to be dull. That was certainly the case on this December day, when the main event was a report from Pascal Lamy, the director-general, on the status of the Doha Round. "Failure could be around the corner, but we need not turn that corner," Lamy told the ambassadors, some of whom, in response, rose to pledge that their countries or groups of allied countries would "continue to engage constructively," "remain committed to an ambitious, pro-development outcome," and "stand ready to find middle ground," even as they reiterated their long-standing stances on the most contentious issues at stake.

The seating arrangement is noteworthy—and in a way, inapt. Lamy was in an exalted position, on a large dais in the front of the room, together with several other senior members of the WTO's Secretariat (the cadre of international civil servants who work at the Centre William Rappard), while the ambassadors were seated below. From this, a misleading conclusion might be drawn that the WTO has a powerful bureaucracy, like other international economic organizations such as the International Monetary Fund (IMF) and the World Bank. In fact, the Secretariat is only about 630 people strong, compared with 2,600 at the IMF and more than 10,000 at the World Bank, and although Secretariat officials exert some influence over key decisions through the technical and professional advice they give to various councils and committees, the WTO is much more a member-driven organization—that is, controlled by the countries belonging to it. In stark contrast with the boardrooms of the IMF and the World Bank, where countries' votes are weighted according to the size of their economies, each country has one vote at the WTO. That doesn't mean that, say, Botswana or Peru or Sri Lanka has as much clout as the United States—far from it—but the strong tradition of making decisions by consensus means that power is more evenly distributed among the member countries than at the other institutions. Unsurprisingly, the WTO's decision-making process is by far the most cumbersome of the lot. "We have 144 handbrakes and one accelerator," Mike Moore, who served as director-general from 1999 to 2002, once wrote. "Sometimes it feels more like one of those old Laurel and Hardy movies, with the car out of control and the steering wheel coming off in your hands. It's like trying to run a parliament with no parties, no whip, no speaker, no speaking limits and no majority voting system. It is consensus by exhaustion."

On the other hand, the General Council seating arrangement is emblematic of something significant—the power of the WTO as an institution, which is greater in important respects than that of either the IMF or World Bank.

Whereas the fund and the bank have leverage over developing countries to whom they lend, the WTO has leverage over industrialized nations as well, including the United States. If a small, poor country believes a big, rich one is violating WTO rules, it can haul the rule violator before a tribunal to obtain redress. And if the tribunal finds the big country to be guilty as charged, the offender must change its behavior, or—if it refuses to do so—accept economic punishment of some sort at the hands of the aggrieved party. (As shall be seen in Chapter 8, the large members enjoy a number of advantages in the tribunal system, but the point is that they are also accountable to it.) Furthermore, the WTO extends its rules deeply into the domestic economic arrangements of its member countries in ways unmatched by other international bodies. One example is the WTO code concerning the standards for assessing the sanitariness of imported animal and plant products, which can affect member countries' regulation of food safety. Another example is the WTO agreement on intellectual property rights, which can shape the ways in which member countries protect patents. Still another is the accord on services, which influences countries' regulation of banks and telecommunications. The depth and scope of these rules help explain the rationale for making decisions by consensus: Because the rules affect all members, they should be agreed by all members.

Finally, the WTO confers on its member nations one of the most important rights—perhaps *the* most important right—provided by any international organization, namely, most favored nation treatment. This right means that each member shall receive all the trade advantages granted to the others; its goods shall not be treated any worse than those of other members, and it thus will enjoy strong protection against arbitrary and capricious trade sanctions. Small wonder that most countries want to join so that they can obtain this right and exert whatever influence they have to shape the rules.

Indeed, trade policymakers from developing countries who want to learn how to use the system to their nations' benefit come to the Centre William Rappard throughout the year to take courses on the basic principles and workings of the WTO. I briefly sat in on one of these courses and found that the course material, in addition to providing a good introduction to the subject, offers a penetrating insight into what makes the WTO tick—and what doesn't.

| * |

The student from Sudan had a yellow scarf covering her head and was fiddling with a cell phone. The pupil from Bangladesh, a man, was wearing jeans, sneakers, and a polo shirt. From the Bahamas came a distinguished black man with graying hair, sporting a blue dress shirt with a white collar. Across from him sat a Qatari woman in a black robe and head scarf with gold trim. Most of the other students—from Indonesia, Eritrea, Kazakhstan, Paraguay, and about twenty other countries—wore business suits. They tended to be in their thirties and forties, and the oldest was in his mid-fifties. They had the titles of mid-to-upper-level government bureaucrats; one was his country's "deputy head of WTO and E.U. Affairs Department," another was "chief negotiator in the Ministry of Trade," and another was "deputy director of the Foreign Trade and Economic Affairs Division." They had been invited to Geneva to take this three-month course, with the WTO footing the bill for transport, food, and lodging from a fund financed by donor nations. The idea is to help such policymakers overcome one of the biggest disadvantages their countries face as WTO members—mustering the technical expertise needed to participate effectively in an organization where the giants, especially the United States and the European Union, have much larger staffs, better equipment, deeper knowledge, and more experience playing the game.

Early in the course, the students spend a day going over the basic economic theory of trade. To refresh the memories of those who are trained in economics and to inform those who aren't, the students examine the principle—which is accepted as valid by economists across the ideological spectrum—that trade between two nations will raise living standards overall in both. They learn that although trade may impose costs on a country in the form of jobs lost to foreign competition, greater gains will result, for a variety of reasons: Low-cost imports help drive down consumer prices; exporters increase production as they obtain access to markets overseas; companies grow more efficient in response to competitive pressure from abroad. With the aid of simple supply-and-demand graphs of the sort used in universities around the world, the class studies the effects of the most common barriers to trade—tariffs (duties imposed on imported goods at the border) and quotas (restrictions on the quantity that can be imported of a given good). A country using such barriers to restrict foreign competition may help its domestic producers stay in business, thereby saving some jobs, and it may generate revenue for the government. But consumers will have to pay so much more for the restricted goods, with a resulting decrease in economic efficiency, that the overall impact will be a "net loss," as the study materials show.

The theory class also quickly covers the great thinkers of the past few centuries whose work has led the vast majority of economists to accept as a matter of faith the virtues of free commerce across international borders. The most seminal of these thinkers, of course, was Adam Smith, whose 1776 book *The*

*Wealth of Nations* discredited the theory of mercantilism—the belief, widely held among Europe's ruling elites in the sixteenth, seventeenth, and eighteenth centuries, that exports provide a country with the main benefits of trade and that imports (especially manufactured imports) tend to be damaging to its economy. Smith turned mercantilism on its head, arguing that a nation's economy gains strength from unfettered trade that enables it to import goods more cheaply from abroad than it can make at home. Just as individuals operate more efficiently when they specialize in producing what they make best—"the taylor does not attempt to make his own shoes, but buys them of the shoemaker. The shoemaker does not attempt to make his own clothes, but employs a taylor"— so too do countries, Smith argued. "In the mercantile system," he wrote, "the interest of the consumer is almost constantly sacrificed to that of the producer; and it seems to consider production, and not consumption, as the ultimate end and object of all industry and commerce."

But although Adam Smith might seem to the casual observer to be the guiding inspiration for the WTO, the course for developing-country officials shows how misleading that impression is. The day spent learning trade theory is only a tiny portion of the three-month course, and that fact speaks volumes about the ethos that pervades the WTO's decision-making. Much more of the course is devoted to teaching the students the practical skills needed to be effective in WTO negotiations, which means, in a sense, instructing them in the art of hard-nosed mercantilism. The special interests that besiege trade ministries around the world are typically exporters seeking opportunities for overseas sales and domestic industries (along with their unions) seeking protection from imports. Ordinary consumers are rarely heard from, if ever, and they tend to be poorly organized in any case. Thus, for the typical trade negotiator, exports are "wins," and imports are "losses," Adam Smith to the contrary notwithstanding.

A perfect illustration comes in the high point of the WTO course—a mock global trade round that the students conduct. The students are divided into teams representing four fictional countries, called Alba, Vanin, Medatia, and Tristat, and starting on a Monday morning, they begin negotiating, with instructions that they must reach a consensus deal by 4:00 p.m. the following Thursday. "The participants sometimes fight, shout, and lose their tempers," says Jean-Daniel Rey, who oversees the course. "They sometimes meet in hotels, or have negotiating lunches, or negotiate until midnight. They are extremely tired at the end. The whole purpose is to create an atmosphere similar to the kind of atmosphere they will face in real negotiations."

Each of the fictional countries has a different sort of economy and different levels of protection for its industries and farms. Alba and Tristat are wealthy,

Medatia is a developing nation that is advancing rapidly, and Vanin is poor. For simplicity's sake, the participants negotiate over many fewer issues than they would in real WTO talks, although there's plenty to haggle about—rules on government subsidies, plus the tariff levels that each country maintains on thirty different products, including grain, fruit, beef, dairy, copper, tin, coal, fertilizer, pharmaceuticals, paint, boilers, air conditioners, lamps, semiconductors, fax machines, T-shirts, and carpets. The teams can meet in bilateral negotiations if they wish (the Alba team meeting just the Tristat team, for example) and form alliances, or all four can meet together. "We don't tell them how to negotiate," Rey says. "The point is to understand the process—the difficulties, risks, and skills that are required."

The revealing part is the secret instructions that each team receives from its country's "cabinet." Rey wouldn't disclose the details of the instructions because that would spoil the exercise for future participants. But the basic idea is that each team is supposed to gain as much access as possible for its country's most competitive exports in the other countries' markets, while giving up as little access as possible in its own market. Suppose, for example, that Medatia is highly competitive in textiles and apparel. The instructions for the Medatia team might be to aim for a 50 percent average reduction in the tariffs that Alba and Tristat maintain on T-shirts and carpets. But in addition to that sort of "offensive" goal, the instructions contain "defensive" ones as well—limits on the concessions that each team should offer the other countries in the form of lower tariffs. Alba's "trade minister" might be instructed to strongly resist any major cuts in its tariffs on grain and beef because of the political clout of Alban farmers, for instance, or Tristat's might be admonished to protect his nation's chemical industry by offering no more than a 15 percent cut in its tariffs in that sector.

In the end, when the participants reach a consensus on a deal, the overall result will be lower barriers in all four countries, because each team will grant some access to its own market in exchange for gaining more access to the markets of the others. In certain cases, a team might not resist a cut in its own tariffs. A country's negotiators might happily agree to lower duties on machinery and fertilizer, for example, without regarding it as a concession, because having access to cheaper machines and fertilizer would presumably help factories and farmers become more competitive. But, as in real-life WTO negotiations, each country is fundamentally interested in mercantilist objectives—maximizing its gains in terms of exports, and minimizing its "losses" on the import side.

So the WTO is a peculiar mix: power and impotence; free trade and mercantilism. How did it get that way? As with many contemporary international institutions, the story has its origins in the mid-1940s.

| * |

Still amazingly energetic for a man born in 1918—even in his early nineties, he was traveling to Geneva to serve as a panelist in WTO dispute cases—Julio Lacarte has many yarns to tell. His career as a diplomat and international civil servant brought him into contact with Indira Gandhi, Konrad Adenauer, and Che Guevara, among other luminaries. He went into exile from his native Uruguay during the military dictatorship that began in the 1970s. And while growing up in New York, he saw Babe Ruth play baseball. But Lacarte has an even more impressive claim to fame, at least for the people he encounters at the Centre William Rappard: He participated in the U.N. Conference on Trade and Employment, in Havana, Cuba, which began in November 1947 and produced a charter the following March. In the world of multilateral trade, that makes him a founding father.

At the Havana conference, "there was tremendous debate," Lacarte recalls. "But everybody had one single aim. It was only a couple of years after the end of the war, and everybody was very keen about this postwar world that we were trying to build." The architects of the postwar order already had the United Nations up and running, and another of their creations, the World Bank, was starting to lend money to rebuild war-torn economies. Also newly in business was the IMF, whose chief goal was the promotion of global financial stability. Now, by turning to trade, the architects were taking another important step toward their goal of preventing a recurrence of the events that had engendered and deepened the Great Depression. Memories were still fresh of the Smoot-Hawley Tariff Act and other protectionist policies responsible for creating a ruinous climate for trade in the 1930s.

Signed by President Herbert Hoover in 1930, Smoot-Hawley was passed by Congress in response to the pleas of many American manufacturers and farmers and over the objections of many economists. The legislation raised tariffs on foreign products to an average of about 55 percent of the value of dutiable goods—the highest levels in at least a century, all but guaranteed to drive up the cost of many imported goods to unaffordable levels. In short order, America's trading partners, which had already begun raising their own barriers, erected their own sky-high protective walls. French tariffs on foodstuffs soared from 19 percent in 1927 to 53 percent in 1931. Over the same period, Germany's went from 27 percent to 82 percent, Italy's from 24 percent to 66 percent, and Austria's from 16 percent to 59 percent. To make sure that Washington would pay a painful price for Smoot-Hawley, the French, Germans, and Italians also imposed duties of well over 50 percent on autos, the crown jewel of American industry. Following a similar path were Mexico, Argentina, Japan, and many other countries. Even Britain, the nation that had pioneered free trade in the mid-nineteenth century by lowering its duties first on corn and then on other products, reversed course in early 1932 by enacting a general tariff.

Canada, the biggest single destination for U.S. exports, imposed stiff tariffs on key American products that accounted for about 30 percent of the U.S. goods shipped across the northern U.S. border, and it reduced duties on goods from the British Commonwealth. An "egg war" that erupted between the two countries offers a classic illustration of how one tariff hike begets another. Smoot-Hawley's increase in the U.S. duty on eggs caused a steep drop in the amount of Canadian eggs purchased by Americans; that increase prompted a retaliatory boost in the tariff faced by American farmers selling eggs to Canada, from three cents to ten cents a dozen. The upshot was that U.S. egg exports to Canada, once a lucrative market for American farmers, dwindled to virtually nothing.

These policies didn't *cause* the Depression; the chief blame for that belongs to the overly tight credit of the U.S. Federal Reserve. And it should be remembered that tariffs had been quite high in many industrial countries before, notably in the United States during much of the nineteenth and early twentieth centuries. Although some economists contend that the outbreak of protectionism severely intensified the economic downturn, even that is a matter of dispute; the 40 percent drop in global trade between 1929 and 1932 was probably much more attributable to the collapse in worldwide demand than it was to higher tariffs. But because steep trade barriers remained in place for years thereafter and proved hard to remove, the world's economies were hobbled as they strove to generate recoveries—on that score, there is general consensus among economic historians.

Equally unfortunate were the geopolitical consequences, which helped fuel conflict among countries. The leading powers established special trading arrangements with their close allies and colonies, splintering the world into blocs by using a combination of bureaucratic allocations, currency controls, and preferential tariffs. Japan's trade pattern offers an illustrative, if extreme, example: The share of Japan's imports coming from Korea, Formosa, and Manchuria doubled to 40.6 percent during the period 1929 to 1938, while the share of its exports going to those lands burgeoned from 12 percent to nearly 55 percent. A similar pattern emerged for the United Kingdom with its Commonwealth, France with its colonies, and Germany with its friends in southeastern Europe and Latin America.

This was the wreckage upon which Lacarte and his colleagues were mandated to build. To repair the damage and to minimize the danger of future trade wars, they sought to create a multilateral institution that would both open markets and limit the ability of governments to restrict imports in the future. Under the new system, tariffs would be lowered and also "bound," meaning countries would pledge never to raise them above certain levels. Each nation specified precise figures for the tariff bindings it would maintain on each of the goods to be covered, which included auto parts, acids, barbed wire, cash registers, fruit, glue, jewelry, liquor, soap, steel, tractors, and dozens of other products. And underpinning the system was a commitment by the participating nations to abide by certain cardinal principles. The first, and most important, was that nations joining the new arrangement would extend most favored nation (MFN) treatment to each other, meaning that they had to treat the products of all participants in a nondiscriminatory fashion. If, say, the United States set its tariff on cash registers from Britain at 15 percent, it would have to impose the same duty on cash registers from France or Australia or Uruguay. (Some exceptions were allowed, notably for national security measures, for free-trade areas, and for countries wishing to give especially favorable treatment to goods from their colonies and former colonies.) Countries outside the system—the Soviet Union being a prime example—would not enjoy these protections; tariffs on their goods could be set at any level. But for participants, MFN treatment was both a right and a responsibility. And participants also agreed to another key principle—national treatment, which meant they had to treat imported and locally produced goods equally, at least after the foreign goods had entered their markets. In other words, although a country could impose duties on imports, it could not impose laws and regulations on foreign goods that were different from the ones applicable to domestically produced ones.

The system that was finally implemented was not nearly as robust as the founders had hoped. A plan approved at Havana for a strong institution, dubbed the International Trade Organization (ITO), fell apart when the U.S. Congress, by then growing suspicious of global organizations, refused to approve it. Surviving the controversy was a more skeletal arrangement, the General Agreement on Tariffs and Trade (GATT), which was signed by twenty-three countries in 1948. The GATT was a compact, not an organization, so the participating countries could not claim the official status of "members." They were described as "contracting parties" (a term that was always capitalized in official documents), and when the GATT took action, it never did so under its own name; rather, it was "the CONTRACTING PARTIES" that did so.

Still, the GATT, whose Secretariat set up shop in Geneva, accomplished many of the key goals that the founders had envisioned, including enshrining the MFN and national treatment principles. And it meant that the noncommunist world had embarked on a grand march toward more-open commerce across borders. Here, in this grand march, was where free trade and mercantilism came together in a sort of harmonic convergence: Countries agreed to lower barriers based on the proviso that trading partners would lower theirs as well. Governments that might otherwise shrink from cutting tariffs for fear of offending powerful domestic industries were willing to join in multination trade-liberalization exercises because their exporters were eager for access to foreign markets, making it possible to mobilize political majorities for freer trade.

The grand march was more like a heavy slog at times, for it consisted of a series of rounds that involved long, arduous negotiations. Although the GATT had elaborate voting procedures, in practice consensus was required, and more countries kept joining as the years went by.

The initial GATT agreement lowered the tariffs of the twenty-three participating countries by nearly 20 percent. Then came four rounds in the 1940s, 1950s, and early 1960s that brought tariffs down a little more; during this period the United States was doing the lion's share of the market opening to help spur recovery in the economies of its Cold War allies. From 1964 to 1967 the participating countries—now numbering sixty-two—negotiated the Kennedy Round, named for the U.S. president who had played a key role in launching it, which reduced tariffs on manufactured goods by another 35 percent. In the Tokyo Round, which was negotiated from 1973 to 1979 among about one hundred countries, industrial tariffs were cut yet again, by about one-third. Moreover, this round included several agreements aimed at stopping countries from using unfair practices to block imports and to give advantages to their exports. The agreements were deemed necessary because a number of countries were subsidizing their exporters, imposing burdensome licensing requirements on importers, and allegedly using regulations concerning health, safety, and the environment in a discriminatory fashion against foreign products. Only a relatively small number of the contracting parties signed these agreements, however; countries were free to pick and choose, à la carte style, the codes to which they would subscribe.

The grand march was not only plodding. It almost completely avoided certain major areas of terrain.

As the political price for agreeing to the Kennedy Round tariff cuts, the United States insisted on sheltering its textile and apparel industry, which was a dominant force in southern states and held sway over powerful members of Congress from that region. Starting in the late 1950s with limits on imports of cotton goods made in Japan, Washington gradually extended restrictions to clothing, fabrics, towels, sheets, and all manner of other textiles—wool, cotton, polyester, nylon—from many other countries. The upshot was a massive abrogation of GATT principles, as the world's rich countries established a system of quotas that limited their imports from individual nations. The system specified, for example, the maximum amount of pillowcases that Pakistan could ship to the U.S. market, or how many pairs of cotton socks could come into the United States from Honduras, or the quantity of handkerchiefs made from artificial fiber that Hong Kong could export to Europe.

Agriculture, too, was exempted from GATT rules, initially because of a request from the United States in the 1950s and later because of the European Community's insistence on protecting its farmers. Moreover, as barriers fell on most manufactured goods, some industries hit hard by imports—the American steel industry being a salient case in point—made effective use of special legal devices that helped keep foreign competitors at bay, at least temporarily. These devices included "antidumping" laws, which empower a government to impose high tariffs on imports found to be selling at unfairly low prices, and "safeguard" laws, which allow the imposition of duties to protect a domestic industry threatened by a sudden import surge.

And then there were the developing countries, many of whom adopted the "Greta Garbo policy"—a reference to the Swedish actress known for the line "I vant to be alone."

The 1950s, '60s, and '70s were the heyday of the Non-Aligned Movement, the Group of 77, and other third world coalitions. Having finally thrown off Western colonialism, these countries aimed to achieve economic independence from the industrialized powers, using state-run development and opposing encroachment by American and European multinational corporations. Their leaders—India's Jawaharlal Nehru, Egypt's Gamal Abdel Nasser, Indonesia's Sukarno, Zambia's Kenneth Kaunda—nationalized industries and emulated some Soviet-style strategies, such as five-year plans, while staying clear of putting themselves under Moscow's thumb. They were not liberalizing their trade regimes nearly as much as the rich countries were; they insisted on "special," "differential," and "more favorable" treatment that largely exempted them from the tariff reductions adopted by the industrialized nations in GATT negotiations. Embracing the theory of import substitution, an approach that was especially popular in Latin America, they nurtured homegrown industries, sheltering them by high protective walls from the chill winds of foreign competition. In these countries, tariffs were so steep for virtually any item manufactured domestically that prices of those items were typically double or even triple the world level.

The rich countries allowed this to go on, even as they lowered their own barriers, and they also allowed low-income countries to exclude themselves from many of the individual GATT codes and other obligations. They did so partly because they wanted to keep the developing countries from joining the Communist bloc, and partly because the markets of Latin America, Africa, and developing Asia did not appear very lucrative from their standpoint anyway.

Having cut themselves loose from the rules of the system, the developing countries could pretty much chart their own economic courses, but they paid a toll. When the time came to write the rules, they were usually out of the room—one room in particular.

| * |

Arif Hussain's eyes sparkle when he recalls the Green Room. A former Indian civil servant who joined the GATT Secretariat in 1984, Hussain even kept the old Green Room furniture in a small chamber across from his office at the Centre William Rappard. The room was named for the tacky color ("goat-vomit green," one of Hussain's former colleagues calls it) of the fabric and upholstery that graced its walls and chairs. It was the director-general's conference room, which became famous in trade circles as the gathering place for representatives from a select group of powerful countries, usually twenty or so, at the invitation of Arthur Dunkel, the director-general from 1980 to 1993.

"There was lots of cigar and cigarette smoke in the air," Hussain recalls. "Negotiators were poring over papers and drafts, with liberal servings of wine and sandwiches." The idea was to create the proper ambience for reaching agreements that could be sold to all the countries participating in the GATT. Although the former Green Room is no longer green—it has been elegantly appointed with wood paneling, modern art paintings, and a polished oval wooden table—neither the tradition nor the term have faded into history. "Green rooms" are held often under WTO auspices—the term will come up repeatedly in this book—and consist of small groups of negotiators who try to strike key compromises in a manageably sized forum before the larger WTO membership considers them.

"English gentlemen's club" is the phrase veterans like Hussain often use to describe the atmosphere in the old days at the Centre William Rappard, where the GATT moved in 1977. Under a tacit understanding, the director-general was always a European, typically a courtly diplomat. It was a simpler era, in which developing countries were largely content to let the wealthier ones call the shots in trade rounds—provided, of course, that the developing nations could cling to their special and differential treatment. "Don't obey, don't object," was the principle they followed. Although Brazil and India were usually included in green rooms because of their leadership status in the developing world, their main goal was usually to ensure that they were exempt from whatever rules the rich were devising.

In fact, most of the major decisions taken during much of the GATT's history were the product of agreements thrashed out between the two biggest economies, the United States and the European Union (formerly known as the European Community).* Other industrialized countries participated in key meetings, especially Japan and Canada, whose trade ministers periodically met with those of Washington and Brussels, forming the Quad, a sort of steering committee for the trading system. But a speech by Pascal Lamy during his tenure as European trade commissioner describes, with a touch of exaggeration, the domination by the Americans and the Europeans: "In the old days, getting a new Round launched and indeed agreed was simply a question of aligning E.U. and U.S. objectives, sidestepping the odd row about agriculture, signing up the rest of the world, and catching the next plane home."

Rickety and jerry-built though the GATT system may have been, it resulted in a gradual melting away of many obstacles to commerce. Average tariffs imposed by industrialized nations on manufactured goods fell from roughly 35 percent to 6.5 percent by the mid-1980s as a result of GATT agreements. Economists widely credit this trend with providing a solid platform for the growth in international commerce that helped raise productivity and invigorated economies in the free world during the second half of the twentieth century.

But by the mid-1980s, the GATT system was in serious trouble, losing credibility and increasingly viewed as ineffective—with good reason.

Imagine a court in which a person could be accused of a crime and be found guilty, but then could, before being sent off to prison, stand up and announce, "I am exercising my right to void the verdict," and walk off scot-free. The GATT's system for settling disputes sometimes worked like that. If, say, the Republic of Freedonia believed that its exports were encountering unfair obstacles in the Kingdom of Sylvania, it could bring a case before a tribunal of specially selected experts in trade law. And if the tribunal agreed that Sylvania was violating GATT

---

*The member states of the European Community were "contracting parties" in the GATT, and as members of the European Union they are still members of the WTO. But because they have ceded control over much of their trade policies to the European Commission (the bloc's executive body), they have been represented in Geneva, and at nearly all GATT and WTO meetings, by commission officials. The member states exert influence over the trade commissioner through the Council of Ministers and other institutions.

rules, it could order Sylvania to change its practices or face punishment—the punishment usually being that Freedonia would be allowed to raise tariffs to punitive levels on some of Sylvania's products. But an odd loophole allowed countries to dodge this mechanism. The tribunal's ruling could be overturned if just one GATT member—including the one found to be violating the rules— lodged a dissent. Indeed, an accused country like Sylvania could stop the case from even being heard, because full consensus among GATT participants was required at every step of the proceeding, including the appointment of the tribunal, the tribunal's decision, and the imposition of sanctions. These rules often led to absurdly long delays, in which countries would refuse for months or even years to allow cases against them to move forward.

So the GATT was in many ways toothless, and that fact helped inflame protectionist sentiment in Washington, especially as angst was arising in the late 1970s and the 1980s about the apparent decline in U.S. competitiveness. The soaring U.S. trade deficit, the seeming invincibility of Japan's industrial juggernaut, and the rampant piracy of American films and music convinced many politicians and commentators that unfair practices by foreigners were tilting the playing field on which U.S. corporations and workers were competing. The trade hawks argued that America had to take matters into its own hands, because the GATT was incapable of remedying the problem. Lawmakers from both parties lined up behind legislation, passed in 1988, that toughened requirements for the U.S. trade representative to impose sanctions on countries that were engaging in "unjustifiable and unreasonable" practices against U.S. exports. The 1988 Trade Act, which was signed by President Ronald Reagan, was part of a mounting move toward a unilateral approach to handling disputes that struck at the very heart of the principles on which the GATT had been created. The same was true of agreements signed during that decade in which Japan promised to limit its exports of autos and certain other products to the United States—deals that were officially dubbed "voluntary export restraints," even though it was obvious that Tokyo's participation was the involuntary result of congressional threats to impose protectionist tariffs. Washington's commitment to multilateralism appeared to wane further with the completion, also in 1988, of the U.S. free-trade agreement with Canada, which was followed soon thereafter by the opening of talks for a similar deal with Mexico.

"GATT is dead," proclaimed Lester Thurow, dean of the Sloan School of Management at M.I.T., in 1989, and derision toward the institution intensified anew as the United States slipped into recession in the early nineties. Laura D'Andrea Tyson, a University of California–Berkeley economist who would become President William J. "Bill" Clinton's first chief economic adviser, published a book in 1992 declaring that "in its present form, [the GATT] is largely irrelevant" to America's most pressing trade concerns; she called for a policy that would "sometimes involve forceful unilateralism."

For the beleaguered defenders of multilateralism, salvation came in the form of an idea, conceived by an American, though his government would resist until the last minute.

| * |

John Jackson acknowledged in the book he published in 1990 that he was advancing his proposal "at the risk . . . of appearing unrealistic or too 'idealistic.'" A professor at the University of Michigan Law School, Jackson had gotten interested in the GATT during the 1960s and spent a few months working in the Secretariat in Geneva. After writing a highly regarded treatise on international trade law, he caught the eye of the Nixon administration, which wanted him to serve as general counsel of the Office of the U.S. Trade Representative. "I am definitely not a Republican," Jackson says, "and they asked me, had I signed any Vietnam War petitions at Michigan? Well, I had. So at first, the job was off. But then after the 1972 election, they decided to have another go at it, and I got the job." Deeply concerned by the problems he saw threatening the GATT, he issued a clarion call after returning to academia in the late 1970s, penning an article titled "The Crumbling Institutions of the Liberal Trade System." A dozen years later, he got his chance to play a part in the solution.

Big changes were afoot. Trade ministers from seventy-two countries had gathered in September 1986 at the Uruguayan seaside resort of Punta del Este. There they had launched the Uruguay Round, which was aimed not only at lowering trade barriers but also at expanding the compact's scope into new areas, in particular services, agriculture, and the protection of intellectual property. As a supporter of multilateralism, Jackson wanted the round to succeed, but he feared it would cause even more trouble for the GATT, which was already riddled with separate codes and treaties on issues ranging from civil aircraft to subsidies to import licensing. So in a 1990 book, he proposed replacing the "weak framework" of the GATT with an "institution which could be variously named, but which I will call (for simplicity's sake) a World Trade Organization (WTO)." In addition to providing a superstructure that could coordinate all the various agreements, the new organization envisioned by Jackson would have a much stronger dispute settlement system, with no more vetoes by losing parties.

Canadian trade minister John Crosbie jumped at the idea and formally proposed that the WTO be created as part of a final Uruguay Round agreement.

The Europeans were also enthusiastic; they had previously stood firmly against the idea of changing the dispute settlement system, but now they wanted a strong new global organization in the hope that it would stop the United States from continuing down the path to unilateralism. A big concern for Brussels was that the name should be "Multilateral Trade Organization"—an "MTO." Chairing the committee of negotiators considering these institutional issues—enhancing his status as a founding father—was Uruguay's Julio Lacarte.

The United States was wary. Policymakers in the U.S. Trade Representative's Office feared arousing the same sort of opposition in Congress that had doomed the ITO forty years earlier. After all, a more robust organization armed with a tough enforcement mechanism could restrict Washington's freedom of action on trade and would probably arouse fresh criticism from people worried about the erosion of American sovereignty. Still, U.S. officials favored a stronger international system for resolving disputes, and they thought they might use the WTO proposal as a bargaining chip in the Uruguay Round—in other words, agree to it on condition of receiving concessions in other areas. Behind the scenes, they indulged in debates about the best name. "We had all these jokes, because we didn't like 'Multilateral Trade Organization,'" recalls Rufus Yerxa, who was a deputy U.S. trade representative in the Clinton administration. "People said, 'Let's make it the Cosmic Trade Organization. No—the Intergalactic Trade Organization!'"

A grand bargain was in the making. Though it was taking years to come to fruition—the Uruguay Round negotiations often bogged down—the outlines of the deal began to take clear shape in the early 1990s, thanks in part to a bold proposal advanced in 1991 by Director-General Arthur Dunkel in a bid to break the deadlock.

The United States and other wealthy nations, including those in Europe, badly wanted to modernize international trade rules by extending them into sectors where commerce was growing rapidly, such as services, and into areas where conflicts were on the rise—intellectual property rights in particular. Some of the most dynamic Western companies were world leaders in industries such as pharmaceuticals, banking, and cinema, and their governments hoped to gain new protections for those firms' overseas operations. Washington was also keen to get greater export opportunities for highly competitive American farmers, and the Europeans wanted, among other things, the "MTO."

Meanwhile, a paradigm shift around the globe was drawing developing countries into the negotiations as never before. Communism had crumbled, with Russia and many of its satellites embracing free markets. The awe-inspiring rise of the Asian "tiger" economies—South Korea, Taiwan, Hong Kong, and

Singapore—was also transforming mind-sets. Many developing countries were abandoning their old models based on heavy government control and import substitution, which seemed to leave them mired in economic stagnation, and they were unilaterally lowering trade barriers in the hope that world markets would provide their salvation. Brazil, for example, reduced its average tariffs from 57.5 percent in 1987 to 13 percent in 1993, and Argentina cut its average tariffs from 40 percent to about 9 percent (though both nations kept much higher bound tariffs—that is, the ceilings they were legally required to honor under their GATT commitments). These countries wanted new and more advantageous rules in areas of trade that they cared about, and they were ready to bargain to get them.

At the top of the developing countries' wish lists were the two sectors that wealthy nations had fenced off from the GATT system—agriculture and textiles. Farmers and clothing makers in Latin America, Asia, and Africa could often undersell their rivals based in the industrialized world. Accordingly, their governments sought an end to the enormous obstacles that were keeping them from gaining full access to rich countries' markets, in particular the complicated quotas limiting their shipments of textiles.

The situation came to a head in mid-December 1993; it was potentially the biggest trade deal in history, with the fate of John Jackson's proposal just one of the issues hanging in the balance. Everyone knew that Peter Sutherland, the forceful Irish barrister and politician who had become the GATT director-general in July, meant business when he set December 15 as the deadline, "engraved in stone," for wrapping up the negotiations. No more extensions, Sutherland warned; the Uruguay Round would be declared dead this time if the negotiators failed again to make the necessary compromises. As the endgame neared, all eyes were on two men who shared a common heritage—Lithuanian Jewry—and little else.

Lean, almost gaunt, Mickey Kantor, who was the U.S. trade representative, speaks with a light Tennessee drawl (he is a native of Nashville), and he brought his talents as a hard-nosed Los Angeles lawyer and Democratic political operative to the negotiating table. His portly counterpart at the European Commission, Sir Leon Brittan, had a penchant for waxing philosophical in his plummy British accent about cerebral matters—a skill the conservative Sir Leon had honed during his days as president of the Cambridge Union. Their predecessors had already moved far toward resolving some of the biggest bones of contention, especially by striking an agriculture deal in late 1992 in which the Europeans agreed to curb subsidies for farm exports. But as typically happens in big negotiations, many concessions were being held back until the very end, so a number of issues remained outstanding. In the first three days of December 1993, Kantor and Brittan hammered out an accord in Brussels that refined the terms of the agriculture agreement, then flew to Geneva to continue grappling on other matters.

Geneva's hotels were filled to capacity with negotiators and lobbyists as the clock ticked closer to the December 15 deadline. The city's limousine and taxi services were running around the clock, and its finest restaurants were ladling out massive quantities of fondue to throngs of expense-account diners. A deal of breathtaking scope was on the table.

This time, tariff cuts on manufactured products were only a small part of the package. Yes, some hefty-looking reductions in tariffs were included; industrialized nations were slated to lower their duties by two-fifths, to an average of 3.8 percent. But other elements were far more important. Rich countries would get a whole new system of rules to protect patents and copyrights worldwide, plus rules covering international trade in the burgeoning service sector. Developing countries would get the elimination of textile quotas over a decade-long period, and agricultural tariffs and subsidies would finally be subject to worldwide limits. The package included goodies sought by other players as well, such as rules governing countries' rights to impose antidumping duties and a ban on "voluntary" export restraints. Japan and South Korea, which had steadfastly refused to open their rice markets even a crack, finally succumbed in early December to pressure from Washington and agreed to allow a very limited amount of rice imports. Riots erupted in Seoul and the prime minister was forced to resign upon word that 1 percent of the Korean rice market, rising over time to 4 percent, would be open to foreigners.

As if all this weren't enough, the whole bundle would consist of a "single undertaking." In other words, instead of the à la carte approach used in the Tokyo Round, when countries could choose which of various codes they wished to accept, all countries participating in the Uruguay Round would have to accept the deal in full (although developing countries would again get more lenient treatment, such as smaller tariff cuts and longer transition periods, than did rich countries). Indeed, all member nations would bind themselves to previous GATT agreements, including almost all of those that had previously been optional. So the rules, henceforth to be applied universally, would cover matters such as the laws and regulations countries could impose concerning health, safety, and the environment—the idea being to halt the discriminatory use of government power against imports.

One hot-button issue was still threatening to wreck the talks. The Europeans were insisting on protecting their domestic movie industry by maintaining tight limits on the number of foreign films aired on their TV networks. President Clinton had promised Hollywood's top moguls—among them some of the biggest donors to his campaign—that he would put the highest priority on getting Europe to give up these limits. The silver-maned president of the Motion Picture Association of America, Jack Valenti, led a small army of Hollywood denizens to Geneva, underscoring how passionately the U.S. film industry cared about the issue.

The final confrontation unfolded across the street from the Centre William Rappard, at the U.S. mission where Kantor and Brittan—already fatigued from several straight days and nights of nearly nonstop haggling—continued through the night until the dawn hours of December 14. Upstairs from them were Valenti and his movie-industry brethren, who were meeting constantly with the U.S. negotiators, exhorting them to take a tough stance. But with the French government strenuously opposed to the U.S. demands, Sir Leon refused to back down beyond giving in on a few minor points.

A forlorn, haggard Kantor met with the U.S. negotiating team at around 4:00 a.m. on December 14 to tell them that he had been "stiffed" and that with only a day left before the ax would fall on the Uruguay Round, he had to call the president to find out what to do. He shooed the others out of the room and reached Clinton in Boston. "I told him, 'In my view, this [film] issue is not that important, because Hollywood is going to dominate the world market anyway, regardless of what regulations the Europeans have,'" Kantor recalls, adding that Clinton agreed but wanted Kantor to call Lew Wasserman, who headed the Music Corporation of America (MCA) studio and who at eighty was the movie industry's godfather. "So," Kantor continued,

I called Lew. It was about 7:00 p.m. in Los Angeles. I told him what was going on. He said to me, "Mickey, isn't this the largest trade agreement ever?" I said, "Yes, it is." He said, "Is this in the interests of our country?" I said, "It is." He said, "This [movie] issue doesn't matter. We're going to dominate this business anyway. They can't keep us out of Europe. The technology [such as video on demand] will make it impossible for them to do that." So he said, "Go with God."

The next day, at 7:35 p.m., the rap of a mahogany gavel wielded by Director-General Sutherland marked the end of the Uruguay Round negotiations, triggering cheers and hugs among the representatives of the 117 participating nations.

And what of John Jackson's proposal? It had been settled that morning, the very last issue in the talks, with the United States accepting the idea provided that the new organization's name would be "World Trade Organization." This deal had come so late that the text released to the press still contained the Europeans' preferred name, so the stories about the accord in major newspapers did too. The *New York Times* reported in its December 15, 1993, edition: "A new international agency, the Multilateral Trade Organization, will replace the GATT."

| * |

Someday, historians may look back on New Year's Day 1995 as the zenith of economic globalization. On that day, as a few cameras flashed and videotapes rolled, down came the sign bearing the words "General Agreement on Tariffs and Trade" at the entrance to the Centre William Rappard. Up went a bronze plaque inscribed "WTO/OMC," the latter initials standing for Organisation Mondiale du Commerce, the body's name in French.

The ceremony came at a time when the principle of liberalizing commerce among nations was enjoying widespread favor, as witnessed by a rapid-fire series of events that took place in a remarkable period shortly before the plaque-changing exercise in Geneva.

Three weeks earlier, in Miami, Florida, had come what Clinton called "a magic moment"—the Summit of the Americas, bringing together leaders of thirty-four Western Hemisphere countries. Salsa star Tito Puente, reggae singers from Jamaica, saxophonist Kenny G, the Ballet Gran Folklórico de Mexico, and Brazilian drummers playing handheld *pandeiros* dazzled the summiteers and 4,000 VIPs who then enjoyed a fireworks display and—for the heads of state—a cruise across Biscayne Bay on a two-hundred-foot yacht to a state dinner. The extravaganza celebrated the leaders' pact to set a goal of 2005 for creating a free-trade zone extending from the Canadian Arctic to Tierra del Fuego. The idea was to effectively enlarge NAFTA, which after passing Congress in a stormy debate in 1993 had eliminated most trade barriers among the United States, Canada, and Mexico.

And about a month before the Summit of the Americas, in mid-November 1994, had come a gathering of the Asia Pacific Economic Cooperation forum in Bogor, Indonesia, where Clinton and seventeen other leaders posed for photos wearing batik shirts in varying shades of brown, black, beige, and ochre. This summit issued a declaration pledging to achieve "free trade and investment in the Asia Pacific" by 2020.

The promises issued at both summits—the Western Hemisphere one and the Asia Pacific one—could be considered windy rhetoric or mere symbolism,

but they were nonetheless another stunning sign of capitalism's continuing advance worldwide following the collapse of the Berlin Wall. The significance of
the declarations was not in their fine points, because the implications depended
critically on follow-up decisions that were yet to be made. They didn't legally
bind the signatories to much of anything. Completely free trade in such large regions was such an ambitious goal that it strained credulity; already in Bogor the
Japanese, along with the South Koreans and the Taiwanese, were quietly suggesting that the Asia Pacific plan's "scope" would have to be limited at future
meetings, an indirect way of saying they were determined to exclude rice and
other sensitive agricultural products from new threats of import penetration.
Even so, these declarations marked a milestone in the forward progress of free
markets that had gathered force during the preceding half-dozen years. Notable among their signers were countries—including China, still nominally a
Communist nation—that had been leaders in the Non-Aligned Movement and
other third world alliances opposed to multinational corporations.

The globalizers were obviously on a roll at these summits. The proposed
free-trade arrangements stirred a little unease even among free traders; it was
unclear what impact such plans would have on the principle of nondiscrimination among WTO members. But the multilateral system was being immeasur-
ably strengthened. Eclipsing both the regional meetings in importance was the
development commemorated by the new bronze plaque at the entrance to the
Centre William Rappard.

The fledgling WTO not only had rules that covered far more areas and sectors than had the GATT, areas such as agriculture, intellectual property, services, and health standards. It also had much sharper teeth. Thanks to new rules
in the Uruguay Round regarding dispute settlement, countries guilty of violating international trade rules could no longer block the creation of panels to
judge their cases or veto rulings that went against them. In exchange for giving
up the right to reject rulings that they considered erroneous, countries could
appeal to a newly established, seven-member Appellate Body, but its decisions
would be final. To be sure, the WTO could not *force* its members—which are
sovereign nations—to do anything. A member found to be in violation of WTO
rules could refuse to change its offending laws or practices. But the cost of defiance could be economically painful, given the right of victorious complainants
to impose retaliatory measures against violators.

Was this tantamount to a surrender of sovereignty? That issue had arisen during the debate in the U.S. Congress in 1994 over ratification of the Uruguay
Round. In response, supporters of the new organization argued that it involved
no more relinquishing of sovereign rights than did, say, treaties banning tests of

nuclear weapons. Just as with most treaties or international concords, the United States was agreeing to constraints on its behavior, in exchange for other countries' agreeing to the same. That argument helped secure congressional approval.

The WTO was greasing the tracks on which the globalization freight train was gathering momentum. And there was more to come.

In the second half of the 1990s, groups of WTO members banded together to reach agreements that liberalized trade even further in three specific sectors—information technology, telecommunications, and financial services. These so-called plurilateral deals were not signed by the entire WTO membership; just twenty-nine nations agreed initially to the Information Technology Agreement, for example, a number that later grew to seventy. But the signatories were responsible for the vast bulk of trade in the covered sectors, and they pledged to extend the terms on an MFN basis to all. For example, under the information technology deal, the participating countries agreed to cut their tariffs to zero on computer chips, fax machines, word processors, and a wide array of other high-tech products, and they agreed to grant the same duty-free treatment to those products from any WTO member, whether it had signed the agreement or not.

Not long after those accords came one of the most expansive lurches ever for the global trading system—the agreement signed by China that put it on the road to membership in the WTO.

Joining the WTO is a lot more complicated than simply mailing in an application form and paying dues. To get in, a country must negotiate bilaterally with any WTO member that wishes to obtain some changes in the prospective new member's trade regime, and all changes that are agreed are extended to the entire membership in accord with the MFN principle. For China, this process was bound to be transformative, because the United States, more than any other WTO member, was demanding a top-to-bottom makeover of the Chinese economy. The nation's economic structure still bore many of the hallmarks of Communist central planning—state enterprises that provided cradle-to-grave benefits for millions of workers; a creaky, bureaucratic banking system designed to fund those enterprises; and heavy interference from government and party officials who had the power to severely restrict opportunities for foreigners when it suited their interests. Under Zhu Rongji, China's modernizing visionary who became premier in 1998, Beijing made it clear that it was prepared to dismantle much of that old apparatus in order to obtain WTO membership. The Chinese had ample motive: By entering the WTO, they could free themselves from the threat of unilateral action being taken against their exports. They could also be assured that the United States, and other countries as well, would have to bring their grievances against China to WTO tribunals, instead of simply threatening Beijing with tariffs.

Prolonged and often-bitter negotiations were required, because the Chinese felt that the United States was taking advantage of the situation to press extreme demands on them. But in November 1999, U.S. Trade Representative Charlene Barshefsky and a team led by Zhu wrapped up a deal. Some of the deal's highlights give an idea of the lengths China went to in the course of securing its place in the WTO: Beijing had to reduce its bound tariffs on industrial goods to an average of about 9 percent by 2005—less than a third of the comparable figures for Brazil, Argentina, India, and Indonesia. Most quotas and license requirements that had restricted imports would be eliminated, and in the auto sector, where tariffs on cars had ranged up to 100 percent, the duty would fall to 25 percent over six years. As for agriculture, average tariffs would be cut to 15 percent, and for some commodities, notably wheat, the tariff would be near zero for a significant amount of imports. In another major concession, Chinese officials agreed that in three years' time they would allow foreign firms full rights to trade and distribute goods within the country, ending a system of state-controlled distribution than had long limited the ability of multinationals to sell products made abroad to Chinese consumers. In services, China made market-opening commitments in more sectors than most WTO members had. Foreign banks and insurance companies would no longer be restricted to operating in very limited areas. Beijing also agreed to embrace competition in its telecommunications system, substantially altering a regulatory regime that had protected the national monopoly.

The "W" in "WTO" had a much firmer basis once China was on its way toward joining. The absence of the most populous country on earth from the WTO's membership rolls had diminished its status as a global institution; that problem was now being corrected.

The forward progress of the globalization express, however, was not going unchallenged. A backlash was brewing.

# 3 | THE WTO AND
## ITS DISCONTENTS

EVERY YEAR GENEVA HOSTS A MAJOR TRADE AND TOURISM SHOW, AND in May 1998, one of the attendees was Don Lorentz, an economic development official with the Port of Seattle, who went to help promote Seattle as a convention destination. Serendipitously, he got a promising tip about an exciting opportunity for his city. The lead came at a reception at the home of the U.S. ambassador to the WTO, who confided to Lorentz that President Clinton was going to invite the trade body to hold its next big ministerial meeting in the United States. As a city with extensive involvement in trade, Seattle was an obvious candidate to host the meeting.

Pleased to be conveying this information, Lorentz flew home immediately after the show in mid-May. Had he stayed an extra day or two and seen what was about to happen in Geneva, he would have been able to temper his enthusiasm with a warning to his colleagues in Seattle that this arcane organization was becoming a magnet for trouble.

A series of often-violent demonstrations rocked Geneva from May 16 to 19. Chanting "The WTO kills people. Kill the WTO," an estimated 5,000 people rallied in the city's streets, with some groups going on rampages that involved smashing windows, spraying graffiti, and throwing paint-bombs. The car belonging to the Jamaican ambassador was overturned.

The protests were aimed at spoiling the fiftieth-anniversary celebrations of the multilateral trading system. To mark the occasion, the WTO was hosting a meeting of leaders from all over the world, including Clinton. The purpose was mainly to engage in a high-profile stocktaking of the system's half century, in the hope that this would inspire WTO member nations to aim even higher.

Homage, not protest, was in order at this Golden Jubilee, as far as the system's boosters were concerned. In a column titled "Why Liberalization Won," Martin Wolf of the *Financial Times* cited compelling statistics to underline the role that global commerce had played in five decades of postwar prosperity: World exports of goods and services had grown sixteenfold since 1950, reaching an annual total of $6.5 trillion; during that same period, the total volume of world output had risen sixfold. "Trade has consistently led output," Wolf concluded. Although tariff cuts were not the only cause—technological changes had helped too, by sharply reducing the cost of air travel and telephone calls—the "growing realization of the benefits of openness to trade" had transformed national policies, Wolf wrote. In Asia especially, "the results were stunning," he continued, noting how rapidly the living standards of ordinary people had risen in the region's four newly industrializing countries of Singapore, Hong Kong, South Korea, and Taiwan. In 1965, incomes per head in those countries had averaged 20 percent of the level in high-income nations; by 1995, that figure was 70 percent. "Their path was followed by other countries—Chile, Indonesia, Malaysia and Thailand, then China," Wolf noted.

But for the militants in Geneva's streets, and others who saw capitalism as exploiting the weak and despoiling nature, the three-and-a-half-year-old WTO made a perfect target. The very strengths that its admirers liked—its wider scope, its tougher enforcement—were arousing the hostility of people who viewed it as an instrument by which giant corporations were expanding their domination of the global economy. This perception had some basis in fact. Lower barriers to commerce meant that multinationals enjoyed greater freedom to conduct business wherever in the world they wished, and some WTO rules undeniably enhanced the multinationals' power—a perfect example being the new protections for intellectual property rights, which shielded big firms in the pharmaceutical, software, and entertainment business from would-be copycats.

In Europe, home of the Green movement, antipathy toward the WTO was rooted in concerns about the environment and public health. Free marketeers have long contended that trade is generally beneficial for the environment because it boosts growth and living standards, thereby giving nations the means to curb pollution. But Greens could legitimately spot some serious conflicts between trade and environmental goals, especially in cases where damage to the ecosystem spills over from one country to another—for example, the destruction of forests, the emission of acid rain, or the extinction of animal species. The WTO could potentially thwart efforts to combat such environmental ills, Greens feared, because the only effective approach might entail the imposition of trade sanctions on nations that engage in irresponsible policies—and it was far from clear that such sanctions were permissible under WTO rules.

Food safety was another issue that raised hackles over trade in Europe, whose consumers are famously leery of artificial elements in their diet. In assessing the health risks of food additives, European governments wanted to use the "precautionary principle," by which they could protect the public from products they suspected of posing a danger even when no scientific certainty had been established. But that policy had already run afoul of a WTO tribunal by the time of the Geneva protests in 1998; indeed, this controversy was one of the factors stoking the demonstrators' anger.

It was a beef over beef—specifically, meat from cattle treated with growth-enhancing hormones. The European Union had banned hormone-treated beef in 1989, an action challenged at the WTO by both the United States and Canada, where ranchers have used hormones on their cattle for years. Washington and Ottawa cited an overwhelming consensus among experts that there was no scientific evidence of hazards in hormone-treated beef, and they said the E.U. policy therefore violated WTO rules, which require that regulations exceeding internationally agreed standards must be justified by scientific evidence.

The WTO's ruling against the E.U. ban in May 1997 infuriated food-safety activists. Why, they asked, shouldn't the European Union be allowed to evaluate health risks based on the societal norms of its citizens, who favor the precautionary principle? In fact, the European Union *could* still base its policies on that principle, and the Brussels ban on hormone-treated beef remained in effect—a classic example of the fact that the WTO cannot force a government to change its policies. The WTO ruling still rankled, however, and the price of defying it would be steep. (Later, after the case was fully litigated, Washington received authorization from the WTO to impose 100 percent tariffs on more than $100 million worth of European items such as French foie gras and Roquefort cheese.) Further upsetting Europeans was the prospect that the hormone case would be just the first in a series of WTO challenges to E.U. health and safety rules, including those on genetically modified food.

In addition to the hormones-in-beef case were WTO rulings that seemed almost comically malevolent because of their apparent callousness toward the fate of some of the earth's most beloved creatures—sea turtles and dolphins.

The sea turtle case was decided only five weeks before the fiftieth-anniversary festivities in May 1998. This time the United States was on the side of the environmental angels. At issue was a U.S. law aimed at saving the reptiles, an endangered species, whose populations had been decimated because thousands of them were accidentally getting caught in shrimp nets and drowning. Under the U.S. law, no shrimp could be sold in the American market except from countries whose fleets used special nets with "TEDs"—turtle excluder devices, which are basically metal grilles that keep the turtles out of shrimp nets. The law drew a challenge at the WTO from Thailand, Malaysia, India, and Pakistan, which argued that under long-standing rules of the global trading system, the United States had no right to impose its production standards on other countries. A sound principle underlay their case: If one country begins insisting that imported goods must be produced in certain ways, the conditions it imposes (workplace safety? gender discrimination?) could easily become excuses for protectionism. But environmental activists were naturally up in arms when a WTO panel agreed with the Asian complainants. Now turtles would join dolphins as a cause célèbre of the antiglobalization movement, because in a similar case a few years earlier, a GATT panel declared illegal a U.S. law banning the importation of tuna from countries that did not protect dolphins from being caught in tuna nets.*

In the United States, the woes of marine wildlife in trade tribunals were causing a stir. But even greater unease over the trading system was mounting for a different reason.

| * |

For an account of the Dickensian world in which many factory workers struggle in low-income countries, it would be hard to top the article published in the *Chicago Tribune* in 1994 that opened with the story of Winarti, a twenty-three-year-old Indonesian woman. She lived in a "garbage-strewn industrial enclave" outside Indonesia's capital of Jakarta, the article reported, in a "one-room concrete hovel, its harsh, bare walls illuminated by a single bulb that hangs from the ceiling." As bad as her life was already, it was getting even worse, because a few months earlier she had been fired from her job sewing clothes for Gap stores in the United States, which paid her $1.75 a day (the minimum wage then in Indonesia) plus 75 cents a day for overtime. Her offense: She had at-

---

*The United States filed an appeal in the shrimp-turtle case, and a ruling some months later by the WTO's Appellate Body substantially softened the impact of the panel's decision. The Appellate Body acknowledged that WTO members have legitimate interests in protecting sea turtles and other endangered species by using policies such as the turtle excluder device requirement. But the body's ruling still found the implementation of the U.S. policy to be discriminatory and thus technically in violation of WTO rules. As a result, sea turtles remained a potent symbol of environmentalists' unhappiness with the trade body.

tended a meeting to learn about workers' rights, and when the plant's managers found out, they sacked her. This was by no means unusual for the Asian laborers who produce the goods lining American store shelves; according to the article, "Employers regularly flout government regulations on minimum wages and maximum hours" in Indonesia and neighboring countries, and "health and safety regulations are either non-existent or not enforced."

Tales like Winarti's were helping fuel the "antisweatshop" movement on American college campuses, in which students boycotted clothing and shoes made by companies that were allegedly mistreating their workers. And as public awareness grew during the mid-1990s about working conditions in the third world, political momentum was building behind the argument that trade rules ought to require countries to enforce strict standards on labor rights and the environment. For U.S. labor unions, this was a powerful rallying cry at a time when American factory workers were losing jobs in droves to fast-growing industrial juggernauts in Asia and Latin America. The unions had never been able to win on the nakedly protectionist claim that American workers should be shielded from competition from countries where workers earn much less than Americans do. They stood on much firmer ground by questioning the fairness of competing with countries where basic labor rights, such as the right to organize and bargain collectively, were absent and where companies were essentially free to pollute in ways that U.S.-based manufacturing operations couldn't.

Among the leaders of the labor movement and their Democratic allies in Congress, the new catchphrase was "race to the bottom"—the contention that as production shifted to countries with the lowest labor costs and the laxest regulations, living standards and environmental quality everywhere around the globe would gradually but inexorably be dragged down. They warned that amid the manic competition to get and keep job-generating investment, governments would have no choice but to succumb to pressure from multinationals to turn a blind eye when worker rights were abused or pollution rules flouted. The way to prevent that from happening, in this view, was not to halt globalization, which was unstoppable, but to change its rules, so that all trading nations would be subject to sanctions if they failed to maintain reasonable protections for labor rights and environmental policies. Countries such as Guatemala, Sri Lanka, or China might pay their workers a good bit less than Americans earned, but they ought to ensure that workers had the right to form unions and strike, for example. And countries that didn't should not have unfettered access to the American market for their products. As Alan Reuther, legislative director for the United Auto Workers, put it in 1997: "We're not saying that every country has to have our minimum wage today. But we don't want to see a race to the bottom, a competition based on who can have the lowest wages or worst health and environmental standards." Union insistence on strong labor protections in trade rules was the main reason for congressional rejection in 1997 and 1998 of legislation that would have given the president authority to negotiate new trade agreements, an ignominious setback for the Clinton administration.

By the time of the WTO's fiftieth-anniversary event in May 1998, strands of the unions' argument were increasingly turning up in Clinton's rhetoric, as the U.S. president was feeling the heat from critics of his moves to dissolve trade barriers. In his remarks to the assembled leaders in Geneva, Clinton—though hailing the accomplishments of the multilateral system—also issued an eloquent warning of his country's growing disenchantment. "We must do more to ensure that spirited economic competition among nations never becomes a race to the bottom," he said. "We should be leveling up, not leveling down. Without such a strategy, we cannot build the necessary public support for continued expansion of trade. Working people will only assume the risks of a free international market if they have the confidence that the system will work for them."

As free traders were at pains to point out, however, historical evidence suggests that the race-to-the-bottom theorists had their directionality wrong.

The first "loser" in the race, after all, was Britain, home of the original Dickensian factories, which churned out cotton textiles cut and stitched by people in the most desperate stratum of the nation's society, mainly women from rural areas and children from poorhouses. Taking jobs from the British in the early 1900s were mills along rivers in Massachusetts and New Hampshire, where thousands of young women from the New England and Canadian countryside toiled at similarly repetitive drudgery, often for more than seventy hours a week, until the industry moved to southern states to take advantage of farm girls (and many *were* girls, thirteen years old and younger) willing to work for wages half those paid in the north. Meanwhile, by the 1930s, millions of young Japanese women, living in squalid company boardinghouses and working twelve-hour days for substantially less than their American counterparts, were producing a large portion of the world's cotton goods. And although Japan's industry revived after World War II—expanding into shoes, toys, and other products—it fell prey to competition from Hong Kong, South Korea, and Taiwan in the 1960s and '70s. In this race—whose latest "victors" are China, Vietnam, and Central American nations—each "defeat" was undoubtedly anguishing for the factory workers displaced. But it was simply a part of the process by which these countries became modern, diversified industrial economies, as their buying power created demand for new goods and services, leading in turn to new jobs.

Apart from the thrusts and counterthrusts of the debate, advocates of labor and environmental standards had an embarrassing problem: Developing countries were vehemently opposed to the idea of incorporating such standards into the rules of the trading system. Policymakers in Brasilia, New Delhi, Cairo, Pretoria, and other such capitals were deeply cynical about the expressions of concern emanating from Washington about the rights of workers in third world factories and the need to protect the water and air in their countries. They were virtually unanimous in suspecting that rich countries would use worker rights as a pretext for depriving poor nations of their main competitive advantage—cheap wages. Standards on labor and the environment, they feared, would keep their economies from ever climbing the ladder of development as the high-income countries had done. So they rebuffed every effort by the Clinton administration to raise the labor issue as a topic for discussion in the WTO, asserting that the proper forum was the International Labor Organization (which has none of the WTO's enforcement power). Typical was the comment by Veerendra Kumar, India's labor minister, who told a 1997 conference that the "rising spectre of neo-protectionism in the name of labor standards . . . need[s] to be recognized, viewed with concern and combated with all force."

In any event, officials of developing countries had their own grievances against the trading system, which they considered much more justifiable than those of Greens and labor unions in rich nations. They had signed on to the Uruguay Round, having bought into the capitalist fervor of the mid-1990s. Now some of them were wondering whether they had gotten a raw deal.

| * |

Spelling out the basic Uruguay Round agreement required 424 pages of text. The lists of tariff reductions and other commitments that individual WTO members made for the myriad products traded on world markets needed 22,000 more pages, because for most countries each type of product has its own "tariff line" involving detailed specifications. A glance at portions of the U.S. tariff schedule offers a taste of the complexity involved. The variety of duties that U.S. customs officers would assess on poultry, which took up an entire page, included a tariff on live chickens of 0.9 cents per bird; a levy on fresh, chilled, or frozen chicken meat that was not cut in pieces of 8.8 cents per kilogram; a charge on "cuts and offal, fresh or chilled," of 17.6 cents per kilogram; a duty of 15 cents per kilogram on turkeys that were "not cut in pieces, fresh or chilled"; and so on. U.S. duties on gloves and mittens ranged from zero to 23.5 percent of the importer's price, depending on whether they were made of cotton, synthetic fibers, or "wool or fine animal hair," on whether they were "impregnated, coated or covered with plastics or rubber," and on what combination of those materials they contained (for example, different tariffs applied to gloves "containing 50 percent or more by weight of cotton, man-made fibers or other textile fibers" versus those "containing over 50 percent by weight of plastics or rubber"), and depending on whether they were hockey gloves, ski and snowmobile gloves, or other gloves.

Buried in all the fine print were some unpleasant surprises for low-income countries, revelations that were coming to light in the years after the Uruguay Round's completion. The concessions they thought they had extracted from the rich were looking more and more chimerical, while the obligations they had accepted were looking more and more burdensome.

The agreement to protect patents and copyrights was proving much more onerous for many developing countries than they had expected. Just establishing patent offices was a jarringly expensive proposition in some cases—as were the costs of complying with other Uruguay Round codes, such as those aimed at keeping health and safety regulations from unfairly blocking imports. "Argentina spent over $80 million to achieve higher levels of plant and animal sanitation. Hungary spent over $40 million to upgrade the level of sanitation of its slaughterhouses alone. Mexico spent over $30 million to upgrade intellectual property laws and enforcement." Those examples, from a World Bank report published in 1999, illustrated the high expenditures that developing countries were facing to fulfill their WTO obligations. Estimating that the cost for many governments would run at least $130 million, the report noted that such a sum was more than the annual aid some of the poorest nations received.

And what were the developing countries getting in return? They had gripes aplenty about that, too, especially given the painfully slow dismantling of the system of quotas that had limited their exports of clothing to rich countries. The Uruguay Round required the United States and the European Union to phase out the system in a series of steps over ten years, but Washington and Brussels were taking advantage of every legal loophole they could to keep their markets protected for as long as possible. Nearly four years after the Uruguay Round went into effect, the United States had ended only 2 of its 750 quotas, and the European Union had ended only 14 of its 219 quotas, Nestor Osorio, the Colombian ambassador, complained in a statement to the General Council in October 1998.

Above and beyond this matter of timing lay a more fundamental, conscience-pricking truth: Even after all the provisions of the Uruguay Round were fully phased in, many of the products that developing countries were most eager to export would still be subject to massive barriers and distortions, thanks to rich-country policies. A report by the U.N. Conference on Trade and Development (UNCTAD) in 1999 highlighted some of the most egregious examples: The United States imposed tariffs ranging from 38 percent to 58 percent on sports, rubber, and plastic shoes, and in Japan, the duty on some leather shoes ran as high as 140 percent. American tariffs on most synthetic, woolen, and cotton clothing ranged between 14 percent and 32 percent.

Nowhere would this problem be more pronounced than in agriculture. The Uruguay Round notwithstanding, agriculture would remain the last great bastion of protectionism.

| * |

Like most of their neighbors, Joseph Nyambe and his family live in mud-walled, thatched-roof huts, spread out in a dusty clearing about two hours' drive from Zambia's capital, Lusaka. Short, with a scruffy beard, a kindly expression, and a gentle, resonant voice, the forty-nine-year-old Nyambe has eight children, and although five of them are in school, the three eldest stopped going after the ninth grade. The family dines mainly on *nshima,* a bland staple of the Zambian diet made from maize that they grow themselves, and eggs provided by the twenty chickens that Nyambe owns. Several of the children sleep on the dirt floors in their huts; the luckier ones sleep on small grimy beds. The only sign of luxury is a battery-powered TV, which gets one channel. For transportation, the family has three bicycles.

Nyambe's main source of income is cotton, which he and his older children plant, raise, and cultivate by hand on about two and a half acres of land, using simple hand tools such as hoes, though he occasionally rents an ox to pull a plow when the work gets really hard. "Sometime back, my parents had oxen," he told me, "but we don't have any more. They died of disease." His total income in the most recent crop year was $210 from cotton, and about $160 from other crops such as beans.

In developing countries, almost half the population live in rural areas and work in agricultural activities, as Nyambe's family does. Moreover, a very large portion of the rural residents in low-income nations survive on less than a dollar a day. Farming areas are home to about 70 percent of the world's poor. So the health of agriculture in developing countries is of no small consequence to the goal of reducing world poverty.

Yet enormous government programs in high-income countries work to the disadvantage of the rural poor in low-income countries, in two main ways. First, rich nations provide lavish subsidy payments to many of their farmers, which can encourage so much overproduction as to create gluts of certain crops on world markets, thereby depressing the prices that peasants in Africa, Latin America, and Asia get at harvest time. Second, high-income countries restrict imports of many agricultural products, thereby limiting the ability of poor-country farmers to sell their goods abroad.

The meagerness of Nyambe's earnings is attributable, at least in part, to a U.S. government program in which Washington pays U.S. cotton farmers billions of dollars in subsidies when the price of cotton falls below certain levels. American growers, who cultivate cotton using huge, expensive machines, know they'll get a certain amount of money for their cotton regardless of what happens to prices, so they produce a lot more than they would otherwise. Their surplus gets sold on world markets, and—this is just simple economics of supply and demand—helps reduce the price received by farmers like Nyambe. Although the exact amount of the "price suppression" caused by U.S. cotton subsidies is impossible to determine, and it varies from year to year, some studies have put it as high as 30 percent.

Nyambe doesn't know much about world cotton markets, but he does know that his life would be improved—significantly so, from his perspective—if he could get more for his cotton crop. Even though the increase in his annual income might only be about the same as, say, the cost of a meal at a trendy restaurant in the United States, that would make a big difference to someone whose yearly cash intake is in the hundreds of dollars. "I could pay my children's school fees," he muses, which might mean the ones still in school could graduate instead of dropping out. "I could purchase some animals. I could pay for medicine that we need."

Thousands of miles away, in Brazil's Paraíba valley, a couple of hours from the megalopolis of São Paulo, Jorge Benedito de Assis remembers what it's like to live like Nyambe. A forty-two-year-old farmworker with thick black hair, wearing a baseball cap, yellow T-shirt, and rubber boots, Benedito recalls growing up in a mud house, with no running water or electricity, where the family cooked on a wood stove inside their home, filling it with smoke. He enjoys a much better lifestyle now, thanks to a job on a dairy farm where he and one of his sons wake at 4:30 a.m. to milk cows by hand and put in long days—often up to twelve hours—feeding, cleaning, and performing other chores. The pay for him and his son is about $6,000 a year, an enviable sum by Brazilian standards. His cement home, which he occupies rent free, has a tin roof but is tidy and furnished with well-made wooden beds, a refrigerator, two TVs, a DVD player, a gas stove, and a washing machine. Gazing out over a pond near his house, with palm trees swaying in a balmy breeze, he says, "If all Brazilian kids could live like this, we wouldn't have so much violence."

That's the problem: Trade barriers in rich lands, especially America and Europe, limit the number of Brazilian kids who can live as Benedito's family does. Brazil is one of the most agriculturally blessed nations in the world, with an abundance of rainfall and hundreds of millions of acres of fertile land for planting and pasture. So the nation's booming farm sector has helped provide employment to people who would otherwise live in the nation's crime-ridden favelas. But tariffs and quotas in high-income countries on the most formidably competitive Brazilian farm products, notably sugar, beef, and orange juice, translate into curbed demand for those goods. Likewise, in the dairy sector where Benedito works, Brazil has the capacity to become a major exporter of powdered milk, but the American and European markets are essentially closed. "A lot of people who live in the suburbs of big cities want to come back to work in the countryside," said João das Mercês Almeida, the owner of another Paraíba valley dairy farm. "But we have no conditions to hire them."

Worlds away from Zambia and Brazil, both geographically and otherwise, are the farmers who benefit from rich-country subsidies and barriers. They collect government largesse in amounts that their competitors in low-income nations can scarcely fathom.

| * |

A few miles outside the medieval town walls of Beaune, in France's Burgundy region, stands the farm of Olivier Cretin, from whose pasture the panorama encompasses rolling hills, grazing cattle, and the steeple of a fifteenth-century church. Just shy of his thirty-eighth birthday, with tousled hair and boyish features, Cretin (pronounced *creh-TAHN*) proudly showed me a large shed, built by his father forty years ago, which houses his ninety Montbeliard cows, whose milk goes to the French company Danone to make yogurt. He emphasizes that he works hard, because the cows must be hooked up to milking machines twice a day, and he also owns parcels of land totaling about 395 acres that are mostly planted in wheat and other cereals. For fifteen years, he went without a vacation, given the need to tend the cows, so to ease the burden he took on an apprentice a few years ago. "Now I can live," he says, recalling holidays he has taken to England and Tunisia. "Today's farmers aren't like our parents—they were happy just to live on a farm. We want to send our children to school, have vacations and free time."

Assisting him in that regard is the support that he gets from the European Union. In 2006, he received about $57,000 in government payments, on top of the farm's gross profit of about $55,750. In addition, his farm benefits from E.U. tariffs that help boost the prices of the products he sells—for dairy products, the average tariff in recent years has been around 38 percent, and for beef, around 76 percent.

The system that buoys farms such as Cretin's was established in 1962 as part of the deal in which six countries—France, West Germany, Italy, Belgium, the Netherlands, and Luxembourg—were forming the common market that would eventually eliminate economic barriers among most of the nations in Europe. West Germany, the continent's fast-growing industrial powerhouse, wanted markets for its manufactured goods, and France wanted in exchange a system that would secure the livelihoods of its farmers. The result was the Common Agricultural Policy (CAP), which in recent years has absorbed more than 40 percent of the E.U. budget (with French farmers being the biggest recipients), while tariffs imposed on foreign farm goods shipped to Europe add well over $600 a year to the food bills of the average European family.

Asked why farmers like him should be entitled to such treatment, Cretin echoes the justification often advanced by French politicians: "We farmers manage the countryside," he says. "France has a beautiful image. And if there were no farmers to keep it up, you'd have to pay someone else to do it." Besides, he continues, he must comply with many environmental, health, and animal-welfare regulations. In his wheat fields, he is required to keep nitrates well away from nearby streams. His cattle all have tags in their ears saying where they were born, who their parents were, and what vaccinations they have received, and inspectors from the dairy cooperative to which Cretin belongs check each cow once a month and make even more frequent visits to sample the milk in the milking machinery for cleanliness.

Maintaining the countryside, however, can be achieved in more efficient ways than by subsidizing farmers, and critics of Europe's CAP point out that the vast bulk of the money has gone to large farms, including many French ones with vast fields of cereals, sugar beets, and rapeseed that aren't any more picturesque than those found in, say, the flatlands of North Dakota. In recent years, well over 70 percent of the subsidies have reportedly gone to the biggest 20 percent of E.U. farms, many of them owned by large corporations. Activists campaigning for full transparency about E.U. subsidy payments have pried loose data showing that some of the biggest recipients include the Irish agribusiness Greencore, which produces Weight Watchers meals and other convenience foods and got $112 million in 2008, and a French chicken giant named

Doux, which reaped $85 million that same year. Among the rich and famous individuals whose landholdings have also earned them huge payments, to the tune of tens of thousands and even hundreds of thousands of dollars a year, are Queen Elizabeth, Prince Charles, the media tycoon Sir Anthony O'Reilly, and Michael O'Leary, the head of Ryanair.

Although Cretin didn't mention it, another justification often cited for government support of European farmers is what some call "gastronomic sovereignty"—the desire among ordinary people, especially in France, to preserve a food culture that prizes fresh, local ingredients. That sentiment is on vivid display every year at the Salon International de l'Agriculture, an annual exposition in Paris, typically attended by more than half a million people who come to admire and sample French farms' most exquisite wares—sausages, hams, foie gras, terrines, cheeses, wines—and enjoy the competition for medals among handsomely groomed cows, horses, pigs, sheep, goats, rabbits, and other animals. But also out in force at the Salon are politicians, ostentatiously savoring delicacies and stroking animals in their eagerness to demonstrate support for the nation's powerful farm bloc—and that zeal, probably more than any other factor, explains why Europe coddles its agricultural sector. France's main farmers' unions are militant, sometimes to the point of violence, and the countryside is overrepresented in the Senate, where members are elected indirectly by local officials, many from rural communes. The clout of the farm lobby increased exponentially when Jacques Chirac, a former agriculture minister, was elected president of France in 1995. Chirac was a fervent champion of farmers who built his political base as a deputy from the rural constituency of Corrèze, his family's hometown.

To such politicians, it is futile to suggest, as some economists do, that European governments could accommodate the food culture of their citizens by opening the continent's markets and letting consumers choose, based on clear labeling, between expensive local food and cheap imports. As elegant a solution as that might be economically, it does not play in places like Corrèze.

France, of course, is by no means the only E.U. member state with a strong pro-farm stance. It can often count on support on agriculture issues from Ireland, Denmark, Greece, and others in the Council of Ministers, a key legislative body of the union. And the European Union is by no means the most extravagant government in dispensing favors to farmers. Relative to farm receipts, several other countries provide greater support, including Japan, South Korea, Switzerland, and Norway. But the E.U. farm program is by far the biggest in absolute economic terms—followed by that of the other agricultural heavyweight of the rich world, the United States.

Piloting a $180,000, six-row combine through his vast fields of corn, John Phipps of Chrisman, Illinois, offers a classic illustration of the U.S. farm program's bounteousness. Phipps was one of the farmers profiled in a series of articles in the *Washington Post* that focused on subsidy payments, which was appropriate because subsidies are a much bigger factor in buoying American agriculture than are import barriers. With a few exceptions—notably the extremely restrictive tariffs and quotas that limit imports of sugar, frozen orange juice, and some dairy products—U.S. barriers on farm goods from overseas are relatively low, at least compared with those of Europe and Japan. But the subsidies paid to many American farmers are so outlandishly high that even some of the beneficiaries find them excessive.

Among them is Phipps, fifty-eight, a sixth-generation farmer trained in engineering who extracts high yields from his fields by using up-to-the-minute technology to help manage his crop, including computerized tracking of the exact number of bushels he is harvesting, acre by acre, row by row. He received $120,000 in government checks in 2005—an "embarrassing" sum, as he put it. "My government is basically saying I am incompetent and need help," he said.

Boosters of U.S. subsidy programs typically credit them with being essential to saving modest-sized, struggling family farms. But Phipps's case provides some insight into where the money really goes. The half million dollars that he grossed in 2005 from corn and soybeans put him in the "large family farm" category (defined as having more than $250,000 in revenue). Such farms account for just 7 percent of all farms but collect more than 54 percent of federal subsidies. Their owners enjoy average household incomes more than triple that of the average American household.

Needless to say, thousands of American farmers are a lot more favorably disposed toward federal subsidies than Phipps is, and so are many of their neighbors in rural America—the machinery salespeople, storage facility operators, and even restaurant workers who depend on a healthy agricultural sector for their incomes. They make their desires felt through one of the best-organized lobbies in Washington, led by the American Farm Bureau Federation, which encompasses about 2,800 county farm organizations plus state farm bureaus. During the 1990s the Farm Bureau was strongly in favor of free trade, on the theory that U.S. farmers and ranchers could prosper if only overseas markets were more open. In recent years, it has tempered its enthusiasm, showing less interest in seeking export markets if that means sacrificing subsidies. Rural land prices often reflect the value of subsidies, which makes farmers all the more reluctant to accept a shrinkage in subsidy programs, because that would translate into a reduction in the worth of their landholdings.

Thanks in part to the Farm Bureau and in part to associations representing growers of certain types of crops and livestock, lawmakers with rural constituencies of any significance are made painfully aware of the severe political consequences in store for anyone who votes against farm programs. Food and agribusiness organizations contribute generously to political campaigns, and it is no coincidence that the commodity groups that funnel the most money to politicians—sugar, dairy, cotton, and rice—get the most support from Uncle Sam. The Senate and House agriculture committees, which write the U.S. farm bill, consist almost entirely of members from rural areas. (Big-city congressmen are not exactly lining up to serve on those panels.) To garner support from their urban brethren for their farm bills, the members of the agriculture committees include funding for popular nutrition programs, notably food stamps. All this explains how the subsidy programs have remained in place despite intense criticism over the billions of dollars they cost and the environmental toll they exact by encouraging farmers to soak the soil with pesticides and fertilizer.

Taking the European and U.S. programs together, it is not surprising that agriculture clearly takes the prize for having the most distorted trade in the world. Whereas tariffs on manufactured goods average less than 4 percent, the comparable figure for farm products was recently above 60 percent (including the duties that low-income countries impose on each other's goods). Moreover, only in agriculture are governments allowed under WTO rules to provide export subsidies—that is, payments that go specifically to producers that ship their goods abroad. In other sectors, export subsidies have long been banned as an unfair trading practice that undercuts the ability of producers overseas to remain economically viable.

The Uruguay Round was supposedly going to make agriculture much more like other sectors. It did put some caps on export subsidies, but soon after the round's mandates went into effect, their paltry impact on farm trade was recognized. "How can a trade agreement with such major reforms result in so little liberalization?" asked one 1996 study by Dale Hathaway of the National Center for Food and Agricultural Policy and Merlinda Ingco of the World Bank. "The devil is in the details."

Besides bringing agriculture under multilateral rules for the first time, the round mandated a 36 percent average cut in farm tariffs for wealthy countries, with a minimum cut of 15 percent. That sounds pretty hefty—but in the world of trade, "cuts" aren't always what they're cracked up to be (a point that will crop up often in this book). An *average* cut, after all, can mean all kinds of things. One way a country can achieve a 36 percent average cut in a sector is to reduce all tariffs on all goods in that sector by 36 percent. But another way is to pick and choose, barely touching the tariffs on the goods the country most wants to protect while slashing the tariffs on the goods it doesn't care about. Suppose, for example, the cattle ranchers are desperate to keep the 80 percent duties on beef that help restrict foreign competition, but nobody gives a hoot about the 2 percent tariff on mangoes because the country's climate isn't suitable for tropical fruit anyway. The mango tariff can be cut all the way to zero, earning credit for cutting that one by 100 percent, and the beef tariff can be cut by the minimum percentage—and the average cut for those two products is close to 50 percent.

In the Uruguay Round, similar sleights of hand were multiplied across hundreds of tariff lines, and that, along with other practices, led Hathaway and Ingco to conclude: "Certain negotiators, supporters, and officials have portrayed the agreement as a sweeping reform of world agricultural trade and a significant move toward liberalization. Scrutiny of the details suggests it is considerably less."

| * |

The global trading system, and the WTO in particular, thus had numerous sources of disgruntlement as the new system took shape in the second half of the 1990s. European Greens, American labor unionists, third world farmers and trade officials—all had serious bones to pick. For them, and other bone-pickers as well, an irresistible target was presenting itself as the idea for a WTO meeting in Seattle, planted so casually in May 1998, morphed into reality.

# 4 | CLUELESS IN SEATTLE

"LOVE, LOVE," SANG A WOMAN'S VOICE OVER A BULLHORN, AWAKENING campers sleeping on a farm near the Cascade Mountains in Washington State. "Cuddle, cuddle. Love." The day's activities would include training sessions in "urban climbing," which involved ascending tall buildings to hang banners, and "direct action techniques," which included chaining people together in public places.

It was mid-September 1999, and about 160 activists were attending the weeklong Globalize This! Action Camp. The participants were honing their skills at civil disobedience, which they intended to put to good use two and a half months later in Seattle, where the WTO was to hold its third ministerial meeting, with President Clinton in a starring role. Led by the Ruckus Society, a group specializing in "guerrilla communication," they also included members of the Rainforest Action Network and a couple of women, ages seventy-seven and sixty-eight, belonging to the Raging Grannies. They rehearsed scenarios that might arise, such as confrontations with police; they held workshops on nonviolent protest; they pored over maps of downtown Seattle. And they fired themselves up, holding hands in a circle while belting out vows of militancy: "I'm here to put my body against the machine and stop it!" "I'm here to put a stake in the heart of the WTO!"

How fanciful it seemed that this ragtag band and their sympathizers would be dancing in triumph at the end of the WTO meeting. Only in their dreams could they conceive the epic proportions of the defeat the WTO would suffer in Seattle, with officials from the world's most powerful nations admitting glumly, amid the glare of worldwide media attention, that the meeting had failed to achieve its stated goal of launching a new trade round.

In the years since, two sharply conflicting accounts have been posited to explain the result of the Seattle meeting. One is the lore of the Left, which is that to a large degree the outcome was attributable to the extraordinary amalgam of students, labor unionists, environmentalists, faith groups, human rights activists, animal rights supporters, Tibetan monks, and graying veterans of the sixties who thronged the city's streets. By contrast, trade experts and officials who participated in the meeting have almost unanimously dismissed the protesters' claims of victory as romantic drivel. According to this narrative, the demonstrations—tumultuous though they may have been—were little more than a distraction; the meeting ended as it did because of internal divisions among WTO member countries, not the action outside the convention hall.

Without doubt, the forces at work in Seattle far transcended such street-level phenomena as human chains, barricades, and tear gas. But a close look at the Seattle meeting also reveals that the protesters played a bigger role in the outcome than their detractors care to admit. Thus, this book's account of the event will devote extensive attention to the demonstrations. The evidence suggests that they contributed significantly to the WTO's humiliating setback—with important and long-lasting consequences down the road. Having been rocked so publicly on its heels in Seattle, the WTO would be even more compelled to undo the damage at its next major meeting in Doha two years later and to focus its agenda on the widely popular theme of providing opportunity for the world's poor.

The protesters encompassed a wide variety of independent groups, and their grievances against the WTO were myriad and diffuse. But if one person could be identified as the movement's chief intellectual spark plug, it would be Lori Wallach, a 1990 graduate of Harvard Law School who had spurned the lure of high-paying legal jobs to join Public Citizen, the organization led by activist Ralph Nader, where she formed and directed a unit called Global Trade Watch. The full gamut of complaints by the Left about the WTO were encapsulated in a book she coauthored in 1999, titled *Whose Trade Organization?* The WTO, according to the book, is the enforcer for a system that "favors huge multinational companies and the wealthiest few in developed and developing countries" and where "global commerce takes precedence over everything—democracy, public health, equity, the environment, food safety and more." As evidence, the book chronicles the shrimp-turtle case, the tuna-dolphin case, the hormones-in-beef case, and a number of others.

The book airily dismisses the WTO's main defenses against these charges. It didn't seem to impress Wallach that the organization is a collection of the world's governments, most of whom are democratically elected, and that its agreed-upon rules might therefore command a certain degree of legitimacy. Nor did she show much regard for the WTO's insistence that its rules—far from interfering in countries' rights to set strict safety and environmental standards—simply require that the standards be applied equally to domestic goods and foreign ones. Just look, she argued, at the WTO's rules concerning the measures countries use to guard their food supplies and farmland from health dangers, plant pests, and the like. Those rules "effectively eviscerat[e] the Precautionary Principle, which says that potentially dangerous substances must be proven *safe* before they are put on the market," the book says. "Governments rely on this principle to protect the public and environment from suspected health risks, particularly in the absence of scientific certainty," and lamentably, WTO tribunals had "consistently" ruled against governments that took such protective actions.

In other words, Wallach wasn't terribly worried about the possibility that overzealous government officials, egged on by powerful domestic interests, might be using safety as an excuse to keep out imported products, even though multinational firms complain that such things happen all the time. In her view, judgments about such matters oughtn't to be made by remote bodies like the WTO because "the effect is to constrain the power of national legislatures to act in the public interest and to disenfranchise ordinary citizens, who have far more capacity to make their voices heard nationally than in international forums."

Acting as a sort of field marshal for the protesters was Wallach's deputy, Michael Dolan. Described by the *Washington Post* as "something of a cross between Lenin and Woody Allen," the forty-four-year-old Dolan flew to Seattle a few days after the January 25, 1999, announcement that the city would host the WTO meeting at the end of the year and set up an office in a downtown storefront next to a Harley-Davidson shop.

Dolan was a master at organizing and mobilizing, having been trained in those skills in the 1980s by the United Farm Workers. He was soon demonstrating his prowess as a coordinator and intermediary among the groups that, despite a wide disparity of lifestyles and priorities, shared a distaste for the WTO and international capitalism. In the spring of 1999 he held meetings of dozens of people from local chapters of the AFL-CIO, the Teamsters, and other major labor groups as well as from environmental and religious organizations. The unions soon decided to hold a large-scale march on November 30, when the four-day WTO meeting was scheduled to open.

During those months of early 1999, Dolan was also in touch with a gaggle of activist organizations, mostly on the West Coast, such as the Ruckus Society and Art and Revolution, a California-based group whose leading figure, David Solnit, was renowned for his giant puppets. These groups coalesced under a common name, the Direct Action Network (DAN), and they settled in July on a well-defined goal: They would encircle the Convention Center in downtown Seattle, using nonviolent tactics, with the aim of shutting down the WTO meeting on November 30. They knew that that was the day scheduled for the union march, and they recognized that their radicalism might alienate some straitlaced elements of the labor movement. Using Dolan as a go-between, Solnit called him to see whether the unions would object to this timing.

Dolan left a message with one of his union contacts, whom he recalls telling: "The Direct Action people want to do something on Tuesday morning the thirtieth [of November] . . . if you have a serious objection, they need to know it soon." No response to that message came that day, so Dolan told Solnit that the unions had apparently given their "tacit" blessing. Not exactly; a union official called to register his opposition the following week. But Dolan told him it was too late. According to his recounting of the episode: "It's really interesting that that missed phone call and that lack of communication" occurred, thereby allowing the labor march and activist protest to take place on the same day. Really interesting, indeed, as we shall see.

By late summer, the Internet was abuzz. "Tens of thousands of people will converge on Seattle and transform it into a festival of resistance," declared a message posted by the Direct Action Network on September 6. "We are planning a large scale, well organized, high visibility action to SHUT DOWN the World Trade Organization on Tuesday, November 30."

The protesters, whatever the rightness or woolly-headedness of their beliefs, had a lot going in their favor. They were up against an establishment that, over the course of 1999, would show an incredible degree of disorganization, lack of preparedness, and internal rancor.

| * |

Previously amiable relationships among WTO ambassadors were ruined. Geneva dinner parties attended by trade diplomats became tense affairs, where guests strained to keep the conversation focused on small talk. A "Spy Versus Spy" atmosphere took hold, in which staffers in certain countries' missions were checking car license plates to detect who was meeting with whom.

This was life in the WTO during the first few months of 1999, when the trade body was riven by an extraordinarily bitter and hard-fought election race. At issue was who would succeed Renato Ruggiero, an Italian, as director-general, when his four-year term expired in the spring. Developing countries had chafed for years under the tradition by which the job went to a European, and now they wanted someone from their own ranks. Though lacking much formal power, and often buffeted by pressures from member countries, the director-general can exert considerable influence over WTO decision-making, mainly because he (they have all been male) may play an important role in surmounting impasses when negotiations stall and often supervises the writing of texts that are submitted for consideration by members at crucial junctures.

The main candidate of the developing countries was Supachai Panitchpakdi, the deputy prime minister and minister of commerce of Thailand, a pleasant technocrat whose credentials included a Ph.D. from the Netherlands School of Economics in Rotterdam. Two other candidates—one from Morocco, one from Canada—dropped out in the spring of 1999 as it became clear that they were far behind Supachai in informal straw polling among member countries. But Mike Moore, a New Zealand politician, clung on tenaciously, thanks in no small measure to backing from the United States.

Moore was a far cry from the "English gentlemen's club" types who had set the tone at the Centre William Rappard in the past. Earthy, pugnacious, and scornful of piety, he littered his utterances with Kiwi colloquialisms—"Back the truck up" was one of his favorites—and even native English speakers often had difficulty understanding his thickly accented speech. When the mood struck, he proved capable of soaring, even inspirational rhetoric; the problem, as he often acknowledged, was that he is "countersuggestive," so when associates implored him to speak more clearly, his manner tended to become even more rough-hewn and populist.

Born in 1949, Moore grew up in a poor farming family loyal to the New Zealand Labour Party and left school at fourteen to start working in a slaughterhouse. He never attended college, taking jobs as a printer, social worker, and trade union official instead. He made up for his lack of polish and formal education with prodigious self-learning, and he read economics books with particular voracity as he embarked on a political career that won him a seat in Parliament at twenty-three. Based on his reading, together with his observations in the real world, he "came to the conclusion that competition is a cleansing agent" that helps rid economies of rot and corruption, he says. So when Labour won a national election in 1984 and Moore became trade minister, he led a fight to open New Zealand's heavily protected markets, which included the sale of nationalized industries and the abolition of farm subsidies. Although the reforms eventually boosted prosperity, they aroused furious opposition, and in 1990 Moore led the party into an election—lasting just eight weeks as prime minister before his government lost power. Having made many enemies, he appeared to be washed up in New Zealand politics, but he spied a chance to revive his career as the contest for the WTO's director-generalship loomed. He threw his life savings into the campaign, flying around the world to woo trade policymakers, sleeping as often as possible on planes and in budget hotels. (The New Zealand government contributed funds, too, as is customary for candidates seeking such jobs.) "I told my wife, 'We'll spend everything, but we'll keep the house,'" Moore recalls.

U.S. officials decided to support him because, as a Labourite, he was sympathetic to the Clinton administration's argument for labor standards in trade rules, whereas Supachai was appealing to developing countries based on his opposition to such standards. With Washington's endorsement, Moore gained not only the advantage of U.S. lobbying on his behalf in capitals around the world but also a formidable top strategist in the person of Rita Hayes, the U.S. ambassador to the WTO, a cunning operator whose manner alternated between imperiousness and southern charm (she comes from a prominent South Carolina family). "At the U.S. mission, we used to call her 'the belle from hell,'" recalls Andrew Stoler, her former deputy. "She was running a very tough campaign [for Moore], and I have to admit I was part of it."

As the race heated up, both sides took umbrage at what they felt were below-the-belt attacks on their candidates. When Moore averred that he would not ride around in a Mercedes nor peddle influence because "that is not the Kiwi way," Supachai's backers took that as a veiled suggestion that Asians are habitually corrupt. The Moore camp, meanwhile, seethed over the circulation in Geneva of articles in the New Zealand press about his alleged uncouthness. "Having Moore in the job would be a liability—a cause for national embarrassment," huffed one columnist.

A much deeper source of animosity was suspicion that skullduggery was afoot in the securing and counting of votes. The selection of a director-general, like all WTO decisions, is supposed to occur by consensus, so the process was aimed at first determining which single candidate could command a clear lead in the number of member-country endorsements, and then seeking a consensus for that person to get the job. The voting, however, was a murky affair, conducted by "confessionals" in which countries' ambassadors met privately or spoke over the phone with Ali Mchumo, the chairman of the General Council and the ambassador from Tanzania, who periodically announced vote tallies without disclosing the preferences of individual countries. In January 1999, when four candidates were still in the running, Supachai led the pack with forty votes, and Moore trailed in fourth place with thirteen. A couple of months later, Supachai was still far in the lead. But in both cases, Moore had the most second-choice votes, which showed, his supporters claimed, that he was probably the most acceptable among the candidates to the membership as a whole and thus should remain in the race. To the irritation of the Supachai side, Mchumo accepted that argument and kept the contest going. The Tanzanian became the butt of criticism that he was allowing himself to be manipulated by America's "belle from hell."

The cries of "Foul" grew louder as the race tightened and campaign tactics became more questionable. The Moore side succeeded in cadging a number of endorsements, partly because Supachai often came across as so bland, diffident, and lacking in leadership qualities that even some of his supporters started to wonder whether he was suited for the job. Another factor was backroom machinations. Garnering the French vote was a particularly glorious coup for Moore, because Supachai had appeared to be on the verge of claiming the support of the entire European Union, only to see it slip from his grasp. How did that happen? "We made a deal," confirms Stoler—the deal being that Moore would choose a Frenchman as one of the deputy directors-general.

Passions peaked in early May when Mchumo announced in the General Council that Moore had taken the lead in the confessionals, 62–59. "This process is over for Dr. Supachai," he said, because a "final" deadline of April 30 had passed. Outraged backers of the Thai, who had been counting on many more votes, rejected the call to join in a consensus for Moore and demanded that either Supachai be declared the consensus candidate or an open vote be held. The United States strenuously opposed taking a vote, arguing that it would set a terrible precedent. But aside from the importance of preserving the consensus principle, another reason for the U.S. objection, Stoler admits, was that "we would have lost in a straight-up vote."

For the next six weeks, as the two sides continued hurling accusations of bad faith, the WTO remained leaderless and paralyzed, with no director-general; Ruggiero had rejected pleas to stay on temporarily. Anti-American demonstrations erupted in Bangkok.

Then, in mid-June, the phone rang in the office of Surin Pitsuwan, the Thai foreign minister, from a caller expressing deep concern that the longer the internecine strife continued, the greater the risk of lasting damage to the WTO. The caller was U.S. Secretary of State Madeleine Albright, who told her Thai counterpart that she was calling from a plane, according to an account that the foreign minister published more than three years later. Albright said that unless Supachai was prepared to back down, both he and Moore would "go down the drain," and the job would go to some new candidate.

Surin called her bluff, pointing out that any such new candidate "would be the symbol of divisiveness . . . and failure," and he asked, "Are you sure that would be good for anyone?" His account continues:

> There was a long pause again. Finally [Albright] responded in a more con-
> ciliatory tone: "Then what are we going to do, Surin?"
>
> [Surin] seized the moment and made a bold suggestion. "Instead of one
> Director-General for four years, why don't we think about six years divided
> between both of them?"
>
> "That sounds interesting," she said.

To make a long story short, that is how the conflict was resolved, though it took until late July to work out the details. Moore would hold the job first, starting September 1, 1999, to be followed three years later by Supachai. The arrangement drew intense criticism because it appeared likely to leave both men hobbled before they could even assume their responsibilities. The director-general depends on a combination of political savvy and moral suasion to bring countries together, so effectiveness in the job requires support and goodwill from the membership. Neither man appeared likely to have that in abundance.

Perhaps more important, the clash had consumed enormous amounts of trade policymakers' time and energy, impairing the ability of WTO members to prepare for the upcoming ministerial in November.

| * |

Millennium Round . . . Seattle Round . . . Development Round . . . *Clinton Round?* This question of nomenclature was an issue of considerable interest to the Office of the U.S. Trade Representative during the period prior to the Seattle meeting. The U.S. mission to the WTO "got lots of messages from Washington," recalls Andy Stoler. "They wanted to know: How did previous rounds get their names?"

The messages reflected the ambivalence of the Clinton administration toward the Seattle meeting, where the main item on the agenda was whether to launch a new round. On the one hand, top White House strategists were growing increasingly concerned that the trade issue could turn into a political albatross for Democratic candidates in 2000, especially for Vice President Albert Gore. A major factor behind the worrisome erosion in support from the party's rank and file was Clinton's trade record, the highlights of which were his aggressive push for NAFTA and the Uruguay Round.

On the other hand, some sectors of the U.S. economy, prime among them agriculture, were eager for negotiations to liberalize global markets further. U.S. farm groups were itching to capitalize on the generally superior competitiveness of American farms vis-à-vis the much smaller farms of Europe and Japan. And initiating a new round at Seattle, some administration officials argued, would not only keep the momentum going for Clinton's policies but would add luster to his legacy, especially if the talks were named for him. A confidential memo drafted in August 1998 by top State Department officials urged: "We should take advantage of the fact that" the WTO would be meeting in the United States "and propose a new round of global trade negotiations—the Clinton Round."

One problem with this idea was that most rounds had been named for the places where they were launched (Tokyo and Uruguay, for example), and this method was naturally preferred by Seattle officials, who were excitedly talking up the name "Seattle Round." But a couple of previous rounds had been named for the Americans who had played key roles in initiating them (Douglas Dillon and John F. Kennedy)—hence the questions for the U.S. mission in Geneva.

The chief advocate of a new round, championing the cause with his flair for well-turned phrases, was Sir Leon Brittan, whose term as European trade commissioner was ending in 1999. His favored name for the round, "Millennium Round," was prominently displayed on his department's website. (Breaking European ranks was Clare Short, the British minister of development, who proposed "Development Round.") A full-blown round, Sir Leon contended, should include not only agriculture, services, and other issues left over from the Uruguay Round but a broader range of topics, in particular four known as the "Singapore issues" because they had first been proposed at a 1996 WTO meeting in that Southeast Asian city-state: (1) investment, (2) competition, (3) government procurement, and (4) trade facilitation (which mostly involved cutting red tape and delays for foreign goods at ports and other border entry points).

Notwithstanding the eye-glazing terminology, the Singapore issues had the potential to become a major new power grab by the WTO by imposing rules on aspects of globalization that been left largely untouched at the international level.

Investment was the most important—and controversial—issue on the wish list of Sir Leon and other enthusiasts of the Singapore issues. Any time a multinational company poured money into a new plant or distribution facility overseas, the country where it chose to put its operation might require it to form a joint venture with a local firm or to export a certain percentage of its output. Investments that fell within certain areas, such as broadcasting, airlines, or brokerage, might be severely restricted or barred altogether. Those practices could heavily influence the pattern of trade, just as any tariff could, so why should there not be international rules governing them to make the world a more pre-dictable and stable place? Closely related was the idea of establishing WTO rules on competition. All too often, companies seeking to do business abroad found themselves stymied by monopolies in countries whose governments sim-ply looked the other way at the collusive behavior of powerful local tycoons. Government procurement was another area that arguably needed international rules because multinational firms trying to win contracts with foreign govern-ments often lost out to local cronies of the political elites. Finally, international rules on trade facilitation could generate significant benefits because the cus-toms procedures of many countries, especially in the developing world, caused goods to sit on docks for days or even weeks—a boon to customs agents but no-body else.

The chief skeptic of the proposed new round was the woman who was to chair the Seattle meeting, in her capacity as trade minister for the host country.

As a student at the University of Wisconsin in the late 1960s and early '70s, Charlene Barshefsky could hardly have imagined the series of events that would one day vault her to this role. Active in protests against the Vietnam War, she had envisioned following her older siblings into academia, a choice that would have pleased her immigrant parents, who prized scholarly pursuits. But job prospects for Ph.D.'s were poor, so Barshefsky went to law school and accepted an offer from the prestigious Washington, D.C., firm of Steptoe and Johnson. Trade law was not her chosen specialty, as became evident when, at a luncheon she attended soon after joining the firm, the head partner asked whether she might be interested in working on a dumping case. Being unaware that "dump-ing" meant the unloading of foreign goods in the U.S. market at unfairly low prices, Barshefsky assumed she was being enlisted to represent a corporation that had improperly disposed of toxic waste. She demurred, saying she wouldn't want to oppose environmental interests.

Thus was launched a stellar career in the trade bar. In eighteen years at Step-toe, Barshefsky rose to become chairman of the firm's international division, representing both foreign and domestic companies in trade disputes. Her rep-utation attracted the notice of the incoming Clinton administration, which in 1993 offered her a post as deputy U.S. trade representative with responsibility for Asia and Latin America. Although torn about shifting to the even higher-pressure and less-lucrative work of a trade negotiator—she was by then the mother of two daughters, ages nine and four—Barshefsky took the job. With her dark eyes flashing beneath short brown hair, tartly delivering her argu-ments—and threats—in complete and orderly paragraphs, she cut a formidable figure, and soon earned the nickname "Stonewall" from fellow administration officials for the unyielding manner in which she dealt with foreign interlocutors, especially the Japanese. Accordingly, she won promotion to U.S. trade representative when the job became vacant in 1996. Announcing her nomination to the cabinet post, Clinton described her as a woman who "has brought tears to the eyes" of foreign leaders.

Barshefsky had a famously discordant relationship with Sir Leon—the tension between the two was often painful to witness, aides recall—and his keenness for a new trade round was just one of the positions he took that elicited an adversarial response from the U.S. trade representative. She was dubious from the start about proposals to launch a round, according to her recollections and those of several colleagues, because in her travels around the world, she found many developing countries unready and unwilling to adopt new international obligations so soon after the Uruguay Round.

Indeed, the stance taken by most developing countries in Asia, Africa, and Latin America was that because they had gotten mere crumbs from the Uruguay Round, whereas the rich nations had walked away with loads of booty, a new round would presumably deliver more of the same. If trade talks had to occur, the main focus should be on revising those aspects of the Uruguay Round that were proving the most disagreeable, these countries' officials asserted. They demanded a lengthening of the time in which they were supposed to comply with the new rules on patent protection and sanitary standards, for example, and faster opening of rich-country textile markets. "There are fundamental problems" in various parts of the deal, Mounir Zahran, Egypt's ambassador to the WTO, told the General Council in 1998, "and if they are not adequately addressed, it would be extremely difficult to convince our public of justification of further liberalization commitments."

One band of refuseniks took a particularly hard line against anything that smacked of expanding the WTO's power—especially the proposal for including the Singapore issues as part of a new round. Calling itself the Like Minded Group, its members included India, Malaysia, Pakistan, Tanzania, the Dominican Republic, and a handful of other developing nations. Their often-strident rhetoric, conjuring up images of the rich trampling the poor, caused eyes to roll among the Americans and other free-market-oriented policymakers in Geneva, who viewed the bloc as a throwback to the early postwar decades, when multinational corporations were scorned in the third world as agents of economic imperialism. But in opposing the creation of new WTO rules in areas such as investment and competition, the Like Minded Group had backing from a number of respectable economists who questioned whether the WTO had any business establishing its authority over matters only tangentially related to trade.

The big question, as preparations for Seattle began to pick up steam, was where the United States would come down on the new round, given both its superpower status and its role as conference host. Some of Barshefsky's colleagues shared her concerns about the wisdom of trying to launch a new round, but she was forced to relent, because others in the administration, especially those in the State Department and on the National Security Council, were insistent on forging ahead. They were hoping for an agreement at Seattle that a new round should include some discussion of labor rights—which would be a political plus for the White House—and they thought the developing countries could probably be brought around. "Their argument against me was, 'How can you be sure until you try?'" Barshefsky recalls, acknowledging that once the decision to support a round was made, she became a "cheerleader to the end," a stance she later regretted.

The upshot: nearly four hundred square brackets.

Square brackets, "[ ]," are the punctuation used in a legal document to denote words, phrases, sentences, and paragraphs that the signatories have not yet agreed. And as discussions proceeded in mid-1999 about the declaration the WTO would issue in Seattle, very little agreement was forthcoming over the language that many countries were proposing.

The Europeans wanted a pledge to launch a new round that would include the Singapore issues—which was anathema to the developing countries. The United States, Australia, and the big farm exporters of Latin America wanted the agenda for negotiations to include proposals that would significantly open up agriculture markets and eliminate certain farm subsidies—which was anathema to the Europeans, the Japanese, the Koreans, the Norwegians, and the Swiss. Another group of countries, led by Japan, wanted the round to consider rules restricting the rights of countries to impose antidumping duties—which was anathema to the United States. The Americans wanted the WTO to begin dealing with the issue of labor rights, at least by creating a working group to study the trade-labor relationship—which was anathema to developing countries. The developing countries wanted to change some of the terms of the Uruguay Round—which was anathema to the Americans, the Europeans, and the Japanese.

In theory, such vast gaps in position could have been bridged at Seattle, where WTO members were to consider only an agenda for a round, not final rules that would govern any aspect of global trade. Each major player or group of players had issues it wanted on the agenda, and a deal might have been struck to begin talks, with all parties retaining their rights to drive a very hard bargain.

But the task was rendered even more challenging by text drafted in Geneva in November for trade ministers to consider at the Seattle meeting. Nearly every paragraph in the thirty-two-page document was riddled with brackets, which meant that in the four-day meeting the ministers would have a huge number of disputes to resolve. One example:

[Building on the work of the Working Group on Transparency in Government Procurement [and on the elements for inclusion in an appropriate agreement contained in the report of the Working Group], negotiations shall take place to conclude an agreement on transparency in government procurement of goods and services [for adoption at the Fourth Session of the Ministerial Conference]. [Negotiations of the Agreement shall take into account the special situation of developing countries and due flexibility shall be accorded to them.] [[Following that meeting, negotiations] [Negotiations] should take place with a view to adapting a multilateral agreement to reduce obstacles to market access in the area of government procurement.]

Under normal circumstances, a director-general and his deputies would take control over such a text and streamline it to make it more suitable for negotiation at a short ministerial meeting. But that was not in the cards, thanks largely to the Moore/Supachai fight. Moore, who took over in early September, didn't even have deputies in place until a week before the Seattle meeting, and the director-general himself was still a source of deep resentment among the scores of WTO countries that had backed his opponent. So nobody stood up to the strong-willed ambassadors in Geneva who were insisting on inserting their preferred wording in brackets at every juncture.

In public, Barshefsky professed to be unperturbed about the prospects for the ministerial. "At the end it will all come together because it has to come together," she said on November 26, four days before Seattle's scheduled start. "Everyone knows that failure is not an option." She didn't mention that a few weeks earlier she had grown so worried about the meeting that she directed her chief of staff, Nancy LeaMond, to ask the State Department whether the U.S. government would have any liability if delegates' hotel rooms were canceled.

In its inability to get its act together, the WTO was matched by the city of Seattle.

| * |

A rude shock was in store for a group of Seattle officials who met a visiting delegation from the WTO on November 12, 1998. As ardently as they were hoping for their city to be picked to host the ministerial, they were taken aback when the WTO team described the violence that had marred the meeting in Geneva in May 1998.

"We all sort of went, 'Whoa!'" recalled Kathy Paxton of the Seattle–King County Convention and Visitors Bureau. "That was the first we'd heard of it."

But after recovering from their surprise at learning of the Geneva riots, Seattle police officials attending the meeting were unfazed, responding to the information by saying, "Well, we've dealt with demonstrations before," according to Paxton's account. And other Seattle officials adopted a similarly blasé attitude, which they maintained after the city was formally selected in late January 1999 to host the WTO meeting. The rampages for which European militants were notorious seemed unthinkable in mellow Seattle, which prided itself on its long tradition of social activism practiced peacefully. At a city council meeting on March 29, 1999, Ed Joiner, the assistant police chief who had been named to oversee security for the WTO meeting, played down concerns. "We understand there were demonstrations in Geneva," he said, but "we've had a history of being able to work very effectively with demonstration leaders and allow them to conduct their event in a way that gives them the coverage they need and can make the points that they make but avoid situations where we get involved in either property damage or any kind of confrontative demonstration."

That confidence—"complacency" may be a better word—continued to dominate the thinking of Seattle authorities even as disquieting signs began to surface during the late summer and early fall that the WTO demonstrations would be much rowdier than those the city had seen before. The Globalize This! Action Camp got plenty of media coverage, as did the vow by the Direct Action Network to shut down the WTO meeting. A confidential FBI report circulated to law enforcement agencies on November 17 stated, in boldface letters, "The threat of violent or destructive criminal activity—to include individual and group acts of civil disobedience—is considered a distinct possibility."

Police and other city officials were by no means sitting on their hands. In February, to coordinate security planning, they set up a committee that included representatives from the Seattle police, the King County Sheriff's Office, the FBI, and the Secret Service, among other agencies. The police department trained officers in crowd-management techniques, bought supplies of pepper spray and gas masks, and established a "flying squad" with the specific responsibility of arresting people engaged in property destruction and other such unlawful activity.

But the department's planners also made many decisions they would rue later. They rejected the ideas of setting up barricades and fences or of surrounding the WTO meeting area with a massive show of force. Although the department contacted neighboring law enforcement agencies to ensure that additional officers would be available if needed, it didn't go to the expense and trouble of holding joint training with those officers, nor did Seattle police arrange in advance for food and shelter for them. And planners repeatedly cut the number of officers assigned to processing arrests.

The tone was set at the top of Seattle's government, by Mayor Paul Schell, a genial lawyer and former university dean who frequently noted that he had participated in protests during the sixties. Schell didn't want the city turned into an armed camp, and he constantly emphasized that the protesters should be given plenty of latitude, on the assumption that they would be loud but orderly. His mental picture of the event, as spelled out in a "Schell mail"—a missive he sent to locals inside and outside the city government—was that "our streets and restaurants will be filled with people from all over the world. Issues of global significance will be addressed in our conference halls and public spaces. . . . (and our many visitors will be bringing something like $11 million of business to our town)."

"We may not know what is going to happen," his communications director, Vivian Phillips, told the press a couple of weeks before the meeting. "But we are prepared."

| * |

Prepared? Oh no, they weren't, as Seattle's police chief, Norm Stamper, saw to his horror early in the morning of November 30, the official start of the WTO meeting. Standing in a cold rain, he watched ten sheriff's deputies braced against a crowd of protesters who were trying to penetrate the underground garage at the Sheraton Hotel, where many delegates to the WTO meeting were lodged. At that moment, Stamper later wrote, he "realized, for the first time, that we didn't have *nearly* enough cops to get the job done."

The police were not only outnumbered but out-hustled as well. As early as 2:00 a.m., some demonstrators had begun gathering, and at 7:30 the largest of the groups, which had assembled at a park near the city's famed Pike Place Market, began marching east toward the Washington State Convention and Trade Center, where the WTO was to meet. Another phalanx approached from the opposite direction, still another headed in from the north, and a fourth came from the south. They seized control of major intersections along the way, chaining themselves to objects and to each other, lying down, moving dumpsters into the streets, and in some cases setting fires. Only two platoons of cops (each platoon had about forty-five officers) were on duty at 6:00 a.m., and the last two platoons did not arrive until 9:00 a.m. Even at full strength, a mere 290 Seattle officers, plus an extra 50 from the State Highway Patrol guarding the major downtown freeway, were up against a crowd of several thousand. As the police department's own after-action report acknowledged: "This well-coordinated early morning protest action with groups converging from multiple directions quickly surpassed the capacity of police to simultaneously maintain access to the Convention Center and make arrests."

The groups who were executing this tactical masterstroke went by names such as the Lesbian Avengers, the Bananarchy Movement, and STARC Naked (the acronym stands for "student alliance to reform corporations"). These were affinity groups, which meant that their members were committed to working together during protests, with each member responsible for certain tasks such as providing medical care or supplying food. Chanting and dancing to music and the beat of drums, many were dressed in costume, with turtles being among the most popular. The vast majority were resolute in support of the Direct Action Network's pledge to refrain from violence against people or property. But also in the crowd were a number of young people clad in black—some estimates were in the dozens, others in the hundreds—who identified themselves as anarchists and who proclaimed that the trashing of buildings and other such acts were a justifiable strike against an inherently exploitative system of private property rights. By 8:00 a.m. they were breaking windows at stores and corporate offices, spraying buildings with graffiti (one example being "Fuck WTO Bitches"), hurling objects at police, and aggressively confronting the few WTO delegates who were venturing outside.

Scrambling to keep the conference center and hotels safe from invasions by protesters, the police disbanded the "flying squad" they had intended to use for arrests because they needed every available officer to protect the most strategically crucial buildings. Delegates were ordered to stay in their hotels, forcing the cancellation of the 10:00 a.m. opening ceremony. Most galling, for officers of the law and civilians alike, was that the dearth of manpower prevented the police from intervening against brazen acts of looting and vandalism. In some cases, lines of cops in body armor had to stand helplessly in formation at hotel entrances while trashing continued in plain sight. Some protesters committed to nonviolence chanted "Shame on you!" at the anarchists, and even stood in front of buildings that were being targeted.

Although the nonviolent protesters were, by and large, willing to face arrest for blocking intersections and the entrances to buildings—in meetings beforehand, leaders of the Direct Action Network had even asked the police to facilitate arrests—the cops had nowhere near the capacity to conduct so many busts. Furthermore, although a makeshift jail had been set up at an abandoned navy brig outside the city, it too was woefully understaffed. So instead of arresting demonstrators who refused orders to move—only sixty-eight were locked up on November 30—the police began spraying them with gas at around 10:00 a.m., and as the violence intensified, they resorted to billy clubs and rubber bullets too. The predictable result was a ratcheting up in the militance of the crowd; as one account in the *Seattle Times* put it: "With each gassing, protesters get more defiant and continue to return to the scene."

Gazing with dismay from the Westin Hotel at the bedlam below, and watching on TV as well, were Secretary of State Albright and U.S. Trade Representative Barshefsky; they were supposed to have been at the opening ceremony, where Albright was the scheduled keynote speaker. According to people who were there, Albright was voicing fury that she was, as she put it, "a prisoner in a hotel in my own country," and she was calling everyone she could think of who might be able to help restore order, including Attorney General Janet Reno and Washington governor Gary Locke, demanding prompt action. Her confinement, and that of most other delegates, continued for hours, as the chaos started worsening in the early afternoon, when the labor march converged on downtown.

Union members, variously estimated at 20,000 to 50,000 strong, had spent the morning in a stadium listening to speeches and then began marching at noon on an officially permitted three-mile trek that was supposed to pass close to downtown before veering away toward dispersal points. Police were hoping that the march would draw protesters out of the central city, giving them a chance to establish a perimeter around the Convention Center. Instead, as the marchers neared downtown, many of them ventured into the zone of conflict, where some got caught up in battles with police. Steve Williamson, executive secretary of the King County Labor Council, who was severely gassed alongside a friend, recalled later that seeing the scale of the mayhem "really transforms you . . . we really had a massive confrontation against the state."

This was the moment of consequentiality for the "missed phone call" and "lack of communication" that Michael Dolan had experienced a few months earlier when he was trying to coordinate the timing of the labor march and the activists' plan for more-militant protests. The march and the protests were now in the mutual-reinforcement stage.

That development was being observed on TV with grave alarm in the command center in Seattle Police Headquarters, where top officials from law enforcement bodies and local government were ensconced. Hard-nosed traditionalists were demanding a tougher response to the protesters than Mayor Schell and Police Chief Stamper were inclined to mete out. Dave Reichert, the King County sheriff, was "apoplectic, his blood boiling over every time Schell opened his mouth," according to Stamper's account. The Secret Service was questioning whether President Clinton, who was scheduled to arrive late that evening, should be allowed to do so. Shortly before 3:00 p.m., Governor Locke—chastened by his phone call with Albright—arrived to inform Schell that he wanted to call out the National Guard and declare a state of emergency. Although the Seattle authorities had earlier rejected proposals to do so, the situation involving the labor march forced them to back down. Schell issued the emergency declaration, which included the imposition of a curfew and the creation of a perimeter around the WTO meeting venue.

The switch in the city's tactics from tolerance to crackdown did not prevent violence from continuing well into the night. Crowds pelted the police with debris, rocks, ball bearings, and bottles, drawing fusillades of tear gas, concussion canisters, and rubber bullets in response. The cops managed to clear the downtown area and drive protesters to another neighborhood, where trash was set ablaze and dumpsters were dragged into the streets.

A few skirmishes were still in progress when Air Force One landed at 1:30 a.m. The president had been trying to play peacemaker that day, publicly condemning criminal acts while defending the protesters' rights to be heard. But unknown to the delegates, even Barshefsky, Clinton had already lobbed his own incendiary device into the mix.

| * |

An atmosphere tinged with surliness prevailed the next morning, December 1, as trade ministers and other delegates began assembling at 9:00 a.m. in the Convention Center. They were relieved to find that they could at least traverse downtown streets safely, thanks to a "no-protest zone" that was keeping most people without credentials from entering a cordoned-off area of about fifty square blocks, patrolled by a beefed-up police contingent, armored trucks, and some three hundred National Guard troops. But many ministers and delegates, especially those from developing countries, were giving American officials an earful about the harassment they had suffered the previous day. "Can you imagine the kind of criticism we would come under if the U.S. ambassador was attacked in our country?" demanded Federico Cuello Camilo, the ambassador to the WTO from the Dominican Republic, whose trade minister had been roughed up by protesters and also gassed.

Speaking on behalf of the U.S. government in her position as meeting chairperson, Barshefsky apologized at a plenary session for the breakdown in order, which she blamed on the "irresponsible actions of a tiny minority." She then spelled out how the meeting was supposed to proceed over the three days remaining before its scheduled adjournment on Friday, December 3. Five working groups would try to reach agreement on the most contentious aspects of the proposed agenda for a new round—agriculture, market access, the Singapore issues, systemic issues (WTO decision-making processes), and implementation and rules (mainly antidumping and adjustments to the Uruguay Round). The groups, to which all member countries could send representatives, would be headed by ministers from WTO countries dubbed "Friends of the Chair"— an innovation devised by Director-General Moore in the hope that influential ministers could cajole their colleagues into consensus. If all went swimmingly, each of the working groups would produce texts that were broadly acceptable, and these would be incorporated into an overall declaration that would be submitted to the entire membership, based on the usual understanding in multilateral trade talks that nothing was agreed until all was agreed. Barshefsky exhorted the ministers to negotiate rather than reiterate long-standing positions, and she coupled her plea with a warning: Failure to reach agreement in the working groups would oblige her to convene a green room—a meeting of ministers from a select number of countries, whose collective decision would be presented to the rest of the 135 members on a take-it-or-leave-it basis.

In addition to having bruised feelings about the protests, delegates were riled over logistical matters. Many had difficulty getting credentials. Poor acoustics hampered meetings of the working groups, which were gathering in a large exhibition hall separated from each other by textile partitions, "so everything being said in one space could be heard elsewhere," recalls Roderick Abbott, who was a top E.U. trade negotiator. Midday Wednesday brought a new irritant for ministers: They had to stand in long lines to pass through metal detectors on the way to their luncheon, because Clinton was scheduled to address them.

These annoyances were nothing, however, compared with the anger that was taking hold over the substance of Clinton's message. That morning's *Seattle Post-Intelligencer* quoted the president as taking a far more aggressive position than before on the issue of labor standards. Up to that point, U.S. officials had been assuring other countries that they were seeking nothing more than the establishment of a WTO committee on the relationship between labor and trade. They also offered assurances that this committee would merely study issues such as child labor and was not intended as a first step toward a system of sanctions against nations that failed to meet international norms. But Clinton blew those assurances to smithereens, telling the newspaper in a phone interview while he was in San Francisco on his way to Seattle:

> What we ought to do first of all is to adopt the United States' position on having a working group on labor within the WTO, and then that working group should develop these core labor standards, and then they ought to be part of every trade agreement, and ultimately I would favor a system in which sanctions would come for violating any provision of a trade agreement.

U.S. negotiators had had no idea the president would stray so far from their previous position. Barshefsky was busy with other duties that morning, so she was not even aware of Clinton's interview until the ministers' luncheon, where she was seated next to Pascal Lamy, who had replaced Sir Leon Brittan as European trade commissioner a few weeks earlier. Lamy handed her a copy of the *Post-Intelligencer* dispatch, and as both of them recall the episode, she turned pale and gasped that it was the first she had seen it.

Clinton's remarks, they knew, would stoke the darkest fears in the developing world that Washington had a secret agenda for a tough labor rights regime. Already the nations of Asia, Latin America, and Africa suspected that the United States would betray its free-trade principles by using labor standards to squash the low-wage advantage that constituted poor countries' main hope for competing in world markets. The president had obvious political motives for moving in that direction, given his desire to help Vice President Gore secure the loyalty of unions.

When he finally arrived, Clinton launched into a speech aimed at defusing resistance to labor standards. "I freely acknowledge that, if we had a certain kind of rule, then protectionists in wealthy countries could use things like wage differentials to keep poor countries down," he said, but "we can find a way . . . to write the rules" so that such an outcome wouldn't happen. His words cut little ice with developing-country ministers, nor did a damage-control operation that White House officials attempted in the afternoon to explain away Clinton's words as meaning something less than what he had plainly stated. Former Clinton aides recall him as being thoroughly briefed on the labor standards issue, and some of them agree that politics was the reason for his outspokenness. For her part, Barshefsky remembers Clinton asking late on the day of his Seattle speech how the effort to mollify developing countries was going. "Not well," she told him, prompting this somewhat enigmatic presidential reply: "I didn't mean to be making policy."

Also having a rotten time of it were Mayor Schell and Chief Stamper, who were facing condemnation for their initial laxity toward the protests and the brutality of the response after the situation had gone out of control. They were succeeding Wednesday in keeping downtown streets navigable, having established the perimeter around the area of the WTO meeting and having dramatically increased staffing to handle arrests. So the obvious question was, why couldn't they have done the same the previous day? "If I had . . . denied the protesters a chance to make their voices heard, we would have been severely criticized for denying free speech and perhaps for provoking more serious violence," the mayor told the press. Those answers, however, did not satisfactorily rebut criticism that the city should have deployed a much larger number of cops to arrest both violent protesters and those conducting peaceful civil disobedience. The woes besetting the mayor and the police deepened Wednesday afternoon when a five-hour riot erupted and when TV video showed an officer kicking an unresisting man in the groin. News reports that out-of-town cops lacked decent sleeping quarters and meals exposed the city's slapdash planning.

The tumult subsided on Thursday, December 2, with demonstrations attracting smaller crowds. But fresh abuse was heaped on city officials by merchants, who were totting up millions of dollars in losses instead of reaping the sales bonanza they had been led to expect. "There's a lot of anger and frustration," the marketing director of the Downtown Seattle Association told the *Seattle Times*, which reported that the group was considering plans to file suit against the city.

Anger and frustration were the order of the day in the Convention Center too as the working groups struggled, mostly without success, to cut through scores of square brackets to reach agreement on the scope of negotiations that a new round would encompass in their assigned areas.

The most fractious was a working group on trade and labor, which had not even been included in the original five announced by Barshefsky and which was convened on Thursday, the meeting's next-to-last day—with the United States obviously its prime sponsor. The group met for a grand total of forty minutes before it adjourned for lack of agreement. "There was a lot of shouting," recalls its chairperson, Anabel González, who was the Costa Rican vice minister of trade. "It was the most contentious meeting I've ever seen." Inflamed by Clinton's newspaper interview, representatives from developing countries vowed that they would never accept the U.S. proposal for a forum on labor in the WTO. A Pakistani delegate asserted that Gonzalez had no right to even hold the meeting. Gonzalez asked delegates who were interested to meet with her in smaller, informal groups, which later began considering some much-watered-down versions of the U.S. proposal.

The sole working group to produce a draft was the one on agriculture, headed by Singapore's trade minister, George Yeo, who used cleverly vague language to help narrow differences between U.S. and E.U. negotiators over the direction that farm-trade talks would take in a new round. In a classic bit of fuzzing, the draft said the round would aim for "substantial reductions of export subsidies . . . in the direction of progressive elimination of all forms of export subsidization"—phrasing that could be interpreted either as an implicit promise to cut such subsidies to zero or merely as a promise to move part of the way toward that goal.

The only practical hope for reaching agreement on a declaration by Friday evening was to begin organizing a green room with a manageable-sized group of ministers, and that was the course Barshefsky took on Thursday afternoon. She set 6:00 p.m. as the deadline for the working groups and declared that if they had not made sufficient progress by that hour, "I fully reserve the right to use a more exclusive process to achieve a final outcome."

At that point, simmering resentment began to boil over.

Delegates from the poorest countries of Africa, the Caribbean, and Latin America were already in a funk over the way the meeting had been run, and the prospect of the green room gave them fresh grounds to conclude that the proceedings were a throwback to the GATT era of cozy deals among the elite. One formal session dissolved into a cacophony of booing and table-pounding by the poor-country delegates. Their militance, it should be noted, differed from that of the protesters; developing-country officials generally wanted no part of the strict labor and environmental standards favored by the people in the streets. But they shared the protesters' animus toward the powers that were running the meeting, even more so for the arbitrariness by which they were being kept out of the green room. Their complaints were arguably overblown; they had been allowed to send representatives to most of the working groups and were assured that the green room would include several African representatives. Still, they had a legitimate beef: Any green room agreement that emerged Friday would confront them with a rush decision about whether to approve a long, complicated ministerial declaration and would give them little time, if any, to consult their governments back home.

They were soon wielding the little leverage they had—the threat to block consensus. In a statement issued late Thursday, a group of low-income Latin American and Caribbean countries said, "We are particularly concerned over the stated intentions to produce a ministerial text at any cost. . . . As long as conditions of transparency, openness and participation . . . do not exist, we will not join the consensus required to meet the objectives of this ministerial conference." A statement by the African Group contained similar language.

The Seattle meeting was now hurtling toward crash and burn.

| * |

Innumerable factors were at work in diminishing the odds that the WTO would achieve success in Seattle. Most were unrelated to the protests. They included the divisive fight over the director-general's job, the disagreements over what a new round should entail, the myriad square brackets in the draft texts, the logistical snafus bedeviling the conference, and the controversy over Clinton's remarks on labor standards. Perhaps the prospects for agreement had been nil all along, as some participants and observers contend. But a plausible case can be made that on Friday, December 3, a chance for some sort of agreement remained alive, and that the events of that day produced the meeting's true "cause of death," which was inseparable from the protests.

The day began amid high stress levels and exhaustion, as a green room of twenty-five ministers from key countries gathered in the morning around a large square table in a conference room on the Convention Center's sixth floor. Top negotiators from the United States and the European Union had been up all night haggling over agriculture, and although those talks had seemed on the verge of a breakthrough at around 4:30 a.m., European Trade Commissioner Lamy had gone off to consult with farm and trade ministers from E.U. member states and hadn't returned for several hours, indicating that he was meeting powerful resistance. Outside the green room, ministers from the left-out nations found themselves in the embarrassing position of having little to do but nibble on pizza, smoke, watch protests on TV, and fume over their inability to influence or even know what was going on inside. When Barshefsky took a break from chairing the meeting and handed the responsibility to Canadian Trade Minister Pierre Pettigrew, one of the Canadian's fellow ministers joked, "Well, you may be the orchestra conductor on board the *Titanic*."

Anxious to avoid a washout in his first big test as director-general, Moore initiated an effort to obtain the only thing that could possibly save the meeting—extra time. Previous global trade gatherings had sometimes managed to reach agreements by extending talks past the official end point, and Moore believed that Seattle might be another such case. Many hours had been consumed on agriculture, leaving no chance to resolve other contentious topics such as antidumping and the Singapore issues. Extra time offered the only hope for dealing with those matters, and it offered the only hope for overcoming another problem—the determination of the African, Latin American, and Caribbean nations to reject any deal that had been put together behind closed doors with no chance for them to even consult their capitals.

The man tasked by Moore with seeking extra time in the Convention Center was Andy Stoler, the former number 2 in the U.S. mission to the WTO, who had just become one of the trade body's deputy directors-general. As the senior American in the WTO's leadership, Stoler had the responsibility of liaising with Mayor Schell.

The answer from the mayor: Get out.

Not only did Schell refuse to allow the WTO delegates to stay beyond the scheduled deadline, Stoler recalls, but "he told us that he was going to remove police protection from the Convention Center"—an unsettling threat, because demonstrations were still going on that day, with five hundred protesters breaking away from a labor march and moving to the Westin Hotel, where many chained themselves to the doors. "The reason was, the Convention Center was right in the middle of the downtown shopping district, and this was the week after Thanksgiving, and all the merchants in town were telling him, 'You moron, you're costing us millions of dollars,'" Stoler says. "He told me, 'I've got the whole commercial downtown of Seattle closed because of your meeting!' I finally negotiated a deal with him, which was, 'If you can just keep the cops here until 1:00 a.m., we'll make sure we end at midnight.'"*

So the protests wrecked most of the meeting's first day, and now they could be credited with depriving the WTO of its chances for getting a desperately needed extra day. Whether that extra day would have helped will never be known. Barshefsky and some other Clinton administration officials have maintained publicly that the situation became hopeless once the European Union backed away from the agriculture text. Many others dismiss that version of events as an attempt to deflect blame; they say the European Union was willing

---

*Another story making the rounds that day was that the meeting could not be extended because the Convention Center had to be vacated for a gathering of eye doctors, which had been booked months earlier. Several press articles at the time cited the eye doctors' meeting as the problem, as have some retrospectives on the Seattle ministerial conference written by economists and other analysts. But the American Academy of Optometry, the group in question, did not start registration until the following Wednesday—five days later.

Thus, the main reason for the WTO's inability to get extra time appears to be the one cited by Stoler. Asked about Stoler's account, Schell says he does not recall the conversation but allows that it may have happened. He also says he was unaware of the eye doctors' convention. "I do remember, we were anxious to get [the WTO] out of town," he says, citing "an exhausted security force and a very unhappy retail core."

to be flexible provided it was "compensated" for concessions on agriculture with gains in other areas. "Had an agreement come together on the other issues, we would have had a deal on ag," says one former colleague of Barshefsky's. In other words, extra time might have made a difference—a view that several people on the U.S. team say they shared on that fateful Friday.

With no prospect that the additional time would materialize, Moore huddled on Friday afternoon with five prominent ministers—the European Union's Lamy and Singapore's Yeo, plus their counterparts from Egypt, South Africa, and Brazil. They concluded that it was necessary to disband the meeting promptly and in as orderly a fashion as possible so as to minimize the damage to the WTO. The Brazilian minister, Luiz Lampreia, tracked down a friend, Richard Fisher, who was Barshefsky's deputy. "I told Richard, 'Call it quits. Convince Charlene that there is no chance,'" Lampreia recalls. That message was conveyed to Barshefsky, who according to Fisher's account, dejectedly told him, "OK, Richard, you tell the troops."

To the banging of drums and the blowing of horns, protesters cavorted in the streets as word spread of what was happening inside. At 10:30 p.m., Barshefsky officially adjourned the meeting, telling the assembled delegates, "It would be best to take a time out."

The WTO had deep wounds to lick. Even its leading players were blasting away at its shortcomings. Lamy called it a "medieval" organization, telling reporters on December 4 that "it will have to be reassessed and maybe rebuilt." One key figure was already starting to think about how to turn things around at the next meeting.

| * |

Even by his usual standards, Mike Moore was in extraordinarily forceful and profane fettle when he met with top members of the WTO Secretariat in early January 2000. Having just returned from their year-end holidays, the WTO staffers were still recovering from Seattle shell shock. They were hoping that the passage of time would enable the organization to start healing the fissures among member nations and quelling the passions that had been inflamed. After all, even if a new round couldn't be launched, the membership had work to do, in the form of the "built-in agenda," a mandate stemming from the Uruguay Round to start negotiations in 2000 on trade in agriculture and services. But Moore, who knew that the next ministerial meeting scheduled for 2001 would be his last as director-general, was of no mind to gently ease back into standard operating procedure.

"We've got to get this fuckin' show back on the road," Moore told the startled group who had gathered in his conference room, according to participants' recollections. "And no way are we going to be seen as just bumbling along with the fuckin' built-in agenda. We've got to re-brand!"

So what brand would give the WTO a new lease on life? What problems of the trading system should it show itself to be tackling? The labor rights issue was a nonstarter; Seattle had proven that any effort to insert labor rights provisions into WTO rules would meet with violent rejection from developing countries. The environmental issues that were of especially keen interest to the Europeans would also have to be addressed gingerly; developing nations regarded much of the Green agenda too as stemming from protectionist impulses.

But there was a much more promising concept—development.

By cloaking itself in that mantle, the WTO could attract support from both the Left, which was sympathetic to the grievances of developing countries, and the Right, which wanted to encourage low-income nations to see trade rather than aid as their salvation. Making the alleviation of poverty a central priority could also help overcome the resistance of those such as the Like Minded Group to a new round.

"After Seattle, I could see how the deal could be done," Moore wrote later in one of his books. "I knew we had to have a development agenda which addressed developing country needs."

# 5 | "THERE ARE ONLY A-PLUSES"

IN A DESERT KINGDOM WHERE LIQUOR IS BANNED AND WOMEN CUSTOMARILY swath themselves in veils, even the boldest protester would presumably think twice about overturning a police car, trashing a McDonald's, or even just blocking an intersection. And it was in the capital of just such a country where the WTO decided on January 23, 2001, to hold its ministerial later that year. A petroleum-rich, Connecticut-sized peninsula with about 120,000 citizens, Qatar had a traditional Islamic code governing personal conduct and meted out strict punishment for criticism of the monarchy. So it was hardly a hospitable venue for the likes of the Ruckus Society to stage guerrilla theater or to form human chains.

The decision to hold the meeting in Doha elicited complaints from labor, environmental, and human rights activists, who cited a U.S. State Department report stating that the Qatari government "severely limits freedom of assembly." In response, WTO spokesman Keith Rockwell said the plan stemmed partly from the dearth of other cities willing to play host after Seattle. Qatari officials, he added, "gave us assurances that peaceful protests can be held, provided a permit is acquired."

In fact, Qatar was considerably more open politically than some other Islamic countries. Its ruler, Sheik Hamad bin Khalifa al-Thani, had established the Al-Jazeera television network, which aired some of the Arab world's most freewheeling news broadcasts; he also staged the country's first elections, for a municipal advisory council. At bottom, however, Qatar remained a feudal kingdom, and there were other reasons why the atmosphere at the Doha meeting was certain to differ significantly from Seattle's. Only 4,400 hotel

83

beds were available—not enough to handle the thousands of delegates, journalists, and WTO officials expected to attend. The Qataris promised to dock cruise ships in Doha's harbor and to rent villas to accommodate the anticipated overflow. But that would still leave only about a thousand beds for representatives of NGOs—quite an obstacle for anyone hoping to marshal a decent protest.

The WTO clearly wanted its 2001 ministerial, which was scheduled for November 9–13, to be the anti-Seattle. Choosing Doha was only one of several moves its leaders would make toward that end.

In the buildup to the Doha meeting, Mike Moore visited Africa six times in an effort to convince the continent's policymakers that their views would be better heeded than they had been in Seattle. The director-general conveyed the same message to countries too poor to maintain missions in Geneva at meetings hosted for their representatives in Brussels and London.

Most important, in making the case for the launch of a round at Doha, he repeatedly stressed that it should be what he called "a true development round," with the chief aim of addressing low-income countries' needs. "The surest way to do more to help the poor is to continue to open markets. A new round of multilateral trade negotiations would bring huge benefits," he declared in a speech at the London School of Economics in June 2000, and he urged his audience to "learn from the example of those developing countries that are catching up with rich ones":

> Take South Korea. Thirty years ago, it was as poor as Ghana; now, it is as rich as Portugal. Or consider China, where 100 million people have escaped from extreme poverty over the past decade. What do these fortunate countries have in common? Openness to trade.

He used nearly the same wording in speeches delivered at other locations around the world, at the same time noting that trade alone would not cure poverty in countries suffering from war and corrupt governments. In another address in March 2001 he asserted:

> Reasonable people can quibble about the exact size of the gains from a new round. But the basic message from study after study is clear: a new round brings huge benefits to all parts of the globe. For instance, a study by the Tinbergen Institute estimates that developing countries would gain $155 billion a year from further trade liberalization. That is over three times the $43 billion they get annually in overseas aid.

Moore's calls for a development round struck a responsive chord among many policymakers, experts, and commentators, and it helped that he genuinely believed in what he was saying. Even before the Seattle ministerial, he had backed proposals for a round that would have a development emphasis. "It was not a new idea, but Mike felt some sort of transformative approach was needed," says Evan Rogerson, a fellow New Zealander who held a senior position in the WTO Secretariat. "For Mike it was not a cynical marketing exercise."

But some gigantic questions were left unanswered: What exactly would such a round entail? Did it mean that developing countries should get more access to rich-country markets, or did it also imply that they should lower their own barriers, and if so, under what conditions? More fundamentally, was the evidence really indisputable that trade liberalization would generate such wondrous growth in the developing world?

| * |

For advocates of opening markets worldwide, one of the most potent intellectual weapons they could wield was work by an economist with the amusingly apt name of David Dollar. Indeed, his studies were cited frequently in Moore's speeches.

Dollar, a senior staffer in the World Bank's research department, was one of the economic profession's leading champions of free trade and investment in developing countries. The data he marshaled showed that the most prosperous developing nations were the ones that had done the most to engage in foreign trade, whereas the most stagnant ones were those that had done the least to integrate themselves into the global economy.

Dollar began formulating his views on the subject when he was working in Vietnam as the country's World Bank adviser in the first half of the 1990s. A bearded, effusive man, with a degree from Dartmouth in Chinese history and language and a Ph.D. in economics from New York University, he marveled at how Vietnam's economy—almost totally closed to trade and investment while under hard-line Communist rule—had started to emerge from impoverishment as it opened up after the Cold War.

"Now you have Internet cafés in Hanoi, they send students abroad to study, and I've seen people's lives improve dramatically," Dollar told me when I interviewed him in 2001. "What I was seeing seemed out of kilter with claims you hear from people in the antiglobalization movement. So it seemed like a good idea to look systematically at the issue."

Back in the World Bank's Washington headquarters, Dollar cranked out a number of papers, one of the most noteworthy of which was published in the spring of 2001. Although economists had long extolled the virtues of trade and linked it to economic growth and poverty reduction, this study, coauthored by Dollar and colleague Aart Kraay, examined the relationship in a more rigorous fashion.

The study started out by dividing about seventy developing countries into two groups—those that embraced globalization during the 1980s and 1990s, and those that resisted it. The "globalizers" were defined as countries that had increased their imports and exports as a share of their gross domestic product (GDP) and those that had reduced their average tariffs the most during the period in question; they included China, Malaysia, Mexico, India, Thailand, Argentina, the Philippines, and Hungary. The "nonglobalizers," where trade as a percentage of GDP had declined and tariffs had been reduced less, included Burma, Pakistan, and a number of countries in sub-Saharan Africa.

The results were impressive: The globalizers had increased their average economic growth rates from 2.9 percent per year in the 1970s to 3.5 percent in the 1980s and 5.0 percent in the 1990s. The countries not in the globalizing group saw growth decline from 3.3 percent per year in the 1970s to 0.8 percent in the 1980s, recovering to only 1.4 percent in the 1990s. Over the years, the cumulative effect of that disparity in growth rates had a very large impact on living standards. Furthermore, gaps between upper- and lower-income people stayed reasonably steady in the globalizing countries, so their poor had evidently benefited.

"Take two relatively similar countries—Pakistan and Bangladesh," Dollar said, warming to his subject. In Pakistan, he observed, trade had dropped from about half of GDP two decades earlier to 35 percent of GDP in more recent years, and by 2001 the economy had turned stagnant. Bangladesh, though still very poor, had enjoyed relatively robust growth during the same period, when trade rose from 14 percent to 28 percent of GDP and tariffs were slashed from about 93 percent to about 26 percent.

Case closed, if Dollar's research is to be taken at face value. Poor countries seeking to prosper should jump on the free-trade bandwagon. But Dollar had a nemesis who also hailed from a bastion of mainstream economics.

At Harvard's John F. Kennedy School of Government, trade economist Dani Rodrik was devoting substantial energy to picking apart Dollar's work. His attacks on the World Banker's arguments vaulted him to the forefront of what might be called the school of skepticism about free trade. Their clash at times seemed tinged with animosity, despite their protestations that their differences were professional rather than personal. "Completely meaningless" was Rodrik's verdict on Dollar's findings when I visited him in his office just off Harvard

Square. "At best, David Dollar's research is not helpful, and at worst it's harmful, to the extent policy conclusions are drawn from it."

The soft-spoken Rodrik grew up in Istanbul—he remains a fanatical supporter of Turkey's national soccer team—and had come to Harvard as "sort of an adventure," later earning his Ph.D. in economics at Princeton. He assured me that he shares the view that nations benefit overall, in the long run, by engaging in trade and reducing barriers to it. But he complained that enthusiasts such as Dollar have made "truly extravagant claims" about the benefits of free trade, thereby "creating expectations that cannot be fulfilled."

In academic papers, Rodrik challenged the methodology that Dollar used in his work, arguing that it confused causes and effects. I asked him to explain, in plain English, the complicated equations and data tables that he deployed in his assault on the World Bank economist.

"He says increasing your participation in world trade is good for you," Rodrik replied. "Well, policymakers don't have instruments to increase trade. It's like saying, 'enhance your technology.' I know enhancing my technology is good for me. The question is, for the successful countries that increased their participation in the global economy, what policies did they follow?"

He gave China as a good example: "Has China been globalizing? If by globalization you mean increasing trade and foreign investment, there is no question, China has been one of the most rapidly globalizing countries in the world," Rodrik said. "But if you ask the question 'Has China liberalized its trade policy rapidly the way the World Bank advises?' the answer to that would be no. China has liberalized, but it has done so extremely gradually, and most of it came about a decade after its period of high growth started in 1978."

As for South Korea: "You hear constantly, without global markets Korea would be nowhere, and that's correct. The explosion of Korean exports was nothing short of miraculous," Rodrik said. "But did Korea follow the kinds of policies that we think of today as being most conducive to rapid integration into the global economy? No; Korea started growing rapidly in the 1960s, and it wasn't until the second half of the 1980s that they got really serious about import liberalization. They did things that are now illegal under the WTO—for example, quantitative restrictions [on imports], reverse engineering [of technologically advanced products], and export subsidies." Meanwhile, some other countries that opened their markets remained economic basket cases—a classic example being Haiti, which lowered its barriers extensively in the mid-1990s.

"The bottom line ... [is that] there is no single model of a successful transition to a high-growth path," Rodrik wrote in a 2001 monograph. Rather than rushing to open up and comply with the many requirements of WTO membership, such as adherence to intellectual property rules, developing countries would probably be better off if they were to pursue their own strategies for growth, he argued. Maybe this would mean following the policies of East Asian countries that, like Korea, sheltered their industries for a while before opening up. "The appropriate conclusion is not that trade protection is inherently preferable to trade liberalization; certainly, there is scant evidence from the last 50 years that inward-looking economies experience systematically faster economic growth than open ones," he wrote. "But the benefits of trade openness are now greatly oversold."

Making extravagant claims, creating expectations that cannot be fulfilled, overselling the benefits of lowering trade barriers further—these concerns that Rodrik was raising would come back to haunt the "development round" down the road. But Dollar had another powerful fan who, like Moore, quoted the World Banker's work often in his speeches. He was the leading trade policymaker in the WTO's leading country, and, like Moore, he was eager to see a round launched at Doha.

| * |

Most people, when nominated for cabinet positions by an incoming president, tend to bask a little in the glow of media attention while they accept congratulatory messages. Not Bob Zoellick, whose relentless discipline inspires admiration in some quarters and distaste in others. On January 11, 2001, when president-elect George W. Bush announced that he had picked Zoellick to be the U.S. trade representative, the forty-seven-year-old Illinois native plunged into his new responsibilities almost as soon as the news conference was over. "He was insatiable, in terms of the meetings he wanted to have," recalls Faryar Shirzad, who headed the transition team overseeing the trade office. "He had a list of forty people and was putting in calls to all of them. There wasn't a member of Congress or outside stakeholder he didn't want to meet."

That was typical behavior for a man with "a resume so impressive it might be mistaken for a parody of overachievement," as the *Washington Post* put it in a profile of him. A Phi Beta Kappa graduate of Swarthmore College, with a law degree from Harvard as well as a master's degree from the university's Kennedy School, Zoellick joined the U.S. Treasury Department in 1985, as Ronald Reagan's second term was getting under way. He swiftly became a top aide to—and keen student of—Treasury Secretary James Baker, the wily Texan who in a series of senior posts was dazzling the Washington establishment with his effectiveness at manipulating the levers of power. Zoellick followed Baker to the State Department during the administration of George H. W. Bush, serving as undersecretary for economic affairs, and then to the White House, where he was deputy chief of staff. Renowned for always being the best-prepared person in meetings—the yellow legal pads he toted were typically filled with pros and cons of the various policy options under consideration—he looked the part as well, with his reading glasses and neatly trimmed, strawberry blond mustache accentuating the intensity of his manner. His reputation as a clever strategist grew as he immersed himself in Uruguay Round and NAFTA negotiations, represented the United States in planning two summits of G-7 leaders, and played a leading role in the talks concerning the reunification of Germany. He was clearly hankering to return to public service during the Clinton years, when he worked as an executive at the Federal National Mortgage Association and held some academic posts. He joined the presidential campaign of George W. Bush as a foreign policy adviser, endearing himself to the candidate by flying to Florida immediately after the November 2000 election and helping beat back the Democrats' effort to secure that state's hotly contested electoral votes.

Zoellick took to heart the basic lessons that Baker was famous for practicing: In Washington, success breeds success; momentum breeds momentum. The policymaker who achieved one goal (say, winning a congressional vote on taxes) would be seen as effective, a doer, a mover and shaker, and would thus succeed at other goals (say, winning a vote on budget bills) and would be considered more formidable when taking on even bigger tasks down the road. In trade, he noticed, the same principle applied; for example, Bill Clinton's victory on NAFTA in Congress led to a rise in his popularity, because despite all the acrimony the debate generated, the success also generated respect. This approach was central to the strategy Zoellick brought to the Office of the Trade Representative. Right from the start, he manifested his determination to make a major mark in the job by building one success atop another, former aides recall; as Matt Niemeyer, who was a top official in his congressional relations office, admiringly put it: "He looked to his last day in office, back to first. It was, 'What am I going to accomplish?' So every day was the most important day, every week the most important week. . . . For Bob, there is no A-minus. There are only A-pluses. A-minus?! That's a bad grade."

Accordingly, Zoellick's list of goals, spelled out in testimony before Congress in March 2001, included trade deals of all kinds. He viewed with barely concealed contempt the Clinton administration's trade record of the second half of the 1990s, when it "deferr[ed] to the new economic isolationists" and showed itself to be "fearful of alienating protectionist political constituents," as he put it in a *Foreign Affairs* article. He blamed the Clintonites for what he called "the stain of Seattle," and he said that the top item on his agenda was launching a new WTO round. In other words, he would succeed where his predecessor had failed.

And he would not confine himself to the WTO. His strategy was also to negotiate at the regional level, the chief aim being a Free Trade Area of the Americas, and at the bilateral level, the aim being free-trade pacts with the individual countries that were the most willing to welcome American companies. "Competitive liberalization" was the term he used for this approach, which meant, as he explained at the March 2001 hearing: "We are willing to open if they open. But if others are too slow, we will move without them."

Zoellick's work habits attest to his rigor and hunger for accomplishment. When scheduled to meet a visiting trade minister or to appear before a committee on Capitol Hill, he would hole up for hours or even days in his office, poring over briefing materials and often sending memos back with the margins full of questions and directions for follow-up in his tiny, tidy handwriting. Almost every morning he was in Washington, he met in a conference room with his agency's political appointees at 8:15, followed by a meeting at 8:40 with the assistant U.S. trade representatives, who had responsibility for individual issues, countries, and regions of the world. Staffers quickly learned that to avoid a tongue-lashing, they had better have something substantial to say or volunteer nothing at all; that in responding to Zoellick's queries, they had better get to the point quickly; and that they had better have flipped through all the major newspapers in case he asked them about an article he had seen relating to their area.

"Especially on Mondays, he would come in with this whole page, filled up in his small handwriting, and there would be all these ticks—Doha, the Singapore Free Trade Agreement, whatever—and for each one, he'd say, 'Here's what we're gonna do,' or 'Here's what I need to know,'" says John Veroneau, who was Zoellick's point man for legislative affairs and later general counsel. "You could tell, he had spent a big chunk of the weekend just thinking about these issues. The guy really cared." (True as it may be that he cared, the Monday meetings were an extra reminder, to staffers whose weekends were burdened with child-care responsibilities, that Zoellick and his wife did not have kids.)

In contrast to most cabinet members, who are usually content to deflect questions at congressional hearings by pleading ignorance and promising to send a properly researched answer later, Zoellick wanted to be able to answer every conceivable query, even the ones about minutiae that often come from lawmakers on trade issues. This might mean delving into matters such as a North Dakota member of Congress's likely complaints about the Canadian Wheat Board, for example, or an Oregonian's pleas to obtain protection from Chilean raspberries, or an Arkansan's desire to fend off imports of Vietnamese catfish.

This solicitousness toward Capitol Hill was based partly on Zoellick's recognition that Congress is highly influential on trade policy, much more so than on many other issues. The U.S. Constitution gives authority over trade to the legislative branch, and lawmakers are notoriously sensitive to the grievances of well-organized constituencies within their districts about the damage caused by imports or the unfairness of foreign practices. To complete trade agreements, the executive branch must secure passage of legislation authorizing it to negotiate based on assurances that deals will be subject to an up-or-down vote in Congress, with no crippling amendments. So Zoellick knew that catering to Congress was an important part of his job, but even though he worked very hard at it, he often performed ineptly, for the simple reason that wooing lawmakers requires the kind of people skills he lacked. His detailed responses to their specific questions at hearings sometimes seemed to make them bristle, because they didn't like being shown up. He even managed to alienate some of the Senate Republicans, his most natural political allies. At one closed-door meeting, Senator Phil Gramm, a Texas Republican, stormed out in response to what he perceived as Zoellick's dismissal of concerns about the way certain legislative provisions might affect U.S. sovereignty. Also grating, at least to some people, was Zoellick's proclivity for dropping the names of the high and mighty with whom he had consorted. At one news conference, for example, when asked about Russia's chances for entering the WTO, he began his reply thusly: "In 1989, I was with President Bush's father on the cruiser *Belknap*, actually, right before the meeting with President Gorbachev in Malta," and he went on to describe how the issue was discussed at that meeting. He couldn't resist adding a few seconds later: "Indeed, in the summer of 2000 I had an interesting conversation with [Defense Minister] Sergei Ivanov. . . ."

Where Zoellick stood out was in having a clear agenda, much more so than most cabinet members, as well as the knowledge of how to advance it. Following one of the Baker school's formulas for success, he was soon launching initiatives and making announcements on his own, staying a step or two ahead of the White House and other departments that might otherwise have slowed him down with a lot of interagency red tape. He cleared his moves with the White House only when it was absolutely necessary, on the theory that Bush was a firm adherent of free trade and couldn't be expected to devote much attention to the details, given his other priorities. At the same time, Zoellick's personal relations with Bush often struck other administration officials as strained, because he sometimes came across as a know-it-all in Oval Office meetings, arousing Bush's penchant for cutting brainy wonks down to size. One former official recalls an episode in which Bush was meeting with a group of Central American presidents in the White

House and, introducing his trade representative, jibed, "Zoellick isn't being too hard on you guys, is he? People around here don't like him too much."

Indeed, many of Zoellick's high- and midlevel subordinates found him unbearable. He seemed to quickly decide which staffers would be useful to him and which wouldn't, and his treatment of those who fell short caused stress even among his fans, one of whom describes the atmosphere, especially during the first year, as "a Stalinist cult of fear" that led to high turnover. Working for Zoellick meant regularly spending twelve to fifteen hours a day at the office; it meant lying awake on a Sunday night, worrying about the possibility of being belittled in the Monday morning meeting; it meant trying to gauge whether his frame of mind was too dark to dare raising a subject that might trigger a tirade. "He just *always* seemed to be in a bad mood," says one of the departees (who, like others who have negative views about Zoellick, insisted on anonymity). "I remember thinking, 'If this is so painful and unpleasant for you, why are you doing it?' I know that underneath, he got pleasure from what he was doing, but he always seemed so unhappy."

On the other hand, for those who won his esteem, working for Zoellick was enormously rewarding, mainly because his demanding, exacting nature brought out the best in them. "If he respected you, he would give you tremendous authority," says Jeffrey Bader, a former assistant U.S. trade representative for China. "So for really good people, you couldn't ask for a better boss." Jason Hafemeister, who worked at the agency as a senior negotiator on agriculture issues, agrees: "From the USTR staff perspective, imagine you're a racehorse, and you wonder what it would be like to have a really good jockey on your back. That's what working for Zoellick was like. He gave people at USTR a chance to produce the maximum." Matt Niemeyer, the congressional relations chief, adds: "The pressure he put on himself, he put on others. I was comfortable with that, because I like to win. Well, Bob wins." In the course of researching this book, I heard from some of Zoellick's former subordinates that gaining his respect was one of the most fulfilling achievements of their careers.

In the trade arena, one man in particular commanded Zoellick's respect. Their collaboration would prove central to some of the highest highs, and lowest lows, in trade policy in the early years of the twenty-first century. This man, too, was a booster of round-launching at Doha.

| * |

Pascal Lamy, the European trade commissioner, had a long history with Zoellick. They met in the late 1980s and worked closely in planning meetings for

G-7 summits, with Zoellick representing the United States and Lamy, a French-man who was six years older, representing the European Community. They soon discovered that they had a lot in common, one shared obsession being long-distance running. Beyond that, Lamy was, like Zoellick, the product of his na-tion's most prestigious schools, with a degree from the university that trains France's civil service elite, the École Nationale d'Administration, where he graduated second in his year among those specializing in economics. He also boasted a sterling résumé along with a reputation as a workaholic, a master of detail, and an autocratic boss. In many respects, the laserlike focus with which the two men drove themselves toward accomplishments in international policy made them two peas in a pod.

One area in which they differed was their political backgrounds. A lifelong member of the Socialist Party, Lamy started his career at a time when French leftists were turning increasingly hostile toward the United States and its capi-talist model. But although he stayed faithful to the party's basic precepts, he gravitated toward economic liberalization and, as a top official in France's Economy and Finance Ministry, argued for American-style market policies. He was in the inner circle of Economy Minister Jacques Delors, and when Delors became president of the European Commission in 1985, Lamy went with him to the Berlaymont building in Brussels, the commission's headquarters, as chief of staff. There, his penchant for icily enforcing Delors's will on department heads and civil servants earned him nicknames such as "the Exocet" and "Beast of the Berlaymont."

He and Zoellick remained in touch during the 1990s, when both joined fi-nancial institutions, Zoellick at Fannie Mae, Lamy at the French bank Credit Lyonnais, where as second in command he helped privatize the bank. And then, the two were thrown together again, because Zoellick's nomination as U.S. trade representative came a little more than a year after Lamy was tapped as Euro-pean trade commissioner. The ties between the two cerebral policymakers soon became the stuff of legend in trade circles, especially after they resolved a long-festering transatlantic dispute over bananas in an all-night phone conversation just a couple of months after Zoellick took office. Media reports recounted that the two often spent two or three hours on the phone discussing trade issues and noted that Zoellick had previously visited Lamy's family at his homes in Paris and Brussels and that Lamy was one of the few guests Zoellick and his wife had entertained at their house in Washington. Adding to their compatibility was their ascetic lifestyles. In addition to being an observant Catholic, Lamy maintains a Spartan diet, which he believes helps his concentration and his fitness. He avoids meals that combine fat with sugar or protein with carbohydrates; thus, although he might eat a lot of cheese at a meal or some fruit, he won't eat both; and although he might eat pasta or meat at a meal, he will eat one but not the other. His workday lunches, unless he has an appointment, almost always consist of brown whole-grain bread and bananas, consumed at his desk. His one salient vice is cigars, in which he indulged at the Berlaymont building despite rules against smoking there, and as one former aide recalls, "Nobody would dare tell him not do it, certainly not me."

For all their vaunted closeness, encounters between Zoellick and Lamy tended to be extremely businesslike rather than warm, according to associates of the two men. E-mails they sent each other were curiously devoid of references to personal matters such as family, and when they met in person they often dispensed with friendly greetings so that they could dive right into whatever substantive issue they needed to discuss. Still, the mutual trust and understanding they developed marked a major step forward for the U.S.-E.U. trade relationship, especially considering how it compared with the antipathy that had characterized relations between Charlene Barshefsky and Sir Leon Brittan. The potential implications for the WTO were enormous, given that their two economies accounted for over 40 percent of global output. Maintaining transatlantic comity was critical, both Zoellick and Lamy believed, not only to minimize clashes between Washington and Brussels over bilateral disputes, but also to maximize the chances for achieving progress on the global stage in a multilateral trade round.

They were still divided, to be sure, on some of the same big issues about the new round's agenda that had separated Washington and Brussels in 1999. Whereas it was politically essential for Lamy to limit the opening of European agriculture markets, Zoellick tirelessly stressed the need for barriers in agricultural trade to come down. "How much more food can Americans eat?" was one of his favorite lines, which he used to highlight the importance of obtaining greater access to overseas markets for U.S. farmers, who reaped nearly one-quarter of their gross income from exports. This was an issue he had to flog hard to overcome concern among farm groups and their representatives in Congress that their interests would be sacrificed in the course of negotiations in the WTO; the chairman and ranking member of the House Agriculture Committee were threatening to use their clout to block congressional authorization for new trade agreements. Zoellick countered this by promising that American farmers would gain plenty. "The biggest payoff for agriculture is in the global World Trade Organization round," he told reporters.

As for Lamy, he was continuing to push the European Union's pet idea, the Singapore issues (which, as explained in Chapter 4, would expand the WTO's jurisdiction into the areas of investment, competition policy, government procurement, and trade facilitation). U.S. policymakers had always had objections to those, and even more troublesome from Washington's standpoint was the Frenchman's determination to include on the negotiating agenda several environmental issues, which were of special interest to Europe's Greens. One of these involved tilting WTO rules more toward the precautionary principle, as E.U. policymakers continued to seek validation for their use of that principle in addressing issues such as hormone-fed beef. At the very least, Lamy wanted an agreement that countries could use the precautionary principle in protecting public health if it was based on pertinent scientific information, even if that information didn't necessarily reflect the views of a majority of scientists. Another key European goal was enabling countries to impose economic sanctions on each other for violating international environmental agreements such as the ones involving trafficking in endangered species.

But the mutual desire of Zoellick and Lamy to bridge those gaps for the sake of success at Doha was much in evidence when the European trade commissioner visited Washington in mid-July 2001. Displaying a level of camaraderie that would have been unthinkable between their predecessors, the two men wrote a joint op-ed article for the *Washington Post* pledging their cooperation in getting a round launched. They also appeared together at the National Press Club, where Zoellick explained, "Pascal and I decided early on that if the United States and the EU did not work together, a new round would not happen." They unveiled plans they had agreed upon to magnify the prospects for a positive Doha outcome; as Lamy put it: "We've achieved a good convergence of positions, even if we are not there on each and every bit of the agenda." To show they meant business, Zoellick announced that the United States "[would] not stand in the way" of the European Union's efforts to put the most contentious of the Singapore issues—investment—on the round's agenda, and he indicated that Washington, although maintaining its basic policy stance, was willing to be more flexible about expanding the talks to include other matters that were of interest to Brussels. "An important lesson that we and other countries have learned from the failure at Seattle was to avoid trying to pre-negotiate the details and the outcomes of a negotiation," he said.

The people with the most at stake in all this, Zoellick told the Press Club audience, were the world's poor. "Here is the bottom line," he said. "The United States and EU are working closely together to try to launch a new global round with a focus on growth and development. The United States believes that one of the best ways to fight global poverty is through expanding trade opportunities around the globe."

If only the poor saw things the same way. The biggest problem facing the Doha meeting was that they didn't. Or at least, their governments didn't, as a "Reality Check" soon made clear.

The Reality Check was the name of a special, two-day General Council meeting that Mike Moore called at the end of July 2001. The minds of WTO member nations, the director-general believed, needed to be focused on the necessity of agreeing on most of the major issues concerning the agenda for the proposed new round so that a coherent draft declaration could be ready when ministers began gathering in Doha in November. Only about fifty working days in Geneva remained before then, Moore reminded the ambassadors, once the traditional August recess was factored in.

Instead of responding as the director-general had hoped, many developing countries chose to emphasize a different reality—that they, the supposed beneficiaries of the development round, were not interested in it. India's representative derided the idea of a new round as likely to worsen the "asymmetries and imbalances" of the Uruguay Round. Malaysia's ambassador described the situation as one of "four D's—disappointing, demoralizing, discouraging, and, at times depressing," adding that the high-income nations were risking a "Seattle II."

Those two countries, it will be recalled, were prominent members of the Like Minded Group, which in 1999 had been the most militant of the groups opposing a new round. Although some developing countries, such as Mexico and Brazil, favored a round, most of them were fervently against holding talks on the Singapore issues, convinced that WTO rules on matters such as investment would hand excessive power to multinationals and deprive governments of the ability to develop their economies as they saw fit. Another major reason for their hostility toward a new round was the European Union's push on the environment. The Like Minded Group and its allies feared that the hidden agenda there was to promote "Green protectionism" in which the European Union and other governments would use overly tight standards to block the importation of food grown in low-income nations. They were relieved that the United States had dropped its efforts to put labor rights on the agenda; the Bush administration was no champion of unions. But the sum and substance of the Like Minded Group's position was that problems with the Uruguay Round should be rectified before another round started, and representatives of many African nations, which belonged to other blocs, agreed. "Most of us are not ready, psychologically, materially and technically, for a new round," Iddi Simba, the Tanzanian minister for industry and trade, said at a gathering of forty-nine WTO members from least-developed countries in late July.

At the Reality Check, Moore used somber rhetoric in highlighting the dangers should the time remaining before Doha be squandered. A second consecutive failure, he told the ambassadors, "would certainly condemn us to a long period of irrelevance." He also admonished that member nations must be ready for intensive bargaining in September.

September, of course, would change the dynamics in a way that none of those present could have imagined.

| * |

On the morning of the eleventh, the plume of smoke rising from the Pentagon was clearly visible to occupants of the Winder Building, where the Office of the U.S. Trade Representative is located, about a block from the White House. That, plus widespread rumors that more planes were unaccounted for besides the four that had been hijacked, helped spur staffers working in Winder to evacuate and go home, as most people working in downtown Washington were doing. To make sure that everyone was gone, M. B. Oglesby Jr., the chief of staff, went from floor to floor, finding to his satisfaction that all offices were vacant. All, that is, but one.

It was close to noon when Oglesby entered Zoellick's office and discovered him still working, despite the advice of the Secret Service to leave immediately. "You've got to get your ass out of here," Oglesby recalls telling Zoellick, who responded by citing the Winder Building's proximity to the White House. "I kind of thought I was in the safest place I could be," Zoellick protested, though he finally relented and had his driver take him home. The next day, he held a staff meeting at the regular time.

Not that Zoellick failed to perceive any implications of 9/11 for his agenda. Quite the contrary; this was a man, after all, who had spent much of his career working on the connections between foreign policy and economics, and he was soon crafting arguments seeking to highlight the seamlessness of those connections. The terrorist attacks, he contended, offered a newly compelling rationale for how trade—and in particular, the WTO—could serve America's security interests as well as its commercial ones. "America's trade leadership can build a coalition of countries that cherish liberty in all its aspects," he wrote in a *Washington Post* op-ed, published on September 20. "Open markets are vital for developing nations, many of them fragile democracies that rely on the international economy to overcome poverty and create opportunity; we need answers for those who ask for economic hope to counter internal threats to our common values." The article angered Democrats on Capitol Hill, who accused

Zoellick of exploiting 9/11 to promote a partisan agenda because he included a call for Congress to approve the administration's request for authority to negotiate new trade agreements. Undeterred, Zoellick maintained a steady stream of public statements for weeks thereafter exhorting Americans and foreigners alike to recognize trade as an important element in the war against terror. As he put it in an October 30 speech, just a week and a half before the WTO meeting:

> America and the world have been attacked by a network of terrorists who are masters of destruction, but failures at construction. They stand for intolerance and abhor openness. . . .
>
> The international market economy—of which trade and the WTO are vital parts—offers an antidote to this violent rejectionism. Trade is about more than economic efficiency; it reflects a system of values: openness, peaceful exchange, opportunity, inclusiveness and integration, mutual gains through interchange, freedom of choice, appreciation of differences, governance through agreed rules, and a hope for betterment of all peoples and lands.
>
> Therefore . . . By promoting the WTO's agenda, especially a new negotiation to liberalize global trade, these 142 nations can counter the revulsive destructionism of terrorism.

In this respect, by giving new force to their cause, Osama bin Laden did a favor—unintentional though it obviously was—for those seeking to launch a new round at Doha. As noted in Chapter 1, other policymakers and commentators also seized on 9/11 as an especially compelling reason for the Doha attendees to come together. In other ways as well, the atmosphere concerning the Doha meeting changed after the terrorist attacks; Pakistan and Malaysia, both prominent Muslim members of the Like Minded Group, began softening their opposition to a new round lest they appear too much at odds with Washington.

Also helpful to the cause of a new round were various studies of its potential impact. These were used to buttress claims that a major push for trade liberalization would, first, help neutralize the global economic downdraft caused by the attacks, and second, provide a crucial boost toward the newly urgent goal of poverty alleviation. By far the most widely cited study was the World Bank's, which estimated that worldwide income would increase by $830 billion a year by 2015—with two-thirds of that amount going to poor nations—if all barriers were removed, subsidies eliminated, and aid provided to help developing countries take advantage of their new opportunities. In its study, the World Bank noted that it was only logical to expect that the low-income countries would gain proportionately more, given that existing trade barriers hit them so much worse than rich ones. "The average poor person selling goods into globalized markets confronts barriers that are roughly twice as high as the typical worker in industrialized countries," the bank said, adding that part of the problem was the developing countries' own high tariffs, which discourage trade among them.

But 9/11 also presented the WTO with new complications. In a world where no one knew where terrorists might strike next, where anthrax-laced envelopes were turning up in the mail, and where the U.S. military was bombing Afghanistan, suddenly Qatar did not look like a secure place to meet after all.

| * |

A couple of weeks after the attacks, George Yeo, the Singaporean trade minister, received a call from one of Zoellick's deputies, who posed an uncomfortable question: Given all the concerns that were arising among WTO members about the risks of going to Doha, how would Singapore feel about hosting the ministerial if it were necessary to change the venue?

The city-state had hosted the WTO's first ministerial in 1996, and Yeo recalls joking, "We're not due to host for another hundred years." But the request was serious, "and we knew how important it was to the WTO, so I swallowed hard and said, 'Let me discuss it with my prime minister,'" Yeo says. Although worried that Singapore was already a potential target of al Qaeda, the country's authorities agreed to be available to host on the conditions that the honor of chairing the meeting would remain with Qatar, that the number of participants would be significantly slimmed down, and that the government could restrict the entry of people from NGOs to keep Seattle-type problems from occurring.

Behind the request was Zoellick's fear about keeping Doha as the meeting's venue. The issue wasn't his personal safety; rather, it was the meeting's chances for success. Zoellick was concerned about whether WTO member countries would send delegations to Doha, and also about whether a last-minute incident might force a cancellation of the meeting.

Accordingly, Zoellick began hinting in late September that the meeting might have to be moved, telling a Washington audience that "at this point" the United States was "committed to going ahead to launch the round at Doha" but that "obviously, the first imperative is security." Word began to leak out that Singapore was under consideration; indeed, the Singaporean government was preparing for the eventuality by spending several million dollars on security equipment, Yeo says, although "some of it was equipment we needed anyway."

The venue issue was the prime topic at a preparatory meeting of twenty-one trade ministers in Singapore on October 13 and 14, where the Qatari minister, Yousef Hussain Kamal, assured his colleagues that his government had complete control over the security situation. But he failed to convince them; many of the attendees were hoping that the Qatari government could be persuaded to voluntarily withdraw as host. Zoellick was clearly leaning toward a move, without saying so explicitly. He told a news conference on October 15: "The common view was that we need to go forward with this ministerial, in one location or the other."

The Qataris, who had spent an estimated $30 million on preparations for the ministerial, fought back. They sent diplomatic démarches to key WTO members stating that switching the venue would be seen as "a measure against Muslim countries, especially at this juncture so rife with attempts to demonize Islam and link it to terrorism." Even so, member nations continued pressing Moore to use his good offices as director-general to get the Qataris to back down.

Moore flew to Qatar on October 20 to personally deliver the bad news that it didn't seem possible to hold the meeting in Doha as planned. As he stepped off the plane, he was greeted by a welcoming party of smiling Qatari officials, and according to his chief of staff, Patrick Low, their smiles prompted him to mutter, "This proves they didn't want the bloody thing anyway." But the Qataris were smiling for a different reason; as they explained, their role as hosts had been finally settled, with confirmation from President Bush, who had stated publicly that day during an overseas trip that the meeting would be in Doha.

What caused this turn of events? The emir of Qatar had telephoned Vice President Dick Cheney, with whom he was well acquainted, and made a very persuasive case. Just what was said, neither man is revealing. But I am reliably informed that the emir, in only slightly veiled terms, used as leverage the air base in his country that the Pentagon regarded as a crucial asset in the war against terror. His Royal Highness's words to the vice president went something like this: "If Qatar is safe enough to host U.S. military aircraft, how could it not be safe enough to host a WTO meeting?"

| * |

"Not acceptable." "Impossible for me to acquiesce." "My delegation is deeply concerned." Those were a few of the phrases uttered by ambassadors from low-income countries at a General Council meeting on October 31, a week and a half before the scheduled opening of the Doha ministerial. They were up in arms because they felt that their views were simply being ignored, another apparent contravention of all the talk about development being the top aim of the new round.

The main target of their discontent was Stuart Harbinson, Hong Kong's chief representative in Geneva who was the council's chairman. A balding man with a friendly face, metal-rimmed glasses, and the mild demeanor of a British civil servant, Harbinson had been charged with drawing up a workable draft declaration for ministers to consider at Doha. Having a preexisting draft with as few points of contention as possible was another part of Moore's effort to avoid a repetition of Seattle, and the attempt had the backing of virtually the entire membership. In soliciting the opinions of member nations about what they would like to see in the text, Harbinson had heard from one ambassador after another that he should take a much different approach from the unwieldy compendium that had contributed to the Seattle breakdown. During the summer, in compiling his early drafts, Harbinson had won plaudits from developing countries for seeking the views of as many members as possible in private meetings about what the text should say and for listening attentively to their concerns. Although many low-income countries raised objections to the early drafts, they generally appreciated the process Harbinson had used.

Harbinson's new text was only eleven pages, about one-third the length of the Seattle one. But here, to the Geneva diplomatic corps, was the shocker: The text had no square brackets!

In moving away from the bracket infestation for which the Seattle document was notorious, the council chairman was swinging to the opposite extreme. Of course, he was expecting that at Doha, ministers would make some changes in his handiwork; in an introduction, he wrote: "This draft does not purport to be agreed in any part at this stage." But, together with Moore, he had decided that it would be best to present a "clean" text representing his best guess of where a consensus could be found on all issues, because if one section contained brackets displaying different options, demands for a similar approach in other sections would arise, leading once again to bracket hell.

In many respects the text was a model of diplomatic artistry, casting in broad terms the agenda for negotiations so as to avoid any precise delineation of the outcome that might alienate one member country or group. It even eschewed the term "round," calling instead for a "work programme," on the theory that the Like Minded Group and other developing countries would find that easier to swallow, and it clearly identified the parties that were to benefit most: "The majority of WTO members are developing countries," it said. "We seek to place their needs and interests at the heart of the work programme adopted in this declaration." This "work programme," of course, would have most of the elements that would be expected in a round—negotiations on farm subsidies, on market access in both agricultural and manufactured goods, and on trade in services, plus a variety of other trade-related topics of interest to large numbers of WTO members. Like the Uruguay Round, it would be a "single undertaking," with nothing agreed until all was agreed. On the most touchy subjects, Harbinson used carefully crafted phraseology aimed at papering over big gaps in positions among member countries.

One example was his language concerning export subsidies in agriculture. Many nations, including the United States, considered it imperative that the negotiations should bring an end to this specific type of subsidies, which were provided mostly by the European Union to its farmers for crops sold in overseas markets. The Europeans, naturally, remained under pressure from their farmers to continue the payments, at least to some extent. In a bid to get all parties to sign on, the Harbinson text stated that one aim of the negotiations in agriculture would be "reductions of, with a view to phasing out, all forms of export subsidies." In another portion of the text, Harbinson tried to steer down the middle between the European Union's demand for negotiations to include the Singapore issues and the developing countries' antagonism toward the idea of WTO rules on investment and competition in particular. His text didn't exactly say that negotiations would commence on those issues, and it didn't exactly say that they wouldn't; it said that preliminary discussions on "clarification" would take place after Doha and that at the *next* ministerial a "decision" would be made on "modalities of negotiations" in those areas. By accepting that language, the Europeans could claim that negotiations were going to start and that the next ministerial would deal with the precise modalities, whereas nations such as India and Malaysia could claim that the question of whether to negotiate seriously on those issues had been put off for at least two years.

Notwithstanding all of Harbinson's wordsmithing, developing countries were upset, and they were by no means the only ones who were disgruntled. The E.U. ambassador, Carlo Trojan, griped that on the issue Brussels regarded as a potential deal breaker, the text gave Europe "a fig leaf so small . . . that it borders on indecency." He was referring to the E.U. demand for negotiations to establish clear rules on environmental matters; the text envisioned only a continuation of discussions by a committee, which would report to the WTO in 2003 on whether negotiations should take place. As for the United States, a big letdown in the text was its plan for the WTO to negotiate new rules on antidumping procedures, a potentially serious problem for Zoellick because members of Congress were adamant in opposing any such talks.

The chorus of complaints could be regarded as a sweet musical prelude, for it showed, as Moore put it, that the text was a "balance of unhappiness," reflecting the nature of the bargain that would have to be struck at Doha. But this episode is Exhibit A for critics who see the WTO as an oligarchy that only pretends to operate on democratic principles. Yes, each country may have one vote, and yes, consensus may be required, but in reality, the critics say, an improvised, nontransparent system for taking important procedural steps means that weak countries often find themselves railroaded into accepting terms dictated by the strong. Texts are drawn up by people who tend to be sympathetic to the views of the most powerful nations, and the documents are presented to the membership as the sole basis for negotiation. Though technically the wording can be changed in any way imaginable, in practice major modifications are very difficult to effect, especially for small countries in the crucible of a ministerial. Doing so may require blocking the consensus, a momentous step for any country, given the opprobrium that may ensue. By eliminating brackets in favor of·compromise language, Harbinson was effectively dismissing the arguments that developing countries had been raising for weeks, or so their representatives asserted.

The WTO has a difficult balancing act to strike in situations like these. Democracy and inclusiveness are desirable goals, but so is efficiency in coming to decisions. The director-general and the General Council chairman, both of whom had been elected by the membership, had decided on a text after extensive consultations; how much more legitimate could the process be without becoming hopelessly bogged down? Backed by Moore, Harbinson stuck to his guns, asserting that the text as written offered the best hope for success at Doha, though the two men did agree to a couple of additional steps at the insistence of India, Zimbabwe, and other malcontents. They sent a formal letter to Kamal, the Qatari trade minister, who was going to chair the Doha meeting, underlining that the text "clearly" was not yet agreed. The letter also outlined some of the main differences among WTO members.

One issue was too contentious to be handled in the same way as the others. It was in a separate annex to the main text, and in this case, Harbinson inserted two distinct options in bracketed form. He had been warned not to even attempt a no-bracket compromise lest it throw all the preparations for Doha into a cocked hat. This issue was not just a matter of dollars and cents; it involved life and death.

| * |

A gruesome and probably short future was facing Vuyani Jacobs of Capetown, South Africa, in early 2001 as full-blown AIDS racked his thirty-one-year-old body. Suffering from the effects of bacterial meningitis and tuberculosis, the former bank clerk recalls that he was afflicted with "nonstop diarrhea. I was losing all my hair. I couldn't even remember my phone number." His girlfriend had died three years earlier, he adds, with "diarrhea, meningitis, thrush in her mouth and in her vagina. I could see myself dying the same way."

But Jacobs's luck turned. He was one of a small minority of South African AIDS victims able to get generic versions, made in Brazil, of the drug AZT, which cost upwards of $10,000 a year for an individual supply in the United States but only about $550 a year per patient at a program administered by Doctors Without Borders. When I met him a few months after his brush with death, he was energetic and speaking animatedly about his undetectable viral load. His weight, which had once fallen as low as 80 pounds, had risen to 140 pounds, his beard was growing back, and he was circulating his curriculum vitae in hopes of finding a job. "I feel like I'm eighteen again," he said.

The Lazarus-like recovery of HIV/AIDS victims such as Jacobs who got treatment—and the plight of millions of others who were not so fortunate—lay at the crux of a tough dilemma facing the Doha meeting: Where does a drug company's right to earn a profit end, and a poor person's right to lifesaving medicine begin?

Such questions had not mattered to trade diplomats in Geneva as long as global trade rules concerned mostly tariffs. But that situation had changed when the Uruguay Round thrust the newly created WTO into the realm of intellectual property protection, with the inclusion in the round of the agreement on Trade-Related Aspects of Intellectual Property Rights (TRIPS).

The protection of patents and copyrights involves an inherently tricky balancing act. If people are allowed to copy movies, books, and pharmaceuticals at will, the incentives for firms to be creative and innovative are eliminated. If protections against copying those products are excessive, financial rewards go to inventors, artists, authors, researchers, and big corporations without benefiting society. The balancing act is even trickier at the international level, because poor countries generally have much lower stakes in intellectual property protection than do high-income ones, which are the main sources of technological innovation and artistic creation. When citizens of Africa, Latin America, or developing Asia must stop buying cheap knockoffs and pay more for "legitimate" Hollywood DVDs, Silicon Valley software, or brand-name American drugs, an income transfer takes place from poor to rich. (In one study, the World Bank estimated that U.S. companies stood to collect an additional $19 billion a year in royalties as a result of the TRIPS agreement, with much of the money coming from developing nations that are net importers of intellectual property.)

That's not to say that developing countries get nothing from strongly protecting intellectual property; they are more likely to draw investment from abroad, attract new technologies, and encourage homegrown innovation if investors and creators are confident of protection for their work. But the gains may not be great enough to offset the losses, and they are certainly not nearly as great as they are in countries where the items in question are created and the profits reaped. Indeed, this calculation of costs and benefits led the United States to flout the intellectual property rights of foreigners in the early stages of its development. Throughout most of the nineteenth century, Washington gave no copyright protection to foreign books; only when an overseas market developed for American books did the United States sign international copyright conventions. More recently, the Japanese miracle of the 1960s and '70s, and the South Korean miracle that came soon thereafter, showed how countries could help pull themselves up the development ladder by copying foreign technology under lax patent systems.

TRIPS was thus a huge leap for the trading system. It required all WTO members to protect patents for twenty years and to enforce their patent laws vigorously, though it allowed transition periods before developing countries were required to comply and even longer phase-ins for the world's poorest nations. It was controversial even among fervently free-trade economists. Some applauded it as a necessary adaptation of global rules to the new reality of trade, as the goods crossing borders increasingly consisted of items with high levels of creative content that were easy to copy. Others denounced it as an abuse of the trading system on the grounds that intellectual property is a separate matter from trade. These critics feared that turning the WTO into an enforcer of patent rights risked putting the institution on a slippery slope, with interest groups demanding that it enforce all kinds of other rights—labor rights being an obvious example.

It didn't take long for controversy to flare beyond the realm of trade theorists and policymakers, and it could hardly have come in a more emotion-laden setting.

South Africa, which had just emerged in 1994 from apartheid, was struggling under President Nelson Mandela to cope with the greatest number of HIV-infected people in Africa. AIDS was not only killing millions of people on the continent; it was ravaging whole national economies by sickening workers and forcing children to leave school. The Mandela government enacted a law in late 1997 aimed at obtaining cheap, generic versions of powerful AIDS drugs that were protected by patents. This could be accomplished in two ways: One was compulsory licensing, in which a government authorizes local firms to manufacture a knockoff of a patented drug (usually with a negotiated fee going to the patent holder). The other was parallel importing, in which importers are awarded the right to obtain drugs from any source regardless of whether the patent holder approves.

What did all this have to do with the WTO? Arguably, not much. The TRIPS agreement contained provisions giving WTO members flexibilities that seemingly took account of situations like South Africa's. It allowed governments to issue compulsory licenses to deal with "national emergencies or other circumstances of extreme urgency," though with several restrictions.

But drug companies filed suit in a South African court against the government, asserting that the law violated their property rights as well as the TRIPS agreement. The industry was fearful that the precedent set by the South Africans would spread throughout the developing world, undermining patent rights and creating a number of risks for pharmaceutical makers in their rich-country markets—for instance, the importation of bootleg drugs into the United States and Europe. Industry officials, citing a $500 million price tag as the cost of the research and development needed to bring a drug to market, warned of a potentially deleterious impact on the willingness of firms to seek cures for deadly diseases. Besides, the industry argued, the real problem in poor countries wasn't the price of drugs; it was the low quality of their health care systems, in which sick people often couldn't find doctors to prescribe and dispense medication properly. The Clinton administration, which had reflexively supported intellectual-property-oriented industries in the past (Hollywood, for instance), backed up the pharmaceutical industry, putting South Africa on a "watch list" of countries that might face sanctions for violating patent rights. Washington brought pressure on Brazil and Thailand for similar reasons, and the White House dispatched Vice President Gore to South Africa to try to mediate the dispute.

Then the issue turned red hot, galvanizing AIDS activists, who honed in on—and attacked—the administration's most vulnerable target.

"Gore's greed kills! Gore's greed kills!" So shouted a gaggle of protesters at the vice president's June 1999 announcement in his hometown of Carthage, Tennessee, that he was running for the presidency. Noisy demonstrations continued at other Gore appearances, and soon the Clinton administration, taking a fresh look at the issue, backed off from its confrontational posture with South Africa. Pharmaceutical companies, also stung by the public outcry, began voluntarily lowering the prices they charged to Africans for AIDS drugs. When George Bush came to office, Zoellick announced that his administration too would take a relatively tolerant stance toward the use by impoverished nations of copycat medicine to combat AIDS, saying that the United States, "consistent with our overall effort to protect America's investment in intellectual property," was prepared to "work with countries that develop serious programs to prevent and treat this horrible disease."

Developing countries and activists were far from appeased. They feared new legal assaults by wealthy nations and the pharmaceutical industry aimed at restricting the rights of governments to obtain cheap generic drugs, and they wanted an explicit statement that those rights could be invoked by all WTO members in all kinds of health emergencies—not just sub-Saharan African countries, and not just HIV/AIDS. Leading this initiative was Brazil, which had created an HIV/AIDS program considered a model for the developing world. The Brazilian government gave free treatment to anyone who was HIV positive, using locally manufactured generics and a nationwide system of clinics; the program had sharply cut the rate of new infections and AIDS-related deaths.

As drafting work intensified in late 2001 over the document the WTO would issue at Doha, Brazil and its allies coalesced around a demand for a special declaration on the drug issue. The key sentence they wanted the WTO to endorse read as follows: "Nothing in the TRIPS agreement shall prevent Members from taking measures to protect public health."

Drug makers were predictably disdainful of this proposal. "Just nutty" is how Harvey Bale, director-general of the International Federation of Pharmaceutical Manufacturers & Associations, described it at a November 1 news conference. Such broad language, industry spokesmen warned, was a naked attack on the TRIPS agreement and would mean that any country could casually claim a public health reason for copying any drug it wished. The United States agreed that the Brazilian-led group was going too far, as did other wealthy WTO members, including Switzerland, Japan, and the European Union.

If the "revulsive destructionism of terrorism" was to be countered with a successful Doha meeting, one side or the other in the TRIPS debate was going to have to move—a lot.

| * |

Extraordinary preparations were under way in advance of the Doha ministerial to keep it secure. The names of all hotel employees, many of whom were guest workers from other Middle Eastern countries and South Asia, were thoroughly scrutinized; anyone who was viewed as suspicious was ordered to take a few days off during the WTO meeting. Cameras were installed at strategic locations as part of an extensive surveillance operation. The U.S. Navy dispatched an Amphibious Ready Group—a fleet including a ship resembling a small aircraft carrier equipped with numerous helicopters and Harrier aircraft, plus a contingent of marines—to patrol the waters just over the horizon. To minimize the danger of a missile attack on the government plane carrying the U.S. delegation, the flight route for the plane was modified from the normal path that incoming jets take, and plans were laid to station troops on the ground in the areas over which the plane would be flying.

Overseeing these arrangements was Doug Melvin, a former Special Forces commander who was chief of security for the Office of the U.S. Trade Representative. Melvin gathered extensive information from the CIA and other sources about possible threats to the meeting, and having made one trip to Doha before 9/11, he visited again in October, when he went scuba diving in the harbor to see what could be done to fend off a seaborne attack. Back in Washington, he organized briefings of people who might be going to Doha, including government personnel, members of Congress and their staffers, business lobbyists, and leaders of NGOs. These were very sobering affairs, because although the briefers withheld information about sources and methods behind the intelligence they had gathered, they were fairly specific about what the "traffic" had turned up, such as the suspected truck bomber (referred to in Chapter 1) who was feared to be at large in Qatar. The briefers gave assurances that all U.S. citizens would have ready access to gas masks, radio communication devices, antibiotics, and antidotes to poison chemicals; at first, they said such equipment would be issued to each individual, though this decision was later modified in favor of keeping the equipment offshore on the navy ships, which were capable of transporting it quickly to the meeting site.

The danger that the meeting might fail because of outside threats—either terrorists or protesters—had been significantly attenuated. The rest was now in the hands of WTO members.

# 6 | REMOVING THE STAIN

THE LAST LEG OF GEOFFREY GAMBLE'S LONG JOURNEY TO THE WTO meeting in November 2001 was a flight from Dubai to Doha, and the young Arab man sitting next to him on the plane was sweating heavily and acting nervously. Deeply suspicious, Gamble, the director of international government affairs for Dupont Company, decided he'd better be ready for action. He got up to use the rest room, bringing his earphones, which he curled tightly around his hand. "I'm thinking, 'If he makes a break for it, I'll get him—I'll garrote him!'" Gamble recalls. "So I walk back to my seat. He glares at me. He leans forward.

"And he says, 'Your fly is open.'"

The man turned out to be perfectly pleasant, Gamble says, adding, "The stress level at that time was *so* intense."

Business representatives like Gamble are ever-present fixtures at global trade meetings, and as previously seen in the example of the movie industry in the Uruguay Round, they are always eager to press their case, mainly with their own governments' officials, though often with officials from other nations as well. The activities of the business representatives from the United States, who are usually the most numerous, closely resemble what lobbyists do on Capitol Hill; although not allowed in the rooms where formal negotiations are taking place, they wait outside, pouncing on negotiators during breaks and, if necessary, flexing their political muscle, perhaps by calling influential members of Congress to exert pressure on the U.S. team.

Gamble's stress level began to recede after he passed through stringent security to reach the newly built Ritz-Carlton, where most of the American attendees were staying. "I've never stayed in such a hotel," he says, recalling the enormous lobby chandelier, gold-plated bathroom fixtures, and solicitous staff, most of whom seemed to be European or Canadian. Moreover, he was pleased to find that because all the U.S. negotiators were staying there too—and many of his private-sector colleagues were staying home—it would be easy to arrange meetings and mingle with the people he needed to see. So before long, Gamble was caught up in the urgency of dealing with the WTO agenda, relegating anxieties about security to the recesses of his mind.

That reaction seemed almost universal among lobbyists, delegates, journalists, and other participants from the United States and other countries alike. Although the constant bag searches and metal-detector screenings made it impossible to forget completely about the danger of a terrorist attack, most attendees became immersed in the press of business at the main WTO meeting venue, the Sheraton Doha, a towering pyramid-shaped hotel and conference center. The corridors were bustling with people of every nationality imaginable, some rushing to meetings, others huddling with colleagues, riffling through briefing papers, yakking on cell phones, or preening before television cameras.

Conspicuous by their near absence were the environmental and labor groups that had led the Seattle protests. Together with other NGOs, they were setting up desks and tables in a tentlike structure behind the Sheraton, well away from the main meeting halls, that the Qataris had designated for their use. Only one person from each group had been granted a visa, which the WTO attributed to the lack of hotel space. In one orderly, rather forlorn effort to show that they couldn't be completely intimidated, a few dozen activists staged a demonstration as official delegates filed into the opening session. They chanted and waved small, hastily printed placards accusing the WTO of being antidemocratic and biased in favor of the rich.

The WTO leadership and the Qatari hosts were doing their utmost to impart a sense of unity to the proceedings. In the inaugural session, which took place on the evening of Friday, November 9, in a large auditorium with a video screen overhead showing images of the speakers, Mike Moore reminded the delegates of what was at stake, using his most elegant diction, free of New Zealand slang. "The world economy needs the signal of confidence in open markets and commitment to international cooperation which agreement here will deliver," the director-general said. "This conference will initiate the next stage in the development of the trading system, whose focus must be the fuller integration of the developing world."

The following morning, at the first business phase of the meeting, delegates were officially informed of how things would work in the four days before the deadline of midnight on Tuesday, November 13, when the gathering must conclude. As at Seattle, six working groups would meet to discuss the issues on which divisions among WTO members were the most pronounced, with the aim of reaching a consensus text. Each group would be headed by a "friend of the chair"—that is, a trade minister deemed reliable and credible by Moore—and member countries were welcome to send representatives to any of the groups. One difference this time was that the groups would have no acoustic and other logistical problems of the sort that had plagued them at Seattle. The conference facilities at the Doha Sheraton, attendees agreed, were first-rate.

No sooner had this organizational session gotten under way, however, than an amusing gaffe exposed the tensions between the powers-that-be and some of the leading developing countries. Yousef Hussain Kamal, the Qatari minister, was chairing, with Moore at his side, when India's "flag" went up—that is, its country nameplate was turned on its side, indicating a desire by its minister, Murasoli Maran, to be recognized. That, Moore suspected, could mean trouble, given the Indians' positions on issues before the meeting, and he whispered to Kamal that the Indians probably wanted to raise a nettlesome point about procedure. "Then we won't give them the time," Kamal replied—a conversation that, to their chagrin, was heard by everyone in the hall, because Kamal had inadvertently left his microphone on. A wave of raucous laughter ensued at this clumsy effort to suppress dissident voices.

There was good reason to believe that Maran could emerge as the spoiler.

| * |

The sixty-seven-year-old Maran was a short man with a thin mustache and long sideburns that made him look "like a comical villain in a spaghetti-western movie," as one Indian newspaper put it. Having suffered a severe heart attack, he was also very frail looking. (He would live only two more years after the Doha meeting.) He held his position as minister of commerce and industry by dint of his leading role in a party in the governing coalition, the DMK, a regional party based in India's southern state of Tamil Nadu and founded on opposition to the nation's long domination by Hindi-speaking Brahmans from the north. Tamils have their own language, and among the party's principles was resistance to the teaching of Hindi in the region's schools, a cause for which Maran had been arrested in 1965. Like many Tamils, he had only one given name, but one of his first jobs was as editor of a party political organ called *Murasoli*, meaning "Drumbeat," and so he became known as Murasoli Maran.

The country he represented, though making major strides toward the status of modern economic power, had long harbored deep antipathy toward the global trading system. International trade was associated with the colonial rule of the British, whose shameful practices included the use of tariffs and other restrictions to keep India as a producer of raw cotton for Britain's factories while preventing Indians from developing their own competing fabric industry. One of the chief rallying cries of the independence movement was *swadeshi*, or "self-reliance," and the independent nation's first government, headed by Jawaharlal Nehru, put top priority on achieving self-sufficiency in manufactured goods while restricting imports to the minimum required. India was a leader of the G-77, the coalition of developing countries that pushed hard in the 1960s, '70s, and '80s to preserve their rights to protect their economies through tariffs, quotas, and investment restrictions. Until the 1990s, the Indian private sector was subject to strict limitations on investment and collaboration with foreign firms; any company trying to establish a large-scale industrial enterprise had to obtain a government license, which of course limited competition. India's tariffs ranked among the highest in the world, peaking in 1988 at an average of between 120 percent and 140 percent. The result of all these policies was an industrial machine of pathetically poor competitiveness, because with the large domestic market pretty much all to themselves, Indian companies had little incentive to meet the world standards necessary to export their goods.

Many of these policies underwent extensive reform in the early 1990s, partly because of an economic crisis and partly because the fall of the Soviet Union called into question India's own model. The government scrapped the requirement for businesses to obtain licenses for private investment, except in eighteen key industries. The authorities also reduced many of the highest tariffs and narrowed the list of imports subject to quotas and other restrictions. Still, the Indian market remained among the most protected in the world. State trading monopolies controlled the import and export of most agricultural commodities, including the two most important, rice and wheat. In May 2001 the Ministry of Commerce and Industry established a war room to monitor a list of three hundred "sensitive" consumer goods, including cars, tea, and pencils, with the goal of guarding against import disruptions.

Maran's predecessors as minister had long positioned themselves in WTO negotiations as champions of Indian nationalism against foreigners, and coming from one party in the ruling coalition, Maran took special pleasure in assuming that role. His Egyptian counterpart, Youssef Boutros-Ghali, recalls being asked, "because I was supposedly his third world friend," to cajole Maran into being cooperative at Doha—to no avail. "Maran told me, 'Look, in the domestic politics of India, it is in my political interest that this thing fails.' He said it explicitly," Boutros-Ghali says. Indeed, tens of thousands of Indians, mostly farmers, rallied in New Delhi on November 6, 2001, demanding that the government reject new WTO negotiations.

In the run-up to the meeting, Maran had frequently hurled verbal thunderbolts about India's determination to resist pressure from rich countries, calling the WTO a "necessary evil." After his arrival in Doha, he showed no sign of tempering his rhetoric; on the contrary, he seemed to revel in goading Zoellick. He told reporters he agreed with the assessment that U.S. officials were exploiting 9/11 in their effort to launch a new round. "They want to strike when the iron is hot," he huffed.

He was on the list of ministers whom Zoellick met on a bilateral basis at Doha—ministers generally try to hold as many such meetings as possible, partly as a diplomatic courtesy, partly to improve the negotiating atmosphere—and in their get-together, though it was cordial, they made no headway on the issues that divided them. This helped crystallize Zoellick's Doha strategy: He would isolate the Indians as the only ones opposed to a consensus supported by all other WTO members. After leaving the meeting with Maran, Zoellick told an aide that he couldn't possibly reach an accommodation with the Indian minister. He planned to line up all the other countries, so Maran would face a "binary choice" about whether he was "with the program or not."

To do that, Zoellick would have to start winning over other countries, which would mean reaching accommodations with them on issues of great political sensitivity in the United States. With the Harbinson text as a starting point—the draft declaration had been decreed to be the basis for negotiation at the meeting—Zoellick began to see if he could strike some deals. He wasn't thinking of the usual model for big international negotiations, which is to hold out until the last minute and then compromise. He wanted to move as quickly as possible, in the hope of creating momentum that would lead to more momentum, success that would engender more success. At a ministerial scheduled to last only five days, there was little time to waste.

| * |

On the U.S. government plane to Doha, name tags designated the seats in which passengers were to sit. Everyone had a tag with his or her name on it, except for Grant Aldonas, the undersecretary of commerce for international trade. His tag said "Sucker."

A folksy bear of a man, with a booming voice, blond hair, and blue eyes, Aldonas was designated by Zoellick to negotiate the antidumping issue at the WTO meeting. Hence the "sucker" label, for as Aldonas, a former top staffer on the Senate Finance Committee, well knew, the antidumping issue was the touchiest matter facing the U.S. team in Doha.

The U.S. antidumping and countervailing duty laws, which are aimed at protecting American industry from imported products sold at unfairly low prices, are much beloved by members of Congress, who fiercely defend them as essential to ensuring a "level playing field." How else, U.S. politicians ask, can American companies combat foreign competitors who sometimes sell their goods below the cost of production, or below the price at which they sell in their home markets? Or who take advantage of hidden subsidies such as loans from state-owned banks? That's why the laws allow U.S. industries to bring complaints to the Commerce Department, which—after an investigation—may rule that duties should be imposed on the offending imports, with the aim of raising the price in the United States market to a "fair" level.

But the U.S. laws are despised by foreign governments, who see the supposedly free-trade Americans using the laws as a disguised form of protectionism. Many economists agree.

Consider the case of pasta. Anyone who has pushed a cart down the aisle of an American supermarket is familiar with the De Cecco brand, an Italian import sold in royal blue boxes with a picture of a peasant woman holding bundles of wheat. And anyone who has compared pasta prices knows that De Cecco costs up to twice as much as many other brands. Yet in response to a complaint filed by U.S. pasta makers against pasta from Italy and Turkey, the Commerce Department found in 1996 that De Cecco was one of the brands being sold at "lower than fair market value," and it fixed the company's "dumping margin" at 47 percent, which meant De Cecco would have to pay duties of roughly that percentage on the value of the pasta it shipped to the United States.

The history of antidumping cases in the United States is replete with similarly bizarre results in which foreign producers get socked with sky-high duties. Part of the problem is the law itself. Although it may be reasonable to prohibit companies from selling goods "below cost"—especially if a dominant firm is using predatory pricing to drive competitors out of business and establish a monopoly—the question is, how should costs be measured? One method is to use the average cost of all items produced; another is to use the cost of producing the last item ("marginal" cost, in economists' jargon). Suffice it to say that the rules are far stricter against foreign "dumpers" than they are against domestic firms charged with predatory pricing.

And then there's the way the law is administered. Commerce Department officials have a fair amount of latitude in interpreting the rules, and much evidence suggests that they systematically bend the rules in favor of U.S. companies at the expense of free-market principles. Foreign companies can get hung out to dry in dumping cases if they fail to provide Commerce with sufficiently responsive and timely answers to the department's myriad questions about their operations. (That was how De Cecco landed in so much trouble: Commerce found that De Cecco's data weren't properly submitted, weren't consistent, and couldn't be easily verified.)

The U.S. laws were under attack at Doha from a number of countries, led by Japan, South Korea, and Chile, which were insistent that the new round must include talks on new WTO rules aimed at preventing the kind of abuses they felt Washington was committing. They pointed out that the Seattle ministerial had cratered partly because of anger among WTO members over the hard line taken by the United States on the dumping issue. They held the high ground going into the Doha battle because the Harbinson text reflected their basic position, stating that WTO members would "agree to negotiations aimed at clarifying and improving" global rules restricting how countries may use antidumping laws. Aldonas's job was to blunt this attack and get the wording changed.

"This is going to be a train wreck," one top congressional staffer warned the U.S. negotiators before they left for Doha, and there was surely the possibility of such an outcome. Leading lawmakers from both parties had made it clear all year that they didn't want the Bush administration even agreeing to negotiate on antidumping. If Zoellick yielded too much on the issue, allowing the text to stand pretty much as it was, Congress would very probably refuse to grant the administration the authority it needed to complete any trade agreements. That would spoil Zoellick's trade agenda—new WTO round and all—before it had even gotten started.

There was one way out, which might be called the "it's not about us, it's about them" gambit.

Many foreign countries, such as India, South Africa, and Argentina, had enacted their own antidumping laws and were using them with abandon—in a number of cases, finding *American* companies guilty of dumping, much to the consternation of the firms involved. In fact, the United States was the second-most-cited target of dumping complaints between 1990 and 2000, with 195 cases filed worldwide, trailing only China's 341. So Aldonas's objective was a deal that would envision negotiations on antidumping laws, on the condition that some new wording would be used to indicate that the talks would focus on flaws in other countries' practices, rather than just in the American ones. The administration's hope was that Congress wouldn't object too strenuously to negotiations of that type.

The "sucker's" first attempt to cobble together such a compromise proved fruitless. In a meeting on November 11 of the working group dealing with the issue, Aldonas tried to cajole the Japanese, the Koreans, and the Chileans into accepting text changes that would shift some of the focus of the text to other countries' antidumping laws. "We need greater transparency and due process, given all the new users of these laws," he pleaded, according to notes of the meeting. He also underscored the necessity of avoiding a revolt in Congress, noting that Zoellick had assured lawmakers of Washington's determination to "maintain effective measures to address trade distorting practices," a reference to hidden subsidies enjoyed by some foreign firms.

This met with a frosty reception from his counterparts, who suspected that the Bush administration's real goal was to ensure that the negotiations couldn't possibly affect U.S. antidumping laws. Chile "doesn't want any change to the [Harbinson] text at all," said Alejandro Jara, the Chilean ambassador to the WTO, and the same went for the Japanese representative, who said that for Tokyo, the text was "the bare minimum." In between meetings, Aldonas pounded out various alternative texts of several sentences in length, all of which were rejected.

It was time to take a walk outside and come up with a new approach. Aldonas did just that with Stephen Jacobs, another Commerce Department official who worked on antidumping issues. During their stroll, they confronted the reality that they were going to be able to get only minor changes in the text—just enough so they could plausibly tell members of Congress that the negotiations over antidumping wouldn't be entirely about U.S. laws. We've got maybe three words; we've got to make them count, Jacobs told Aldonas, and he proposed a solution he thought might win consensus at Doha while providing the administration with enough cover on Capitol Hill. His idea: to insert two phrases. One would state that the negotiations would "preserve the instruments and objectives" of existing antidumping rules. The other would state that the negotiations could include proposals for new "disciplines on trading distorting practices."

Even this was too much for the others, who smelled a rat.

*Doh iu imi?* What does it mean, wondered the Japanese, whose language is so different from English that even bureaucrats educated at the most prestigious U.S. universities have difficulty with the nuances. Perhaps, they thought, the U.S.-proposed wording was designed to create a giant loophole that the Americans could use to avoid negotiations concerning their laws. As Yoichi Suzuki, who was a member of the Japanese team, recalls: "We had a few bitter memories of drafting texts, in the GATT and WTO, thinking that the English text was good enough, only to discover later that there were different interpretations."

So the two sides were deadlocked. The futility of further negotiations among the lower-level negotiators was evident to Aldonas, who told Zoellick: "I've taken this as far as I can." If the impasse was to be resolved, it would have to be done trade minister to trade minister.

The stereotypical member of the Japanese cabinet is a politician who heads a ministry for a few months, all the while complying faithfully with the policy guidance of the highly educated and experienced bureaucrats who hold most executive-branch positions in the government. Fortunately for Zoellick, Takeo Hiranuma, who headed the Ministry of Economy, Trade, and Industry, was willing to defy the stereotype at Doha. Hiranuma wanted a deal and, overriding the reservations of his bureaucrats, concluded after meeting with Zoellick that the Americans were looking for just enough weasel wording in the antidumping text to minimize the political damage at home. The Korean and Chilean ministers likewise accepted the modest changes in the text.

Now that an agreement was at hand on the antidumping issue, Zoellick did not want to delay in spreading the news. Momentum, he hoped, would build on momentum; his flexibility would lead to more flexibility by others. In a humorous address to a general meeting of ministers on Monday, November 12, he announced that the United States had finally dropped its resistance to negotiations on the antidumping issue. "I understand that there are 143 countries that agree to this text, and one that doesn't," he said. "And in spite of the fact that all of you are on the wrong side, I will agree."

Strong backers of Washington's antidumping laws were predictably upset. Bill Klinefelter, legislative director for the United Steelworkers, who had come to Doha to try to fend off the kind of concession Zoellick had made, noted that any move toward weakening the laws would be enormously unpopular in states like Ohio, Pennsylvania, and West Virginia. "There will be political consequences," he vowed. But in the corridors of the Sheraton, the development generated a positive buzz. "This is a major shift that could help unlock doors . . . in other sectors," reported the *Bridges Daily Update*, a newsletter that closely tracks WTO ministerial meetings.

Even more electrifying was word that the United States was moving on another, even higher-profile issue.

| * |

Prior to coming to Doha, Shannon Herzfeld had attended the briefings about the security risks. But there was no way she was going to stay home. She was the chief Washington representative for the Pharmaceutical Research and

Manufacturers of America (PhRMA), which was girding for battle over the TRIPS issue. "I really needed to be there. The pharmaceutical industry had so much vulnerability," Herzfeld says. After arriving, she adds, she didn't worry much about her safety, except for one terrifying moment, which came during a meeting with industry colleagues in the hotel room of a top U.S. official. She stepped out onto the balcony to take a cell-phone call from her boss, unaware that the balconies had been declared off-limits for security reasons. Hearing a noise, she spotted two Qatari guards in firing position, aiming their rifles at her. "I thought, they're going to shoot me on the frigging balcony!" recalls Herzfeld, adding that she gasped an excuse to her boss and fled back into the official's room.

As that story suggests, the pharmaceutical industry was hovering tightly over U.S. negotiators as the TRIPS negotiations proceeded. The industry's main priority was to prevent a declaration that would roll back the protections for intellectual property that had been established in the Uruguay Round. Drug companies acknowledged that TRIPS contained an exception allowing governments facing public health emergencies to take action that would compromise the rights of patent holders. The questions were, how big an exception, and how could it be applied? Did it apply only to epidemics, or to less urgent public health matters? Deeply anxious about creating legal precedents that might undermine the value of drug patents around the world, many of the industry's leading firms were digging in for battle over a key paragraph in a special declaration on TRIPS that the ministerial was expected to issue.

Two very different versions of the paragraph were on the table. The industry was determined to block the first, dubbed "Option 1," because it indicated that developing countries would have broad authority to break patents using compulsory licenses, parallel importing, and other such tools. Backed by nations in Africa, Latin America, and South Asia, it read:

> Nothing in the TRIPS agreement shall prevent members from taking measures to protect public health. Accordingly, while reiterating our commitment to the TRIPS Agreement, we affirm that the agreement shall be interpreted and implemented in a manner supportive of WTO members' right to protect public health and, in particular, to ensure access to medicines for all.

Far more acceptable to the industry was "Option 2," which was designed to keep the patent-busting of developing countries within carefully circumscribed limits. Backed by the United States, the European Union, Switzerland, and other high-income nations, it read:

We affirm a member's ability to use, to the full, the provisions in the TRIPS agreement which provide flexibility to address public health crises such as HIV/AIDS and other pandemics, and to that end, that a member is able to take measures necessary to address these public health crises, in particular to secure affordable access to medicines. Further, we agree that this declaration does not add or diminish the rights and obligations of members provided in the TRIPS agreement.

But Zoellick, although publicly supporting Option 2, was also making it clear to his lieutenants that he wanted an agreement with the developing countries, and that he wanted it to happen fairly quickly. This was a poisonous issue, he told them; failure to resolve it could bring down the ministerial. By the same token, an early agreement would show the developing countries that success was possible. The result would be pressure on other WTO members to make concessions. Moreover, developing countries would have a gigantic incentive to accept an overall agreement at the ministerial because if the whole conference failed, any TRIPS deal that had been struck would become inoperative. Nothing could be agreed until everything was agreed.

Fortunately for Zoellick, the industry was not united in its rejectionist stance. Although many companies wanted to rebuff anything resembling Option 1—Pfizer Corporation, whose CEO chaired PhRMA, was especially hawkish—there were some doves as well, foremost among them Raymond Gilmartin, the CEO of Merck & Company. In Merck's view, the industry was risking a disastrous backlash by appearing to put intellectual property rights over the needs of the poor and the sick, according to Thomas Bombelles, who represented Merck at the Doha meeting. Whereas other pharmaceutical firms feared that giving an inch on the issue would lead the rest of the world to take a mile, "our view was that if we didn't give an inch, we would lose everything," Bombelles says.

Accordingly, the man Zoellick designated as his chief TRIPS negotiator, Undersecretary of State Alan Larson, went with instructions to be flexible when he participated as the chief U.S. representative in the small working group of negotiators handling the issue. His main adversary was, like him, a veteran diplomat—Celso Amorim, Brazil's ambassador to the WTO, who naturally took leadership of the developing-country forces by dint of his country's widely admired HIV/AIDS program and his skills as a wordsmith.

The talks, which took place in one of the Sheraton conference rooms, were hardly easy. Hour after hour was spent haggling over the words "must," "can," "shall," and "should" in one of the sentences. Each camp was under intense pressure to hang tough. The negotiators from developing countries were besieged by representatives from groups such as Doctors Without Borders, Third World Network, and ACT UP (AIDS Coalition to Unleash Power), a militant gay and lesbian organization. Not only did Larson have to remain in constant contact with Herzfeld and other pharmaceutical industry lobbyists who were in Doha, but he was also instructed by Zoellick to speak directly with drug company CEOs in conference calls, "and some of them had very serious reservations" about the text that was being considered as a compromise, Larson recalls.

The CEOs' concerns were not surprising, because this text—hammered out between Larson and Amorim—was essentially Option 1 with a few of the most extreme phrases watered down a little. Instead of the very strong "Nothing in the TRIPS agreement shall prevent members from taking measures to protect public health," the compromise said, "We agree that the TRIPS agreement does not and should not prevent members from taking measures to protect public health." And instead of saying that the agreement should be interpreted "to ensure access to medicines for all," the word "promote" was substituted for "ensure." But the basic integrity of Option 1 had survived.

Hands were shaken on this slightly altered version of Option 1. Then, suddenly, it looked as if the agreement was falling apart. A letter strongly objecting to the compromise arrived by fax in Doha, signed by Alan Holmer, the president of PhRMA. Amorim got the unpleasant news from Ernesto Derbez, Mexico's economy minister who had chaired the working group, that some of the parties favoring Option 2 wanted to reopen the text.

Absolutely not, Amorim said. We had a deal.

To this, Derbez replied that Amorim was not a minister; he didn't have full authority to speak for the Brazilian government. At that point, Amorim and his Brazilian colleagues were in a predicament. They knew they had to maintain a credible threat to blow up the Doha meeting if the text were watered down any further, and they doubted whether they would get full support from the head of their delegation, Foreign Minister Celso Lafer, a pipe-smoking international law professor and former ambassador to the WTO. But they had an ace in the hole, because another, much more militant member of the Brazilian cabinet was also in Doha—José Serra, the health minister, who was the leading architect of the country's HIV/AIDS treatment program. Frantically, Amorim's team tracked down Serra, who was out on a tour and rushed back to the Sheraton. The health minister backed Amorim to the hilt.

Check, and mate. The Option 2 forces were beaten, and the text was unveiled on Monday, November 12, significantly raising hopes that in the full day remaining before the official deadline, concessions would be forthcoming in other hotly disputed areas.

The terms sparked elation among developing-country officials and most NGO representatives. "Even six months ago, this was unthinkable," Paulo Teixeira, Brazil's top AIDS official, told the *Wall Street Journal,* and in an article I wrote for the *Washington Post,* James Love, who was representing a Ralph Nader–backed group, exulted, "Is the WTO turning into the General Assembly of the United Nations? Is it no longer the playground of the rich and powerful?" Also revealing was the crestfallen expression on the face of Harvey Bale of the International Federation of Pharmaceutical Manufacturers & Associations. When I encountered him in the Sheraton lobby, he was grimly predicting that the "ambiguous" language on intellectual property rights protection would adversely affect medical innovation. "If I'm an R&D director with $500 million that I'm thinking of investing on developing an AIDS drug or a cancer drug, I'm going to be careful," he said. "If a CEO asks me, 'What does this [text] mean,' I'm going to say, 'I don't have a clue.'"

The text left for later a tricky legal question concerning how poor countries in sub-Saharan Africa, which lacked their own capacity for making pharmaceuticals, could take advantage of compulsory licensing. Some drug company officials were soon claiming—in an apparent effort to minimize the damage to their legal rights—that the text had little practical import because it simply confirmed what was already in the TRIPS agreement. But whatever its precise legal implications, the declaration reassured developing countries that they had gained an appreciable degree of protection from WTO cases being brought against their generic drug programs. The political obstacles to bringing such a case would be higher than ever.

So far, so good for Zoellick's strategy to build a coalition at Doha in favor of launching a round. He had secured deals on Washington's two most contentious issues—antidumping and TRIPS—so the vibes were getting better and better. Still, nothing was agreed until all was agreed. And quite a bit remained to be agreed.

"This is what it looks like when it's about to work," Keith Rockwell, the WTO spokesman, told me on the afternoon of the twelfth. "That doesn't mean it *will* work."

| * |

Pascal Lamy's bodyguard, a hulking Irishman named Val Flynn, made sure that everywhere the European trade commissioner went in the Doha Sheraton conference center, a stash of brown bread and some bananas were available. As was his wont at high-pressure events, Lamy was restricting himself to the dietary regimen that he believed would best help him think clearly. He needed to be sure his concentration was at its peak, for as the Doha meeting headed into its final hours, with the antidumping and TRIPS issues settled, the European Union was now on the hot seat.

The Europeans were in their usual dither over agriculture. Trade and agriculture ministers from all fifteen member states were in Doha, and some of them—France, of course, being the most vocal—were giving Lamy a very hard time about the concessions that were being demanded of Brussels on farm-trade issues. Although these member states could not legally stop the commissioner from conceding on issues at the stage of launching a round, they could conceivably block it at the time of completion, and they wanted to bring as much pressure to bear as they could early on. It was bad enough, they thought, that the Harbinson text would commit the WTO to negotiations aimed at "substantial improvement in market access" for agricultural products and "substantial reductions" in general farm subsidies. That wording was subject to interpretation; much less ambiguous—and more objectionable—was the language that the new round would aim to reduce, "with a view to phasing out," export subsidies, of which E.U. farmers received several billion dollars specifically for crops sold overseas. Pounding the table at a meeting of the Council of Ministers, François Huwart, the French trade minister, declared that Paris could not accept the text's implication that such subsidies were to be eliminated. Other Europeans policymakers, although resigned to the inevitability of giving in on agriculture, were adamant that Brussels must be compensated with wins in other areas—namely, the Singapore issues and the environment. The trouble was, many developing nations were equally determined to deny the European Union any such booty.

That was the situation facing twenty-three ministers who were invited to a do-or-die green room meeting starting at 7:00 p.m. on Tuesday, November 13. By this time, it was clear that the conference was not going to finish by the official midnight deadline. All manner of tricks had been attempted to convince delegates that the deadline was firm, including frequent reminders that the holy month of Ramadan was about to start and signs posted in the press room by the Qataris stating that by Wednesday at noon, reporters must have vacated the premises. Those efforts had failed to get all parties close to consensus on all points, so it was necessary for Moore to seek, as he had at Seattle, an extra day of meeting time. The hope was that the green room would reach agreement on a complete text that could be presented to the entire membership as early as possible on Wednesday. In this case, the director-general found the WTO's hosts to be far more accommodating than the Seat-

tle authorities had been; Qatar's Kamal agreed to allow the delegates to remain in the convention center. The extension could not run very long, however, because some ministers from developing countries were starting to leave
to catch scheduled flights home, and it was important to keep the number of
attendees from dwindling to an embarrassingly low figure. Kamal proposed,
with a twinkle in his eye, a solution to this problem. "He said, 'I'll have the airport closed. We'll say it was terrorism,'" recalls Moore, who says he replied
that such a step "wouldn't be necessary."

The European Union's difficulty in coming to terms on agriculture was not
the only reason the ministerial was dragging on longer than expected. The proceedings had nearly ground to a halt Tuesday because of a ploy by dozens of
poor countries from Africa, the Caribbean, and the Pacific islands. They were
effectively holding the whole meeting hostage, threatening to block the consensus unless they got one specific thing they wanted.

As former European colonies, these countries had long enjoyed duty-free
access to the E.U. market for many of their products, and to maintain this
arrangement—which technically violated WTO rules—they needed the WTO
membership to approve waivers from time to time. With the old waiver expir-
ing, a new one was under consideration in the General Council. The issue
wasn't supposed to come up at the Doha ministerial, but the former colonies,
fearful about their chances of achieving their goal, decided they had better get
it while they held the trump card of being able to jeopardize the new round.
This stance prompted a furious reaction from other countries, especially Thailand, the Philippines, Ecuador, Honduras, and Panama, which argued that
some of their most competitive products, notably bananas and canned tuna,
were suffering unfairly in the European market as a result of the preference
given to the former colonies. They, too, threatened to block the consensus unless their problems were addressed. For many policymakers, the whole flap was
a source of exasperation, but there was no getting around it, and extensive talks
were required to work it out.

"Everywhere you looked, there were people trying to blackmail the system," recalls Andy Stoler, then a WTO deputy director-general, who tried to
convince one of the leaders of the former colonies, Kenya's WTO ambassador
Amina Mohamed, that the matter should be postponed until after everyone
returned to Geneva. "I said, 'You understand, Ambassador, you can't do these
things over the space of just a couple of days,'" Stoler recalls. "And she said,
'Well, then, it won't be possible for you to launch a round.' She's very nice,
very soft spoken. But it was clear, she was no dummy, and would maximize
her leverage to get this done."

This game of threat and counterthreat was still being played Tuesday evening as the ministers invited to the green room began arriving, passing through a corridor guarded by kaffiyeh-wearing Qatari policemen and American security agents murmuring into the microphones on their lapels. Zoellick came bearing a supply of sandwiches. He and the others gathered in a windowless conference room with gray walls and a rectangular table, around which were places for Australia, Botswana, Brazil, Canada, Chile, Egypt, the European Union, Guatemala, Hong Kong, India, Japan, Kenya, Malaysia, Mexico, Nigeria, Pakistan, Qatar, Singapore, South Africa, Switzerland, Tanzania, the United States, and Zambia. Several of the attendees were representing "constituencies," or groups of countries, such as the African Group and the Least Developed Country Group, and to ensure that those who weren't invited didn't feel as badly excluded as they had at Seattle, regular communication was planned between those inside and their constituencies outside.

The meeting opened with pleas from Moore and Kamal for all participants to do their utmost for the success of this ministerial. Stacked in front of the director-general was a pile of plastic folders concerning each of the main issues still to be addressed. It soon became apparent that few could be resolved quickly. Lamy sent a note to the ministers from E.U. member states: "This is still taking a long time. Go to bed. If it's necessary, I'll send word. As soon as we have a result, no doubt in the early hours of the morning, we'll get together and I'll inform you."

Indeed, empty coffee cups were strewn on the table, and the clock had passed 2:00 a.m., when Moore—having successfully put a number of folders in the "agreed" pile—finally turned the discussion to the knottiest subjects, namely, agriculture, the environment, and the Singapore issues. Lamy asked for the floor, knowing that, as he later wrote, "the hour of truth" had arrived for him.

The E.U. commissioner knew that some developing countries would be content to let the meeting fail if they could pin the blame on him. "Let's not say, 'Europe is the problem,'" he implored; rather, the group should try to find solutions. He averred that he was ready to make an effort to accommodate demands in agriculture, provided he got help on the other issues. So he hoped he could learn first how far the group could go on subjects other than agriculture.

Here was a supreme test of Zoellick's and Lamy's talents. And by all accounts, they were at the top of their form, acting in concert in ways that other ministers had never seen between Washington and Brussels. All through the ministerial, the duo had been reaping a payoff for the long hours they had spent strategizing in previous months. Not that they were averse to disagreeing on certain points or to putting pressure on each other when they found it advantageous to do so; but their shared desire to see a round launched at Doha was so fervent that to keep the European Union from becoming hopelessly isolated on an issue, Zoellick would often exhort other ministers to cut Lamy some slack, and Lamy would do the same for his American counterpart. Zoellick, for instance, was saying things like "We've got to think about Pascal because he's going to take a big hit on agriculture, so we ought to do something for him on the Singapore issues," according to the recollections of people who were present. In a like vein, Lamy was using his clout to ease the strain on Zoellick, with entreaties such as "This is a particularly sensitive issue for Bob. The Americans haven't gotten much on market access. So let's not push him too far on antidumping."

That dynamic was very much in evidence when Moore turned the green room discussion to the environment issue. On this matter, the European Union was virtually alone. Developing countries had not shed their worries that if the new round included negotiations on the environment, protectionism might be the result, especially if Europe's Greens succeeded in making the precautionary principle an acceptable standard for judging the safety of food and other products. The Bush administration shared this concern, and Washington was also wary of the insistence by Brussels that the new round should address the linkages between WTO rules and the terms of international environmental agreements. The Europeans, after all, were interested in making sure that environmental deals were enforceable, with punitive tariffs available as a potential sanction for countries that failed to comply. The Bush team, which rejected the most important environmental agreement of all—the Kyoto Protocol on global warming—could hardly be expected to look favorably on the possibility that the European approach would be used to penalize American goods.

With the debate at an impasse in the predawn hours of Wednesday, Zoellick threw Lamy a lifeline. He had exhorted his staff to come up with compromise language, and now he was ready to put it on the table. The United States was prepared to accept negotiations on the environment, he said, under certain conditions. The European Union would have to agree to a written pledge aimed at keeping it from using the precautionary principle to justify protectionist trade barriers. More important, Zoellick wanted explicit language in the text that would, in effect, protect countries from facing sanctions under environmental agreements that they weren't a party to—the United States being the most prominent example, as a nonratifier of Kyoto.

Zoellick's proposal was far from what Europe's Greens were hoping for. It risked giving countries an extra incentive to stay out of environmental agreements like Kyoto because it provided holdouts from such agreements with a layer of legal protection against sanctions. But Lamy, recognizing that this was as much as he could get, took it. Likewise, he accepted the compromise language that Harbinson had drafted concerning investment and other Singapore issues, though it was not nearly as strong as Brussels would have preferred. Even then, overcoming objections from the developing countries was not easy; many of them were still unhappy over allowing any WTO negotiations on these issues.

"Things looked like they were going down the toilet at one point," recalls Stoler, "and Mike Moore was wringing his hands and rubbing his head. He said, 'This is just something we have to do. We all have to swallow something we don't like. We can't afford two failures. Two failures will be more than the system can handle.'" That sentiment drew powerful support from two of the most respected ministers from developing countries, Brazil's Celso Lafer and South Africa's Alec Erwin. Exhortations from them and others about the imperative of success helped propel the green room discussion past its most difficult moments.

At 5:00 a.m., the biggest issue of all—agriculture—came before the group. The discussion got off to an unpromising start: Franz Fischler, the European agriculture commissioner, said that he was sorry to repeat once again that for Brussels the text under consideration was unacceptable, as it indicated so strongly that the negotiations on export subsidies would end with their elimination. But then Lamy told the group that he was making good on his promise to be flexible on farm trade, since he had gotten a reasonably favorable result on the other subjects. He said he could accept the shoehorning of one modest phrase into the text. He wanted the words "without prejudging the outcome of the negotiations" inserted into the sentences that spelled out the aims of the new round in agriculture. That wording was almost meaningless; it did nothing more than take note of the obvious, namely, that the negotiating agenda for the round could not determine how the talks would come out. Its purpose was to give Lamy a little political cover with the French and other agriculture hard-liners in Europe who were upset over appearing to surrender too much in advance.

With dawn breaking, Moore, eager to wrap the package up and bring it to the general membership, told the green room attendees: "Well, Ladies and Gentlemen, I think that all this constitutes an excellent result." Kamal chimed in with a "bravo," saying that thanks to their work, "the Doha Summit will be a big success."

But as they filed out into the eerily empty corridors of the Sheraton at 6:00 a.m., Lamy recalls thinking, "The optimism was without doubt a bit forced."

The green room's handiwork still had to undergo scrutiny by scores of delegations that had not been included, many of whom would have to consult their capitals before conferring their approval. At that moment, Lamy gauged the chances at about 50–50 that the package would pass muster at the plenary session that was to be held later that morning.

It would still be necessary, as Zoellick had anticipated, to confront one minister with a "binary choice."

| * |

The expression on the face of Matthew Baldwin, one of Lamy's top aides, told the European commissioner that something was wrong. Baldwin's cell phone had rung as Lamy was conducting a 10:00 a.m. briefing of the E.U. Council of Ministers about the results of the green room that had ended a few hours earlier on Wednesday, November 14. Responding to Lamy's inquisitive look, Baldwin leaned close to him and explained: India was rejecting the text as negotiated. Moore and Kamal wanted to see him right away.

India's Maran had impressed few people at Doha, if any, with his grasp of the issues. He was no match intellectually for Zoellick or Lamy; indeed, his sometimes-rambling diatribes struck many as unhinged. But he had won grudging respect for his sheer stamina. Despite needing physical support from his aides to stand, he had remained present throughout much of the grueling ordeal of long meetings. In an interview afterward with an Indian journalist, Maran gloated, "Many of them who didn't want me there thought they could exhaust me and force me to go and sleep while they finalized the declaration," and he recalled telling Zoellick, "My heart is okay. It is in the right place."

Maran had participated in the all-night green room, and though other attendees thought he had gone along with the package approved by the group, he was now making it clear that India would not join the consensus. The text, he claimed, had been altered from what he had been led to believe it would say. His main grievance was over the Singapore issues; he wanted no negotiations that might expand the WTO's role into investment, competition, government procurement, or trade facilitation. He was unwilling to countenance even the compromise language of the Harbinson text, which fuzzed over the question of whether negotiations would commence immediately on investment and competition or whether the decision would be postponed until the 2003 ministerial.

With the Doha ministerial now well into overtime and with all the delegations in attendance except India willing to approve the text as an official WTO declaration, the pressure on Maran to relent came from every quarter imaginable. Many of those seeking to bring him around invoked the importance of international solidarity in the wake of 9/11, though the Indian minister had already evinced his contempt for that line of reasoning. Kenyan officials railed at him that a failure at Doha would keep the new TRIPS deal from going into effect. Some heads of state placed calls to the Indian prime minister, Atal Bihari Vajpayee; it is doubtful that this did any good, because had New Delhi tried to strong-arm Maran, he could have resigned and dramatically enhanced his political stature, according to Indian officials who worked closely with him.

Moore and Kamal decided to take matters into their own hands. They brought Maran into a small conference room, refusing to admit other Indian officials, and closed the door. The director-general entreated Maran to consider the dangers facing the international trading system, and when that approach didn't seem to be working, the Qatari minister tried a different one, according to people who were present.

"His Highness the Emir will be very displeased if this conference is not a success," Kamal said, adding, "Do you know how many Indians work in this country?"

Meanwhile, other ministers were gathering for scheduled meetings of the full membership, and since India's refusal to join the consensus meant there was no serious business to conduct at that point, it was necessary to keep the ministers occupied lest the meeting disintegrate and cause more people to head for shops or the airport. Minister Hiranuma of Japan gave a lengthy speech about nothing in particular at the request of the WTO Secretariat, and Canada's Pierre Pettigrew kept the crowd entertained by filibustering for an even longer period. After finishing some remarks in English, Pettigrew made similar comments in French, even though interpreters had been providing simultaneous translations of his first riff. And then he displayed his fluency in the WTO's third official language, Spanish, repeating his sentiments all over again. "I got the message that more time was needed, as some of my colleagues were speaking to Maran," recalls Pettigrew. "Everyone was just laughing, because it was so obvious what I was doing. I was really just gaining time."

The binary choice confronting Maran boiled down to this: He could blow up the meeting and let India take the blame, or he could accept a face-saving offer. The face-saver consisted of a proposal, hastily drafted in the morning by members of the Secretariat, concerning the procedure for handling negotiations on the Singapore issues. Under this proposal, negotiations on those issues would proceed after the 2003 ministerial only if an "explicit consensus" of WTO members backed the idea. Exactly what this meant wasn't clear. How, after all, did an "explicit consensus" differ from an ordinary one? Some Indian officials felt that the statement was substantively meaningless. But the offer was that the words "explicit consensus" would be inserted into the Doha text and a special statement would be issued at the Doha ministerial.

Maran remained resentful and recalcitrant during this siege on him and concerned about the political reaction in India if he were to give in. In the end, according to several Indian officials, it was his country's WTO ambassador, Srinivasan Narayanan, who cajoled him into dropping his opposition. Even though India hadn't gotten all it wanted at Doha, it had secured some important goals, Narayanan told him—the TRIPS declaration being the most prominent, as well as a promise to negotiate some changes in Uruguay Round obligations. If India were to continue blocking the consensus, it would lose all it had gained, and as for the Singapore issues, those could be fought later, at the ministerial two years down the road, Narayanan argued.

Finally, in a meeting starting at 6:00 p.m., the revised text, committing the WTO membership to a new round, was presented at a meeting of all ministers. The clarification granted to the Indians concerning the Singapore issues was read aloud. This elicited from Maran a grudging but affirmative "India is supporting the text."

The text launched a new round, so what should it be called? As director-general, Moore regarded the name as his sole prerogative. He had been refraining from announcing it until the last minute because he thought he might need to use the moniker as a bargaining chip. One thing he was sure of: The word "development" must be included, to assure low-income countries that their needs were being addressed and to provide a constant reminder to the high-income countries of the overarching goal that the negotiations were supposed to achieve. Another thing: The word "round" must be replaced with a term that was more politically palatable, even though "round" would be commonly used in unofficial settings. Beyond that, Moore decided, the Qataris would have the honor of bestowing the name, given their successful hosting of the meeting in difficult times.

"I sent notes to Kamal, saying, 'What do we call this? The Qatar Development Agenda?'" Moore recalls. "And he wrote back, 'No! Make it Doha! English speakers can't pronounce Qatar.'"

Thus was it decided. Officially, the ministerial was launching the Doha Development Agenda. Moore's announcement of the name took the Americans by surprise; some of them fretted that putting "development" in the name would reinforce the attitude among the most militant third world countries that they should not be required to contribute anything. But there was nothing they could do about it, as Kamal read the following words: "I should like to propose that the ministerial conference adopt the draft ministerial declaration. . . . May I take it that this is agreeable to members?" He paused, then said: "It is so agreed."

Applause rang out in the meeting hall. Zoellick rose to shake Lamy's hand, to even louder applause. Members of the Indian delegation, stony-faced, sat with arms folded.

"We have removed the stain of Seattle," a triumphant Zoellick proclaimed to the news media.

True enough. That was the reward for the enormous effort that had gone into making the 2001 ministerial different from the one in 1999. Disruptions from protesters had been preempted. The groundwork for the meeting had been well laid beforehand. Developing countries were made to feel more involved in the decision-making. The United States and the European Union had cooperated beautifully and played their hands with consummate skill.

Still, this accomplishment was not the conclusion of talks. It was only the beginning. Inserting the word "development" into the round's name and issuing congratulatory rhetoric about how the world's poor could look forward to a much more beneficent trading system would go only so far. The WTO now had to deliver on the Doha promise. And even before that, it would have to sort out what a "development round" meant—whether it entailed liberalization by developing countries, or just concessions by rich countries for the benefit of the less fortunate.

These challenges were only one matter on the minds of those who boarded the plane that carried Zoellick and his team back to Washington. They knew they could not truly exhale until the aircraft was out of surface-to-air missile range.

Jeffrey Bader, who sat near security officer Doug Melvin, recalls that Melvin told him he would be very pleased after they had risen above 17,000 feet.

"I was watching the altimeter the whole way up," Bader says.

# 7 | THE UPRISING OF THE REST

IT WAS TO BE A GLORIOUS FINALE FOR THE WTO AND FOR THE TWO protagonists from its most powerful members. That was the implication of the Doha Declaration's paragraph 45, which stated: "The negotiations . . . shall be concluded not later than 1 January 2005."

This deadline for completing the Doha Round, as it happened, would come just around the time that Bob Zoellick and Pascal Lamy were likely to be leaving their positions. Lamy's five-year term as European trade commissioner was scheduled to end in late 2004, and assuming that Zoellick stayed in his job as U.S. trade representative until the end of President Bush's first term, he would be moving on to a new post about that time as well. So if everything worked out as planned, the two men would lead the way, during their tenure as trade ministers, to both the launch and the completion of a multilateral trade round. Extraordinarily ambitious as this feat may have been, they evidently considered themselves well suited—indispensable, even—to the task. I asked Zoellick about this in an interview in 2002, and although he was careful to note that he served at the pleasure of the president, he acknowledged, "It is not a coincidence that we pushed at Doha for the 2005 deadline."

Alas, the fantasy of a speedy round soon ran afoul of reality.

The conditions that had contributed so much toward unity among WTO members at Doha proved fleeting. The atmosphere of late 2001, when the world was recoiling from the terrorist attacks and governments around the globe were strongly inclined toward shows of solidarity, began to turn more fractious in 2002 and 2003. Sympathy for the United States was dissipating amid anger over the Bush administration's high-handed policy on matters such as climate change, and the buildup toward the invasion of Iraq further deepened divisions among nations.

All these factors complicated the challenge that WTO members faced as they began work on the first major goal of the round—an agreement on "modalities." This specimen of bureaucratese is so vexing that even lifelong trade specialists, when using it in conversation with people who are not experts, will often hesitate apologetically, pronouncing the word with exaggerated clarity or holding up two fingers on each hand to depict quotation marks. Actually, the concept is reasonably straightforward, and grasping it is important in understanding the mess that the Doha Round is in today, because a modalities deal is what the WTO has spent the better part of six years trying—and repeatedly failing—to achieve.

To produce a meaningful trade agreement, WTO members needed to make much more specific the gauzy principles they had espoused at Doha. In agriculture, for example, the Doha Declaration left scope for a vast range of possibilities. Its call for "substantial reductions" in farm subsidies and "substantial improvements in market access" for farm products could be subject to widely disparate interpretations; negotiators from agricultural powerhouses like Brazil and Australia would obviously view the meaning of the word "substantial" much differently than would their counterparts representing, say, the European Union, Japan, and South Korea.

This was where modalities came in. Would the cuts in tariffs and subsidies be very deep—say, on the order of 70 percent to 80 percent—or a relatively shallow 20 percent to 30 percent? Would the cuts be based on averages, so that each country could decide which tariff or subsidy to cut as long as its average reduction reached a certain number? If so, what would the average number be? Alternatively, would the formula be "progressive," so that the highest tariffs and subsidies would be reduced the most? And if progressivity was chosen, how deep would the cut be for the highest ones, how deep would the cut be for the next-highest, and so on? Would the cuts be across the board, or would allowances be made for exceptions? And if exceptions were to be allowed, how many could there be, what sort of products might be involved, and how would they be treated? Would they be fully spared from cuts, or just partially, and if just partially, by how much?

To produce a full modalities deal, these questions would have to be answered for both agricultural and manufactured goods. Not that those issues were the only matters at stake in the round; the Doha Declaration also called for negotiations on the rules governing antidumping duties, government subsidies for fisheries, the liberalization of services, and the elimination of duties on exports from the world's poorest countries, among other things. But a modalities deal would be the round's defining element and would pave the way for resolution of the remaining issues.

The conclusion of a pact on modalities was supposed to occur by early 2003, leaving plenty of time for negotiators to fill in the myriad details by the round's final deadline. As spelled out in the schedule agreed at Doha, the membership would roll up its collective sleeves and put realistic proposals on the table for negotiation in 2002, and at the next ministerial conference, which was scheduled to take place in Cancún, Mexico, in September 2003, the round would get a solid blast of momentum propelling it toward the finish line, with the modalities having been settled.

Ah, Cancún. White sandy beaches, turquoise waters, swaying palms, free-flowing libation. Amid such convivial surroundings, how could a WTO meeting lead to anything but a harmonious conclusion?

| * |

The acclaimed novel *Killer Angels* tells the story of the Battle of Gettysburg through the eyes of participants. A passionate Civil War buff, Zoellick sent copies of the book to Lamy and a handful of top E.U. trade officials in advance of a private retreat to the Pennsylvania battlefield that he arranged in May 2002 for the Europeans, who were visiting the United States, and his own senior aides. On the morning of May 3, Zoellick and Lamy jogged for about an hour to Little Round Top, the scene of one of the battle's most crucial encounters, and the whole group then took a tour of the battlefield, guided by a retired military officer. Some of the Europeans were rolling their eyes when Zoellick corrected the guide on certain minor details of the battle that were of little interest to them. "He said things like, 'Excuse me, wasn't it in fact the Fifth New York Brigade that made that attack?'" one of the attendees recalls with amusement.

Despite the U.S. trade representative's smarty-pants behavior, both the Europeans and the Americans who attended found the bonding session to be constructive, because the milieu allowed them to relax more readily than they could have in an urban setting, and they spent a lot of time getting educated about each other's political system. For Zoellick, the locale provided another advantage—a sense of the sweep of time. "When I go to battlefields, it puts things in a certain perspective," he told me a few weeks later. "You realize what life and death is all about, versus other sorts of disputes."

The retreat was necessary because those "other sorts of disputes" were, in fact, plaguing Washington's relationship with Brussels, and with many other

U.S. trading partners as well. The Bush administration, for all its rhetorical support of free trade, was not hewing to its stated principles and stood accused in 2002 of taking almost as haughty an approach on trade as it was in its policy regarding the war against terror.

In March, following pleas for help from U.S. steel companies and their unions, the administration had imposed tariffs ranging as high as 30 percent on imported steel, based on "safeguard" rules that allow countries to raise such duties when suffering from a sudden flood of imports. The European Union, together with a number of other countries, denounced the American move as a gross abuse of the rules, and while complaining to the WTO they also threatened to retaliate immediately with sanctions against U.S. products. Zoellick thundered that such a step would abrogate WTO principles; Lamy staunchly insisted that quick-fire retaliation was permitted in this case. (A WTO panel declared the steel tariffs illegal the following year, and the U.S. backed down.)

Another major irritant in the spring of 2002 for the Europeans—and other governments the world over—was the imminent congressional passage of a farm bill that would drastically increase federal subsidies to American farmers. Farm bills set U.S. agriculture policy for five-year periods, and this one, written mainly by House Agriculture Committee chairman Larry Combest, contained a cornucopia of taxpayer-funded goodies for the American heartland. Not only did the bill continue payments farmers were already receiving and established new subsidies for growers of lentils, dry peas, and chickpeas, but it also included new "countercyclical payments," which ensured that if crop prices dropped below certain targets—$2.63 a bushel for corn, for example, and $3.92 a bushel for wheat—farmers would get additional money. The administration, though preferring a more market-oriented approach, had been helpless against the farm lobby on Capitol Hill, and Bush—anxious to maintain the GOP's rural base in upcoming congressional elections—was promising to sign the legislation.

The United States was still talking a good game in the initial stages of the Doha negotiations. Zoellick unveiled proposals on agriculture that envisioned significant market liberalization, and he proposed the complete elimination of tariffs worldwide on consumer and industrial goods by 2015. But the farm bill undercut U.S. efforts to position itself as the champion of free markets, especially in agriculture; in the words of Australian trade minister Warren Truss, the bill sent "an appalling signal to the world." U.S. trade negotiators tried to minimize the damage by pointing out to their counterparts in other countries that, regardless of the farm bill, the United States stood ready to strike a Doha deal in which agriculture subsidies and tariffs would undergo major cuts globally. The 2002 farm bill, they noted, applied only until 2007, after which time new WTO rules, agreed in the Doha Round, could presumably shape U.S. agricultural policy. But the legislation was, at the very least, a severe public relations problem for the Americans, because it gave more-protectionist WTO members a basis for justifying their positions. Looking back at this period, Jason Hafemeister, who was one of Zoellick's senior agriculture negotiators, says, "We spent the year after the bill was passed going around the world, explaining to people, 'It's not as bad as you think, and anyway, when we negotiate in the Doha Round, everything will be on the table.' But it was exploited by people, either cynically or not. It became part of the conventional discourse, that the U.S. isn't serious about reform."

Why was the Bush administration caving in to domestic interests like steel and agriculture? Political expediency was part of the reason. But a reasonable argument could be made on free-trade grounds that the farm bill, the steel tariffs, and other such concessions were necessary evils, justifiable because they served a grand purpose. The congressional beast had to be appeased, lest Zoellick's whole agenda come to grief on Capitol Hill.

| * |

"Trade Promotion Authority" is—let's face it—an uninspired and confusing name for a major piece of legislation. Based purely on its moniker, it sounds like a bill to fund the marketing of U.S. products to foreign buyers. But finding a suitable alternative had proven impossible for Zoellick and his team. They had considered "Trade Negotiating Authority," which was the most apt combination of words for what they had in mind. That choice, unfortunately, suffered from an insurmountable problem—its initials, "TNA." How would the administration secure approval of a bill that opponents could ridicule as sounding like the abbreviation for "tits and ass"?

So "Trade *Promotion* Authority" it was for the legislation that the administration needed before its ambitious trade representative could negotiate the raft of deals he was contemplating. Up until the Bush presidency, such bills had been dubbed "fast-track" authority. Zoellick wanted to scrap this old nomenclature, partly because fast-track bills had gone down to defeat during the second term of the Clinton administration and partly because the term conjured up images of the American people being railroaded into trade agreements.

Whatever the name, the purpose of such bills was the same—to provide U.S. negotiators with the congressional backing required to cut deals with trading partners. Given Congress's constitutional authority over U.S. trade policy, lawmakers must do more than simply authorize the executive branch to conduct negotiations; they must also provide assurances that they won't pick apart any deal the executive branch happens to strike when the deal comes up for approval on Capitol Hill. In the absence of such assurances, no foreign trade negotiator in his or her right mind would bargain seriously with U.S. counterparts for fear that the resulting pact would be subject to all manner of amendments from members of Congress eager to protect particular industries and interests. So Trade Promotion Authority, aka fast track, guarantees that for some limited period (most versions of the bill specified five years), trade accords struck by the Office of the U.S. Trade Representative will be considered by Congress under special legislative procedures. Lawmakers guarantee they will hold an up-or-down vote on those deals, with no amendments allowed.

The Bush administration faced daunting hurdles in obtaining approval for Trade Promotion Authority, especially in the House. Even though Republicans held a twelve-vote majority in the lower chamber, every major trade bill since NAFTA had drawn opposition from at least fifty GOP House members. And House Democrats were generally even more hostile toward trade pacts, as witnessed by the refusal of many in their caucus to back fast track in the late 1990s. All this reflected the fraying of the bipartisan consensus that had enabled trade agreements to sail through Congress in decades past. (The Tokyo Round, for example, passed the House 395–7 and the Senate 90–4; even the Uruguay Round won approval by the comfortable margin of 288–146 in the House and 76–24 in the Senate.) Lawmakers' willingness to cast votes for trade agreements had eroded steadily, thanks to layoffs, corporate downsizing, and the burgeoning U.S. trade deficit, which had swelled to record levels following the 1997–1998 Asian financial crisis as plunging currencies sharply lowered the cost of goods from South Korea, Indonesia, and other stricken countries. The anti-free traders in both parties were unmoved by the insistence of mainstream economists that most job losses were attributable to technological advancement and other non-trade factors, that greater openness to foreign goods still benefited the U.S. economy, and that the trade deficit was largely a function of America's low savings rate rather than its low import barriers.

Even among lawmakers who were not instinctively antitrade, many were willing to cast pro-trade votes only on terms favored by their respective party's most powerful interests. Democrats were thus demanding that the Trade Promotion Authority bill must instruct U.S. negotiators to include labor and environmental standards in trade deals, standards that would be both strict and enforceable, through the imposition of sanctions. Republican free traders were implacably opposed to this on the grounds that the Democratic proposals could lead to protectionism and, by holding the United States accountable to these labor and environmental standards, might force Washington to make its own laws more pro-union and more pro-environment (and hence, they argued, more antibusiness). From Zoellick's standpoint—he was itching to get a bill passed so that he could get on with his negotiating agenda—the dilemma was acute: Although stronger labor and environmental provisions might sway some House Democrats into voting yes, an equal number of GOP lawmakers might be driven into opposition.

There were tears and shouts of anger in the House as a cliff-hanging vote on December 6, 2001, gave Trade Promotion Authority its first big push forward. The bill contained labor and environmental provisions, though not tough enough to satisfy most Democrats. When the normal fifteen-minute voting period had expired, opponents outnumbered supporters by several votes, so Republican leaders held the balloting open for about twenty minutes to cajole and browbeat a handful of their members into switching sides. As Democrats bellowed for the gavel to come down, the GOP leaders finally got the last holdout they needed, Jim DeMint of South Carolina, by promising to do a favor for textile factories in his district—namely, circumventing some key rules in a Clinton administration trade accord with poor Caribbean countries. The final vote was 215–214, with only 21 Democrats in favor. Defending the horse-trading, Zoellick was quoted as saying that it was "necessary to achieve a larger good."

This was the sort of Faustian bargain that the administration also had to make in the aforementioned cases of the steel tariffs and the farm bill, because Trade Promotion Authority remained mired on Capitol Hill for months thereafter. During this time lawmakers skillfully used their leverage to extract more concessions from the White House, knowing that the administration could not afford defections from its razor-thin House majority. The Senate did not pass its version of the bill until May 2002, and the reconciled version of the two chambers' bills finally passed the House at 3:30 a.m. on July 27 by 215–212.

Though it had come at a price, at least Zoellick now had the deal-cutting authority that his predecessors had not enjoyed since 1994. He was soon wielding it with characteristic gusto.

| * |

Jaws were agape among the trade ministers and other top-ranking officials from twenty-five countries. The vitriol that Bob Zoellick was aiming at Japanese foreign minister Yoriko Kawaguchi and two of her cabinet colleagues was far harsher than most of them had ever heard in a high-level international meeting.

According to notes of the gathering, Zoellick capped a denunciation of the Japanese position with the following rant: "Please start to take some responsibility. Go back and think about this! Or quit coming to these meetings. You're just a drag!"

The outburst came at a "mini-ministerial" in Montreal at the end of July 2003 that was convened in advance of the pending WTO meeting in Cancún. Mini-ministerials were held in various locales every couple of months prior to Cancún, with invitees coming from two dozen or so countries that included the WTO's most powerful as well as a few representing smaller and poorer nations, much like a green room. The idea was for ministers to get to know each other, gain some insight into their partners' positions, and start some wheeling and dealing on the big issues they would confront at the ministerial, in the hope of narrowing differences enough to make consensus at least somewhat easier to achieve. As Zoellick's verbal blast showed, the getting-to-know-you process could take unpleasant turns.

Discourteous though he may have been, his ire was understandable. Among countries that have benefited the most from the multilateral trading system, Japan surely ranks near the top, given the tremendous role that exports played in its postwar economic miracle. Yet Tokyo seemed congenitally incapable of contributing to the success of trade negotiations by showing flexibility on issues of importance, especially in agriculture, thanks to the political hammerlock that Japanese farmers hold on the ruling Liberal Democratic Party. In mini-ministerials, Japanese representatives would typically recite talking points that had been drafted for them by their ministries' powerful bureaucrats, full of flowery sentiments about the need for progress but devoid of substantive concessions that might help move the talks along. Zoellick complained privately to associates that every time the meetings appeared to be on the cusp of making some incremental advance, a stilted intervention by a Japanese minister would kill the mood.

Japan's stance was only a symptom of a much deeper problem facing the ministers at Montreal: With just six weeks to go until the meeting in Cancún, the Doha Round was going nowhere, most notably in its biggest issue, agriculture. Even Stuart Harbinson, whose text had worked such wonders at the Doha meeting, seemed to have lost his mojo; he got a barrage of negativity for a draft text on farm trade that he presented in early 2003 to serve as the outline of an agreement on modalities by the March 31 deadline. By midsummer negotiators were expressing growing doubts about whether they could even manage to agree on modalities by the Cancún meeting, which was scheduled to start September 9.

That was the state of play in Montreal, where a fateful decision would be made.

Zoellick's most important differences on agriculture were not with the Japanese; they were with his *cher ami*, Lamy. There was nothing new about such a schism in the multilateral trading system. The United States had almost always been on the "offensive" in farm trade, pushing for lower barriers (except in a handful of cosseted sectors, such as sugar), whereas the European Union was almost invariably on the "defensive." But as Zoellick and Lamy themselves repeatedly emphasized, the chance for a broader deal among all WTO members was nil unless the world's two trade superpowers could reach some kind of accommodation. Although a U.S.-E.U. understanding might not be sufficient to ensure a broader WTO pact, it was necessary.

Lamy came to Montreal with a newly strengthened hand. Several weeks earlier, the European Union's fifteen farm ministers had accepted a major reform of the Common Agricultural Policy. This was a long-overdue makeover of a program that was notorious for inducing European farmers to produce in wretched excess, the result being surpluses dubbed "butter mountains" and "wine lakes." Recognizing that the unloading of such surpluses on world markets was likely to become illegal as a result of the Doha talks, E.U. agriculture commissioner Franz Fischler successfully pushed to transform the program so that farm aid would be "decoupled" from production. Rather than rewarding farmers for every ton of grain they grew or head of livestock they raised and thus giving them incentives to overproduce, the new system would create a basic safety net for their incomes by giving them flat payments based on acreage. In return, farmers would have to manage their land responsibly and promote food safety and animal welfare. So proud were European policymakers of CAP reform that they trumpeted it as their contribution to the Doha Round's agriculture talks; as Fischler put it when the agreement was announced: "We have done our homework, and it is now up to others to do their homework."

But genuinely important though CAP reform may have been, other WTO members did not regard the European Union as having gone nearly far enough in liberalizing its agricultural markets. For one thing, the reform was loaded with loopholes, at French insistence. Moreover, although the European Union would change the *way* it spent its farm budget, it wouldn't change the *size* of the budget, which totaled 43 billion euros (about $50 billion in 2003).

Most crucially, Brussels was leaving unaltered its high import duties for agricultural products. And that was where the differences with Washington were starkest. The United States was pushing for WTO members to make deep cuts in agricultural tariffs, based on a very progressive formula under which the highest tariffs would get cut much more than the ones that were already low. The European Union, strongly backed by Japan, was insisting that tariffs be cut by an average of 36 percent—a simple and clean formula, but one that (as noted in Chapter 3) had produced little change in market access when it was used in the Uruguay Round because it had allowed countries to leave tariffs on certain key products almost untouched.

The discussion at Montreal started off acrimoniously, with Alec Erwin, South Africa's veteran trade minister, asking, in light of the fact that the European Union and Japan appeared to be sticking to their positions, "What do we gain from further negotiations?" The E.U.-Japanese approach implied "no opening" in farm goods, he said, so on the issues Brussels and Tokyo cared about, he asked, "What's the point for developing countries making concessions?" After much huffing and puffing back and forth, Luis Ernesto Derbez, the Mexican foreign minister, issued a plea for a middle ground. "Let's get real," he said, because although the E.U.-Japanese stance was "not on," neither was the U.S. proposal for radical tariff cuts, given that such an approach was politically unpalatable in Brussels, Tokyo, and other capitals. "What's in between?" he asked. "That is what we should be concentrating on."

A critical moment came when Lamy put an idea on the table. "There is a clear challenge for the U.S. and ourselves to move the process forward," he said. "I suggest that the E.U. and the U.S. try to work on a paper" that would contain broad proposals on all major agriculture issues, including a blending of the two sides' tariff proposals.

So it was settled: The Americans and the Europeans would attempt to strike a compromise on agriculture, and their proposal would serve as a basis for negotiation at Cancún. Although cast as an exercise in leadership, this was a risky plan, because it smacked of the bad old days of the GATT, when Washington and Brussels worked out deals between themselves and then presented them to the rest of the world as faits accompli. Lamy promised to avoid overbearing behavior this time, and the suggestion was guardedly welcomed by others. Zoellick said he was "comfortable with Pascal's idea" though "differences between us are still very sharp." Carlos Pérez del Castillo, the Uruguayan who chaired the General Council, said he looked forward to receiving the U.S.-E.U. paper by August 11. "No one wants Seattle II," he said.

Looking back at the details of the Montreal meeting is illuminating because the U.S.-E.U. agriculture deal of 2003 would come to be regarded as one of the most colossal cock-ups of the Doha Round negotiations. In justifying their decision to draft a joint paper, American and European officials would later maintain that the other countries virtually begged them to do it. But as the notes of the Montreal meeting show, it was Lamy who put the proposal forward. He and Zoellick deserve plenty of blame for the events that were about to unfold.

| * |

The flushing of toilets was distinctly audible during a transatlantic conference call among senior U.S. and E.U. trade negotiators that took place in early August 2003. The sound was, in retrospect, apt accompaniment.

The call was booked for ninety minutes. Instead, it lasted ten hours, which turned out to be the time required to finalize the details of the joint paper on agriculture that the Americans and Europeans had promised to present to the rest of the WTO membership. So lengthy was the call that the mobile phone belonging to one of the European officials became too hot to hold, and he had to put it down with the speaker function on.

Many of the key players, having gone on August holidays, were calling in from vacation homes or other travel destinations in far-flung locations, including the south of France and the Italian countryside. That is why toilets were heard in the background; when participants had to go to the bathroom they left their phones connected to the call lest they lose their place in the conference. (The identity of the flushers, of course, was a mystery to the others.) Other noises on the line distracted people, including the barking of a dog belonging to one of the Europeans.

The product of that phone call, a three-page document agreed by the two sides, was unveiled on August 13 in a presentation at the Centre William Rappard by Peter Carl, the top civil servant in the European Union's Trade Directorate, and Allen Johnson, the chief U.S. agriculture negotiator. They emphasized that their proposals were just that—proposals—that must still be negotiated with other WTO members. But the paper was galvanic, in the negative sense of the word.

As they scrutinized the three-page paper, officials from the developing world drew this overarching conclusion: They were being asked to lower their trade barriers, while at the same time the United States and the European Union were intending to keep a lot of their subsidies, which meant that poor farmers would be exposed more than ever to competition from subsidized imports. Rather than providing a text that could be used as the basis for negotiation at Cancún among all WTO members, Washington and Brussels were mainly showing concern for the sensitivities of their own agriculture lobbies.

Indeed, some key elements of the paper made it look like an unholy bargain in which each big power was giving the other license to engage in the practices that everyone else found most offensive.

For the European Union, the special goody in the document was that export subsidies would survive, at least partially. Ridding the world completely of these types of subsidies was a long-standing goal of both developing countries and the United States, given the highly distorting effect of the $4 billion that European farmers were receiving to grow crops for sale in foreign markets. The Doha Declaration had strongly implied that export subsidies would be eliminated; it called for "reductions, with a view to phasing [them] out." But the U.S.-E.U. paper said that export subsidies would be zeroed out only for certain "products of particular interest to developing countries," which were unspecified. (The European Union's own agriculture reforms would curb export subsidies somewhat, though not entirely.)

American farm groups, meanwhile, got their own plum, a provision in the paper that would shield one of the big subsidy programs in the recently passed farm bill from deep cuts. This was a gambit that critics of farm subsidies denounced as "box-shifting," and they were all the more incensed because of the difficulty of explaining it, which requires a little background information about the WTO's kaleidoscopic world of "boxes."

Amber, green, blue—these are the colors of the boxes in question, which the WTO uses as a rating system to grade subsidy programs based on their trade impact. "Amber box" payments are the worst; they're the subsidies that, by rewarding farmers for growing more crops, encourage the most overproduction. "Green box" payments are the most benign; they're the subsidies that reward farmers for, say, protecting the environment, without regard to how much the farmers produce. "Blue box" payments are in between. Like any big subsidizer, the United States wanted to count as few of its farm payments as possible in the amber box, because those are the subsidies that would be most vulnerable to the deepest cuts in the Doha Round. And under the terms of the U.S.-E.U. paper, Washington could count its new countercyclical payment program in the blue box instead. U.S. officials insisted that the program merited inclusion in the blue box, though officials of some other countries strongly disagreed, arguing that the program had as bad an effect on world crop markets as most other subsidies.

No sooner had the U.S.-E.U. paper been presented than an uprising began among developing countries in the Centre William Rappard.

Luiz Felipe de Seixas Corrêa, Brazil's ambassador to the WTO, approached his Indian counterpart, K. M. Chandrasekhar, to present an audacious idea. He proposed forming a developing-country alliance that would unite in opposition to the approach on agriculture advanced by the Americans and the Europeans.

Though they were friends, the Indian ambassador looked at the Brazilian quizzically—a natural reaction, given the vast disparity between the agricultural sectors of their two countries. Indian farms average less than 1.4 hectares (about 3.5 acres) and typically rely on laborious, primitive methods of cultivation. They could hardly be more different from the fields of soybeans, corn, cotton, and cattle pasture that stretch to the horizon in Brazil's tropical savannah, called the *cerrado*, a swath of land about a thousand miles long in the country's heartland where highly mechanized production is the rule. By 2003, Brazil, which was already the world's largest exporter of sugar, coffee, and orange juice, was also surpassing the United States as the number 1 exporter of soybeans.

"The Indian ambassador said, 'Brazil's interests are offensive. India's are defensive. How can we work together?'" recalls Rajesh Aggarwal, who was counselor in the Indian mission. "And the reply was, 'Don't worry. We'll figure it out, and we'll all fight together.'"

Up to that point, the Indians had been collaborating loosely with the European Union on agriculture because both governments were anxious to maintain protection for their farmers. But the U.S.-E.U. paper convinced the Indians that they needed new allies, and Chandrasekhar quickly got clearance from New Delhi to join forces with the Brazilians. Within days, the two ambassadors were signing up more of their colleagues—from Argentina, South Africa, Thailand, China, and about a dozen other countries—who, after checking with their capitals, agreed to become members of the new group.

Thus emerged a new phenomenon that would alter the balance of power in the WTO for years thereafter. The alliance named itself the G-20,* though its numbers often fluctuated above and below that figure as countries dropped in and out. Its formation elicited both apprehension and scorn among officials from wealthy countries, who had no idea what they had unleashed, in part because they couldn't figure out what G-20 members had in common other than a desire to band together in a united front against the world's fat cats.

As far as U.S. and E.U. trade policymakers were concerned, the ringleaders of the G-20 were almost deliberately overreacting to the U.S.-E.U. agriculture paper. The paper had, after all, fulfilled a promise by Zoellick and Lamy to propose a compromise between their rival formulas for cutting farm tariffs. And although it

---

*This G-20 should not be confused with the group of the same name, consisting of rich and emerging market countries, that rose to prominence in late 2008 in the midst of the financial crisis.

failed to go nearly as far toward curbing farm subsidies as developing countries wanted, it was intended to be only a basis for negotiation; it left open the clear possibility that hard bargaining among all WTO members could lead to a much better outcome. If the developing countries had been studying the paper with an open mind, U.S. negotiators argued, they would have seen that the idea was to advance the ball some distance toward needed reform and that reaching final goals would come only in full multilateral talks. For instance, says Allen Johnson, "We thought people understood that we *have* to eliminate export subsidies," even though the paper didn't say so. "We felt this was essential as strongly as anyone did." But the Americans and the Europeans could not undo the damage they had caused by reinforcing the impression that their top priority was appeasing their farmers. As Cancún approached, the G-20 continued to gain momentum and new members, heightening the prospects for a titanic clash between high-income and low-income nations.

Some hopeful signs did emerge prior to Cancún. On August 28, 2003, one major source of tension evaporated when WTO ambassadors in Geneva announced a landmark agreement on access to medicines under the TRIPS rules. The deal resolved an issue that had been left over from the Doha meeting about whether and under what conditions countries with generic drug industries could export generic medicines to poor nations. The battle over that question had threatened to wreck the ministerial, with the United States squaring off against the rest of the WTO membership. So the compromise, U.S. officials thought, would generate enormous goodwill, thereby keeping Cancún from turning into another Seattle.

The meeting had other things going for it, including good security to protect delegations against the thousands of protesters who were planning to show up. The convention center where the WTO was to meet stood on a long sandy spit, and an eight-foot fence would be erected around it. Furthermore, the meeting's goals had been steadily scaled back during the summer. Supachai Panitchpakdi, who had taken over as director-general from Mike Moore the previous year, was playing down any talk of reaching a deal on modalities. Instead, he was expressing hope for incremental steps that could breathe a little life into the round—modest aims for which consensus seemed eminently reachable.

Another problem was heating up, however. It would catch U.S. policymakers flatfooted.

| * |

Nicholas Imboden is an unlikely champion of poor African farmers. He is the former chief trade negotiator for Switzerland, one of the world's most protectionist countries in agriculture. But in early 2003, Imboden, then the director of a Geneva-based NGO, went to a meeting of officials from western African countries on a mission to help them figure out their strategy for the Doha Round. Paying his way were several European governments, including those of Switzerland and France. He suggested that given their limited clout, the Africans should forgo the temptation to try to have an impact on all issues; instead, they should pick just one crop, where they had a real grievance, and make a fuss about that. "How about cotton?" he recalls asking them.

It was a good question.

Cotton prices were down by half since the mid-1990s, to 42 cents a pound. That drop was a devastating problem for western Africa, where cotton is a very important crop, accounting for two-thirds of Burkina Faso's export revenues and about half of Benin's. The U.S. cotton program obviously deserved a hefty portion of the blame. Despite the price slump and despite the higher cost of production in the United States, American cotton growers were producing more and more of the fluffy white stuff—about 40 percent more in 2001 than in 1998—and shipping much of it abroad. This trend looked sure to continue, because cotton had gotten a particularly generous deal in America's 2002 farm bill, with even more subsidies per acre than corn, wheat, or soybeans.

Lending an emotional charge to the case of the 10 million Africans who depend on cotton was "Cultivating Poverty," a report produced in 2002 by the British aid group Oxfam. "Cotton prices are too low to keep our children in school, or to buy food and pay for health," the report quoted a small cotton grower from western Burkina Faso as saying. "Another season like this will destroy our community." The report noted that Burkina Faso is one of the world's lowest-cost producers of cotton, with planting, weeding, and harvesting done by hand, yet its growers were finding it almost impossible to compete with the 25,000 subsidized American cotton growers. Also powerful was a 2002 article in the *Wall Street Journal* that contrasted the life of Mody Sangare, a farmer in Mali who tills his cotton field with a one-blade, oxen-pulled plow, to that of Kenneth Hood, one of four brothers running a 10,000-acre cotton plantation in the Mississippi Delta, who rides in an air-conditioned $125,000 tractor. As chairman of the National Cotton Council, Hood had been the first person to shake hands with President Bush after the signing of the 2002 farm bill at a White House ceremony. In defense of the subsidy program—which paid his family farming operation $750,000 in subsidies in 2001—he had this to say to the *Journal*: "Maybe the farmers in Africa should be the ones not raising cotton. The Delta needs cotton farmers, and they can't exist without subsidies."

Cotton had gone all but unnoticed in the Doha negotiations until Imboden's meeting in early 2003 with the western African ambassadors. The formal submissions filed by western African nations in the early stages of the talks barely mentioned the issue. Imboden urged them to form a coalition to seek concessions from rich countries on cotton as their main "win" in the round. The Africans were nervous.

"The decision was not easy," recalls Samuel Amehou, who was Benin's ambassador to the WTO. "The worry that some people had was, 'Perhaps the Americans and the Europeans will get angry, and end [aid] cooperation with us.' So it was very important to convince these people that no, the WTO is a place where everyone can defend their economic interests."

The Africans finally took the leap in April 2003. The four countries with the greatest dependency on cotton—Benin, Burkina Faso, Mali, and Chad—filed a submission in the Doha Round demanding that WTO members agree on a phaseout of cotton subsidies in three years, plus compensation to the Africans of $250 million a year for the impact of past subsidies on their export revenues. In June, Imboden stepped up the heat by arranging an unusual event—an address to the General Council by Blaise Compaore, the president of Burkina Faso. Some Geneva denizens could not help noticing that the entourage accompanying the president of this impoverished country traveled in luxury and was incongruously decked out in designer clothing and expensive jewelry. But the speech attracted some media attention, giving the Africans confidence that when they had a potent message to convey, their voices would be heard. Compaore declared:

> Our countries are not asking for charity, neither are we requesting preferential treatment or additional aid. We demand solely that, in conformity with WTO basic principles, the free market rule be applied. Our producers are ready to face competition on the world cotton market—under the condition that it is not distorted by subsidies.

It was grossly unfair to ascribe all the problems burdening western African cotton farmers to subsidies. Development experts had long identified other reasons for the poverty afflicting cotton growers in Compaore's country and those of his neighbors, including state and private monopolies, price-fixing, and unscrupulous behavior by middlemen. But there was no gainsaying the blatant hypocrisy of rich countries, especially the United States, in spouting free-market rhetoric at the same time as they were defending subsidies, and subsidies to mostly southern, mostly white cotton farmers, no less, which conjured up unpleasant memories of America's treatment of Africans.

With African anger over cotton supplementing the G-20's militancy over the agriculture issue in general, the stage was set at Cancún for a North-South smackdown.

| * |

Bob Zoellick had not wanted to meet the G-20. Indeed, he refused at first. He was convinced it was an artificial alliance that wouldn't last very long, given the conflicting interests of its leading members—especially Brazil and India—and he didn't want to elevate its status by granting it a special meeting. He saw it as a modern-day incarnation of the G-77, the antimarket alliance among developing countries of decades past. He and his deputies were using all manner of pressure to keep countries from joining, the most common being warnings that G-20 membership would ruin a country's chances for a free-trade agreement with the United States.

But as the WTO's Cancún ministerial opened on September 9, 2003, Zoellick encountered a different point of view from a man he could not ignore—George Yeo, the Singaporean trade minister. Yeo was designated to lead the negotiations on agriculture at Cancún, as he had at the two previous ministerials, and upon arriving in Cancún he was struck by the force that this new agglomeration of developing countries was projecting. There is a new power triangle in the WTO, Yeo concluded—the United States, the European Union, and the G-20. If he was to coordinate a deal on agriculture, he told Zoellick, he needed Zoellick to interact with this group. Grudgingly, the U.S. trade representative agreed.

On the ministerial's second full day, a glowering Zoellick entered an amphitheater in the Cancún convention center that was packed with G-20 officials from Latin America, Asia, and Africa. The scene was like something out of a sixties protest, participants recall; the developing-country policymakers were perched on desks and sitting on the floor and any other place they could find. They had just been discovered by the world media, which was agog over their unity and strength in numbers. Now, having left the TV cameras and the microphones behind, they were girding for their private confrontation with the Man, the establishment heavy, the representative of the ruling class.

Zoellick sat down, a bottle of water on the desk in front of him, and opened the meeting, as he often does, with this question: "What's on your mind?"

The leaders of the G-20—with Celso Amorim, the Brazilian foreign minister, and Arun Jaitley, the Indian commerce minister, in the main speaking roles—presented the conditions that, they said, were required for a successful Doha Round. In general, they were demanding much deeper reductions in farm subsidies than the United States and European Union seemed willing to accept. Specifically, they insisted on very ambitious cuts in amber box subsidies, the ones that have the biggest impact on trade by encouraging farmers to overproduce. For green box subsidies—the most benign ones, such as payments for conservation—they wanted caps on the amounts that individual countries could spend, plus strict criteria for determining the types of subsidies that qualify. They wanted to eliminate the blue box entirely, thereby blocking the U.S. plan to categorize its countercyclical payments program in a way that would protect it from the butcher's knife. And they wanted a firm date for the elimination of export subsidies.

Zoellick, who had been taking notes and occasional swigs from his water bottle as he listened to the presentations, waited until they had stopped speaking. Then he invited them to continue.

We're finished, Amorim said. But Zoellick, with exaggerated courtesy bordering on sarcasm, urged them again to keep talking. An awkward silence ensued.

You've just given me a long list of the things that you want, Zoellick said. But this is a negotiation. You haven't said what you're going to give. Are you going to provide that half of your presentation?

Again there was silence, and Zoellick said he guessed the discussion was over. He rose and left.

This was Zoellick at his most supremely confident—or arrogant, depending on one's point of view. Participants from the G-20 sheepishly admit, in recalling the episode, that they had been unprepared for the challenge he threw down. But it was a challenge they would have to take up, if they were to be something more than an ephemeral assemblage of obstructionists. They were mostly middle-income, rapidly advancing countries, angling to play bigger and bigger roles on the world stage, and Zoellick's words were an uncomfortable reminder of the demands they were facing to make contributions to the international system commensurate with their growing place in it. They were resolutely determined to stick together, using their solidarity to enhance their impact in the trade realm. The question was, how long could they remain a cohesive force? And how would they use their power?

The answers would hinge to a large extent on Amorim, a silver-haired man with a neatly trimmed beard who had once worked as an assistant film director and who proudly talked of his days as a student leftist. The facts that he was a foreign minister and that he hailed from Brazil, the linchpin nation of the G-20, were only part of the reason he would become the group's natural leader. He had risen through the ranks of his country's diplomatic service, one of the world's most rigorous, with a primary expertise in trade; there probably was not a trade minister on the face of the earth who knew as much about the ins and outs of the WTO.

A lover of movies—his early favorites were tales, like *Grapes of Wrath*, about social injustice and poverty—Amorim joined the foreign ministry in the mid-1960s, when Brazil was lurching from one military regime to the next. In 1979 he was able to parlay his interest in cinema into a job as head of Embrafilme, the state-owned movie company, which landed him in trouble when he approved funding for a film about the military's torture of its opponents. His punishment was to be dispatched to a minor diplomatic post in Europe, but from there he began a long march to the top that included two stints as Brazil's representative in the multilateral trading system—the first, during the GATT years, from 1991 to 1993, and the second at the WTO from 1999 to 2001. Those Geneva postings put him in prime position for the external relations minister's job, a position he held briefly in the mid-1990s as well as starting in 2003, because the ministry takes trade very seriously; it is one of the world's few foreign ministries where trade is part of the ministry's portfolio. (Amorim's two predecessors had both served as ambassadors to the GATT or WTO before becoming ministers.) For all his diplomatic experience, he had a volatile temperament, and in meetings he had a distracting tendency to show his disagreement with other speakers by throwing his hands in the air, rolling his eyes, or turning to colleagues and whispering. He was, in short, a man of gravitas with whom few cared to pick a fight.

He and his government were clearly making more of a political choice than a purely economic one by casting Brazil's lot with India, the other lead partner in the G-20. Although the Brazilians and the Indians shared one economic goal—ending rich-country subsidies—they were at opposite poles on the issue of opening global agriculture markets. But Brazil had more cosmic ambitions than getting extra export opportunities for its farmers. Under President Luiz Inácio Lula da Silva, the Brazilian government was making a spirited bid for leadership of the developing world, a goal with which Amorim, as foreign minister, was only too glad to assist. The country had long harbored ambitions for a seat on the U.N. Security Council, and "Lula," a former union leader and head of the left-wing Workers Party, had another reason to raise Brasilia's diplomatic profile. Since taking office in 2002, he had been obliged to continue the free-market policies of his predecessor in order to stave off a financial crisis, which meant he had to find other ways to keep the left-wing base of his party happy. One way to do that was for Brazil to head a coalition that would confront the world's richest countries.

The G-20, which could claim to represent more than half the world's population, was the perfect vehicle. In Cancún, it was the straw that was stirring the drink, as reporters crammed into its news conferences to find out what act of insurrection it was planning next. Its leaders could not disguise the degree of empowerment they were feeling. "This is truly a historic moment," crowed South Africa's Alec Erwin, "when we have been able to unify our position across economies."

Even for developing countries not in the G-20, this sentiment was contagious in the Mexican resort town.

| * |

Supachai had been director-general for a year at the time of the Cancún meeting, and it was clear he was out of his depth. To be sure, he was much better educated than Mike Moore, and more easygoing too. Whereas Moore had been prone to black moods that drove staffers in the Secretariat crazy, Supachai was always pleasant company. He was ever ready for convivial conversation about chess or botany or wine, all of which he could discuss knowledgeably; on his many travels to foreign cities, he made a point of spending as much time as possible in museums. But Supachai was utterly lacking in the head-banging skills that the director-general's job requires. Though normally a director-general plays a crucial role at a ministerial conference by leading the discussion in green rooms and other key meetings, the chairman at Cancún, Foreign Minister Luis Ernesto Derbez of Mexico, felt obliged to assume most of those responsibilities himself.

One of Supachai's admirable qualities was that he was capable of subordinating his ego to greater causes. He had a deep sense of wanting to serve and was willing to take on thankless tasks, ones that might not necessarily make him look good. That's exactly what he did at Cancún, when he agreed to act as a facilitator to help find a resolution to an issue that others feared was intractable— cotton. On September 10, the ministerial's first day, he took a surprisingly strong position on the matter, saying in an address to ministers that although he didn't usually intervene in debates, the proposal submitted by the four western African cotton-producing countries (Benin, Mali, Burkina Faso, and Chad) had "strong moral and economic merit." He observed that the four "are not asking for special treatment, but for a solution based on a fair multilateral trading system." The following day, he announced that he had accepted a request from Derbez to chair the small working group negotiating the cotton issue. Nobody else had agreed to do it; Supachai did, partly because *someone* had to, and partly, some Secretariat officials suspected, because he was flattered that he was finally being asked to do something meaningful.

The U.S. team in Cancún was extremely irritated at being under siege on cotton. Zoellick and his aides were aware that one of the main instigators of the "Cotton Four" was a European (Nicholas Imboden). So in Washington's eyes, the cotton furor looked suspiciously like an attempt to make the United States into the bad guy on agriculture while deflecting attention from the Europeans' own multitude of farm-policy sins. The Africans' demands, the Americans thought, were ridiculous. The compensation the Cotton Four wanted to remedy the problems caused by past subsidies would mean handing millions of dollars to some of the most corrupt governments on the planet, with little likelihood that the benefits would reach poor farmers. And the Africans' other main objective, the immediate phaseout of cotton subsidies even before an overall Doha agreement was struck, was a complete nonstarter on Capitol Hill. Although the American negotiators realized that any final Doha deal would have to include major cuts in the U.S. cotton program, they needed wins in other sectors to offset the losses in cotton before enough members of Congress could be mustered to approve such a package. Unilaterally phasing out the program simply wouldn't fly.

But in their defensive crouch, the Americans responded to this challenge in an astonishingly ham-fisted way. Taken by surprise at how much attention the cotton issue was getting in the media, they sought to defuse it by presenting officials from the Cotton Four with a hastily conceived package of palliative measures that succeeded only in making matters worse.

"I remember looking at the Africans when I heard the phrase 'diversification,' which was the first I had heard it," says Joseph Glauber, who was then deputy chief economist in the U.S. Agriculture Department. "I had spent time in Mali in the Peace Corps, so I was especially interested in their reaction. I remember thinking, 'This is not good.'"

Diversification was the main theme of a plan that Zoellick and Agriculture Secretary Ann Veneman set forth to the Africans in meetings on September 9 and 10. The basic idea was that western Africa needed to export something more than raw cotton, and the United States was ready to help them move up the value chain into the manufacturing of cotton fiber and clothing, using aid and World Bank loans. The plan was, in one sense, based on impeccable logic, for what did these wretchedly poor nations need more than the creation of a manufacturing base? But the Africans, with equally impeccable logic, saw it as a maneuver to divert attention away from the subsidy issue. They knew aid money—of which they were already getting plenty—was not going to turn their countries into manufacturing hubs anytime soon. They continued to press their demands.

The Americans had a nightmare scenario: They feared being confronted late in the meeting with a text that, by incorporating most of the African position on cotton, would put Washington in the hugely awkward position of blocking the consensus. Determined to keep Supachai from drafting a text that went in that direction, Zoellick went all out in strong-arming the director-general. In a private meeting, he reproached Supachai for overstepping his bounds by showing sympathy for the Africans. "My Congress raised with me the fact that you're taking sides on this issue. You're no longer seen as neutral," he blustered, according to notes of the meeting. He warned Supachai against drafting "language that is further than I can go," and he described the African demand for compensation as a "financial shakedown." The hapless director-general protested, "I can't understand why you think I'm partial," and he assured Zoellick, "I won't try to push anything on you."

The result was a total U.S. victory—and a totally Pyrrhic one.

The release of a new draft ministerial text at midday on Saturday, September 13, showed that Supachai had given Zoellick almost everything he wanted on cotton. Subsidies for U.S. cotton growers were to be cut only as part of an overall Doha deal, according to the text, which also parroted the U.S. proposal by proposing that the WTO should work with aid donors to "effectively direct existing programs and resources toward diversification of the economies where cotton accounts for a major share of their GDP." Even some of the American negotiators recall feeling worried that the text was, as one later put it, a "slap in the face" to the Cotton Four that would only heighten the sense of victimhood then taking hold among developing countries. Encapsulating the reaction in the developing-country camp were the words of an African delegate, reported that day in the *Bridges Daily Update*: "We are used to hardship, disease and famine. Now the WTO is against us as well."

At the same time, another long-festering dispute looked as if it was ready to boil over, as witnessed by the lanyards, printed with the words "Explicit Consensus," that many developing-country delegates were wearing to hold their ID badges. The lanyards were a symbol of defiance, a warning that developing countries intended to take a combative stand on the Singapore issues. The phrase printed on them was a reminder about the final day of the Doha meeting, when the WTO had promised India that no negotiations would proceed on any of the Singapore issues in the absence of full unanimity among member countries. The

European Union was still leading the effort to ensure that the round would include these issues, which many others at Cancún viewed as a hopelessly lost cause.

By Saturday night, the eve of the final day in Cancún, the prospect of a failed meeting was clearly growing, despite the modest initial goals. Ministers from developing countries delivered angry, sometimes militant speeches at a plenary session that evening. "We are engulfed in a sense of deep disappointment that the development dimension envisaged under the Doha Work Programme has been given short shrift," India's Arun Jaitley said.

In the hope that a green room planned for the next day would prove fruitful, a small group of ministers met in a strategy session that lasted until nearly 4:00 a.m. There Lamy told his colleagues that he would reluctantly offer a compromise on the Singapore issues on the morrow.

Too late.

| * |

Better prepare to stay for an extra day, U.S. delegates were told as the scheduled final session at Cancún began a little after 8:30 on Sunday morning, September 14. Little did they or others realize how swiftly and suddenly events would unfold in an entirely different direction.

Chairing the green room was Mexico's Derbez; although Supachai was sitting next to him, the director-general remained silent during virtually the entire meeting. Early on, the no-nonsense Derbez made it clear that he would put the kibosh on speechifying and posturing. When a Japanese minister ploddingly recited Tokyo's stance on one issue, the reaction from the chair was mortifying: "I am really not looking for you to repeat your well-known positions," Derbez said. "This is not why we are in this room. Let me recall that we will be done at 4:00 p.m. today." Because several of the ministers from the thirty-two countries participating in the meeting were there as representatives of large groups—Botswana's Jacob Nkate, for instance, was representing the Group of 90, an alliance of the smallest and poorest developing countries of former European colonies—Derbez reminded them of their responsibilities to keep those outside the green room informed and consulted.

The first matter for discussion, Derbez announced, would be the Singapore issues, "since these are clearly a deal-breaker." In short order, participants were clamoring for Lamy to drop at least some of the four. There was no way, they said, that the European Union could have negotiations on investment *and* competition *and* government procurement *and* trade facilitation. "If the proponents insist on the package approach then I will be on a 3:00 p.m. flight," said Rafidah

Aziz, the tart-tongued Malaysian trade minister, who aimed the following query at Lamy: "Are you ready to unbundle?"

At last Lamy made his move, saying that although he would have to get approval from European trade ministers, he was indeed prepared to deal. "We are now in a situation where negotiations on the four issues is impossible," he acknowledged, adding: "Let's go for a couple of areas and drop those that are too difficult." His flexibility drew approval from Mark Vaile, the Australian minister, who said, "There is a significant concession on the table here."

But now this group had to decide, in a very short period of time, which of the four issues to keep on the agenda and which to jettison—another matter about which they differed. "Why did you wait two years to do this?" Rafidah asked Lamy.

A cascade of proposals came from the ministers. Zoellick urged keeping government procurement and trade facilitation. Lamy preferred keeping competition and trade facilitation, as did Rafidah, who warned that Malaysia could never accept negotiations on government procurement. (The country has a program aimed at giving preference in government contracts to companies owned by locals, especially from the ethnic Malay majority.) As the morning wore on, confusion reigned over which issues were being dropped and which kept. "We need clarity about which ones we are talking about," pleaded Botswana's Nkate.

At around 1:00 p.m., Derbez adjourned the group for lunch, telling them to consult with constituent groups and return at 2:15 ready to move on to the agriculture negotiations, "or we're finished." The preferred option turned out to be "finished," at least for many delegations.

Delegates from African countries were loaded for bear when their green room representative, Nkate, arrived to ask for guidance on how to proceed. Thanks in large part to the cotton text, which NGOs and others had been denouncing as a travesty, Nkate's colleagues made it clear that they were not in a compromising mood. "When someone said, 'We should consider one or two of the Singapore issues,' people just switched on their mikes and said, 'No! No! No!'" recalls Dipak Patel, who was Zambia's trade minister. "It was very militant. We would just literally shout them down." Youssef Boutros-Ghali, the Egyptian trade minister, who had also been in the green room, tried to calm his fellow Africans, telling them Lamy had offered an important concession. "It makes no sense for us to block the whole process, because we are the main beneficiaries of the multilateral system," Boutros-Ghali recalls saying. "But the feeling [of wanting to confront the rich] was too strong."

The green room reconvened at 2:25. There, the word from the poor countries that Nkate represented could hardly have been more jolting: "We cannot negotiate on *any* of the Singapore issues," Nkate declared. Flags shot up all over the room, as ministers clamored for the chair to recognize them. The South Koreans said that they would take the exact opposite position from the Africans—namely, continuing to demand negotiations on all four Singapore issues. Singapore's Yeo, appealing for restraint, suggested that perhaps the green room should move on to agriculture, the idea being that perhaps some kind of breakthrough on that would make the rest at least possible. But Derbez rejected that idea.

"My job as chairman of the conference is over," he said. "There is no possibility of finding an agreement. There is no purpose in discussing this any further or talking about anything else. All of you can take your flights back now."

The end had come so unexpectedly and so suddenly that it took a few minutes for the import of the words to sink in. Had Derbez just announced that the meeting had collapsed? Only two years after the stain-removing achievement of Doha, would there now be a new stain of Cancún?

Arancha González, Lamy's spokeswoman, was having her first relaxed lunch in several days when a call from the E.U. trade commissioner came in on her cell phone. "He said, 'Would you come here? We are done,'" González recalls. "I said, 'You mean, we are done for the day?' He said, 'No, we are done for the conference.' I couldn't believe it. I said, 'What?!'"

As her recollection suggests, E.U. officials were in shock over the outcome. They knew that with the breakdown occurring over the Singapore issues, they would get a healthy portion of blame. They immediately began to suspect a plot: Derbez, they concluded, had gaveled the meeting to a close prematurely, at the behest of the Americans. He could have kept the meeting going, with some chance of success, by moving on to agricultural issues. The reason he didn't do so, the Europeans concluded, was because Washington was anxious to avoid a breakdown over cotton, for which *they* would be depicted as the bad guys.

There is at least some evidence for this theory. Zoellick acknowledges that just before the meeting's halt, he passed a note to Derbez, which said, "I don't think this is going anywhere." But he didn't write the note with the aim of dodging a confrontation over cotton, Zoellick contends; he wrote it because he genuinely saw no chance for a consensus. "People weren't there to solve problems," he says. "It was to posture. My view is that sometimes it's better to have the shock effect. Sometimes in negotiations you have to say, 'You've pushed too far. We're done.'" His anger at the time was manifest in his postmeeting news conference:

A number of countries just thought it was a freebie; they could just make whatever points they suggested, argue, and not offer and give [Zoellick said]. And now they are going to face the cold reality of that strategy: coming home with nothing. That's not a good result for any of us.

It is fair to accuse many developing-country officials of having chosen the posturing option at Cancún. That they had done so was evident in the joy and triumph that reigned among African delegations at the end of the meeting, when television pictures showed some of them raising clenched fists. It was evident too in the behavior of the NGO members, who had exhorted the Africans to take unyielding positions and who danced in the halls of the convention center to celebrate their success, singing "Money can't buy the world" to the tune of the Beatles' "Can't Buy Me Love." The inability of the G-20 to answer Zoellick's question about what *they* would contribute was further evidence. Although developing countries had demonstrated that they could bat down proposals advanced by the rich, they had evinced little, if any, capacity for making the sort of tradeoffs that would be necessary to change the trading system in the ways they wanted.

But just who pushed whom too far at Cancún is a matter of perspective. The United States had shown gross insensitivity on cotton. The European Union had waited much too long to show some flexibility on the Singapore issues. Both Washington and Brussels had bungled the agriculture issue overall. Taken together, these positions had given developing countries the sense that the rich were merely talking the talk of a development round, rather than walking the walk. The U.S. farm bill had accentuated that impression.

The legislative, or rule-making, function of the WTO had ground to a halt. There were some grounds for hope, because the formation of the G-20 meant that developing countries had a vehicle through which they could find their voice. The group had the potential for transforming the way WTO negotiations worked, by giving new actors central roles on the main stage. Still, it was hard for many of the key players to see that possibility at the time. "I said in Seattle that the organization is medieval, but I'm now wondering whether Neolithic isn't a more appropriate term," Lamy wrote in an op-ed a few days after Cancún.

Meanwhile, another part of the WTO's machinery—the judicial system— was proceeding apace. It was about to give the United States another punch in the nose.

# 8 | JEWELS AND PIRATES

*OYEZ, OYEZ, OYEZ.* COURT WAS IN SESSION.

On the morning of October 7, 2003, three judges took their places on a dais of raised tables at the front of Room E in the Centre William Rappard, a long rectangular room that commands a splendid view of Lake Geneva and the Alps. Below them were lawyers and witnesses who were about to present testimony in one of the most important cases ever brought before a WTO tribunal.

This was no ordinary courtroom. For one thing, the judges—or panelists, as the WTO prefers to call them—were not full-time jurists. One was a former Polish foreign minister, another was a Chilean foreign ministry official specializing in trade issues, and the third was an Australian attorney, and they had come to Geneva specifically to adjudicate the single case before them. Moreover, the proceedings were closed to the public. And perhaps most important, the parties to the case were not individuals or companies but sovereign governments—specifically, the United States and Brazil.

As in most WTO cases, the presentations that day tended to be dry and technical, with the exception of one witness, who livened up the proceedings with his salt-of-the-earth manner.

The witness, a Brazilian farmer, had a problem: He didn't look or sound like a Brazilian. His name was Christopher Ward, and having been raised in New Zealand, he spoke English like a true Kiwi. So he started off by explaining to the panel: "You may not believe it from my accent, but I can assure you that I am Brazilian, with three Brazilian children and a Brazilian wife, and I have farmed in Brazil for more than twenty years."

Once he had clearly established his national identity, Ward proceeded to present devastating testimony on the central issue in the case—Brazil's complaint that U.S. cotton subsidies were in violation of WTO rules because they were driving down world cotton prices and severely affecting the livelihoods of

Brazilian farmers. Although Ward wasn't poor like the African cotton growers introduced earlier in this book, he had a compelling tale to tell about the impact of the American cotton program. He patiently explained to the panel why, under the normal laws of economics, his cotton operation ought to be highly profitable. In the state of Mato Grosso, where his farm was located, weather conditions and the soil "are ideal for cotton production," he said, noting that given regular rainfall, irrigation wasn't required. Accordingly, he could produce "high-quality cotton at very high yields per acre," an average yield more than two and a half times the American level. "But even with these high yields and the excellent quality of our land," he said, "we were not able to fully recover all of our variable costs of production during the 2000–2001 and the 2001–2002 season[s]," thanks to low world prices. In fact, he said, the low prices received by him and his Mato Grosso neighbors had "caused many producers to drop plans to expand cotton acreage, reduce their area planted to cotton or go out of the business of producing cotton."

This snippet from case DS267, *Subsidies on Upland Cotton*, offers a glimpse into the workings of the system often described as the WTO's "crown jewel"—its mechanism for handling conflicts among member nations. Just as governments have courts that interpret the laws passed by their legislatures, the WTO has its Dispute Settlement Understanding. It is the system by which the institution renders judgment as to whether one nation or another is violating the basic tenets of trade such as the MFN principle, or is failing to adhere to commitments made in WTO agreements, or is abrogating rules promulgated at ministerial conferences. It is "clearly the most powerful dispute settlement system at the international level that we have today or perhaps ever in the history of the world," as John Jackson, the law professor who first proposed the WTO's creation, once put it.

The impact of the Dispute Settlement Understanding on the trading system extends far beyond the rulings handed down in individual cases, because its very existence helps defuse the tensions that inevitably arise in commerce among nations. When a country's politicians and citizens are up in arms over another country's trade practices, bringing a case to the WTO can help lower the political temperature. Instead of lashing out by unilaterally imposing sanctions, which might well provoke retaliation and counter-retaliation, a country's trade minister can call a news conference and righteously announce that his government is pursuing litigation in Geneva with the aim of bringing the offender to justice. Aggrieved parties can take comfort in knowing that their case has been turned over to an impartial body for adjudication, and that the body has potent methods of enforcing its decisions.

To be sure, there are limits to the potency of that enforcement. Recall that, for all the WTO's fabled powers, a nation found to have violated the rules doesn't have to change its offending practices; the guilty party can exercise its sovereign right to keep those policies in effect. In such instances, the WTO wields its clout by granting the winning country the legal right to retaliate against the loser—which typically means imposing punishingly high duties on some of the loser's products. Sometimes, the mere threat of such sanctions helps spur the losing country toward accepting the WTO's verdict. A classic example was the 2002 dispute over steel (mentioned in Chapter 7), in which the European Union and several other governments won a WTO ruling that the Bush administration's tariffs on imported steel were illegal. In that case, officials in Brussels let it be known that if the time came for retaliation, they intended to impose duties of up to 100 percent on U.S. exports from politically important states—notably citrus products from Florida, textiles and furniture from the Carolinas, and farm machinery from the Midwest. The Bush administration, facing the prospect of suffering electoral pain in the Sunshine State and elsewhere in 2004, terminated the steel tariffs in late 2003. In most cases, such saber-rattling isn't necessary, because by and large countries abide by verdicts that go against them.

Under the GATT, the system tended to be "diplomacy oriented," with a chief aim of reaching a negotiated settlement between the disputants, a rather flimsy method of dispensing justice that, given its lack of enforceability, ultimately proved inadequate to containing trade tensions. With the creation of the WTO came a much more "rules-oriented" and "sanctions-based" system. It was based on the theory that countries ought to be encouraged to settle their differences, and to be given plenty of time to do so, but if they can't, a decision will be rendered as to who's right and who's wrong, backed by the threat of punishment against noncompliers. The WTO version of the system incorporated several crucial innovations, the most important of which was "automaticity," meaning that rulings could no longer be overturned by the vetoes of a losing party. Another was the creation of the Appellate Body, giving countries a chance to bring appeals to a higher court of regular jurists. A third was a schedule of faster deadlines for getting cases processed.

All this is what sets the WTO apart from other international institutions and gives it a special claim to evenly balance the world's nations on the scales of justice. "Rich and poor countries alike have an equal right to challenge each other in the WTO's dispute settlement procedures," boasts the WTO's website. As this chapter will show, that claim is somewhat misleading; the crown jewel has a number of flaws beneath its shiny surface.

The system has certainly worked to America's mercantile benefit at times. Washington has filed several dozen cases, sometimes winning commercially significant gains for U.S. firms. A 1998 ruling against Japan's liquor taxes, for example, forced Tokyo to remove its discriminatory levies, resulting in an 18 percent increase in U.S. whiskey exports to the Japanese market the following year. More recently, in a case brought by the United States, the European Union, and Canada, China was found to be violating WTO rules by requiring automakers there to buy components from local suppliers.

But *Upland Cotton* offers a powerful illustration of the system's capacity for leveling the playing field at least to some extent. And because it involved the issue of subsidies—one of the main bones of contention in the Doha Round—the case would have a major impact on the negotiations as well.

| * |

Pedro de Camargo Neto had been spoiling for a fight against the farm-subsidy programs of rich countries for a long time. He finally got his chance in 2000, when Brazil's agriculture minister hired him as a deputy.

Camargo came from a family of cattle ranchers and sugar farmers. Although he had spent much of his working years as an engineer, he switched careers in 1990 to become the head of one of Brazil's most influential farm lobby groups. The farmers who belonged to the organization frequently complained to him about the competitive pressure they faced from subsidized foreign crops, with American soybeans being one of the prime examples. So once he attained a high position in the government, Camargo was determined to do something about it. He latched onto the idea of using the WTO dispute settlement process, and initially set his sights on bringing a complaint against the U.S. soybean program.

One of his first steps was to hire Sidley Austin, a Chicago-based law firm. Only about four firms handle WTO cases regularly; they are all American, and Sidley has the biggest practice. Even though the firm is headquartered in the United States, its Geneva-based attorneys are happy to litigate on behalf of other nations against Washington.

The initial advice from the Sidley lawyers was not what Camargo wanted to hear: There was almost no way to win a case against soybean subsidies, because Brazil would have to show that its farmers were suffering injury, which would be a hard claim to make at a time when soybean prices were going through the roof. But an economist in the agriculture ministry pointed out that cotton would offer a much better case, and Camargo seized on it as the perfect weapon.

His counterparts in the Foreign Ministry, which has primary responsibility for trade policy, weren't so sure. They wanted to be confident that the case was watertight. There were lots of ways the case could go wrong for Brazil, and if the United States were to win, Washington would feel more unconstrained than ever about expanding its subsidy programs. But Camargo was not easily dissuaded; he pushed and agitated for the case to go forward, and after carefully studying the legal ramifications, the Foreign Ministry came around. In mid-2003, the government filed its first submissions to the panel. "This is a case involving basic economic principles of supply and demand," the Brazilians said. "It is a case about too much upland cotton being produced and exported by high-cost U.S. producers. . . . This case is about equity."

In its counterargument, the U.S. government contended that its main cotton-subsidy programs didn't affect global trade and therefore weren't breaking any WTO rules. The government checks received by American cotton farmers were, for the most part, completely unrelated to the amount of cotton they produced at the time they got them, U.S. lawyers asserted; rather, the payments depended on past cotton production and acreage. So the programs could not be inducing growers to overproduce.

The Brazilians, however, held a trump card. Not only had they hired top-notch American lawyers, but they had retained the services of a highly respected American agricultural economist.

Like most academics, Daniel Sumner is not favorably disposed toward farm subsidies in general because he sees little rationale for protecting farmers from market forces, and he believes that some of the goals subsidies are supposedly aimed at—preserving rural communities, for example—could be achieved much more effectively using other programs. A pleasant, soft-spoken professor at the University of California–Davis, he had served as assistant secretary for economics at the Agriculture Department during the administration of George H. W. Bush. In the *Upland Cotton* case, he produced a study for the Brazilians that was filled with math equations and symbols, using Agriculture Department data. Its most damning portion was an estimate showing how big a role subsidies had played on world markets in 1999–2002. Had no subsidies been in place during that period, Sumner concluded, the 25,000 cotton farmers in the United States would have shipped about 41 percent less cotton abroad, and this would have raised the world price by about 12.6 percent.

American farm groups reviled Sumner as a traitor for accepting tens of thousands of dollars in fees to work for Brazil, and some of their leaders vowed to teach him a lesson by cutting off funding for other work he does. "He joined forces with the enemy to cut the heart out of our farm program," said Don

Cameron, vice chairman of the California Cotton Growers Association. Cameron said such an act was "unethical" because Sumner was an employee of California's public university system, and he added menacingly: "There are research projects that he's been involved with in the past that we'll direct elsewhere." This was no idle threat; it evidently unnerved the dean of Sumner's agricultural school, who said that although Sumner had the right to express his opinion, "I question his judgment" in agreeing to work against the interests of U.S. farmers. Sumner, however, was unrepentant. "I'm trying to do the best economics and put it into the system," he told me. Likening the growers' threats to witness tampering, he said with a chuckle, "What is this, the Mafia or something?"

Vindication came in April 2004, when the WTO panel decided almost every issue in the case in Brazil's favor.

The ruling struck fear in U.S. farming communities because the big question now was how many other agriculture programs funded by Washington would be in jeopardy. "This has the potential to have extraordinary consequences up and down every Main Street in rural America," Senator Kent Conrad of North Dakota said after the ruling was disclosed. Not long thereafter Brazil won another case against subsidies, this time beating the European Union in a case over its coddling of sugar farmers. The WTO's Appellate Body upheld the cotton ruling, and Brazilian officials, claiming their country had suffered $3 billion in losses as a result of U.S. cotton subsidies, warned that they would seek the right to retaliate by an equivalent amount against the United States unless Washington changed its cotton program.

Justice had triumphed. Superpower America had been forced into submission in the WTO docket, only months after being thwarted at the negotiating table in Cancún. Here was fresh evidence that even if globalization is proceeding apace, Western powers no longer have nearly the ability to control it that they once enjoyed.

Should the ruling also lead to the conclusion that the WTO dispute settlement system is a finely honed process, meting out justice fairly to all? Not so fast. The cotton case was still not fully resolved. The system has many estimable qualities, but it also has some aspects that are highly controversial and some that are deeply troubling to anyone concerned about equity between rich and poor countries.

| * |

"We do not wear robes. We do not wear wigs. We do not wear the white bibs that are often worn by jurists on other international tribunals." So wrote James

Bacchus, a former U.S. congressman from Florida, in a memoir of his years in Geneva as a member of the Appellate Body, for which he was selected when it was first established in 1995. Though the Appellate Body is similar in function to a supreme court, Bacchus and his colleagues did not even have formal titles; rather than referring to themselves as "judges" or "justices," they called themselves simply "members of the Appellate Body."

The six other members selected along with Bacchus came from Egypt, Germany, Japan, New Zealand, the Philippines, and Uruguay. All were nominated by their countries' governments, selected by a committee of senior ambassadors to the WTO, and approved by the membership. (The term of an Appellate Body member is four years, with the possibility of being reappointed once.) Although they came from vastly different cultures and although some of their decisions drew criticism, the Appellate Body established a solid reputation for integrity and independence. The members' deliberations take place at a round table in a room on the third floor of the Centre William Rappard, where they review panel decisions that often run hundreds of pages long, and in deciding whether to approve, modify, or reject them, they engage in debates and drafting sessions that last for days and sometimes weeks. In Bacchus's words, the process involves sitting for "hour after hour, day after day, plumbing the depths of meaning of the words of the WTO treaty, slicing the layers of logic in the interpretation of those words."

The high esteem in which the Appellate Body is held is especially important because the same esteem does not always extend to the panels who issue the initial decisions in WTO cases. Panelists are often juggling their regular jobs while plowing through thousands of pages of evidence and briefs. (Ambassadors to the WTO, for example, sometimes moonlight as panelists.) Although potential panelists are proposed by the Secretariat staff from a permanent list of qualified candidates with experience in trade matters, both sides to a dispute must agree on their appointment, and because one side or the other often exercises its right of rejection, the people who end up serving on panels are sometimes far from the first choice. When the disputing parties can't agree on who should serve, the director-general makes the appointments.

The difficulty of finding highly qualified panelists, however, pales by comparison with some of the other problems with the dispute settlement system.

First, it is no model of transparency. How did I learn the details of Christopher Ward's testimony in the *Upland Cotton* case? Sorry, I can't tell you; the source who gave me that information made me promise not to reveal his name, because under WTO rules such information isn't supposed to be disclosed, even when it's innocuous. Although panels' final rulings are made public, as are decisions by the Appellate Body, the hearings, testimony, and documents submitted by the disputants are confidential unless one side or the other voluntarily publishes the submissions it makes.* That's what critics of the WTO are referring to when they attack its "secret tribunals."

In justifying these practices, a number of WTO member governments contend that the material submitted in their cases sometimes includes proprietary corporate information. They also argue that disputes pitting one sovereign government against another are most appropriately handled behind closed doors to encourage negotiated settlements. The idea that WTO panels are conducting business affecting the public, and therefore ought to be open to scrutiny, apparently doesn't persuade them. This is too bad, because a lot of information about WTO cases leaks out anyhow, and by maintaining secrecy over its panel proceedings, the WTO only perpetuates its stereotype as an undemocratic, sinister institution.

Worse still is the system's combination of slowness and lack of retroactivity. Imagine an extremely lengthy trial of a defendant who is sued by banks for robbing them and who, during the trial, keeps robbing banks right up to the day of the verdict, claiming that he's not violating any laws. Then when the court rules that bank robbery is indeed illegal and prepares to assess damages, the defendant jumps up and says, "I hereby agree to stop robbing banks," a pledge enabling him to walk away scot-free, without even having to pay back the money stolen during the period of the trial.

The WTO dispute settlement system sometimes works like that. It isn't as bad as the GATT system, because it doesn't allow the defendant to veto the ruling. A country found by the WTO to be guilty of violating the rules has to change its policies so as to comply with the ruling or accept punishment. But cases often take a good three years to go all the way through the panel stage to the appeals process, and the violator may continue its practices with impunity until the time of the final ruling, with no fear of suffering any consequences for its actions up to that point.

Again, the 2002 dispute over steel is illustrative. Although the White House terminated the tariffs that the WTO ruled illegal, it did so only after American steelmakers had enjoyed twenty months of protection. Do governments sometimes recklessly violate WTO rules, secure in the knowledge that the worst that

---

*WTO dispute panel hearings may be open to the public if both parties agree to waive secrecy. The first time a waiver was granted was in August 2005, in a dispute between the European Union and the United States.

would happen is losing a ruling and paying for legal talent? Here's what Gary Horlick, one of Washington's savviest trade lawyers, has said:

> Prudence, diplomacy, and client confidentiality forbid me from naming too many names, but every major WTO member has consciously done something that violated the WTO, on the assumption that the member could deal with it through litigation and stall for at least 3 years. If anyone doubts that, they are dreaming.

Even more fundamental is this question: Do poor countries really stand a fair chance in WTO dispute cases? By some measures, developing nations are behaving as if they perceive a genuine opportunity to exact justice; they filed a little more than half of all WTO cases in the 2001–2006 period. But these complaints came mainly from relatively large and fast-growing nations, with the most frequent filers in the developing world being Brazil, India, Argentina, Thailand, and Chile.

It is one thing, after all, for a country like Brazil to beat the United States. More revealing is what happens when a truly tiny country files a complaint against one of the major powers. It so happens that at pretty much the same time as *Upland Cotton* was proceeding, the United States was embroiled in another case involving one of the WTO's smallest members.

| * |

Locked in his prison cell, tortured by the distant lights of the Las Vegas Strip, Jay Cohen couldn't stop thinking about getting even with the government that had put him behind bars, and he had a unique revenge fantasy.

The crime for which Cohen was incarcerated was running an Internet gambling site based in the Caribbean nation of Antigua and Barbuda that took bets from Americans. Not long before beginning his sentence, Cohen had learned that the federal crackdown on online betting might violate global trade rules. So he played a key part in instigating a complaint by Antigua and Barbuda at the WTO. "It kind of helped keep my spirits up," he says.

Never before has such a tiny nation—69,000 people live in Antigua and Barbuda—brought a WTO complaint against the United States. Therein lay Cohen's plan for vengeance. The world's lone superpower would capitulate to a country whose entire population could fit comfortably inside the Rose Bowl. Could it happen? Case DS285, *Gambling*, reveals a great deal about the pluses and minuses of the WTO's dispute settlement system. Whatever one's feelings about gambling, this quirky saga has much to commend it for anyone who enjoys seeing Washington get its comeuppance. But the case also shows that the Davids of the world trading system need more favorable rules if their disputes with the Goliaths are to be resolved on terms that most people would consider fair.

Setting global precedents wasn't what Cohen had in mind when, in late 1996, he quit his job as a floor trader at the Pacific Stock Exchange and moved to Antigua with a couple of friends. "Life was fine," he recalls wistfully. Gambling was legal in Antigua, so Cohen and his buddies figured they would have no problem operating a business that took sports bets from people in the United States by phone or Internet. Between golf rounds and fishing trips, they built World Sports Exchange Limited, one of several dozen Internet betting parlors then springing up in Antigua and elsewhere. Their goal was to get a slice of the billions of dollars Americans illegally bet on pro football and other sporting events. Money was soon rolling in as bettors put up initial stakes by sending checks or charging their credit cards, with the understanding that their losses would be deducted from their accounts or sent by check in the mail. The Antiguan government was delighted, both because the industry became the country's second-largest employer after tourism and because the companies paid fees to operate there.

The U.S. government did not share that enthusiasm. Justice Department officials viewed as a legal fiction the argument that the bets were taking place in locations where gambling was permitted, outside U.S. jurisdiction. Members of Congress, together with a host of state attorneys general, were becoming worried that the convenience of online gambling would increase addiction and lure underage bettors who wouldn't be admitted to casinos. So law enforcement agencies threatened to prosecute broadcasters and publishers that took ads for online gambling sites, and financial regulators persuaded many banks to stop processing credit card payments to the sites.

Most drastic of all, the feds vowed to charge people like Cohen with violating a 1960s-era law forbidding the use of the telephone wires for gambling. "You can't go offshore and hide; you can't go online and hide," warned Janet Reno, the attorney general at the time. Cohen, who was indicted in March 1998, returned voluntarily to U.S. soil to fight the charges under the assumption that, as he put it, "No judge is going to let this stand," because in his view, the United States was wrongly trying to dictate what is legal in Antigua. But a jury convicted him, the judge gave him twenty-one months, and the Supreme Court refused to consider his appeal.

Then out of the blue came a break, shortly before Cohen was about to begin serving his sentence. A strange, rambling letter arrived in Cohen's mailbox from someone who had seen the publicity surrounding the case, suggesting that the U.S. government's position left it vulnerable to a WTO complaint. Cohen recalls that he phoned a lawyer friend from his student days at the University of California–Berkeley and said, "Check this out—is there anything to this?"

The friend, Bob Blumenfeld, and his law partner, Mark Mendel, were hardly giants in the trade field like the attorneys at Sidley Austin who represented Brazil in *Upland Cotton*. Quite the contrary: Mendel-Blumenfeld was a modest practice in El Paso, Texas, handling securities issues and other corporate matters. But after researching the points made in the letter, the lawyers soon agreed that the U.S. position was at odds with its WTO commitments because in the services portion of the Uruguay Round, U.S. officials had included the American "recreational, cultural and sporting services" market in its list of those areas that would be opened to foreigners. Mendel flew to Antigua in January 2003 in the hope of persuading the government to bring a case.

At this point, one of the biggest inequities in the WTO system came to the fore. One of the reasons small countries rarely file WTO cases is because of their lack of resources and legal expertise, which can put them at a huge disadvantage relative to nations with large, well-staffed trade ministries. Antiguan officials figured it would cost about $1 million to pursue a case properly—no trivial sum for a government whose total budget was less than $150 million a year.

The country didn't even have a full-time representative at WTO headquarters in Geneva, and the diplomat whose responsibilities included the WTO—Sir Ronald Saunders, then the Antiguan ambassador to Britain—recalls, "I was somewhat skeptical" about bringing the case, especially given the adversary's clout and experience in trade disputes. Still, Antiguan officials were upset about U.S. policy, which was contributing to a shrinkage of the country's online gambling industry. So the government gave the go-ahead for the case—provided the industry footed the legal bills. (It is worth noting in this context that such a solution wouldn't work for, say, cotton farmers in Burkina Faso.) "Did we not have a duty to our citizens to protect their jobs?" Sir Ronald asks.

The initial result came on March 24, 2004—"the single worst day of my professional life," recalls John Veroneau, who was then general counsel of the Office of the U.S. Trade Representative. His unpleasant duty was to inform Bob Zoellick that the United States had lost the case.

The ruling by a three-member WTO panel was such a sweeping victory for Antigua that it was widely predicted that the Appellate Body would overturn it. The panel's decision came despite the insistence by Washington that it had never intended to include gambling when it agreed to open the "recreational, cultural and sporting services" market. The panel was also unswayed by another seemingly compelling argument by the United States known as the "public morals and public order" defense, which essentially means that WTO members can ban goods and services that they fear might harm their social fabric (a classic example being the prohibition of liquor in Muslim countries). That defense appeared sure to prevail at the appellate level.

There was, however, a gaping hole in the American position: The U.S. government was tolerating Internet betting on horse races and, in some states, lotteries and other games. Numerous U.S. sites, going by names such as Youbet.com and Xpressbet.com, were letting users wager on races from the New Jersey Meadowlands to the Louisiana Downs. This was blatant hypocrisy, claimed the Antiguans, who contended that the U.S. stance violated the bedrock WTO principle of national treatment. The principle, as noted previously, essentially requires a government to treat foreign goods and services the same as it does domestic ones. To outlaw liquor imports, for example, a Muslim country must ban domestic brewing, too. Likewise, the Antiguans contended, the United States can bar citizens from using overseas gambling sites only if it bans domestic sites as well. Yet Congress had refused to enact a comprehensive ban, in part because the politically influential horse racing industry depends on phone and Internet wagers.

So if the United States was going to tolerate a limited amount of vice while banning a foreign supplier of vice, it would run afoul of WTO rules. That argument carried the day with the Appellate Body, which ruled in April 2005 that Washington must either crack down on all forms of online gambling, including horse racing, or Antigua won.

It looked as if Jay Cohen's revenge fantasy was truly on the verge of realization. But at this point, another major inequity in the WTO system was coming into play. When a government like the European Union wins a case and threatens to retaliate, as Brussels did in the steel dispute, the losing country is obliged to pay heed because of the size of the European market. The effectiveness of such a threat is far more questionable for nations of Antigua's scale. The danger of losing export sales in the Antiguan market would barely arouse notice in U.S. corporate circles. In other words, the ability to inflict punishment on opponents and to muscle them into compliance with WTO rulings is reserved for the fairly rich and fairly big. Developing countries may win cases against wealthy adversaries at the WTO, but that doesn't necessarily mean they have the leverage to attain their objectives.

Or do they? Of all the bizarre twists in this case, the most dramatic may be yet to come—Antigua's transformation into the Pirate of the Caribbean.

| * |

Fast-forward to the spring of 2009, as this book is being finished. Despite having won a WTO ruling in its favor in 2004, and another victory at the appellate level in 2005, Antigua still hasn't been able to get satisfaction, in the form either of changed U.S. policy or of a clear right to inflict severe punishment on the United States. And much the same goes for Brazil in the *Upland Cotton* case.

In the Internet gambling case, Washington has been able to use a series of legal ploys to keep the Antiguans tied up in endless litigation. For a while, the Bush administration, using the flimsiest of pretexts, claimed that the United States had complied with the WTO ruling.* The frustrated Antiguans went back to the WTO for a ruling that Washington was still not in compliance, and again Antigua won, though only after many months of wrangling. The U.S. government then used yet another maneuver to keep the Antiguans at bay, the complex details of which need not concern us; suffice it to say that even members of Congress decried the tactic as setting a bad precedent that could undermine international respect for the WTO.

All the while, the Antiguans have been brandishing a new kind of weapon, never before used in a WTO dispute, which has some leading U.S. companies squirming.

Picture a factory in Antigua that is churning out millions of dollars' worth of uncopyrighted versions of American DVDs, music CDs, or computer software, with full support from the Antiguan authorities. Ordinarily that would violate the WTO's intellectual property rules. But the Antiguans asked the WTO for the right to do something like this, which involves a technique called "cross-retaliation." The reasoning is that because raising Antiguan tariffs on American

---

*The administration first vowed to secure legislation "clarifying" that all forms of online betting are illegal in the United States. But the horse racing industry blocked such legislation on Capitol Hill. In its next attempt to claim that it was in compliance with the WTO ruling, the administration cited some April 2006 testimony by a Justice Department official asserting that all Internet wagering across state lines, including that on horses, violates existing laws. This assertion was news to the horse racing industry, and it seemed to have little effect on the actual wagering, which continued without prosecution.

goods isn't an effective means of punishing Washington, Antigua ought to have the right to abridge U.S. rights in another area of the WTO rule book.

There's a delicious irony in this situation, because the United States was once the chief advocate of establishing the right to cross-retaliate. Washington insisted during the Uruguay Round that if it was to gain the effective ability to protect American firms' intellectual property, it should be allowed to impose tariffs against the goods of countries that were found guilty of allowing the piracy of American movies, drugs, and other such products.

Now the shoe is on the other foot. Shortly before Christmas 2007, a WTO panel agreed that Antigua had the right to cross-retaliate. But whether this right would be worth much still isn't clear. For one thing, the panel said that Antigua had the right to only $21 million worth of retaliatory damages, which was the panel's estimate of Antiguan losses attributable to illegal U.S. policies. This left legal scholars scratching their heads over how $21 million of cross-retaliation should be calculated. Should it be based on the production costs of making the copycat products, or on the market value of the legal versions of the products being copied? An even more important uncertainty concerns Antigua's right to export the copycatted material. U.S. officials have emphatically maintained that any copycatting Antigua does must be confined to products sold in Antigua's small domestic market. For the time being, the Antiguans are waiting out this ambiguous situation, hoping that a Democratic president and Democratic Congress may be more willing to negotiate a satisfactory outcome.

Meanwhile, back in Room E, another hearing was held in the *Upland Cotton* case on March 3, 2009. At stake this time: Should this case also end with the awarding of a license to commit piracy—a truly gigantic one, held by Brazil?

| * |

Introducing the Brazilian argument that day was Roberto Azevedo, the country's ambassador to the WTO. "It has been a very, very long time" since the original set of hearings in 2003, Azevedo observed to the panelists, who included an Irish economist, a Mexican government official, and the same Australian attorney who had served on the 2003 panel. "This is now the fifth WTO proceeding [in the dispute] spanning a period of more than six years."

As the envoy's remarks suggest, even Brazil, though endowed with a much bigger market than Antigua, has also encountered plenty of frustrations in its efforts to obtain its just deserts following its landmark victory on cotton subsidies. The United States did take some remedial measures in response to the WTO ruling in 2004; Congress eliminated one of the most outrageous parts of

U.S. cotton policy, a program that paid U.S. textile mills to buy American-grown cotton. But U.S. lawmakers and administration officials insisted that other, bigger cotton subsidies ought to be negotiated in the Doha Round rather than subject to litigation. The dispute went back to court at the WTO, where tribunals repeatedly ruled that Washington was out of compliance. The Americans still managed to prolong the proceedings by arguing that market conditions for cotton had changed drastically over the years. That phase of the dispute was also judged in Brazil's favor, though only after another delay.

So at long last, on that early March day in Room E, the case was coming down to the question of what Brazil would be allowed to do in retribution, including whether the country should, like Antigua, get the right to cross-retaliate. U.S. lawyers argued that Brasilia shouldn't be authorized to do much—the damage from the cotton subsidies wasn't that great, the Americans contended, and in any case, given the size and diversity of its economy, Brazil could easily "exact a serious economic cost" on Washington by using the traditional method of raising tariffs on U.S. exports.

That argument "entirely misses the point," according to Azevedo's statement to the panel. "The reality that the United States cannot hide is that this is not a dispute between equals—not even close to that." He noted that the U.S. economy is "some ten times larger than Brazil's" and that exports to Brazil account for only about 1.7 percent of U.S. exports. This meant that Brasilia could exert scant leverage over Washington by raising tariffs; in fact, doing so would only hurt the Brazilian economy, because the vast bulk of the U.S. goods coming into Brazil are items the nation badly needs, such as agricultural and industrial components and machinery. "Your decision in these proceedings will bear directly on the health of the multilateral trading system," Azevedo concluded. "The credibility of that system is at stake," because by giving Brazil the right to cross-retaliate, "you would be signaling that the WTO system of enforcement works not only for the developed members." A ruling was expected in the summer of 2009, too close to the publication of this book for its inclusion here.

| * |

Both the *Upland Cotton* and *Gambling* cases may drag on for still more years. They should be kept in proper perspective. These disputes are highly illuminating, because they show that developing countries may face an unfairly uphill battle in obtaining enforcement of WTO rulings that go in their favor. But these cases are not representative. In many instances, rich countries comply fairly readily with WTO judgments rendered against them in cases brought by developing nations. One of the first WTO cases, for example, involved a complaint by Costa Rica against the United States involving underwear quotas. When Washington lost, it promptly brought its policies into compliance.

In sum, the defects of the Dispute Settlement Understanding should not obscure its considerable virtues. It fosters stability and serves to some extent as a great equalizer. Perhaps most important, the dispute settlement side of the WTO instills the whole institution with credibility that was lacking during the GATT era. And the dispute settlement side functions at a relatively high degree of effectiveness. Trade negotiations, to which our narrative now returns, are a different matter entirely.

# 9 | HIS HOLINESS, POPE BOB

"JACK'S BACK" MEANT THAT BOB ZOELLICK WAS IN AN ESPECIALLY foul mood. It was an expression his aides coined after hearing Zoellick seethe, "That guy doesn't know jack shit!" Accordingly, when his temper seemed to be getting the better of him, the word at the Office of the U.S. Trade Representative was that "Jack" had returned. The expression was in especially common use during the fall of 2003, in the aftermath of Cancún. "Boy, was Jack back then," shivers one of Zoellick's former aides.

As well he might be. Cancún had thrown Zoellick's agenda into peril. With the Doha Round stuck, his hope of building one trade success atop another, culminating in a finish for the round by 2005, appeared remote at best. Moreover, according to the prevailing wisdom, little would happen on the trade front in 2004 because of the presidential election. Democrats would surely pounce on any moves the Bush administration made that might put American jobs at risk from globalized commerce, and Republicans would strongly resist any U.S. concessions on farm-trade issues that might cost them votes in rural areas. Thus progress in liberalizing markets would have to wait.

Anyone who knew Zoellick knew that he wasn't going to lie down and give up during the final year of Bush's first term. Having publicly derided the Clintonites for failing to match their free-trade rhetoric with action in the late 1990s, he was determined to ensure that he and the president he served would produce a much different sort of record. But in his resolve to make a mark, he was pursuing a policy course that took the global trading system in a new direction— a disturbing one, even to many who were sympathetic to his overall goal of trade liberalization.

Reflecting his frustration over the events in Cancún was an op-ed he wrote in the *Financial Times* on September 22, 2003, a few days after the meeting. He blasted his adversaries—Brazil was mentioned five times—for having fostered a "culture of protest that defined victory in terms of political acts rather than economic results." He made it clear that he was going to reward cooperative countries and punish uncooperative ones by intensifying his "competitive liberalization" strategy of pursuing trade deals on multiple levels:

> The key division at Cancún was between the can-do and the won't-do. For over two years, the U.S. has pushed to open markets globally, in our hemisphere, and with sub-regions or individual countries. As WTO members ponder the future, the U.S. will not wait. We will move towards free trade with can-do countries.

America's market of 300 million free-spending consumers, in other words, would be used as both a carrot and a stick. Countries that shared Washington's enthusiasm for freer trade would obtain preferential access to that market by signing bilateral and regional agreements eliminating most trade barriers between them and the United States. Meanwhile, the ranks of the reluctant would be left at a disadvantage; their products would be subject to the tariffs that Washington maintained on MFN terms for members of the WTO. Eventually, they would recognize that their self-interest lay in joining the U.S.-led bandwagon, the result being that small deals would prove to be "building blocks" toward bigger ones and, ultimately, a worldwide one.

Regional and bilateral free-trade agreements were nothing new, of course. The European Union was the granddaddy of the regionals; its success had inspired several imitations, including NAFTA, Mercosur (Brazil, Argentina, Uruguay, and Paraguay), and the trade agreement among members of the Association of Southeast Asian Nations (Thailand, Indonesia, Malaysia, Singapore, the Philippines, and several others).* Long-standing bilaterals included the United States–Israel deal in 1985, Canada-Chile in 1996, Mexico-Chile in 1999, and European Union–Mexico in 2000. The European Union also signed a number of agreements during the 1990s with neighboring countries, such as Norway and Iceland, and with a passel of nations that were candidates for E.U.

---

*The European Union and Mercosur are customs unions, which are different from free-trade areas such as NAFTA. In a customs union, the member nations not only reduce or eliminate tariffs on trade among themselves but also maintain common external tariffs on goods produced outside the union. In a free-trade area, the members don't have common external tariffs.

membership, including Bulgaria, Poland, Romania, and the Czech and Slovak republics. Indeed, Zoellick often cited these arrangements as justifying an aggressive U.S. effort to conclude free-trade agreements, on the grounds that Washington needed to catch up with its competitors.

But the trend really went into overdrive after Zoellick secured the legislative authority he needed in 2002 and began rapidly expanding Washington's portfolio of free-trade accords. By the fall of 2003, he had completed two bilateral agreements that had been launched during the Clinton years—with Chile and Singapore. In addition, he had initiated negotiations with Australia, Morocco, and five Central American nations (Guatemala, Honduras, El Salvador, Nicaragua, and Costa Rica) plus the Dominican Republic. He was also exploring similar deals with Thailand, Bahrain, Colombia, Peru, and a group of southern African nations.

In Zoellick's view, these pacts offered an array of advantages. They gave Washington a chance to get more from willing partners than it could extract in the WTO context, because not only did the deals involve cutting tariffs all the way to zero on a broad range of products, but they also gave American companies certain benefits that went beyond WTO rules. In particular, these deals usually contained provisions protecting the rights of U.S. investors and service providers, plus rules on intellectual property rights protection that were stricter than the WTO's. By keeping the U.S. domestic debate focused on free trade rather than stopping protectionist initiatives, bilateral accords also enabled the executive branch to stay on "offense" with Congress. Also important to Zoellick were the synergies between these accords and U.S. foreign policy goals. The agreements with Morocco and Bahrain, for example, would help encourage free-market reforms and American-style rule of law in the Islamic world, serving as a model for other Muslim nations.

Moreover, the agreements provided a new raison d'être to the Office of the U.S. Trade Representative.

"While the WTO was the right thing to do and we did some good things, thank God Bob Zoellick did FTAs [free-trade agreements] too," said Allen Johnson, the former chief agriculture negotiator. "If all I could have worked on was the WTO and the [Free Trade Area of the Americas], at times I think I probably would have considered killing myself." Matt Niemeyer, who was the chief congressional relations man in Zoellick's office at the time, echoes that sentiment, saying that the bilateral agreements "chewed up the [assistant U.S. trade representatives], but they loved the victories. They loved them, because once they had done one, they had a trophy on the wall," which, of course, would enhance their employment prospects when they were ready to go into the private sector.

But the more bilateral agreements Zoellick finished and the more negotiations he initiated, the more misgivings arose: Were these "trophies on the wall" just that—trophies, to make the administration's trade agenda (and its trade representative) appear active, aggressive, and successful? And even if bilateral deals were commonly thought of as advancing "globalization," did they really help the globalization cause? Or might they do that cause more harm than good?

| * |

Grant Aldonas vividly remembers the day he found out that the United States was launching negotiations with Morocco on a free-trade agreement, because both he and his then boss, Commerce Secretary Donald Evans, learned about it in the newspaper. As commerce undersecretary for international trade, Aldonas would have liked to have been informed beforehand, so that he could have expressed his reservations.

Within the administration, Aldonas was one among a few voices dissenting from Zoellick's penchant for bilaterals. He was hearing from Republican friends on Capitol Hill that the sheer volume of agreements was eroding support for trade in Congress. For lawmakers of either party, supporting a trade pact often means giving an opponent ammunition in the next election. So Aldonas could not help questioning what great purpose lay behind Zoellick's bilateral wheeling and dealing. It would have been one thing if the deals Washington was striking had involved big economies, but eliminating trade barriers with those trading partners posed too many political problems; the European Union, for instance, was not about to fully expose its agricultural market to U.S. competition. Canada and Mexico, which were major markets for U.S. exporters because of their proximity, were already part of NAFTA. That left Zoellick with a motley assortment of partners available for bilateral talks, most of them having relatively puny markets of limited interest to American exporters. Australia, one of the biggest economies with which Zoellick was negotiating, was already relatively open.

"We were ignored," Aldonas shrugs.

Others outside the administration had more fundamental objections—namely, that Zoellick, in his zeal to transact agreements, was making a hash of the principles of multilateralism. This criticism came mainly from academic economists, led by Jagdish Bhagwati of Columbia University and Ross Garnaut of the Australian National University. They ranked among the world's most distinguished and ardent advocates of free trade, but they were horrified by the bilateral arrangements Zoellick was pursuing. Yes, they acknowledged, the architects of the GATT had included special provisions allowing for free-trade agreements. "But that misses the point. There is no evidence that they had in mind an epidemic of FTAs that would spread far more effectively than severe acute respiratory syndrome," Bhagwati and Garnaut wrote in a July 2003 op-ed opposing the U.S.-Australian pact. The problem, they fretted, "has turned systemic," and they blamed the Bush administration for making bilateralism all the rage in the world's trade ministries, noting that "hundreds more possible FTAs have been the subject of discussions since Australia first responded to the Bush team's new approach to FTAs in late 2000."

The "epidemic" of which they spoke was spreading because each free-trade agreement that was struck—or even rumored to be in the works—tended to beget others. When policymakers saw their counterparts in neighboring countries negotiating them, they often concluded that they had better join the club lest they end up encircled by trade blocs from which they were excluded.

Thus, even countries that had once been the staunchest supporters of multilateralism were hooking up in bilateral arrangements. The trading giants of northeast Asia—Japan, South Korea, and China—had long spurned all deals other than multilateral ones, but in 2002 Japan signed an accord with Singapore, and it was pursuing talks with Malaysia and several other trading partners. "Back in the 1980s and early 1990s, we were not interested in free trade agreements, but since then, we have started to become surrounded by these groups, in Europe and the United States," Noboru Hatakeyama, chairman of the Japan External Trade Organization, explained to the *New York Times*. South Korea, not to be outdone by its rival, was soon linking with Chile and with the Southeast Asian bloc, as was China. Australia, whose only previous agreement had been one with New Zealand dating from the 1960s, signed agreements with Singapore in 2002 and with Thailand in 2003. Singapore hooked up with India, not long after the Indians did the same with Thailand.

Many of these agreements were more symbol than substance. They typically exempted certain politically sensitive sectors, especially agriculture, and thus only marginally enhanced opportunities for commerce between the participating countries. But each added another noodle to what Bhagwati called global trade's "spaghetti bowl." Each entailed a set of complex rules to make sure that goods receiving duty-free treatment were really supposed to do so. NAFTA, for example, requires some two hundred pages of rules spelling out how products qualify as North American—for in the absence of such rules, what would prevent, say, a Vietnamese shirt maker from shipping its shirts to Mexico, sewing on labels stamped "Made in Mexico," and selling them in the United States duty-free? And what exactly would qualify the shirts as Mexican-made—the stitching, the fabric, or the yarn, or would all three be required? Adding even more strands of pasta to the spaghetti bowl were a plethora of one-way agreements in which rich nations give special treatment to some of the products made in poor ones; examples include the African Growth and Opportunity Act in the United States and the European Union's preferential treatment of its former colonies.

The potential damage to multilateralism caused by free-trade agreements goes much deeper than the additional complexity involved. Bilaterals and regional deals may undermine the WTO's authority by relegating it to the status of bit player in the setting of trade rules. At the very least, such agreements play havoc with the MFN principle by promoting discrimination within the WTO's ranks. After all, every time two beaming trade ministers stand before the television cameras to shake hands and announce the completion of a free-trade agreement, one dirty aspect of the deal almost invariably gets overlooked—the impact on outsiders, who lose some trade opportunities they otherwise would have had.

Then there's the problem that economists call "preference erosion." Each new free-trade agreement or preferential arrangement creates constituencies that fight against worldwide liberalization because their special access to a lucrative market loses value when their competitors in other countries gain the same low-tariff treatment. As a result, bilaterals and other such deals can easily turn into stumbling blocks, rather than building blocks, for global pacts.

To all these objections, Zoellick consistently argued that his critics were hopelessly idealistic and naive. In his view, bilaterals were not inimical to multilateralism. Quite the contrary: They were essential to the WTO's success. "The ability to be able to say, 'We'll do bilaterals' is very important when you're trying to negotiate a WTO agreement," he says. "The academics have never sat in these negotiating rooms or negotiated with Congress. I'm a believer in the multilateral system and worldwide free markets. But I also understand how to use national power. Bilaterals have been a very useful means of exerting influence. They also have benefits in their own right."

Some countries, no doubt, can be cowed by threats that the United States will forge bilaterals with other nations. But how many? Because U.S. tariffs are already low in general, the prospect of being excluded from Washington's list of free-trade partners is not necessarily terrifying for policymakers in all capitals.

A few weeks after Cancún, the limitations of the competitive liberalization strategy became starkly apparent.

| * |

Completing the Free Trade Area of the Americas was one of George W. Bush's top trade priorities. As a Texan who had campaigned on the importance to the

United States of deepening ties with its southern neighbors, the president was personally enamored of the proposal to create an expansion of NAFTA that would span the Western Hemisphere. His administration's big chance to advance the pact came at a meeting in Miami in November 2003, where representatives of thirty-four nations from North America, Latin America, and the Caribbean gathered, with Zoellick leading the U.S. delegation.

As in the case of other free-trade agreements that Washington had struck, the Bush administration was insisting on making the agreement comprehensive—"the gold standard," as U.S. officials liked to say. This meant the deal would include provisions ensuring that all member nations would provide new access to each other's companies in investment and services, while also affording extensive protection to those companies' intellectual property rights. Backing the United States in its vision for the free-trade area were several influential hemispheric powers, notably Canada, Chile, and Costa Rica.

Unfortunately for Zoellick, one of the countries that had given him heartburn in Cancún was leading the resistance to the U.S. approach. Brazilian president Lula da Silva had won office campaigning on a view of hemispheric integration that was almost the polar opposite of Bush's—namely, that the regional trade accord would be tantamount to U.S. "annexation" of Latin America. As the biggest Latin American nation, Brazil had few qualms about rejecting Washington's all-encompassing vision of the deal, and the Brazilians could take comfort in the support they were getting from Argentina, South America's second-largest power. Once solidly pro-American, Argentina was recovering from a wrenching economic crisis that had left its policymakers much less infatuated than before with the U.S. capitalist model. These countries' governments were taking the stance that the only Free Trade Area of the Americas they could consider joining was one stripped to its bare essentials— tariff reductions for the goods traded between its member nations. That was unacceptable to Washington.

Notwithstanding the supposedly fearsome power that Zoellick was wielding, he could not bully the Brazilians and Argentines into submission. The U.S. trade representative's repeated warnings that the United States would strike free-trade agreements with their neighbors failed to move either Brazil or Argentina from its position. Martín Redrado, who was then Argentina's trade secretary, recalls shrugging off concerns that exporters in other Latin American nations would have moderately better access to the U.S. market than would Argentine exporters. "At this point, the E.U. is our number 1 market, then Brazil, then Asia excluding Japan, and the *fourth* is NAFTA—that is, mainly the U.S.," Redrado says. "I told Zoellick and the other American negotiators, 'This is not a matter of ideology. I have been trained as an economist in the U.S. I want closer relations with the U.S. But I am defending my country's interests.'"

To avert another Cancún-style blowup—just two months after Cancún itself—Zoellick had to work out a face-saving accord with Brazil's Celso Amorim that glossed over their differences. The Miami meeting ended with a pledge to continue pursuing a Free Trade Area of the Americas but little that went beyond that. The countries of the hemisphere might integrate with each other fully or narrowly; the details would be left to future negotiations.

Nobody was fooled when, in the closing press conference, the attending ministers claimed their meeting had been a success. Privately, U.S. negotiators admitted that plans for the free-trade area were stalled because major participants couldn't even come close to reaching common ground on the most basic terms. Ever since then, the hemispheric pact has remained moribund.

The long and the short of it was, competitive liberalization had come a cropper. Big countries with big markets had refused to be intimidated by the use of the ploy. Not that Zoellick would admit it. Undaunted, he announced plans at Miami for even more talks aimed at striking bilateral agreements. Colombia, Peru, Panama, Ecuador, and Bolivia joined the already-long list of potential free-trade partners for the United States. For the spaghetti bowl, more penne, farfalle, and capellini were to be added to the mix.

Then Zoellick did something completely unexpected. Having arguably ravaged the multilateral system, he turned his attention to giving it a new lease on life.

| * |

Global trade talks often follow a pattern of death and resurrection in which a highly publicized falling-out tends to force negotiators toward convergence at their next meeting. Death had come in Seattle. Resurrection had followed in Doha. Death had come again in Cancún. Now the question was who, if anyone, could play the role of resurrector.

The answer came in a letter, dated January 11, 2004, addressed to trade ministers of all WTO member nations, which began with the following words: "New Year's Greetings! I hope this finds you well." The letter exhorted member nations to try to make significant progress in the Doha Round in the coming months and set forth some ideas for how to do so. It was the kind of thing the WTO director-general might have done, but the occupant of that job, Supachai Panitchpakdi, was showing no sign of the dynamism required to galvanize the membership. In fact, the author of the letter was Zoellick, who—with his conviction that the United States must exercise leadership and with confidence in his skill at making big things happen—was ready to step into the breach. Zoellick wrote:

> Here is my frank assessment: there is a general interest in advancing the Doha Development Agenda, and even a sense that our struggles at Cancún may have laid some useful foundations. Yet there is uncertainty about how to reengage productively so that we can make the necessary decisions.
>
> I do not want 2004 to be a lost year for the WTO negotiations.

That was a surprise, because as noted in the *Financial Times*, which broke the news of Zoellick's initiative, "with the U.S. presidential elections coming in November, many WTO members had resigned themselves to making only minimal progress this year." Yet here was the U.S. trade representative, an appointee of the man running for reelection, essentially stating that he was willing to take some political risks—provided, of course, that his counterparts were as well.

It was surprising also because Zoellick's disgust with the balky WTO, and his preference for going the bilateral and regional route, had seemed so pronounced after Cancún. But Zoellick was above all a transactions-oriented policymaker who wanted to post achievements on the trade liberalization front in whatever way he could. Some forward movement in the Doha talks seemed possible; for one thing, Zoellick's agricultural aides were advising him that U.S. farm groups were much more interested in a worldwide pact than they were in the bilateral accords Washington was contemplating.

In the seven-page letter, Zoellick held out some olive branches to developing countries. Importantly, he backed away from the U.S.-E.U. paper on agriculture that had so riled low-income nations prior to Cancún. Whereas the paper had envisioned that some export subsidies for farm products might survive, Zoellick wrote in his letter that there was no way the Doha Round could be concluded "unless we have an agreement to eliminate export subsidies by a date certain." Because the termination of export subsidies would mostly entail pain for the European Union, he said that Washington would be willing to offer some related concessions in return—specifically, changing U.S. farm policy to eliminate programs that are similar to export subsidies, such as federally funded credit for exports. He also hinted that he would be willing to offer some concessions on the cotton issue. (At that point, the WTO panel decision in Brazil's cotton case was still four months away.)

It was a plucky initiative, and, as on other occasions, Zoellick did not bother to vet his plan with the White House prior to launching it. He had gotten indirect encouragement from President Bush after Cancún, when the president asked at a cabinet meeting how he planned to revive the round. That was enough for him to feel comfortable closing his letter by reemphasizing that 2004 should be "a year that exceeds expectations and delivers for the Doha Development Agenda."

Zoellick did need to ask the White House for one thing—a plane—because he followed up his letter with a two-week, round-the-world trip in February to meet with his fellow trade ministers and promote his idea of making progress on Doha in 2004. The 32,000-mile journey made him the most traveled of any cabinet member, including Secretary of State Colin Powell; he stopped in Japan, China, Singapore, Pakistan, India, South Africa, Kenya, Switzerland, and France. On February 13, during his stop in Singapore, he unveiled his proposed plan for the year: WTO members would hold a major meeting in Geneva over the summer—not a full-blown ministerial, but one in which some ministers would attend and other countries would be represented by their ambassadors. "Our goal," he said, "would be to try to get done this summer if possible what we didn't get done in Cancún."

To do that, a new process would be needed for advancing the negotiations. Zoellick took a leaf from the Chinese military strategist Sun Tzu, who famously advised, "Keep your friends close, and your enemies closer." He had not even wanted to meet with the G-20 at Cancún; now he would accept the inevitable. He would welcome their leaders into a new WTO power elite.

| * |

Celso Amorim was in Argentina for a meeting in January 2004 when a phone call came from Zoellick. The Brazilian foreign minister thought the topic would probably be a tiresome one—the Free Trade Area of the Americas. To his surprise, their conversation on that subject lasted only a few minutes. "The rest of it was about how we should resume the WTO negotiations," Amorim recalls. "Zoellick told me, 'I've been thinking about a number of countries, both developed and developing, which might lead the game.'"

The multilateral trading system has always governed itself with a "concentric circle" system, in which small groups of nations first try to reach agreements that are then passed on to wider groups for consideration, with consensus ultimately required from the entire membership. As noted in Chapter 2, the most exclusive clique during much of the GATT period was the Quad, consisting of the United States, the European Union, Japan, and Canada. Their four trade ministers met periodically at various locations around the world to discuss key issues in the multilateral system while reporters camped outside awaiting the possible dissemination of a joint decision that would presumably have major influence over global trade policy. Nobody could claim that this self-anointed group was democratic; the main justification for its existence was that agreement among its members was a necessary first step toward the adoption of any formal policy, given their dominance over trade flows in the sectors (primarily manufacturing) for which rules were being drafted.

The Quad continued to meet during the first few years of the WTO's existence, but it gradually went into eclipse as the Doha Round got under way. Its exclusively rich-country membership seemed more anachronistic than ever at a time when large developing countries were growing by leaps and bounds in economic importance and assertiveness. The inclusion of the Japanese, moreover, was obviously a turnoff as far as Zoellick was concerned. The replacement for the Quad, he reckoned, needed to be roughly the same size as before, with both U.S. and E.U. trade ministers still included, but with the rest of the participants reflecting the shift that was taking place in global economic clout.

Who would make the cut, and who wouldn't? This distinction was important, because although those in the innermost circle could not force their agreements down the throats of outsiders, they could put the onus on others to reject it.

Pushing and tugging went on for months. Brazil was an obvious choice, as the leader of the G-20. The European Union wanted India included because of their shared defensive position on agricultural tariffs. Zoellick likewise insisted on bringing in an ally on the farming issue—namely, Australia, which led the coalition of agricultural exporting countries. Out went Japan and Canada, over especially vigorous protests from the Japanese. A Brazilian policymaker recalls that Tokyo sent a high-ranking official to Brasilia "begging to be let in"—a futile effort, given Zoellick's low esteem for their prior contributions.

By May 2004, the updated and slightly expanded version of the Quad—the "Five Interested Parties," as they called themselves—were meeting often. They consisted of officials from various levels of the U.S., E.U., Brazilian, Indian, and Australian trade ministries, and they had a self-assigned mandate to negotiate the outlines of an agreement on agriculture for submission to the rest of the WTO membership. They had a relatively short deadline for doing so, because that month, plans were announced for the WTO ministerial meeting that Zoellick had proposed. The ministerial would take place in late July in Geneva, with the aim of producing a "framework" to guide the rest of the Doha negotiations.

"The WTO volcano is smoking again," Lamy triumphantly declared on May 14, when the plans for the ministerial were unveiled.

The European trade commissioner had done his part to activate the volcano. A few days earlier, he had offered a number of substantive concessions to help create auspicious conditions for the forthcoming meeting in Geneva. On May 10, over strenuous objections from France, Lamy jointly announced with Agriculture Commissioner Franz Fischler that Brussels could agree to the full elimination of export subsidies as a key component of the Doha Round. The European Union had already cut such subsidies by two-thirds since the early 1990s, to about $4 billion, and Fischler said, "Provided we get a balanced deal . . . we are ready to put all export subsidies on the table."

And Lamy was proffering even more goodies. He said the European Union was finally dropping its demands that the round include negotiations on those Singapore issues that were most objectionable to developing countries—namely, investment, competition, and government procurement. (The one issue that would remain on the agenda was trade facilitation, which was much less controversial than the others.) This concession removed a major sticking point from the talks. Moreover, Lamy proposed a "round for free" for the WTO's poorest members—in particular, those that qualified as least-developed countries, which were mostly located in sub-Saharan Africa and the Caribbean. A free round meant that those nations would be exempt from having to open their own markets beyond their existing WTO commitments, even though they would benefit from the market-opening measures taken by wealthier countries.

Not all WTO members were grateful for Lamy's sacrificial moves. Fans of the Singapore issues, such as the Japanese and South Koreans, were unhappy over being abandoned by the European Union. Also upset were officials of some developing countries that were not poor enough to be included in the "round for free" offer. "Saying some members don't have to do anything is the wrong approach," grumbled Youssef Boutros-Ghali, Egypt's trade minister.

But Lamy got his way, underscoring that he, like Zoellick, was still a potent force in the WTO. Indeed, the Five Interested Parties boasted some extraordinarily high wattage in terms of the expertise and experience of the participating ministers. Zoellick was in the fourth year of his tenure, and Lamy was in his fifth, as was Australia's Mark Vaile. For his part, Amorim could match or even surpass the others in his mastery of the agenda before them; although he was not as long-serving a minister as they were, he could draw on his service in Geneva as Brazil's WTO ambassador.

The Five Interested Parties also included a newbie, however. In this group, he stood out. Nobody would mistake him for a trade technocrat. And it was easy to tell that, sooner or later, he was likely to tangle in a major way with the U.S. trade representative, whoever that might be.

| * |

"Kamal Nath!" bellowed a young man, pumping his fist skyward as he stood in a rutted dirt road, surrounded by a crowd consisting of weather-beaten laborers with long beards and turbans, old women in saris with bangles on their wrists, and little boys with skullcaps.

The responding roar from the crowd— "*Zindabad!*"—is Hindi for "long live." The chant was repeated to the hypnotic beat of drums as a brightly dressed troupe of teenagers danced ecstatically. "Kamal Nath! *Zindabad!* Kamal Nath! *Zindabad!*"

An open jeep bearing Nath, India's commerce and industry minister, was inching through a town in the impoverished central Indian district he has represented in the Indian Parliament for nearly thirty years. As the jeep wended past tin-roofed hovels and ramshackle shops, people thronged the vehicle seeking to thrust garlands of flowers over Nath's head, to touch his feet (a traditional gesture of respect), or to hand him letters seeking favors. Dressed in a traditional loose-fitting shirt and trousers called a *kurta-pyjama*, Nath managed to make appearances in six towns and villages that day, flying around in a helicopter. In each place, he got similarly enthusiastic receptions from crowds numbering in the thousands.

As this scene suggests, Nath is a political animal through and through. That set him well apart from his colleagues in the Five Interested Parties; the closest Zoellick or Lamy might come to arousing frenzies among masses of people would be earnest applause for their speeches at think tanks. Nath's style in the negotiating room was also in sharp contrast to that of the others. Often bored by the discussions, his hands would slip every couple of minutes into his pockets for his cell phone or BlackBerry, with which he fiddled constantly. When he spoke, his dark eyes darted and his speech erupted in rapid-fire bursts. Limited though his attention span and capacity for lucid analysis might have been, his storehouse of one-liners was not. "Next time can you bring a picture of an American farmer?" he reportedly quipped at one of his first international trade meetings. "I have never actually seen one. I have only seen U.S. conglomerates masquerading as farmers."

Short, with his jet-black hair swept back, Nath comes from an extremely privileged background. He flies to his constituency on his personal jet, a Hawker 850 with five plush leather seats and a couch, and the chopper he uses to helihop around also belongs to him. Yet he has a keen grasp of what the common Indian wants.

He is the scion of a family that built a business empire based in Kolkata (or Calcutta, as it was previously known). Educated at the Doon School, a private boarding school for boys, he became very close to Prime Minister Indira

Gandhi's younger son Sanjay, who died at age thirty-three in a plane crash. After graduating from a Jesuit college, Nath joined the ruling Congress Party as a youth worker, and he launched his political career in 1980 by running for Parliament from Chhindwara, in the state of Madhya Pradesh, where his family had substantial landholdings, though with its heavily tribal population and tropical forests, the area was as far from his upbringing as could be imagined. "I had had little exposure to or direct experience of the indigence, the desperation, and the utter helplessness that defined my district," Nath recalled in his book *India's Century*, noting that "very few" of his constituents were literate, only a few hundred of the 2,000 villages were electrified, and "even an oil lamp was a luxury." His prospects for victory got a crucial boost from Mrs. Gandhi, who was highly popular among the tribal peoples and traveled to the area to tell them in a speech: "This is my third son. You have to make him win." They did, and Nath quickly learned that the way to boost his fortunes was to use his influence to effect the spread of electrical power, roads, medical clinics, and other such necessities of life to as many of Chhindwara's denizens as possible.

In a country where voters regularly throw out incumbent politicians, Nath won reelection over and over, even when the Congress Party was out of power. As the party's general secretary, he played a key role in the 2004 contest in which Congress wrested control of the government back from the ruling Hindu Nationalists. Congress politicians inflicted heavy damage on their foes by accusing them of ignoring the needs of the rural population amid the nation's high-tech boom. Nath's reward was his appointment as commerce and industry minister, which includes the trade portfolio.

All Indian trade ministers routinely vow to protect Indian agriculture. Nath elevated the practice to high art. Understandably, he wanted to protect the Congress Party from the same accusation—neglecting the residents of the countryside—that had been used to such devastating effect against the Hindu Nationalists. So in meetings among the Five Interested Parties, Nath tended to remain quiet until the time came to discuss the question of how Indian farmers would be sheltered from steep tariff cuts. He dwelled constantly on the threats facing the nation's rural populace, which he almost invariably (and hyperbolically) described as consisting of "650 million subsistence farmers," and he frequently reminded his colleagues that for Indian farmers who fall heavily into debt, suicide is an all-too-common escape. "For us, it's life and death" was one of his constant refrains.

Behind Nath's concern lay some cold mathematics. If concluded, the Doha Round was certain to cut agricultural tariffs progressively—that is, with the highest tariffs reduced by the greatest proportion—to achieve maximum liberalization in sectors that had been the most protected. The Americans and other farm exporters were insisting on this, and the European Union had effectively conceded the point prior to Cancún. The exact formula was still uncertain, but the widespread assumption was that tariffs above, say, 50 percent might well be cut by as much as three-quarters. Obviously this would have a major impact on India if it were strictly implemented across the board with no exceptions. New Delhi maintained higher barriers on farm products than all but a handful of countries; its duties on agricultural goods, typically ranging between 35 percent and 50 percent, were two and a half to six times higher than those in other large developing countries such as China, Brazil, or Indonesia. Its protective walls were especially lofty in the main staple crops, notably wheat (with a 50 percent tariff) and rice (87 percent).

Accordingly, defensive countries like India were demanding that such a formula would have to allow a significant number of exceptions, for which tariffs would be cut much less than the progressive formula would dictate. The high-income WTO members, led by the European Union, Japan, and Switzerland, were emphatic on getting a loophole for what they called "sensitive products." This was a bow to political reality, for all parties realized that those governments could not easily survive if they allowed extensive liberalization in every single agricultural product. In Japan and Korea, this meant rice farmers could count on relatively modest tariff cuts; in the European Union, the same would apply to beef and dairy farmers. Even the United States had some products, notably sugar, that it would want to shelter under the "sensitive" label. The only caveat was that for each sensitive product, a country would have to allow some additional quantity to be imported at very low duties before it could apply its high tariffs.

As far as Nath and his allies were concerned, the sensitive products exception was not enough. Together with other countries from the South, including Indonesia, Pakistan, and Jamaica, the Indians were insisting on another set of exceptions for what they called "special products," that is, staple foods such as wheat and rice that were largely grown by small-scale, low-income farmers. This exception would be exclusively for the use of developing countries and would include some products for which tariffs would be left completely untouched. The chief rationale was that countries with large numbers of farmers living at or near subsistence level are especially needful of insulation from the ups and downs of world food prices. The "livelihood security" of these farmers must be paramount, it was argued—meaning that they must be protected from the utter destitution they would probably suffer if they were forced to compete with cheap imports.

"I am here for one reason—special products," Nath often told his counterparts in meetings of the Five Interested Parties. The rubric "special products" covered not only the exclusion of a sizable number of special products from tariff cuts but also the creation of a related loophole, known as the "special safeguard mechanism." Under this mechanism, a WTO developing-country member whose farmers were suffering from a flood of imports in special products could raise tariffs temporarily on those products, even above bound levels.

These loopholes would become major points of contention in the round. Nath's obsession with them can be put in perspective by glimpsing life among those "subsistence farmers" of whom he so often spoke.

| * |

Arjan Singh's turban is checkered, and his white beard is about eight inches long. Together with his sons, one of whom got through fourth grade, the other of whom is completely uneducated, the fifty-five-year-old Singh raises wheat on the four acres he owns in a village called Gobindpura Jawaharwala in India's Punjab state. Singh's house has cement walls and floors, which makes it better than many of the other village homes, but it is still squalid. A cooking room, where water is stored in clay pots, buzzes with flies. Singh, his wife, one of his sons, and two other family members sleep in one room, on dusty cots; a battered, dirty trunk stores clothes. He is indebted to moneylenders; he owes them more than $1,000, on which he pays 18 percent to 20 percent interest. Such debts have led 21 farmers in the village of 3,000 to kill themselves since 1993, according to local officials.

Singh is a good example of a subsistence farmer, in the sense that his family consumes an enormous quantity of its own production. In 2007, when I met him, he told me that over the previous year he had taken about two tons of his wheat to a mill, where it was ground into flour that his wife turned into chapatis (Indian flatbreads) for family meals.

Subsistence farmers shouldn't need protection from imports, as World Bank economists are fond of noting in their criticism of farm policies in India and other developing countries. By definition, subsistence farmers eat what they grow; they are indifferent to prices, so by maintaining high duties on foreign grain, the Indian government must be mainly trying to shelter rich farmers. But Singh's case shows the flaws in that argument. He grows a surplus that he sells, accounting for about half his crop, which is fairly typical of India's small grain farmers, according to Indian agricultural economists. So these farmers do care, quite intensely, about the price their crop fetches, and Indian politicians would be daft to ignore that. On purely political grounds, it is hard to blame officials like Nath for trying to limit the extent to which crop prices might fall; to do otherwise would expose them, too, to charges that they are callously disregarding the welfare of villagers. About 70 percent of the country's 1.1 billion people live in villages, and they vote in astonishingly high percentages.

So is India's government doing the right thing overall for its poor by showing such solicitude for growers of staple foods? The answer to that question is quite a separate matter from the political calculation. A quick look at some of the facts about the Indian economy underlines what many of the country's experts know all too well—that the politicians' professed sympathy for the plight of poor farmers represents the height of hypocrisy.

"Friendly fire" is what Amartya Sen, the Nobel Prize–winning Indian economist, calls the country's antipoverty policies, because just as in the case of a military mistakenly shooting its own troops, the government in New Delhi recklessly victimizes the very people it is claiming to help. High wheat prices may be a boon to Arjan Singh; they are not so for poor Indians who have to spend a huge portion of their daily expenses on food. "The overall effect of high food prices is to hit many of the worst-off members of society extremely hard," Sen writes, "and while they do help some of the farm-based poor, the net effect is quite regressive on distribution." Among groups whose living standards are the most adversely affected, he notes, are slum dwellers, migrant workers, and rural artisans. To be sure, the Food Corporation of India, the giant state enterprise that controls most of the crop trade in the country, distributes staple food, especially wheat and rice, at subsidized prices to people at or near the poverty line. But in many parts of the nation, this program has long been plagued by corruption in which inventory mysteriously gets siphoned off for the benefit of the well-connected, while poor consumers who go to government-run shops typically find the shelves empty or supplied only with grain so pest-riddled as to be inedible. Meanwhile, who gains from the minimum support prices that the government guarantees for growers of wheat, rice, and a number of other staples? Studies have shown that large farms—India does have these; they are owned by relatively wealthy people—get more than ten times the benefits that accrue to small, marginal farmers.

The inescapable conclusion, to which virtually all reputable authorities subscribe, is that instead of coddling its farmers so much, India needs to move the bulk of them into nonagricultural activities. Keeping such a huge portion of the population eking out livings on tiny plots of land, especially with water getting scarcer and scarcer, is a recipe for stagnation and social unrest; the country must rapidly generate alternative sources of income for a population that is on track to surpass China's by the mid-twenty-first century.

To some extent, India's famously thriving information technology (IT) sector is helping create opportunities for job seekers. This industry not only employs software engineers and call-center operators but also creates demand for lawyers, accountants, janitors, drivers, groundskeepers, security guards, maids, and untold other sorts of workers. But the IT sector can absorb only a fraction of India's labor pool. It employs about 1.3 million Indians, according to a report issued in 2007 by the National Association of Software and Service Companies (NASSCOM), the industry's main trade association, and provides indirect employment for about 5.2 million more. A much more promising source of job growth would be light industry—apparel, furniture, metal fabrication, and other labor-intensive businesses—but India's laws and regulations have stifled the country's potential in those sectors. This is yet another example of "friendly fire."

Still, the point remains: The political considerations driving India's farm-trade stance are compelling, even if the long-term economic logic is cockeyed. India can't be expected to make the transition overnight from an economy in which the majority of people depend upon agriculture to an economy in which most people rely for their incomes on manufacturing and the service sector. The United States and Europe made that sort of transition long ago, over many decades, and America *still* heavily subsidizes farmers. Americans, of all people, ought to understand the pressure that causes a politician like Nath to fight for as much protection as possible in the agriculture sector.

"If the U.S. will not reduce its support to farmers when only 2 or 3 percent of the population is engaged in farming, how can you ask much of a country where 60 percent of the population is in agriculture and where it's a life-and-death question?" asks Ashok Gulati, one of India's premier agricultural economists.

A fair point, well worth bearing in mind amid the combat over agricultural issues that would dominate much of the Doha Round in the years to come—the first step being the round's 2004 resurrection. This would be the ultimate illustration of Bob Zoellick's talent in the art of the deal.

| * |

Oh, the shame of it: To be an ambitious politician holding a responsible position in one's government and to travel some distance to an international meeting, only to be shut out of the key discussion, with members of the media observing one's consequent, embarrassing idleness. That was the fate of about two dozen ministers from WTO member countries, who gathered in Geneva during the week of July 26, 2004, for the meeting that Zoellick had envisioned, the one that was supposed to keep 2004 from being a lost year for the Doha Round. The majority of countries were represented by their WTO ambassadors, but some of the larger governments had sent their trade ministers in the expectation of participating in a conclave of major significance. The goal was for the entire membership to approve a "framework" for the round by a deadline of midnight, Friday, July 30. Haunting the proceedings was the specter of Cancún; warnings abounded from policymakers and independent commentators alike about the dangers of a repeat performance. "A second such failure could severely undermine confidence in the Doha Round and even in the WTO and the system it oversees," Supachai wrote in an op-ed in the *International Herald Tribune*.

The problem was that the Five Interested Parties were meeting—and meeting, and meeting some more—in the U.S. mission because they had arrogated to themselves the responsibility of "guiding" the text on agriculture. There was little point for others to conduct much business until it was certain that the ministers representing the United States, the European Union, Brazil, India, and Australia could reach a common understanding. According to an announcement by Shotaro Oshima, the chairman of the General Council, a draft text would be issued for the perusal of delegations on Wednesday the twenty-eighth. But the promise of a text on Wednesday morning gave way to a promise of one on Wednesday evening, followed by a new promise of one on Thursday morning, followed by yet another delay until late Thursday evening. As a result, the Centre William Rappard was the scene of much milling around, cooling of heels, and stewing about whether an attempt would be made to impose a deal on everyone before they had a chance to consult with their capitals. Unkind questions arose: Who did these guys in the Five Interested Parties think they were? And why were they taking so long, when so much was hanging in the balance?

"It is catastrophic," Luzius Wasescha, the chief Swiss negotiator, told reporters, adding that the Five Interested Parties "consider themselves to be the leaders of the world and they are not. They are not even able to negotiate properly." Japanese trade minister Shoichi Nakagawa told journalists from his country that it was "unbearable" that so much should hinge on an agreement among only five countries, obviously reflecting Tokyo's resentment at having been booted out of the charmed circle. To mollify the malcontents, the Friday night deadline was extended by twenty-four hours.

Tiresome as it was for those on the outside, the Five Interested Parties were themselves undergoing an intense trial of their stamina. Two negotiating sessions among the five went into the wee hours of the morning, with Nath's demands concerning the special products loophole nearly causing the meeting to break down. In addition to those talks, Zoellick went to a nearby hotel for a session with ministers from western African cotton-growing countries on cotton subsidies that lasted until 4:00 a.m.

Even after a text finally materialized on Friday, July 30, the endurance test was far from over. Getting to "yes" at Geneva would prove to be a lot dicier proposition than many of those present had expected. Another full night of talks lay ahead on Friday evening as the debate moved to a larger concentric circle of countries in a green room meeting. The events of that night were kept from the press at the time. But looking back on the tumultuous episode, many would later say that the Doha Round came very close to premature demise.

| * |

It certainly didn't help that the venue for the green room meeting was so hot and sticky. The Centre William Rappard was not very efficiently air conditioned; the Geneva lakeside usually affords enough cooling in the summer, but not so on this Friday night, when a crowd of about thirty ministers, along with top aides and Secretariat officials, thronged the director-general's conference room, starting around 5:00 p.m. An effort to provide some relief by opening the windows resulted in an invasion of insects, so the participants had to persevere as best they could by shedding jackets and loosening ties. For those who were already smoldering over having to wait for the Five Interested Parties, the discomfort was another cause for irritation.

Some attendees went into the meeting assuming that the debate would be relatively smooth and uneventful, among them Tim Groser, New Zealand's ambassador to the WTO. A clever man, though viewed by some of his colleagues as a showboating self-promoter, Groser was reveling in the central role to which he had been assigned—chairman of the agriculture negotiations. As such, he was the primary author of the document that was the main focus of the meeting, the agriculture text. To produce it, he had sat through endless hours with the Five Interested Parties, listening carefully to the understanding reached among the Americans, Europeans, Brazilians, Indians, and Australians and consulting with delegations from numerous other countries, in the hope that the text would undergo only slight modifications in the green room before becoming the principal element of a new Framework for the Doha Round approved by all WTO members.

But as the early hours of the evening passed, it was becoming increasingly clear that many of the green room participants were upset with various provisions in the text, and Supachai, who was chairing, seemed incapable of keeping the discussion focused. Fearing that serious negotiations would never get started and that the proposed framework was thus on the verge of unraveling, Groser went into the director-general's office during a break at around 8:30 and told a small group: "I've got to take over this meeting, or we're not going to get there."

Groser had a plan for making the meeting productive: He would apply the "sweaty underpants theory" (a name he had learned from a veteran European negotiator). Crude but simple, this theory holds that sometimes the only way to force people toward convergence is to wait until they get so clammy that they simply can't wait to leave and take a shower. The heat and humidity in the room seemed bound to help in that regard, and when the meeting reconvened shortly after 9:00 o'clock, Groser forcefully asserted his authority as the meeting's new chairman. He recalls telling the group, "You've only got one thing to do tonight, which is agree to a text. I will walk out if I hear speeches, and you can explain to your governments why this didn't work. So let's go through the text systematically."

On a number of fundamental issues, there was little or no dispute, so at last a realistic prospect was emerging for advancing beyond the negotiating agenda agreed at Doha. The text produced by the Five Interested Parties contained a number of important principles and concepts regarding which tariffs and subsidies would be cut, how they would be cut, and what sorts of exceptions would be allowed. It fell well short of a modalities deal; it did not set forth hard numbers or percentages, so WTO members realized that agreement on it would still leave the round less far along in 2004 than it was supposed to be a year earlier. Still, agreement would provide a clearer idea than before of what type of accord the round would eventually be.

In some respects, the text envisioned a round of highly ambitious liberalization. To cut agricultural tariffs, a "tiered formula" would be used, with the highest duties being cut more than lower ones.* (What level of tariff would be defined as "high," and how much those would be cut, was left for future negotiations.) A similar type of tiered formula would be applied to farm subsidies, so that countries having the greatest amount of government payments to farmers would cut their subsidy programs more deeply than other countries. Export subsidies, as Lamy had conceded in advance, would be "eliminated by an end date to be agreed."

But whether global farm trade would undergo true reform—or just pretend to—was unclear, because the text also contained provisions for a number of "flexibilities" that would give countries the means to keep some of their most cherished policies protected from major change. All member nations could choose "an appropriate number, to be designated" of farm products that would be treated as "sensitive" and thus subject to less drastic tariff cuts. Developing

---

*Developing countries would be allowed to cut their tariffs by a smaller percentage than high-income ones, but they would use a tiered formula as well, so that their highest tariffs would be cut more than their lower tariffs. The very poorest of the developing countries would not have to cut tariffs at all, in keeping with Lamy's proposal that they should get the "round for free."

countries would, in addition, get the exceptions that the Indians were insisting on, notably the right to choose "an appropriate number of products as Special Products" that would also be sheltered from liberalization. Although the size of these flexibilities was not specified, their inclusion in the text was clearly a departure from U.S. goals. Zoellick had been forced to accept them in part because he himself had fought tooth and nail to extract a concession from the others that would limit the amount by which U.S. farm subsidies—specifically Washington's countercyclical payments program—would be cut.*

The text included a deal on cotton as well, because this time, U.S. officials seemed to have learned how to avoid making proposals that would insult their counterparts from western Africa. Instead of urging the Africans to diversify away from cotton growing, as they had at Cancún, the Americans had tried a more persuasive approach in a marathon negotiating session at a Geneva hotel the night before the green room meeting.

Under the compromise that emerged from that meeting, the text promised that the cotton issue would be "addressed ambitiously, expeditiously and specifically, within the agriculture negotiations." In plain English, this implied that once an overall Doha agreement was struck, cotton subsidies would be cut more deeply and rapidly than other subsidies. Furthermore, special talks on cotton would be held within the negotiations on agriculture, to ensure that the issue would be properly addressed as the round progressed. The Africans had accepted this compromise only grudgingly; they feared it didn't bind Washington to do much. But they understood that it was politically impossible to push a cut in cotton subsidies through Congress in the absence of a broader deal containing sweeteners for American farmers. And they took seriously U.S. warnings about the catastrophic consequences should the negotiations fall apart.

"We did not want to be the ones who caused the breakdown of the multilateral system," says Sam Amehou, Benin's ambassador to the WTO, who was one of the chief African negotiators. "If there were no place like the WTO, how do you think countries like mine could deal with the U.S.?"

In sum, quite a few major problems had been resolved by the time hard bargaining began in the green room under Groser's chairmanship on July

---

*As he had prior to Cancún, the U.S. trade representative wanted to ensure that the countercyclical payments program would not be counted in the amber box, where cuts to subsidy programs would be deepest because of their particularly distorting effects on prices. His case was based on the argument that the program, which compensates farmers when global prices fall below target levels, did not link payments to production and should therefore be counted in the blue box, the category for less-harmful subsidies. Critics of the U.S. position regarded it as a smoke screen aimed at keeping Washington's damaging subsidy spending relatively unscathed.

30. But the night was still young, and the prospects for consensus still fragile, when the meeting was jolted by an eruption of obscenity ending with the
words, "I'm leaving, Bob Zoellick! You're buggering up the markets for all
of us!"

| * |

Canadian trade minister Jim Peterson is a cheerful career politician from On-
tario, not at all the sort of person one would expect to disrupt an international
meeting with a tirade. Yet at around 9:00 p.m. on July 30—his sixty-third birthday, as it happened—Peterson was unleashing a string of profanities at Zoellick, getting up from his seat, putting on his jacket, and heading for the door, an
apparent threat to put an end to the green room talks and, presumably, doom
chances for an agreement at that time.

At play in this conflict was a hoary tradition in multilateral trade negotiations—
namely, that ministers who spill blood will insist on others in similar circumstances spilling an equivalent amount. The reason for this tradition is a variation
on the old adage that misery loves company; a minister who makes a concession
adversely affecting one of his or her country's interest groups may be able to
mollify that group by showing that corresponding groups in other nations are
also suffering.

In this case, the blood-spilling had started with Lamy when he pledged to
eliminate export subsidies on farm products as part of a Doha deal. To make
that concession palatable to European farmers, Lamy had insisted on the
condition that the United States must change a much smaller but analogous
program that gives subsidized credit to agricultural exports. Although accepting Lamy's condition, Zoellick in turn was demanding similar concessions
from other countries with programs resembling export subsidies, lest American
farmers complain of unfair treatment. One of those programs was the Canadian Wheat Board, a government-backed marketing agency for wheat and barley from western Canada that has long been a source of trade friction between
Washington and Ottawa.

There was no way he would agree to this demand, said Peterson, who told
the green room that dismantling the Wheat Board "would be political suicide
in Canada." He excoriated Zoellick for Washington's high farm subsidies, saying they were the reason Canada had to take such unique measures to protect
its producers, and he maintained that agencies like the Wheat Board were not
tantamount to export subsidies. His profane outburst and walkout came in response to a caustic remark by Zoellick on the issue.

As Zoellick watched Peterson rise from his chair and put on his jacket, he said, according to notes of the meeting: "Well, if that's your position, I'll take my stuff off the table and so will Pascal"—a threat that the E.U. and U.S. concessions on export subsidies would be withdrawn, which would throw the negotiations back to square one. Only after Groser implored Peterson to stay, with a promise that the issue would be resolved later, did the Canadian return to the table.

Peterson's blowup set the tone for much of what followed as other participants also insisted on changes to the text as the meeting resumed. Argentina's Martín Redrado lodged a strong complaint about a proposed restriction on the use of taxes on exports, which his country was depending on to shore up its finances as it recovered from its devastating 2001 crisis. China protested that its state trading enterprise shouldn't be subject to the same sort of disciplines as others because the objective was simply to keep consumer prices stable. And so it went—on and on. "Switzerland and Japanese taking the whole thing down," one note taker jotted in his pad around midnight, referring to demands by the Swiss and the Japanese for milder tariff cuts in their agricultural sectors.

It was time for another gut check. "Gentlemen, we are risking the end of the Doha Development Agenda," Groser said, and he called for another break at 12:40 a.m.

What happened next was a remarkable moment, referred to later by some of the participants as "coming to see the pope," with Zoellick in the role of pontiff. Together with his deputy for agriculture trade, Allen Johnson, the U.S. trade representative took over a reception room in the Centre William Rappard where he received a series of visits from delegations seeking modifications to the text. While many others went to sleep in nearby offices or on hallway sofas, Zoellick—who had already been up negotiating for several nights previously—spent hour after hour in this reception room, listening to the supplicants' objections and offering wording to accommodate their concerns. At times Lamy joined in these discussions and at times Groser did too, mainly to ensure that the deals hammered out by Zoellick and his team were properly drafted for insertion into the text. But it was Zoellick who was effectively running the show, even though he was obviously a key party to the negotiations himself. When the Chinese came, they were bought off with amendments to the text asserting that state trading enterprises that "preserve domestic consumer price stability" would "receive special consideration for maintaining monopoly status" over the trading of food. The Indians, Canadians, and others likewise got some concessional wording.

As dawn approached, the "pope" and his sidekicks had drafted about a dozen amendments to the text, some of which they knew would be controversial, and now the question facing them was whether to present those amendments to the green room one by one, in batches, or all together as a package. The decision was quick: The amendments must go as a package, on a take-it-or-leave-it basis, or the whole thing would be picked apart anew.

Groser recalls that he was "spaced out, operating on pure instinct," when the green room participants reassembled at 6:00 a.m. on Saturday morning. "I have a text. I'm afraid it's all up or all down. And I can't take on board all of your suggested changes," he told them. After reading through the proposed amendments, he got up to leave, with a parting bit of brinkmanship: "If you're not going to do this, you're going to have to take responsibility for killing the Doha Round." With that, he left the room and headed home on his motorcycle.

Wasn't it highly irregular for the U.S. trade representative to essentially take over the writing of the text that would be presented to the membership on such terms? Of course it was, but at that hour, under those circumstances, especially given the general relief that the meeting had not collapsed, nobody was going to raise serious procedural objections. So the framework was finalized—though not that morning. Another full day was required, with more green room talks on other, less controversial areas of the round, such as tariffs on industrial goods, followed by a formal General Council meeting beginning at 10:00 p.m. at which all WTO members approved the revised text. It was not until 2:00 a.m. Sunday morning, August 1, that Zoellick and Lamy appeared at press conferences to proclaim their mission accomplished.

"After the detour in Cancún, we have put these WTO negotiations back on track," Zoellick said, to which Lamy added: "I said in Cancún that the WTO was in intensive care. Today I can say that it is not only out of the hospital but well and running."

| * |

The contrast with Cancún could hardly have been starker. This time, there were no raised-fist salutes from ministers parading before TV cameras, and bombast about the tyranny of the wealthy was kept to a minimum. Instead, the July 2004 meeting that produced the framework ended with a series of mutually congratulatory statements. In one particularly touching scene of hatchet-burying in the closing moments of the green room, Canada's Peterson told his colleagues: "We owe a special debt of thanks to two people: Bob Zoellick and Pascal Lamy." Peterson's positive attitude, to be sure, was influenced by wording he had secured addressing some of his concerns about his country's Wheat Board. Still, singling out Zoellick and Lamy was appropriate. Zoellick's letter to ministers the previous January, his round-the-world trip, and his assumption of the "pope" role in Geneva were the highlights of a stunningly successful demonstration in how to gin up and ram through an international agreement. Lamy's proactive offering of concessions had also been essential to the outcome.

Explanations are myriad, but one factor probably accounted for the result more than any other—fear of the fate that might have befallen the multilateral system. In the end, for all the fierceness of their differences over specific issues, the representatives of the WTO's 147 member countries stepped to the brink and saw that the abyss into which they might plunge was deeper and scarier than the one they had leaped into in Cancún. They worried that the Doha Round, and conceivably the trade body itself, might not be able to withstand another Cancún-style blow.

As the meeting was wrapping up on the morning of August 1, I met a morose-looking Celine Charveriat, the head of Oxfam's Geneva-based trade campaign, on the steps of the Centre William Rappard. She was dejected because the counsel she had given African countries, to reject the cotton agreement, had gone unheeded. The main reason that African nations had joined the consensus, she acknowledged, was that governments from the developing world have potent reasons for wanting to keep the WTO alive and well. "Even if developing countries think the WTO needs radical reform, they know they have greater leverage in the WTO than in bilateral agreements," she told me.

Now, more than two and a half years after it started, the Doha Round was reaching the point of agreement on basic guidelines concerning how tariffs, subsidies, and other distortions would be reduced or eliminated. Although a deal on modalities still loomed as a huge challenge for the future, progressivity had been firmly entrenched as an overarching principle.

Yet there were grounds for unease about this achievement, and not just because it had been patched together amid so much perspiration, sleep deprivation, and text-writing usurpation. The framework created some potentially huge exceptions from tariff cuts. The loopholes for sensitive products and special products in agriculture were the price of "success," as was the special safeguard mechanism that was designed to help developing countries cope with surges in imports of staple foods. Although the size of these loopholes was yet to be determined, they gave the whole undertaking the vague feel of a Leonardo da Vinci helicopter, with many extra wings, propellers, and stabilizers. It remained to be seen whether this contraption the WTO had devised would amount to anything worthwhile once it was up and flying, or whether it would ever truly get up and flying at all.

# 10 | ONE CHICKEN McNUGGET

THE GIFTS THAT BOB ZOELLICK AND PASCAL LAMY EXCHANGED ON October 18, 2004, were emblematic of their shared interests—jogging, global travel, and trade wonkery. To Lamy, Zoellick gave a world atlas and a running suit with a White House logo. In return, the European trade commissioner gave his American counterpart a framed caricature depicting Zoellick surrounded by a few products that had been the subject of WTO disputes between their two governments, including bananas, cows, corn, and airplanes.

The dynamic duo of trade was meeting for the last time in their official capacities as trade ministers, because Lamy's term was drawing to a close. They had not achieved what they had hoped to, which was to finish the Doha Round by 2005. Even so, they felt there were grounds for mutual self-congratulation, at least for advancing the round to the stage of the framework; certainly their relationship had been critical in that regard. With their impending departures from their jobs, links between the world's two economic giants appeared bound to change, with potentially adverse consequences for the multilateral trading system. "Some analysts . . . fear that relations between Europe and the United States could sour after Mr. Zoellick and Mr. Lamy part," the *Wall Street Journal* noted in an article about their October meeting. Those worries would prove to be well-founded.

It was not that Lamy was leaving the trade realm; quite the contrary. He set his sights on succeeding the ineffectual Supachai Panitchpakdi as WTO director-general, and he would reach that goal the following year. But his job in Brussels was being taken by a very different kind of person.

Replacing Lamy, the "Exocet" known for his relentless focus on policy and for his quiet, abstemious lifestyle, was Peter Mandelson, whom the British press had dubbed the "Prince of Darkness" for his cunning in the art of political manipulation, and whose private life had provided endless fodder for London's gossip columns. "Love Triangle Ended Spin Agency Contract" and "'Exotic' Party Animal Stands Out from Dull Cabinet Pack" were just a couple of the headlines that had been published about Mandelson. How many trade policymakers could boast that sort of coverage?

| * |

The grandson of a venerable Labour Party leader, Mandelson, who was born in 1953, graduated from Oxford and became Labour's director of communications in 1985. At that time, the party seemed doomed to unelectability because of the power wielded over its policies by trade unions and the "loony Left." Making good use of his silken charm, Mandelson played a crucial role in the transformation that led to the emergence of "New Labour," which followed the lead of the Democratic Party in the United States by embracing a more moderate, pro-market, smaller-government form of progressivism. Ideologically extreme policies such as unilateral disarmament were jettisoned, and party conferences changed to slick exercises in image promotion, with leaders standing before banners emblazoned with slogans such as "Looking to the Future." This approach went over poorly with Labour's old guard, whose members reviled Mandelson for his use of focus groups and insistence that party members stay on message. His zealotry on behalf of the party's fortunes gave him a reputation, deserved or not, as a spinmeister with a capacity for shading the truth. A 1989 profile in the *Independent* reported: "He wheedles journalists, cajoles them, takes them into his confidence, spurns them, adapts his tone to theirs— either earnest or joking, companionable or distant. Then, if they fail to present the party his way, he bullies, pesters and harries them."

After his election to Parliament in 1992, Mandelson's star continued to soar along with that of Tony Blair, who counted Mandelson among his closest allies and advisers. When Blair became prime minister in 1997 following a smashing Labour victory that Mandelson helped mastermind, Blair put him in his cabinet, naming him trade and industry minister in July 1998, and the prime minister continued to rely heavily on him for counsel on political matters large and small. By this point, Mandelson was a much-sought-after guest at the soirees and country-house parties hosted by London's glamour set, an example being Prince Charles's fiftieth-birthday celebration, to which he was the only cabinet member invited. Together with his political prominence and waspish wit, a major reason for his appeal was what he once called his "exotic personality"—which included the fact that he is gay.

During much of his young adulthood, Mandelson was living with a bisexual man, whose son he helped raise, and by the mid-1990s he had a new partner, a Brazilian-born linguist who is two decades his junior. None of this might have come to public light—Mandelson, though acknowledging his sexual preference to friends, worked hard to keep it out of the news media—but by the late 1990s he had become such a lightning rod for controversy, with so many detractors in both old Labour and the Conservative Party, that the press could not restrain itself from dishing about him. And the attacks on him in the media often turned viciously homophobic after scandals forced his resignation from the cabinet, not just once but twice.

Six months after Mandelson became trade and industry minister, the news broke that when he was a member of Parliament in 1996 earning $73,000 a year, he had received a low-interest loan of $627,000 from a fellow Labour Party politician and former business executive to buy a townhouse in London's Notting Hill neighborhood. Some of the lender's business dealings had been under investigation by Mandelson's department, and although the minister had recused himself from the investigation, his critics highlighted his failure to disclose the loan when he joined the cabinet. Suddenly the press was full of reports claiming that Mandelson, who had lived modestly until the mid-1990s, had fallen prey to the desire for accoutrements commensurate with his newfound status as a social lion—not just the exquisitely appointed townhouse but also membership in a tony health club and sharp, tailor-made suits. Bowing to the inevitable, Mandelson stepped down. Less than a year later, he was back in Blair's cabinet, this time as Northern Ireland secretary, but in 2001 he again had to quit because of allegations that he had improperly helped an Indian businessman with a British passport application. He was cleared of wrongdoing in that matter and remained an important adviser to Blair, who offered him a chance at redemption by helping him secure the European trade commissionership.

Soon after Mandelson took over the trade post in Brussels, it became clear that in one area, at least—relations with Zoellick—he would stack up poorly by comparison with Lamy. In a heated transatlantic phone conversation in March 2005 concerning a dispute about subsidies for Boeing and Airbus, the two men hung up the phone on each other; Zoellick accused Mandelson of "spinning" and of conducting negotiations through the media. "That is not the way I did business with Commissioner Lamy," he huffed to the press, to which

Mandelson replied caustically: "Bob said he and Lamy managed everything brilliantly. I'll do my best to live up to their high standards."

Whoever was at fault in that incident, Mandelson would not have to deal for long with Zoellick, who was heading to the State Department as deputy secretary in the second Bush term. And Zoellick, like Lamy, was being replaced by an individual very unlike himself.

At a time when the U.S. Congress had become poisonously divided along partisan lines, Rob Portman, a Republican member of the House from Ohio, was one of a rare breed—a lawmaker who elicited gushing affection from colleagues on both the Republican and the Democratic sides of the aisle. Lanky, with graying hair and green eyes, Portman had a gift for coming across as kind and caring to almost anyone he encountered, without the slightest hint of pretense. His amiability shone through at the March 17 news conference in which Bush announced his intention to nominate the forty-nine-year-old Ohioan, who related the reaction of his three children. "Sally, who's a fourth grader, had to admit that she had never heard of the U.S. Trade Representative," Portman said to laughter from the press. "However, Mr. President, she said, 'Dad, it sounds like a really neat job.'"

Portman grew up in a wealthy suburb of Cincinnati. Fresh out of Dartmouth College in 1979, he worked as an advance man for George H. W. Bush, who would soon become vice president—the first of many roles that would make him an intimate of the Bush family. He earned a law degree from the University of Michigan, worked several years as a trade lawyer in Washington, and then joined the elder Bush's presidential campaign in 1988, which led to a job in the White House counsel's office and then to the post of the president's chief lobbyist. When his mother was diagnosed with cancer, he returned to Cincinnati to prepare for a run for Congress and in 1993 won the first of six terms. His relations with the younger Bush blossomed when, like Zoellick, he helped with debate preparation in the 2000 election—he played the role of Vice President Gore in practice debates—and served as a Bush campaign spokesman during the conflict over the Florida vote recount. As a lawmaker, he was known as a legislative workhorse who took pleasure in getting bills enacted by cosponsoring them with moderate Democrats; his achievements included bills on pension reform and the overhaul of the Internal Revenue Service. Summing up his capacity to disarm opponents with an air of goodwill and sincerity, a *New York Times* profile in 2003 reported:

> In interviews around the Capitol this week, no one could be found who would say anything unfavorable about Mr. Portman. The closest was a

Democrat on the Ways and Means Committee who insisted on not being identified and then said in almost a whisper that Mr. Portman's pleasant manner masked an extremely conservative philosophy. But even this Democrat said he admired Mr. Portman's ability to master tough topics and have friendly relationships across party lines.

A collective exhale was the reaction to Portman's nomination among many of the people who worked in the Office of the U.S. Trade Representative. No longer would they have to quake through morning staff meetings in fear of being chewed out; the new man at the top simply didn't convey displeasure so harshly. Foreign trade negotiators, too, noticed a distinct change in atmosphere. "Portman made it seemed like he cared about you. That's the major difference between him and Zoellick," says one Latin American policymaker who dealt often with both men. "Zoellick always acted as if he needed something, and whenever he was flexible, people somehow felt they were still being cheated. Portman could make the same gesture, the same sort of deal, and it felt like genuine movement."

But pleasing as it might be to relate the tale of a Mr. Nice Guy who produces miraculous results for the global trading system, the Portman era would not fit that description. Around the time he came to office and in the years immediately thereafter, the benefits and costs of trade liberalization were undergoing a major recalibration, especially in the developing world. And the United States and the European Union remained disinclined to confront their powerful farm lobbies very aggressively. For those reasons, the story of this chapter and the three that follow is of the Doha Round heading into a long, sickening, downward spiral.

| * |

When he became U.S. trade representative, Portman knew he would be hearing calls for the United States to shrink its crop subsidies. He could scarcely have imagined that some of the most radical demands would come from his colleagues in the Bush White House.

In the late summer of 2005, a debate was raging within the administration over what to do about the Doha Round. A major action-forcing event was looming—the WTO's next ministerial meeting, which was scheduled for Hong Kong in December. As one of the world's great entrepôts, Hong Kong was being touted as the perfect setting for a breakthrough in the round. Ideally, the meeting there would finally produce an agreement on modalities, the goal that had been eluding the WTO since 2003. Even though the framework agreement had been approved in 2004, real numbers were still needed to give concrete meaning to the framework's broad principles concerning the ways tariffs and subsidies would be cut and the exceptions that would be allowed.

The prospects for such an outcome at Hong Kong did not appear bright, however, because the round had been stuck in very low gear during the first half of 2005. Progress was hung up on a battle of stupefying complexity concerning how to convert different types of farm tariffs (some using percentages of import price, others using fixed amounts of money per ton) to a common measure. If the WTO were again to fall short of a modalities deal at Hong Kong, the trade body would miss one of the last best chances for the round's timely completion.

On this much, the Bush administration was agreed: The United States was going to have to deliver new stimulus to the Doha talks—the equivalent of a shock from a defibrillator for a patient with no pulse. Little was likely to be forthcoming from other WTO members, administration policymakers knew. The unsettled question was how to do it.

Pressing for an all-out approach was the White House National Economic Council, which coordinated policy among economic agencies and was headed by Allan Hubbard, a close personal friend of the president. Hubbard and his team wanted the Office of the U.S. Trade Representative to offer a complete end to farm subsidies, and they had Bush's own words to lend force to their argument, because in a speech to the United Nations, the president had stated Washington's willingness "to eliminate all tariffs and subsidies and other barriers to the free flow of goods and services as other nations do the same." Why, Hubbard asked, shouldn't U.S. trade negotiators advance a position that was consistent with the president's rhetoric?

Even-tempered though he was, Portman responded to this idea negatively and forcefully. "I had some relatively heated conversations at high levels and said that if they wanted to propose this, they could find another USTR [U.S. trade representative] to do it," he recalls.

Based on his experience in Congress, Portman was convinced that a proposal to zero out subsidies would never pass muster in the agriculture committees. It was one thing to insert such high-flown ideas into presidential speeches; it was quite another to use them as the basis for concrete proposals in WTO negotiations, where other countries would deride them as pie in the sky. Portman's preferred approach was to consult closely with the most powerful members of the agriculture panels, as well as with farm organizations, to develop a proposal that would have an energizing impact on the Doha talks while still maintaining the political support on Capitol Hill that would be required to get a WTO deal approved. Aiding him in this effort was the new agriculture secretary, Mike Johanns, a former governor of Nebraska, who delivered speeches warning farm groups that U.S. policy was going to have to undergo major changes. Brazil's success in getting Washington's cotton program declared illegal meant that "the status quo is very high risk for American farmers," Johanns told the Senate Agriculture Committee. Rather than waiting for other U.S. subsidies, such as those for rice, to be challenged in WTO tribunals, it would be much better to negotiate curbs in those subsidies as part of a round and get substantial concessions in return, the Agriculture chief asserted.

The administration finally got its ducks lined up in early October 2005, and a carefully coordinated public relations blitz heralded the launch of a new U.S. plan. Portman, who had won the right to craft the details as he saw fit, traveled to Zurich to make a presentation to fellow trade ministers on October 10, and an op-ed with his byline, titled "America's Proposal to Kickstart the Doha Trade Talks," was published in the *Financial Times* that day. "Our ambitious initiative demonstrates a seriousness of purpose," he declared at a news conference. "The United States is committed to breaking the deadlock in multilateral talks in agriculture, and unleashing the full potential of the Doha Round."

Under the plan, Washington would cap at $22.6 billion its overall spending on farm subsidies that distort crop prices, including a reduction in the most objectionable sorts of farm subsidies—those in the amber box, where the effects on crop prices were the greatest. The $19.1 billion ceiling on U.S. amber box spending would be lowered by 60 percent, limiting outlays for such subsidies to $7.6 billion annually. And other U.S. agricultural programs would be cut as well. All these proposals, of course, were contingent on several big "ifs."

In exchange for Washington's concessions, other countries would have to take their own steps toward liberalization. The European Union and Japan would have to cut their subsidies by even greater percentages, given their higher starting points. Most important, almost all WTO members would have to accept steep reductions in their tariffs on farm products, including an eye-popping 90 percent cut in the highest duties imposed by rich countries, with very limited allowances for exceptions. In addition, developing countries would have to lower their barriers further to foreign manufacturers and service companies.

The package was based on a hardheaded political calculation, in the finest tradition of WTO- and GATT-style mercantilism. Curbing farm subsidies might be a desirable policy for the United States as a whole, but it was a "sacrifice" that American politicians could accept only if most farm groups were assured that their export opportunities would burgeon. A Kansas wheat grower who might ordinarily rebel at seeing his federal check shrink would presumably acquiesce provided his crop stood a better chance of gaining access to European consumers or the booming emerging markets of India and China. To buttress the case for insisting on lower tariffs abroad, Portman used a moral argument as well: Economic research, he noted, showed that developing countries would gain more from reduced farm barriers than from any other move contemplated in the round. "By improving market access for agriculture, the greatest benefits can be realized," he wrote in his *Financial Times* op-ed.

Not everyone was swallowing the U.S. claim that its proposal was so far-reaching. Leading the attackers was Oxfam, which called the plan "smoke and mirrors." To understand the reasons for this cynicism, it is important to recall the crucial difference between "bound" and "applied" tariffs. Bound rates are the maximum allowable based on commitments that countries have made in WTO agreements; a country with a bound tariff of 30 percent on beef, for instance, is legally obliged to keep its beef duties at or below that level. Applied rates, which refer to the tariffs that governments actually impose, can be—and often are—much lower than bound levels. Likewise, with subsidies, countries legally bind themselves to certain ceilings, although their actual spending levels may be substantially less. WTO negotiations concern bound levels, not applied ones. A "cut" in tariffs or subsidies, in other words, may be no such thing, at least not as measured by the duties imposed or dollars spent.

This was the basis for Oxfam's main complaint about the U.S. proposal. The highly-touted "cut" in amber box payments would be from the legal ceiling of $19.1 billion, and Washington was already spending considerably less than its allowable amount; furthermore, other types of spending were simply being shifted from one box to another. As a result, "the United States will have to make only negligible cuts to the subsidies it pays to farmers," asserted Celine Charveriat, the group's chief trade expert, in an argument echoed by some WTO members.

American officials insisted that the critics didn't understand how much the plan would affect U.S. farm programs. The countercyclical payments program, for instance, would be subject to real cuts because Washington was proposing to put a much lower cap on those types of subsidies—$5 billion—than the $10 billion to which it had previously agreed. These arguments were at least somewhat persuasive to other countries' policymakers, who after scrutinizing the U.S. proposal offered measured praise for it. "The U.S. proposal is a good start," said Australia's Mark Vaile.

Whatever the merits or demerits of the U.S. proposal, its presentation did change the dynamics of the Doha Round. Because it was bolder and more specific than anything any major player had previously advanced, it put the onus on other WTO members—especially the European Union—to respond with offers of their own.

In the process, it threw a spotlight squarely on a crucial question: How ambitious was the round going to be? An epithet—"Doha Lite"—was starting to circulate to describe a hypothetical deal involving minimal contributions by all countries, with few significant cuts in trade barriers. Would the round be deserving of that appellation? Free-trade enthusiasts were soon to be disappointed with the answers.

| * |

The phone call for him was a matter of some urgency, Peter Mandelson was told during a visit to Geneva a few days after the unveiling of the October 10 U.S. proposal on farm trade. On the line was the office of Dominique de Villepin, prime minister of France, who wanted to discuss why, in his view, the E.U. trade commissioner should not offer major concessions in response to the U.S. plan.

Mandelson said he would be happy to talk and promised to have his office arrange a meeting. That was not good enough, however; Villepin's aides said he wanted to have a discussion promptly. Realizing that avoidance behavior was futile, Mandelson decided that a touch of stoutheartedness was in order. He said he would fly to Paris that day and meet the prime minister in the evening.

After his arrival at the airport, a car delivered Mandelson to the back garden gate of Matignon, the mansion that is home to French prime ministers, an eighteenth-century masterpiece of archways and courtyards furnished in tapestries and paintings. He was ushered into Villepin's office, where the prime minister, a protégé of President Jacques Chirac with an aristocratic mien, informed him that owing to an evening engagement they could meet for only forty-five minutes. But, the prime minister said, under no circumstances would France support a fresh offer being made by the European Union on agriculture at this stage, given the weakness of the U.S. proposal and the lack of offers from other WTO members. Mandelson remonstrated with him, explaining why he felt compelled to show some flexibility. After three quarters of an hour, Villepin arose to signal that the meeting had come to an end. He said that if Mandelson were to make the proposal, it would be disavowed by the French government, and with that Villepin swept from the room.

This development was hardly welcome, because Mandelson was already under fierce pressure to match, or at least come close to matching, the concessions put on the table by the United States on October 10. In meeting after meeting in mid-October of the Five Interested Parties, Mandelson's counterparts from the United States, Brazil, India, and Australia had goaded him, and when he balked at their demands, they had publicly upbraided him, asserting that if the European Union failed to offer significantly better access to European agriculture markets, the Hong Kong meeting would turn into another Cancún.

Almost all fingers were pointing at Brussels. "The E.U. are the ones putting the round under threat," Australia's Vaile said at a news conference after two days of meetings in Geneva among the Five Interested Parties broke up on October 20 with no sign of progress. Portman told reporters in a conference call that day: "The failure of the E.U. to put forward a real market access proposal has put the benefits of Doha at risk. . . . I'm not trying to be melodramatic, but we are very close to [a] drop-dead date" for preventing a collapse at Hong Kong. Even Oxfam's Charveriat, who had been so unimpressed with the U.S. proposal, agreed: "Rear-guard action by the French and other E.U. member states is undermining even the minimal progress made."

The chief reason for these attacks was Mandelson's insistence on sticking by the European Union's position regarding how many "sensitive products" should be exempt from steep tariff cuts. Brussels was adamant that 8 percent of tariff lines could be classified as sensitive—a stance that, as Portman put it, would create "a big enough hole to drive a truck through." It would mean that for more than 160 products, duties would be subject to only modest reductions; these would obviously include beef, dairy products, poultry, and a host of other goods, precisely the ones that E.U. trading partners were most eager to sell in the European market. By contrast, under the U.S. proposal, only 1 percent of tariff lines could be designated as sensitive, and the G-20 group of developing countries had advanced a proposal in which the allowed amount for high-income countries was only slightly higher.

With the European Union under such withering fire, Mandelson had no choice but to offer something in response to the U.S. proposal. By itself, France couldn't stop him from negotiating as he pleased, because a supermajority of E.U. member states was required to overrule him, and though the French strove mightily, they could not muster such a large number of European governments to their side. But Mandelson was constrained by one huge factor—the negotiating mandate that the member states had approved. Under that mandate, the 2003 reform of the Common Agricultural Policy set the limit for what Brussels could accept; the theory was that a solemn promise had been made to European farmers that they would not have to endure any additional changes in the fundamental nature of their government support for ten years. By the reckoning of the French government, Mandelson's negotiating stance was already violating the mandate with regard to beef, poultry, tomatoes, sugar, and butter, so to go further toward an even more ambitious proposal would surely step over the line. As Mandelson and his staff continued to work on their new proposal, French president Chirac escalated the pressure by taking an extraordinarily tough stance, publicly threatening that Paris might use its veto over any deal negotiated during the Doha Round. "France reserves the right not to approve" any deal it didn't like, Chirac admonished on October 27, and that threat was at least legally credible, because although Paris may have ceded negotiating authority to Brussels, it was still a member in its own right of the WTO, where consensus was required.

A high-noon shoot-out came the following day, October 28. Video screens flickered on in the offices of trade ministers in Washington, Brussels, Brasilia, New Delhi, and Canberra. The Five Interested Parties were holding a videoconference in which the European Union would present its counterproposal. Each minister—Mandelson, Portman, Celso Amorim, Kamal Nath, and Vaile—saw a screen split into four, with one of his counterparts in each quarter of the screen.

"Serious and credible" were the words Mandelson used to introduce his proposal to the other ministers. "It pushes our margin of maneuver to the limit. We cannot go for a new mandate," he said, adding that it was a "one-shot" offer—the implication being that there would be no second one.

Explaining the details, he noted that the tariff cuts for farm goods under his proposal would go "significantly further" than those of the Uruguay Round—an average of 46 percent for high-income countries, compared with the Uruguay Round's 36 percent. As with the U.S. proposal, everything was conditional; other WTO members would have to open their manufacturing and service sectors significantly.

The reaction from the others was scornful, not least because Mandelson had held fast to the European Union's demand for keeping 8 percent of tariff lines designated as sensitive. "For many Brazilian products the E.U. proposal would be no real market access," Amorim asserted in the videoconference, and he also took strong exception to the finality with which Mandelson had made his offer, saying it "cannot be presented as take it or leave it." Vaile pronounced himself "disappointed" and disputed some of the European Union's arithmetic, asserting that a back-of-the-envelope calculation by Australian government trade experts showed the average tariff reduction would be several percentage points less than Brussels was claiming. Portman then piled on, saying, "This is not meeting the standard of 'substantial improvement in market access,'" and he described himself as "discouraged," saying, "I cannot go to Congress [for approval of a Doha deal] without true cuts [in tariffs] for the E.U. and developing country markets."

For some insight into this negativity, consider the criticism of the E.U. proposal that came to be known as the "one Chicken McNugget" argument. Poultry was one of the products that the Americans hoped to export more of to Europe. The E.U. tariff on chicken leg quarters was 53 percent, and if, as seemed likely, Brussels selected that as one of its sensitive products, the duty would be cut by as little as 15 percent, to 45 percent—still a prohibitively high level. Under Mandelson's proposal, the European Union would compensate for that minor tariff cut by allowing an additional 10,000 metric tons of chicken annually into its market at low duties, but that would add up to only 0.02 kilograms per capita, which as U.S. government trade experts noted, was "less than one chicken nugget per person per year."

To this sort of argument, Mandelson was unmoved. In the October 28 videoconference, he shot back at his tormentors, especially the Americans, by observing, "We've already reformed [agriculture policy, with the 2003 CAP reforms]. You have not." He warned the group that they needed "to get real," and he voiced the hope that due consideration for the E.U. proposal might change their minds. "Everyone needs more time to reflect and digest," he said.

Reflecting and digesting indeed took place, and it led to an inescapable conclusion: Given the vast differences among the leading parties in the WTO, a major attitude adjustment was in order for the Hong Kong meeting.

| * |

For most of the WTO's existence, the corridor outside the director-general's office at the Centre William Rappard was dark and stodgy. Poster-sized photos from the GATT era adorned the walls, commemorating the various rounds that had taken place since the 1950s, with scores of trade ministers posing solemnly for posterity. Down they came in late 2005, replaced by modern paintings and sculptures, tastefully displayed amid bright lighting. Instead of being steeped in history and tradition, the new design gave an open, forward-looking feel to the place. The change was duly noted by members of the Secretariat: A new regime had come.

The new regime was Lamy's. His election to the director-generalship had been refreshingly free of the acrimony and accusations of double-dealing that had characterized the 1999 donnybrook. This time, the voting process had been widely acknowledged to be fair and transparent, with a committee privately polling all delegations in three rounds. Although developing countries had again agitated for one of their own to get the job, their votes had been split among candidates from Brazil, Uruguay, and Mauritius, and Lamy managed to overcome concern that he would act as an agent of the European Union, stressing that as European trade commissioner he had often broken with policies favored by his native France. He took office in September 2005 amid high hopes that he would prove vastly superior to Supachai at shepherding the Doha negotiations.

But Lamy's vaunted competence, depth of knowledge, and leadership skills amounted to very little in the face of deep divisions among the WTO membership. That was the situation he faced when he chaired a somber meeting of ministers in Room E of the Centre William Rappard on November 9, a few days after the fruitless videoconference among the ministers from the Five Interested Parties.

Lamy told the ministers in Room E that it would be best to abandon the goal of achieving full modalities at the Hong Kong meeting. As much as he had hoped to see Hong Kong—the first ministerial that he would oversee—make great strides, "keeping that objective, and not getting there, is too risky for the organization," he said, an assessment to which few if any participants dissented. Amorim, expressing the downbeat consensus, said, "We've made no progress at all on the main issues. What is on the table is not a basis for any agreement."

So the word went forth to the press: Expectations for Hong Kong were being officially downgraded. The new objective for the meeting was to "consolidate" gains that had been made since the July 2004 framework and to determine what would be needed so that modalities could be agreed at some point in the near future. Officials tried to put the best face on the outcome, emphasizing that they remained resolute in seeking a meaningful Doha accord. "We have not given up; we will not give up," Portman told reporters.

From Mandelson came a comment striking for its gloominess: "My fear is that in lowering expectations for Hong Kong, we will cause the overall ambition for the round to fall," he said. Making such a lamentation required a certain amount of chutzpah, because he had played a starring role in the events that had led to this turn of fortune. He blamed the Brazilians and the Indians for refusing to cut industrial tariffs, though he had shown little willingness to lower European agricultural barriers as part of a broader deal.

The downgrading of Hong Kong was not the only problem besetting the Doha Development Agenda. An even more existential issue was bubbling to the surface: Would *any* deal the negotiators might reach do much good for the world's poor?

| * |

On a potholed road in Livingstone, Zambia, stands a company that makes long-life milk, the kind that can last for months without refrigeration. Named Finta Danish Dairies, it is owned by the Parbhoos, a family of entrepreneurs who immigrated to Zambia from India decades ago. Inside is a surprisingly modern facility, with gleaming stainless-steel pasteurizers used for heating milk to ultrahigh temperatures, along with large storage tanks, coolers, packaging equipment, and even a machine that attaches straws to the little "Tetra Pak" cartons in which the milk is contained when it's ready for shipping.

One might think that Finta would be a successful exporter. After all, refrigeration is sadly lacking in this part of the world, so long-life milk ought to be a popular product in neighboring countries. But the firm's sales are confined to the Zambian market, for reasons that have nothing to do with tariffs. The problem is that this is sub-Saharan Africa, and the logistical challenges facing anyone trying to ship goods across national borders are overwhelming.

"There could be huge markets for us in Mozambique, the Democratic Republic of the Congo, and Angola, all of which border Zambia," says Ron Parbhoo, the firm's managing director. "But infrastructure is just a huge problem. There are no roads. Forget 'terrible roads.' There are *no* roads." The Democratic Republic of the Congo, he notes, "has a population of 60 million, with no dairy industry, but there's no roads going into it from here. The Angolan border is only 100 miles away, but the only way we could transport milk there would be to ship it by road or train to Durban [in eastern South Africa] and then by ship around the Cape of Good Hope." Another nearby country, Zimbabwe, has an excellent road network, but the country has plunged into such political and economic chaos that it lacks the foreign exchange with which to pay for imports. "And fuel in Zimbabwe is non-existent," adds Brush Parbhoo, Ron's brother, the firm's technical director. "Not to mention the uncertainty of what would probably happen to a 30-ton truck with thousands of dollars of stuff on it."

As this story suggests, landlocked Zambia needs a lot more than an end to foreign barriers to get plugged into the international economy. In fact, Zambia enjoys duty-free access for many of its exports to the United States, the European Union, and other rich-country markets under special programs established for the benefit of the world's poorest nations, such as America's African Growth and Opportunity Act and the European Union's "Everything but Arms" initiative. Although these programs have generated some export-related jobs in countries like Zambia, they haven't helped much, partly because each program has a different set of complex rules concerning the products that qualify, and companies often find the required paperwork overwhelming.

So what does the Doha Round offer for countries like this? Does Zambia make a lot of products it could sell in overseas markets if only tariffs were lower? These are important questions, because with a per capita annual income of $630, Zambia is precisely the sort of country the delegates in Doha supposedly had in mind when they vowed to put the needs of developing countries foremost in the round's priorities.

In late 2005, some disheartening answers were coming from an unexpected quarter.

| * |

For years, the World Bank had been the source of those numbers cited most often to bolster the case that a development round would generate an abundance of opportunity for the world's downtrodden. At the time of the Doha meeting in 2001, it had estimated that an ambitious trade deal would increase global income by as much as $830 billion in 2015, with about two-thirds of the benefits going to developing nations. By the bank's reckoning, the impact would lift 320 million people above the two-dollar-a-day poverty line. As will be recalled from earlier chapters, those figures had provided potent ammunition for politicians, trade ministers, and commentators—Bob Zoellick and Mike Moore prominent among them—who were seeking to prod WTO members toward an agreement. But new estimates based on more current and more refined data, which the bank released a few weeks before the 2005 Hong Kong meeting, suggested that the impact would be much more modest.

The bank's revised "headline number" was that global income would rise by just $287 billion in 2015, with developing countries reaping only 30 percent of the gains, if WTO members were to strike a deal for completely free trade in goods worldwide—that is, if all farm subsidies were eliminated and all tariffs were reduced to zero. This would reduce by 66 million the number of people living below two dollars a day—a fraction of the previous figure. "These numbers are significantly lower than earlier World Bank estimates," the bank acknowledged. Moreover, the numbers were based on the hopelessly unrealistic assumption that WTO members would agree to wipe out all trade distortions. Using a much more likely scenario regarding the outcome of the

Doha talks, the bank projected a reduction in global poverty of only 12 million people.

Perhaps most disturbing, the bank's new estimates indicated that a number of countries would be worse off under completely free trade. "In North Africa and the Middle East, as well as in sub-Saharan Africa . . . there are more losses than gains," one of the bank's studies stated. Other net losers included Mexico and Bangladesh. One reason was that many of these countries were big importers of food; the elimination of farm subsidies would actually hurt those nations' economies, the bank observed, because their national food bills would rise as the United States and other rich countries stopped paying their farmers to overproduce.

A number of countries would come out ahead—notably Brazil and Argentina (which would be able to export significantly more farm products) and China (which would be able to export significantly more manufactured goods). But the gains for many individual nations would be marginal. Zambia was an example of such a country. The elimination of cotton subsidies would boost Zambia's economy and reduce poverty there, because once Zambian farmers were able to sell cotton at higher prices, they could use their increased income to buy nutritious food and good medicine for their families. But "it is clear that the magnitudes are quite small," the bank said in a study that projected an increase of just 1 percent in Zambian household income resulting from subsidy-free trade in cotton.

Critics of trade liberalization gleefully seized upon these new estimates as validation for their arguments. Lori Wallach, still beating the anti-WTO drum at Public Citizen's Global Trade Watch, organized a conference call for reporters with Frank Ackerman, a researcher at Tufts University, who wrote a paper called "The Shrinking Gains from Trade." The paper stated:

> What a difference two years makes. In the discussion leading up to the WTO negotiations in Cancún in 2003, it was common to hear about the hundreds of billions of dollars of benefits available from trade liberalization. Exact numbers and definitions varied, but $500 billion of benefits to the developing world was a widely quoted figure. By 2005, leading up to the next round of negotiations in Hong Kong, it was difficult to find estimates of benefits to the developing world as high as $100 billion—and easy to find figures much lower than that.

The bank's economists, anxious to avoid creating the impression that their research undercut the rationale for global trade liberalization, scrambled to contain the damage. Reporters were summoned to briefings at the bank's head-quarters, where they were told that the correct "takeaway" from the new esti-mates was that WTO members should strike a far-reaching accord, because that would generate greater benefits for the poor than a Doha Lite compromise that left most trade barriers intact. "While it's important not to oversell the impact, it's hard to think of any single measure that countries could take collectively that would have a more significant effect on poverty than a successful Doha Round," Richard Newfarmer, an economic adviser in the bank's trade depart-ment, told journalists.

The new projections were very conservative, bank staffers emphasized, and it was misleading to compare them with the earlier estimates because they in-volved different assumptions. The 2001 estimate of an $830 billion increase in global income had been based on assumptions that lower barriers would gen-erate improvements in productivity, thereby enhancing economic growth world-wide. Because critics had sharply questioned the precision of those assumptions, the bank was erring on the side of prudence by refraining from incorporating them in its new $287 billion estimate of global gains. Furthermore, none of the estimates included any gains from the liberalization of the service sector, a po-tentially major source of higher productivity whose effects are much more dif-ficult to measure than those of tariff and subsidy cuts.

It is important to keep these new estimates in perspective. They certainly didn't mean that the trade liberalization of previous decades had been pointless; rather, they suggested that so much had been accomplished in the past as to dwarf the incremental benefits of going further, at least where trade in goods was concerned. Nor did the new estimates mean that the Doha Round was with-out value. Ridding the global economy of farm subsidies and lowering rich-country tariffs that blocked the importation of goods from low-income nations would make the trading system more just and would improve the fortunes of millions of destitute people, even if only modestly. Millions more would con-ceivably benefit from developing countries' reducing their own tariffs. Although there was considerable disagreement on this point, especially from countries such as India, the evidence suggested that many more poor people would gain from the lowering of prices for imports—especially for food—than would lose.

But there was no escaping the implications of the bank's new findings: The world's preeminent advocate of trade liberalization in developing countries was acknowledging that the impact of trade on development was much more limited than it had thought. "Are some of these numbers small? Clearly, smaller than one would wish," Alan Winters, the bank's director of research, told reporters. And the reason for that was not just that the bank had used conservative methodology; it was also that the model the bank's economists were using was more sophisticated and up-to-date than the earlier version.

The new model was more sophisticated because it factored in the impact of trade preferences—that is, the unrestricted access that some developing countries already enjoyed in rich-country markets under special arrangements. Those nations stood to lose something if all the world's trade barriers disappeared. Mexico, whose exporters could ship goods duty-free to the United States under NAFTA, offered an illuminating example. The more Washington lowered its barriers to all WTO member countries, the more Mexico's competitors could gain sales in the U.S. market at Mexico's expense. Thus, the bank's calculations showed Mexico as a net loser from global free trade.

The new model was more up-to-date, too, because it incorporated the effects of one of the most significant changes to hit the global economy in recent years—China's entry into the WTO, which had been finalized in 2001. The earlier model—the one that had led the bank to estimate global gains from a far-reaching trade deal at $830 billion—had been based on 1997 data, including the high tariffs that Beijing was imposing before it joined the trade body. The new model took account of the fact that the gains from China's liberalization were already in the past; this lowered the overall estimate of the benefits from freeing trade worldwide.

What, then, were the practical implications of this new analysis?

To the bank, and to other supporters of trade liberalization, there was fresh evidence of the need to slash tariffs, not just trim them, if the Doha Round were to generate much new trade that could advance the cause of development. As one of the bank's studies stated: "The liberalization targets under the DDA [Doha Development Agenda] have to be quite ambitious if the round is to have a measurable impact on world markets and hence poverty."

Furthermore, the liberalization would have to be especially far-reaching in one key area—agricultural market access, because that was where about two-thirds of the potential worldwide gains were to be found. Cuts in farm subsidies and lower tariffs on manufactured goods were both desirable, but those measures would not affect incomes much, either globally or in individual nations. The greatest economic value, according to the bank's calculations, was to be derived from lowering barriers to farm trade. Not only should agricultural tariffs be cut significantly, but there should be as few exceptions as possible for "sensitive" and "special" products. "Exempting even two percent of tariff lines [from deep cuts] could eviscerate the round" by wiping out most of the gains to be had from farm-trade liberalization, bank economists wrote.

The bank had a ready answer, too, for what should be done about the countries—such as Mexico, Cameroon, or Mozambique—that would apparently lose out for one reason or another as a result of global trade liberalization: Their losses "could be easily offset by extra foreign aid" that would help them adjust to the new world of lower trade barriers. Generous dollops of "aid for trade" would also be essential for countries with problems such as poor infrastructure that prevented them from taking advantage of lower barriers; they could make great strides in overcoming poverty if they received assistance targeted at helping them build the roads and ports they needed to bring their goods to market.

But another conclusion could be drawn from the bank's research—namely, that a sharp lowering of global trade barriers would bestow gains mainly on a few large, dynamic exporters in the developing world, like Brazil and China, whereas poorer nations would get much less than they had been led to believe.

Peter Mandelson, for one, seized on this point in a bid to rally the least-developed WTO members to his side in the battle over farm tariffs. The Doha Round "should benefit all and not just a tiny minority of competitive exporters," he said in a speech to a group of officials from impoverished countries on November 30, 2005, a couple of weeks before the Hong Kong meeting. So the best approach, the European trade commissioner contended, was not a radical reduction in barriers to agricultural trade, as the Americans were proposing, but a more modest one, which would help poor countries preserve the value of the preferential access they enjoyed in rich-country markets under various programs (such as America's African Growth and Opportunity Act). "Be aware," Mandelson said, in an ominous reference to the proposal Portman had advanced on October 10, "that some of the alternative tariff cutting proposals on the table will destroy completely your preferences."

Regardless of one's perspective on the bank's new data and the desirability of an ambitious Doha Round, the outlook for Hong Kong was bleak. Neither a deal that cut tariffs a lot nor one that cut them a little was even going to be discussed there, because of the fear that WTO members would fall on their faces trying to overcome their divisions.

| * |

With breathtaking views of Asia's most fabled harbor, fifty-two meeting rooms, seven restaurants, commodious auditoriums, and whiz-bang audiovisual gadgetry, the Hong Kong Convention Center offered a superlative venue for the delegations from the 149 WTO member nations who convened from December 13 to 18, 2005. The hosts from the former British colony bent over backward to accommodate their visitors' every need. Did a delegation want mobile phones? No problem; how many would they like? Trays of dim sum and other delicacies were available in copious quantities outside meeting rooms. Although a few thousand demonstrators mounted noisy protests, they encountered 9,000 police who had implemented elaborate security precautions.

Likewise, the WTO Secretariat, led by Lamy, had carefully planned meeting arrangements to guard against some of the problems that had contributed to failures at previous ministerials. Much effort went into ensuring effective communication between the green room insiders and outsiders. The *Bridges Daily Update*, the newsletter published during ministerials, reported the heartening result in its December 14 edition: "In terms of the negotiating process, the loud complaints . . . with respect to inclusiveness and transparency have all but disappeared. From a practical standpoint, most Members seem to have effectively accepted that the [green rooms] are the only realistic way to move forward in a 149 Member-strong organization, so long as all delegations are kept informed of the process and the discussions."

The logistics, then, were ideal. But what would the meeting participants talk about? That was the awkward problem confronting the ministers, because with expectations having been downgraded nearly a month earlier, they were under no pressure to pull any rabbits out of the Doha Round hat. On the other hand, they had to do *something* to impress the legions of journalists from newspapers and television stations all over the world who were prowling the halls. The result, despite the paucity of big issues, was some of the most memorable histrionics of any WTO ministerial. In the process, Hong Kong laid bare some of the WTO's worst traits—in particular the tendency of its meetings to degenerate into bureaucratic point-scoring exercises. In the WTO, the triumph that ministers exhibit in extracting concessions is often way out of proportion to the economic benefits they have reaped, and the stubbornness of those who resist making the concessions often conflicts with economic common sense.

So it went in the debate that took center stage at Hong Kong—whether, and if so when, to put a firm deadline on the elimination of export subsidies. As noted in previous chapters, these subsidies are not the most important form of support given to farmers—the European Union was pretty much the sole user of them, to the tune of about $4 billion a year—though they are widely viewed as the most egregious, and the July 2004 framework deal had included a pledge to scrap them by a "credible end date."

The upshot was that Mandelson found himself cast in the role of Franken-stein's monster, with the rest of the WTO membership playing the parts of a vil-lage mob brandishing pitchforks and torches.

At one of the first green room meetings, a four-hour session that began late in the evening of Wednesday, December 14, every country in attendance ex-cept for the European Union and Switzerland endorsed an end date for export subsidies of 2010. And during the next three days, as the pressure mounted on Mandelson in one late-night green room after another, he responded with a se-ries of outbursts ranging from the petulant to the explosive. On one occasion, he flung his glasses on the table; on another, he angrily left the room, com-plaining of having been "picked on all week"; on yet another, he lashed out at Lamy, whom he accused of abusing his position as meeting chair by trying to frame the E.U. position. "You're not the European Commissioner anymore, Pascal," Mandelson spat at the director-general. To add to Mandelson's dis-comfort, Portman was drawing raves for the genial manner in which he was conducting himself; at one point, during a discussion about cotton, the U.S. trade representative walked across the green room and knelt by his counterpart from Benin to engage in whispered conversation—a gesture that melted ob-servers' hearts.

At first, Mandelson refused to consider any specific termination time for ex-port subsidies, despite the vigorous entreaties of others such as India's Nath, who barked at the European trade commissioner, "I want a date! I want a date! I want a date!"—adding, to the general hilarity of the green room, "But not with you!"

Mandelson remained resolute, pointing out that he was being offered little of value in return. Only grudgingly did he accept the idea of terminating the subsidies by 2013; this was not a hugely meaningful move, because Brussels was already phasing out its use of such subsidies in important sectors (grains, beef, and sugar), leaving only dairy products and a couple of other sectors where the end date was still contentious. A majority of E.U. member states were insistent that 2013 was the earliest point at which export subsidies could be fully abol-ished, and Mandelson refused to violate this mandate.

The battle reached a climax on the final night in an eight-hour green room. Outside the Convention Center, TV cameras were trained on hundreds of pro-testers who broke through security cordons and, armed with bamboo sticks and wooden two-by-fours, fought their way to within a block of where delegates were meeting, prompting police to use pepper spray, water cannons, and trun-cheons. (Most of the demonstrators were South Korean farmers, who were once again rising up against the threat to their livelihoods that they said would result from any agreement allowing more rice to be imported into their country.) Inside the green room, far from the media's prying eyes, another clash was materializing, the highlight—or lowlight—of which came when Brazil's Amorim stormed out in such a rage that many participants thought that this ministerial, too, would end in an impasse.

Amorim was the leader of the forces demanding a 2010 end date for export subsidies; he had staked his prestige, and that of the G-20, on getting an agreement on the issue. His fury mounted as some of his G-20 allies, notably including Nath, began voicing the view in the green room that perhaps 2013 was the best that could be achieved, given the apparent lack of flexibility in Mandelson's position. To Amorim, this was a betrayal of a firm G-20 agreement to accept nothing short of 2010, and as other ministers watched with dismay, he headed for the door, fuming, "I'm not prepared to stay here and see people, one by one, cave in to the European Union!" Two of his aides, unsure where their boss was going or whether he would ever return, looked at each other and then, after a few moments, gathered their papers and walked out too. But then, a stroke of serendipity helped turn things around.

After leaving the green room and starting toward the exit of the Convention Center, Amorim bumped into the Japanese trade minister, Shoichi Nakagawa, who was munching on some hors d'oeuvres in the hall. Unaware of what had happened in the green room and assuming that Amorim was taking a snack break, Nakagawa waylaid the Brazilian minister to inquire about an unrelated issue. Just as Amorim was starting to extricate himself from this encounter, Portman burst through the doors of the green room and caught up with him.

"I literally begged him to come back," recalls Portman. "Celso is capable of theatrics, but this was real frustration on his part." Applying every bit of his self-effacing charm, the American implored Amorim to consider the possibility of a compromise, and after about fifteen minutes, the Brazilian relented, returning to the green room. A deal was indeed struck after he came back: The European Union would be allowed to keep the 2013 end date, but with the proviso that the phaseout of export subsidies would be front-loaded—that is, with a "substantial part" of the reductions taken well before 2013. Of this episode, Amorim would later say that had it not been for Nakagawa slowing him down, the Hong Kong meeting would have had an entirely different outcome.

| * |

So time-consuming was the Hong Kong haggling, and so often did the meetings continue late into the night, that Lamy ended up getting only seven hours of sleep during the five days of the meeting. When it was all over—after the director-general had held the closing press conference, and when ministers were racing to catch their flights to Chek Lap Kok Airport and protesters were folding up their banners to carry home—Guy de Jonquieres of the *Financial Times* authored one of the drollest leads in the annals of trade journalism. His story, which appeared in the *Financial Times* editions of December 19, 2005, began as follows:

> It is tempting, and scarcely an exaggeration, to sum up the meeting of World Trade Organization ministers in Hong Kong, which ended yesterday, by paraphrasing Winston Churchill: rarely in the history of international negotiations have so many laboured so long to produce so little.

At least the meeting had ended in agreement—for that, minister after minister was quoted as voicing relief. The compromise on export subsidies had made it possible to reach consensus on a text, thereby keeping the Doha Round from sliding backward. The text contained the following solemn passage: "We agree to intensify work on all outstanding issues to fulfill the Doha objectives, in particular, we are resolved to establish modalities no later than 30 April 2006." In other words, having once again failed to achieve this important goal, the WTO was compensating by setting a new deadline that was four months in the future.

To be sure, the termination of export subsidies was not the sole topic of discussion at Hong Kong. Other issues of greater potential import got attention as well. Rich nations announced plans to ramp up spending on "aid for trade" projects, such as the building of roads and other infrastructure that might make it possible for companies like Zambia's Finta Danish Dairies to export. The aid increases, however, were the source of much skepticism, and with good reason: They consisted mainly of grand promises to hike outlays over five or ten years— the kind of pledges that have a way of going unfulfilled, because they are not legally binding on the governments that would be in office so far in the future. Another noteworthy development at Hong Kong was the advancement of an initiative for high-income countries to eliminate all tariffs and quotas on goods exported by the world's poorest nations, specifically the thirty-two WTO members that qualify as least-developed countries. But this plan was shot through with loopholes, mostly because of the insistence of the United States that it not be required to grant duty-free access to these poor nations across the board. The textile barons of the American South, who feared a deluge of imported clothing from countries such as Bangladesh, were once again flexing their political muscles.

A fitting coda to Hong Kong came a couple of days after the delegations had returned home.

Mandelson was at his desk in Brussels when he received a phone call from Prime Minister Villepin to congratulate him for his performance. France saluted him for his mettle, for fighting like a lion on the export subsidy issue, Villepin told the European trade commissioner. Mandelson replied that he appreciated the sentiments but could not guarantee that Paris would always be so enamored of his actions as the negotiations progressed. Villepin said he realized that, but still wished to express his commendation.

The satisfaction that Europe's leading protectionist government took in the outcome at Hong Kong showed how unlikely it was that a Doha deal would imminently transform the settled arrangements governing global trade, especially insofar as they concerned agriculture. And another hammer blow was about to befall the round.

# 11 | WHEN PETER
# MET SUSAN

RIO DE JANEIRO'S COPACABANA BEACH IS JUSTLY RENOWNED FOR ITS picturesque setting, and Rob Portman enjoyed a run along the surf there while he was in the Brazilian city in late March 2006. That was just one of the positive aspects of his trip to Rio, where the U.S. trade representative attended a meeting hosted by Celso Amorim for purposes of discussing the next steps in the Doha Round. The other attendee was Peter Mandelson, and after meeting together with their aides, the three ministers gathered for a lunch that was so congenial, and so productive, that it went for an hour over schedule. Portman was relieved to see a much friendlier relationship taking hold between the Brazilian foreign minister and the European trade commissioner after their heated clash in Hong Kong. "It was one of those conversations where you're actually talking to each other, rather than past each other," recalls Mandelson. "We were sitting there using the backs of envelopes, putting down figures, and getting a sense of ambition and parameters. Don't get me wrong. I'm not saying we negotiated final figures—nothing of the sort. But it was a moment of frankness and trust."

Afterward, Mandelson took Portman aside to ask a sensitive question. The two men enthusiastically agreed that their discussion that day held great promise if they could build on it, but Mandelson was anxious about a rumor sweeping Washington that, he feared, could spell big trouble for the round. The rumor was that Portman, whose winsome ways had proved so effective with fellow trade ministers, was about to be promoted to a higher position. Asked point-blank whether that was true, Portman replied that it was not; he was totally committed to his job and was staying put.

At that time, the U.S. trade representative was giving an honest answer. The job he was rumored to be getting was Treasury secretary, and Portman already knew that he was not in the running; indeed, he was helping the White House persuade Henry Paulson, the chief executive of Goldman Sachs, to accept the Treasury post. Besides, Portman loved the trade job, which he had held for only eleven months, and, what was more, he knew that for the Doha Round, crunch time was coming in a matter of weeks.

The deal on modalities for agriculture and manufacturing trade, which had again proven elusory for the WTO in 2005, was supposed to be struck by April 30, 2006. This was a mandate of the Hong Kong declaration, and although that formal promise might have meant little given the number of self-imposed deadlines that had already slipped, now a different deadline was looming that could not be ignored. The Trade Promotion Authority bill that Congress had passed in 2002 was due to expire on June 30, 2007, and chances for its renewal looked sketchy at best because of growing hostility on Capitol Hill toward trade deals. Once that authority had expired, any agreement the Bush administration might strike in the Doha talks would be in mortal danger when it was submitted for approval on Capitol Hill, because it would not be guaranteed a straight up-or-down vote and could thus be picked apart with all sorts of destructive amendments. Although June 2007 was a long way off, WTO members would have to complete a huge amount of work before then. Even if a deal on modalities established the broad formulas setting the size of the cuts and exemptions in tariffs and subsidies, finalizing a Doha accord would also require months of negotiations about other issues, such as services and antidumping rules, that were also part of the round's agenda. Furthermore, drafting and scrutinizing the thousands of pages of schedules for each country's myriad tariff lines would probably take a good half year. Lamy spared no effort in spelling this out to WTO members as he sought to convey the urgency of reaching a deal on modalities as early as possible in 2006. The director-general warned in late March that delay until later in the year would be "a huge collective mistake."

But any momentum that might have been building in the negotiations came to a halt after Portman returned from Rio to Washington and got a phone call from Joshua Bolten, the newly appointed White House chief of staff. Portman *was* going to be changing jobs after all.

The president had decided, Bolten said, that Portman should take the job that Bolten had just vacated as head of the Office of Management and Budget, a powerful post. Flattered as he was, Portman turned the offer down; he felt that the Doha Round was at a crucial juncture, and he was also making progress on several bilateral deals. But Bolten, who had known Portman for years, replied in a friendly tone that perhaps Portman wasn't listening: This decision had been made by Bush himself. Although several members of Congress were qualified for the job, the White House didn't want to risk losing Republican seats in a tough election year. The chief of staff reminded Portman that as budget director, he would have far more access to the Oval Office than he had in the trade job. And Bolten laid it on thick where he knew it would work best: *The president has decided you should.* So Portman relented. "It was not something I said yes to initially," Portman says. "But it wasn't put to me as an option they wanted me to think about. It was, 'The president wants you to do this.'"

Portman set one condition: The White House must announce both his nomination and his successor on the same day, so as to minimize any perception of discontinuity in Bush administration trade policy; and further to that same goal, his strong preference was that his successor be one of his deputies. He knew the person he wanted.

Deputy U.S. Trade Representative Susan Schwab was attending a play on Friday, April 14, when during intermission a call came from Portman with some staggering news: The White House was going to announce early the following week that she was going to replace him. Sure enough, a few days later Schwab was standing next to the president in the Rose Garden, with her parents beaming in the audience as Bush named her as his choice for the top trade post. Knowing that Portman's job switch would draw criticism because of the potentially negative impact on the round, Bush aides made sure that the president's remarks highlighted his commitment to finishing the talks and Schwab's record as a trade negotiator. "Now she will use her experience to help complete the Doha Round and create other new opportunities for American exporters," Bush stated. But many outsiders saw through such spin. "To have Rob Portman leaving that post at this crucial time . . . is bad news as far as the Doha Round is concerned," Charles Grassley, the Iowa Republican who chaired the Senate Finance Committee, told reporters. A statement issued by Mandelson reflected the widespread sentiment among other countries' negotiators that the loss of Portman would significantly damage the talks' prospects. "We will, of course, manage without him, but at this stage of the round, it would have been easier to manage with him," the European trade commissioner said.

Without question, Sue Schwab brought a skill set to the trade job that differed from Portman's, just as Portman's strengths had contrasted with Zoellick's. At fifty-one, she had spent nearly three decades in the trade field, honing an agreeable but steely manner in the process.

Schwab's training in dealing with foreigners came early. The daughter of a U.S. Foreign Service officer, she had moved with her parents to Togo, Nigeria,

Sierra Leone, Tunisia, and Thailand before earning a B.A. from Williams College and a master's degree from Stanford. As a child, she was "very self-motivated and very self-directed," according to her sister. Part of the family lore is that she decided one day at age six to become an Olympic swimmer and went to a pool in Togo to begin training immediately; her mother had to fish the half-drowned Susan out of the water.

Her early career established her reputation for toughness in dealing with people across the negotiating table, notwithstanding her honey-colored hair and cheery disposition. After joining the Office of the U.S. Trade Representative in 1977 as a junior agricultural negotiator, she was dispatched a couple of years later to the U.S. embassy in Tokyo, where she tangled with Japanese bureaucrats in prying open the market for American beef, citrus products, and telecommunications equipment. Her influence soared in the 1980s when she joined the staff of Senator John Danforth, the Missouri Republican who chaired the International Trade Subcommittee. Danforth entrusted her with enormous responsibility for shaping trade legislation, and she gained notice as one of the leading "hawks" in the effort to clamp down on Japan over its trade practices—so much so that critics accused her of being a closet protectionist. ("Free-trade pragmatist" was how Schwab described herself.) A skilled infighter in the art of bill writing, she was a key drafter of the 1988 bill that substantially increased the threat of unilateral U.S. sanctions against countries that were "unreasonably" blocking U.S. exports. During the administration of the elder George Bush, she further enhanced her image as a champion of American exports by heading the Commerce Department agency that assists U.S. firms in gaining access to overseas markets. Following a brief stint at Motorola Incorporated, she concluded that she had better hedge her career bets by getting more academic credentials. So she finished a Ph.D. in public administration and international business and became dean of the University of Maryland School of Public Policy, before rejoining the trade representative's office in 2005 as Portman's deputy.

For all her accomplishments, her personal life was a source of anguish. In 1995, while on a cruise, she had met and soon thereafter married a professional magician named Curtis Carroll—who, given his occupation and lack of education past high school, was hardly a classic match for a woman with Schwab's career and good-girl persona. He was "hysterically funny and incredibly talented," in Schwab's words, but he also had a serious problem, as she later explained to *Fortune* magazine:

> Curtis became an alcoholic, or maybe he was and I didn't know it. It got
> worse and worse, and the last couple of years it was pretty strained because

I was doing what all spouses and loved ones of alcoholics do—beg, plead, threaten, try to rescue. And then at some point you figure out there isn't a damn thing you can do. No matter how much you love the guy, no matter how much he loves you. . . . He'd go to rehab. He was in and out. I didn't realize how sick he was, quite frankly.

After an unsuccessful effort to revive Carroll's career by investing their savings in a magician's theater, the couple separated. Instead of sobering up, Carroll plunged even further into the depths and developed cirrhosis of the liver. (He would die a few months after Schwab's appointment to succeed Portman; Schwab later told the *New York Times* that she had been "lucky to have found him" and "I miss him a lot.")

The trade representative's job gave Schwab more than ample reason for moving on. She needed to channel enormous energy into getting up to speed, because although she had in a sense been in training for the post her whole adult life, she had been back at the agency only six months and had spent very little of that time on the Doha Round. As Portman's deputy she had worked mainly on free-trade agreements with Colombia and Peru and on a lumber dispute with Canada. Her exposure to the Doha talks consisted of attending the Hong Kong meeting, where she had privately expressed bafflement to some of her U.S. colleagues about how a deal was supposed to get done. After looking even more closely at the terms of what was on the table, she began to conclude that she and the other Doha negotiators had been handed a massive problem, thanks to the design of the July 2004 framework. "The way the framework was set up made it almost inevitable that countries would focus on protecting their defensive interests instead of going after their offensive potential," she told me. "The theory was right on target—the highest tariffs get cut the most. But then there are the flexibilities"—that is, the sensitive and special products loopholes. "Because of them, you don't know whether your exports will get any market access at all."

Schwab had none of Portman's personal connections to Bush, and she could hardly hope to match Portman's ability, as a well-liked former congressman, to pull levers on Capitol Hill. Nor did she have his gift of instant rapport with people.

What she did have was the tenacity of a veteran trade warrior who wasn't afraid to say no, especially when she felt that U.S. exporters were being shortchanged. Concerning the Doha Round, she repeatedly stated that only an ambitious agreement—one that significantly opened markets around the world—would be acceptable; Doha Lite "would waste a once-in-a-lifetime opportunity." Just in case her spine wasn't stiff enough already, members of Congress made sure she understood that they would insist on terms aimed at generating abundant new exports for U.S. farmers. "If Plan B might be a minimalist approach, don't bother bringing Plan B to me," Finance Committee chairman Grassley warned her at her confirmation hearing. Farm groups, too, were emphatic in admonishing her to take account of their expectations about the round, which dated back to the promises Zoellick had given them in 2001. For every dollar Washington gave up in subsidies, she must extract a dollar's worth of exports for them; as a June 1, 2006 letter signed by most major agriculture organizations put it: "If negotiators are forced to scale back" the amount of market access they get for American farm goods overseas, their offer to cut subsidies "must be commensurately reduced."

So it was that Schwab sallied forth, flying the flag of ambition. In her view, she was following the classic American tradition of pressing aggressively to expand the frontiers of free trade, with the expectation that this would boost growth and development. In her negotiating partners' view, she was practicing mercantilism, just as Portman and Zoellick had, seeking to ensure that the United States would be richly compensated for curbing subsidy programs that ought not to exist in the first place. In any event, she would have to trim her sails as evidence grew that grand ambition was not to be the Doha Round's guiding principle. The framework was only part of the problem. When it came to demands for lower trade barriers, other countries' policymakers were coming up with more reasons all the time to resist. Ambition, in liberalizing trade? That was so 1995.

| * |

Of all the rooms in the Centre William Rappard, the library is one of the most elegant, with its carved ceilings, encirclement of balconies, and windows overlooking the lake. That is where Lamy decided a major green room meeting would be held in June 2006. The original Green Room (the director-general's conference room) was too small for the meeting he had in mind, and other conference rooms in the building were, he thought, too sterile. Lamy wanted an atmosphere that was both warm and stately, in the hope that this would be conducive to breaking down the defensiveness of the thirty or so ministers who would attend. Bookshelves were hauled away from the main library floor and replaced by a large table and chairs. Because the room isn't air conditioned, a ventilation tube was installed to pump fresh air in from outside.

The stage was literally being set for the long-awaited accord on modalities. Lamy had been forced to abandon his plan to hold a ministerial in April, thanks in part to the replacement of Portman with Schwab, but he was still gung ho to advance the Doha Round to the point where it could be wrapped up before the expiration of Trade Promotion Authority. So he was calling a meeting that would be very similar in format to the one that had produced the framework in 2004—that is, with a few dozen countries represented by ministers and the rest by ambassadors. Provided this meeting was successful, there was still time, he believed, to finish the round during the remaining months of 2006, leaving time for the U.S. Congress to consider the deal on a strictly up-or-down vote, with no amendments, in accord with Trade Promotion Authority procedures.

If only dislodging governments from their entrenched positions were as easy as moving furniture.

To further enhance chances for a deal, a new elite club of ministers, called the G-6, met with Lamy at the U.S. mission a couple of days in advance of the scheduled June 30 meeting in the library. The premise of this meeting was that the six must reach agreement before the library group would have any prospect of doing so. The group consisted of the ministers from the Five Interested Parties—the United States, the European Union, Brazil, India, and Australia— plus Japan. (The Japanese had been invited back into the innermost council mainly because their trade minister, Shoichi Nakagawa, was proving a more active give-and-taker than his predecessors who had so riled Zoellick.)

It was Schwab's debut in the global arena, and it could hardly have been rockier. Previously, fingers had been pointing at the European Union and Mandelson for the round's slow progress. Now the United States and its rookie trade representative would take a turn at feeling the heat.

The other ministers were in full cry about U.S. farm subsidies, insisting that Washington offer deeper cuts in its agricultural support programs than it had in its much-ballyhooed proposal of October 2005. They understood that as a newly minted trade representative with little stature on Capitol Hill, Schwab would want to prove her mettle by taking a very hard line against their demands. But that did not stop them from trying.

"What do you need to do more?" That question, posed by Mandelson to Schwab early in the meeting, established the theme for much of the discussion, in which she was repeatedly—and unsuccessfully—challenged to show signs of willingness to make concessions.

Cleverly, Mandelson positioned himself as an ally of the G-20, which had presented its own proposal. Under the G-20 plan, the United States would have to cap at $12 billion all farm-subsidy programs that distort trade, which was far below the $22.6 billion that would be allowed under Washington's offer. To induce the United States to accept a much lower ceiling on subsidies, Mandelson said Brussels was prepared to "move as close as possible" to the G-20 plan on the issue the United States cared about most—increased market access for farm products. That would presumably mean an average cut in European farm tariffs of as much as 54 percent, which was a considerably deeper reduction than the European Union had previously put on the table. But he could make that move, Mandelson added, only if the United States first indicated its willingness to take a significant step on subsidies.

"The bottom line is, you have to improve your October offer," the European trade commissioner declared. "So tell us what you need for that." His remarks were warmly seconded by Brazil's Amorim and India's Nath.

Schwab, who was accompanied by Agriculture Secretary Mike Johanns, countered that any additional concessions they might offer on subsidies would simply be pocketed, so it was the responsibility of the others in the room to step forward with clear pledges to reduce their import barriers. She stuck to the U.S. argument that in evaluating whether the round was truly successful or not, the best metric would be the degree of new openness in world agriculture markets rather than cuts in farm subsidies. "Market access is where the benefits of the round will come from," she said, reminding the others of the World Bank studies showing that lowering barriers across the board in agriculture would give developing countries the greatest gains.

In making this case, Schwab's style caused her counterparts' teeth to grind, because she sometimes came across as a schoolmistress lecturing inattentive students. She would occasionally take note of her academic background and knowledge of development issues, which the others took as an attempt to cloak her political concerns about the U.S. farm lobby by infusing her positions with high-mindedness.

Still, they could not effectively rebut her main point, which was that they simply weren't offering anything very meaningful on the market access issue. For all of Mandelson's claims to be showing new flexibility in opening Europe's agriculture markets, he had only suggested he might accept something like the G-20 tariff cut number, and he hadn't changed his position at all on the critical loophole issue—that is, how many sensitive products the European Union could exclude from deep cuts. The Indians, meanwhile, were sticking to a proposal advanced by a group of developing countries, called the G-33, that had coalesced around the idea of ensuring that their poorest farmers would get strong protection from being overrun by foreign competition. Under their plan, developing countries would get an especially broad special products loophole by being allowed to designate up to 20 percent of their tariff lines as special, with the majority of those undergoing no cut whatsoever. This degree of flexibility appalled the U.S. negotiators, who reckoned it would stifle any hopes American farmers might have had for growth in agricultural exports to the developing world. According to U.S. government calculations, just 5 percent of tariff lines could account for more than 90 percent of the U.S. farm goods imported by many large developing countries.

Amorim, too, hammered away at Schwab on the subsidy issue, demonstrating firm solidarity in G-20 ranks. The Brazilian minister derided the $22.6 billion figure that Washington had promised as a cap on its subsidy programs, saying: "It's difficult to accept a level that was surpassed only twice in the last 11 years." But Schwab made it clear she wasn't going to even discuss offering deeper subsidy cuts.

"There is nothing in market access on offer that is anywhere near our expectations," she said, and there the group remained stuck. A disappointed Lamy steered the conversation toward how to handle the impasse. "We have before us two options," he said. "One is an open crisis, and the other one is a managed crisis."

The library redecorating exercise thus turned out to have been in vain. The larger group of ministers gathered as planned in the library on June 30, but no amount of warmth in the surroundings could produce a meeting of minds given the rupture in the G-6. To the profound annoyance of many ministers, Nath came very late to this meeting, telling the others that he had been watching a World Cup soccer match between Argentina and Germany. It was a disrespectful way of conveying the message that he regarded the larger meeting as a waste of time, but he knew that nothing important would transpire.

"The result of these discussions is pretty clear: there has been no progress, and therefore we are in a crisis," Lamy told a press conference. Yet all was not lost; the crisis was to be of the "managed" variety. "I still believe the differences and the gaps are not unbridgeable," the director-general said, explaining that he planned to conduct an intense round of "shuttle diplomacy" during the following weeks in the hope of bringing the parties close enough together that an agreement could be struck in late July. Part of these talks would involve confessionals—meetings in which ministers would tell him, in utmost confidence, just how far they could go.

As the ministers streamed out of the Centre William Rappard following a series of press conferences, I snagged a brief interview with Schwab. She did not dispute that the United States had now emerged as the outlier in the talks—the country getting most of the opprobrium from the others for holding up an agreement.

"Isn't that what leadership is all about?" she asked rhetorically.

Maybe so, and if being an outlier means being a leader, Schwab was soon to find herself even further out in front of the WTO parade.

| * |

To say that Schwab and Mandelson weren't hitting it off would be a gross understatement. She told colleagues, in disgust, that the European trade commissioner seemed much more interested in how he would be portrayed in the news media than in reaching an agreement, to the point where he sometimes stopped paying attention in meetings while working on his press statements. For his part, Mandelson complained to other European officials that Schwab was nervous, brittle, and unforthcoming, seemingly unable to overcome her fear that she would run afoul of Congress and industry groups for offering too much in the negotiations.

As preparations got under way for another meeting to repair the breach that had occurred in June 2006, the two sparred repeatedly. They attended a mid-July summit of the G-8 leaders in St. Petersburg, Russia, that issued a communiqué calling for "a concerted effort" to finish the round, starting with "agreement on negotiating modalities . . . within a month." Despite the leaders' appeal for cooperation, tension between Schwab and Mandelson flared almost as soon as they walked into a postsummit meeting in Geneva with a few other ministers. A snide comment by Schwab drew a rebuke from Mandelson that he considered her words "inappropriate," to which she responded that she wanted to show everyone what *she* considered inappropriate. At that point, she personally handed out copies of a newspaper article containing some leaked information from the negotiations—a leak that, she suggested, could have come only from Mandelson or his lieutenants.

The exchanges got uglier still once the real negotiations got under way on July 23, when the G-6 met at the U.S. mission in what was billed as a last-ditch effort to get the round on track in 2006.

The meeting started with a reproof from Lamy. The WTO members outside the G-6 were "not happy" with how the six had failed to produce results, the director-general said. He regretted to inform them that during the shuttle diplomacy he had conducted over the previous couple of weeks, he had detected "not much movement" in the confessionals he had held with the key players. "We need to improve the numbers," he implored them, and "define the landing zone" where an accord was to be found.

He then proposed to start the discussion by focusing on agricultural market access. This proved a good way to get the talks going, because the parties who had resisted opening their markets for so long were indicating at least some willingness to be more forthcoming. Nath, who had steadfastly insisted up to that point on India's right to designate 20 percent of its tariff lines as special products, assured Schwab, "I'm happy to negotiate the 20 percent," though he didn't say how much lower he would go. "India is prepared to negotiate numbers and treatment," he said. Mandelson committed himself to more specific numbers than before, accepting a 51 percent average cut in E.U. farm tariffs, and he indicated that he could reduce the amount of products he would protect under the sensitive products designation to perhaps 4 percent or 5 percent of tariff lines, a figure much closer to a level Washington considered acceptable.

These signs of flexibility, however, were insufficient for the Americans, who felt there were still too many unanswered questions about how open foreign markets would really be for U.S. agricultural exports. Never mind about the *average* tariff cut that Mandelson was offering; what about the cuts that would apply to the *highest* tariffs? As for sensitive products, what exactly would happen with those in the European market? The European Union was proposing that for each sensitive product, a certain amount of increased tonnage could enter European markets at very low duties, but how much extra U.S. exports might that entail? The often-vague, sometimes unsatisfactory answers they got to these questions left the U.S. negotiators uneasily imagining the time in the future when they would be scrutinizing the thousands of pages of tariff schedules for specific products that would be incorporated into a final Doha Round agreement. If those schedules did not translate into significant new opportunities for U.S. exporters, there would be hell to pay in Washington.

"We have to know now what the rules [about market access] are going to be," Johanns protested. "We can't wait until we see the schedules."

Accordingly, when Lamy moved the topic of discussion to subsidies, the meeting suddenly hit an insurmountable roadblock, because Schwab took just as unbending a position as she had a few weeks earlier. "I see no new market access," she said. "Because of that, we're in no position to do anything more."

Furious sputtering ensued over her prim refusal to budge. "Do you mean to insult everyone, or is it just a ploy to hide the fact that you can't move?" Mandelson asked, according to notes of the meeting. "We can understand if it can't be done now," the European trade commissioner continued, implying that the White House was trying to help Republican candidates in rural districts in the upcoming 2006 elections. "But don't blame us. It's not credible. . . . [I]t's a position dictated by politics. You should be straight. . . . This is shabby. I don't know whether to react in horror or anger."

Others then piled on, though in less harsh tones. "I've always taken your word when you said you could do more [on subsidies] when you saw movement in market access," Amorim said. "The U.S. showed leadership with its 2005 proposal. Now the E.U. has shown movement. Kamal showed movement. . . . The U.S. must show leadership." Even Japan's Nakagawa, who had barely offered anything new, pronounced himself "astonished at the U.S." But Schwab retorted, "We won't negotiate with ourselves."

Then it was Lamy's turn to intervene. The director-general made it clear that he thought Schwab was abusing the process; although the others had put some chips down during the discussion about the issue she cared about, she had failed to reciprocate in any way during the discussion about their most important issue. "There's a lot more on the table today than has been previously expressed in the negotiations," he told Schwab. "Surely you can indicate what direction you can move. In fairness you owe it to the group." She held fast to her position, however, and after some additional recriminations, the meeting broke up for dinner.

It was an awkward meal, given all the conflict that had just arisen. While the others were eating, Schwab huddled with Lamy for a private chat. She suggested that she could offer *something* on subsidies—a $19 billion cap, down from the $22.6 billion that Washington had officially put on the table. But this concession was so piddling that the director-general advised against it. The United States was currently spending about $20 billion on farm subsidies, Lamy observed, so offering to trim that by a mere $1 billion was only going to anger her interlocutors even more.

The time for managed crises was over. An open one was in order.

Lamy declared the Doha Round "suspended" the next day, in a somber address to ambassadors in the General Council chamber. "There are no winners and losers in this assembly today," he said. "There are only losers."

What the suspension of the round meant, and how long it would last, nobody could be sure. One thing was clear: It was going to take quite a while for passions to cool, especially the animosity between Schwab and Mandelson. The U.S. trade representative returned to Washington livid over Mandelson's treatment of her in the meeting as well as his public statements afterward, in which he accused the United States of being the only participant that had failed to comply with the St. Petersburg summit's mandate for greater flexibility. She could barely conceal her ire when she met with reporters, recalling that she had turned to Mandelson just as the meeting ended, "but he didn't want to talk."

Some analysts predicted that the negotiations would remain moribund until after a new U.S. president was elected, because only then would there be any chance that Congress would pass a new version of Trade Promotion Authority. And who could be sure that, even then, much sentiment would remain for continuing? The potential implications of this scenario were aptly depicted by the July 29 cover of the *Economist*. "The Future of Globalisation" was its title; the illustration was a photo of a rusty boat heaved on its side near a sandy shore.

The suspension left an enormous amount of unfinished business. It had resulted from a clash over agriculture, and although that was the main issue in the round, the negotiations had barely touched on another major subject on the agenda—manufactured goods, the chief topic during so many trade rounds of yore. In this realm, too, globalization was showing signs of running aground.

| * |

When Danubia Rodriguez walked away from her mountain village in Honduras in 1998 to work in an apparel plant, her act demonstrated the implicit bargain Honduran officials had struck in hopes of improving the lot of their country. They had scrapped inward-looking policies and turned the economy into one of the most open developing countries in the world, according to the World Bank. Foreign clothing makers were welcomed to invest, so shipments of bananas, coffee, and shrimp were gradually eclipsed by exports of garments and fabric churned out by the new plants, or *maquilas*, where employment surged to 130,000 by 2003, a substantial number in a country of just 6.8 million. It was, Honduran officials hoped, the start of a cycle of development and wealth creation whose virtues could be glimpsed in the small steps forward taken by people like Rodriguez.

In the village where she and her six sisters grew up, a place called Las Mangas, life had been difficult. Getting there from the nearest dirt road required an hour-long hike up a steep, rocky trail, including fording a small river. The home built by her father, a coffee farmer who never went to school, was an earthen-walled structure covered partly with a corrugated-zinc roof and partly with thatched coconut leaves. The worst part of living there, she said, was picking, washing, and drying coffee beans. "We woke up at 4:00 a.m., and came back at 5:00 p.m. during the cutting season," she recalled, shuddering at the memory of the swarms of mosquitoes that would bite her and her sisters as they worked. She attended school up to the sixth grade; the village had no school for the grades beyond.

By 2004, when I met her, Rodriguez was living in a cinder-block house in a town called El Progreso, and though cramped and rickety by U.S. standards, it held luxuries undreamed of in village life: A gas stove. Indoor plumbing.

Television and the electricity to power it. A diet that had moved beyond rice, beans, and tortillas to include regular portions of meat, fish, and fresh vegetables. She was able to afford these middle-class accoutrements thanks to the wages of $1.50 an hour she had earned stitching Hanes brand sports shirts at a *maquila* owned by Sara Lee Branded Apparel, whose businesses include the Hanes line. "It has really been hard for me to achieve all this," said Rodriguez, a twenty-four-year-old single mother, gesturing around her home.

But Rodriguez was now out of the job that had made her rise in living standards possible. A few weeks earlier, Sara Lee had shut down the *maquila*, depriving her and 470 of her coworkers of their incomes. The chief reason, company officials confided, was competition from China.

Imagine: Even a Honduran "sweatshop" job was vulnerable to being undercut, now that China's export juggernaut was ramped up. Rodriguez's plight highlighted concerns that were growing fast among WTO member nations, especially developing ones: Could their manufacturers survive in a world where Chinese factories were expanding their dominance over one industry after another? Would they have a chance to industrialize before Chinese competition wiped them out? If not, how would their peoples' living standards ever advance? In other words, could the global trading system truly work to their advantage?

There is nothing new, of course, about industries pulling up stakes in one country and putting them down someplace else. But the speed at which such moves take place has accelerated dramatically in recent years, in no small part because of China's success in turning tens of millions of its peasants each year into low-wage, highly productive factory workers. Nowhere was this truer than in the sector where Danubia Rodriguez worked—the traditional first rung on the ladder of industrialization. Beijing had scrapped a network of outmoded, state-run textile and apparel factories in the late 1990s, at the cost of more than 1 million Chinese jobs. On the ashes of that industry arose a vibrant, privately run new one that invested heavily in state-of-the-art plants with advanced weaving machines and other modern equipment. To top it off, the Chinese authorities poured billions of dollars more into roads and ports that allowed speedier delivery to American customers across the Pacific. By the time Rodriguez lost her job, 18 million Chinese were working in competing mills earning average wages of about sixty-eight cents an hour.

The full force of globalization's accelerating pace came home to me during my trip to Honduras when, over beers in the lobby of the hotel where I was staying, I chatted with a fifty-two-year-old American named B. J. Robbins, who worked for Garan Incorporated, a children's apparel company. In his deep southern drawl, Robbins told me about his background, which had eerie parallels with that of Danubia Rodriguez.

Like her, Robbins was one of seven children (although his siblings were all boys instead of all girls), and he was the offspring of illiterate parents. Like her, he grew up doing backbreaking farm labor; "I started cutting cotton at age five," he told me, explaining that his family members were the only white sharecroppers on the Arkansas plantation where they lived. Like her, he stepped on the escalator to a better life by going to work in an apparel factory.

Here, though, was a huge difference: Whereas Rodriguez had worked in *maquilas* for only six years before seeing them close under pressure from foreign competition, Robbins had stayed employed in the industry for thirty-four years, moving eventually into lower-level management, which gave him a decent enough income to buy a farm in Mississippi and to send his wife, who also worked for a clothing concern, to college. Sure, many of his company's factories in Georgia, Alabama, and Mississippi had migrated about five years earlier to Honduras, El Salvador, and Nicaragua, but only after staying put long enough in the American South to help propel the region well down the road to modernization. Sourly, he predicted that Honduras was destined to suffer the same fate, only more quickly. "Yeah, work will go out of here," he said. "Just like it did in the States."

One major reason for worry about Honduras—along with a host of other developing countries—was that on January 1, 2005, WTO rules governing the textile trade were undergoing their biggest revision in thirty years. As noted in Chapter 2, developing countries' textile industries had been forced to operate for decades under a complicated system of quotas that set limits on the amount of slacks, tops, nightgowns, sheets, and other such products each nation could export to the United States and Europe. They fought during the Uruguay Round to end this system and got Washington and Brussels to agree that the quotas would end in ten years. Now that the expiration date for the quota system was imminent, however, governments throughout the developing world were having second thoughts, because the quota system at least ensured each of them a portion of the world market—a market that China appeared poised to capture. Already, in a handful of categories where quotas had been eliminated (baby clothes, robes, and knit fabrics, for example), Chinese exports to the United States had surged, in some cases by twentyfold, at the expense of exporters from other nations. If buyers for companies like J. C. Penney or Banana Republic could purchase as much as they wanted of any item from whoever gave them the best price, they were bound to give Chinese suppliers an enormous amount of business. Wal-Mart, for example, which had been buying apparel in about sixty-three countries under the quota system, was planning to reduce its supplier nations to around four or five, with China topping the list.

So dozens of developing nations were scrambling to stave off the Chinese menace to their textile and apparel companies, lest they become mere way stations for multinational firms looking for places to set up factories. Some were negotiating preferential trade arrangements with the United States, a notable example being the Central American Free Trade Agreement, which would give Honduras's clothing makers some hope of salvation by permanently making Honduran clothing duty-free in the U.S. market. Others were lobbying for measures that would extend the quota system to a certain extent (and they would have some limited success in that regard). Among them was Turkey, whose textile companies lost about a tenth of their workforce in 2005–2006 in the face of Chinese competition.

For the Doha Round, the fearsome specter of China's industrial machine posed a problem that became increasingly manifest in 2007 as the focus broadened to the talks on access for manufactured goods—or NAMA, in WTO-speak. (The acronym stands for "nonagricultural market access," and, alas, it is uttered so commonly by trade negotiators that its use in this book is unavoidable.)

Securing an ambitious deal in NAMA was a top priority for rich countries. They already have very low tariffs on most manufactured goods, and in industries where they were especially competitive—chemicals, machinery, and medical equipment, for example—they wanted fast-growing emerging markets to lower their barriers significantly.

But at a time when China was bestriding the manufacturing world like a Colossus, the idea of cutting tariffs wasn't going over well in parts of Latin America, Africa, and developing Asia. A new argument was coming to the fore—or, rather, an old argument updated for the new reality: Perhaps developing countries needed to maintain relatively high tariff walls for their most promising industries, as they had during the era of import substitution in the 1960s and '70s, because the alternative might be decimation at the hands of Chinese imports. For adherents of this school of thought (who included Harvard's Dani Rodrik, the globalization skeptic introduced in Chapter 5), the buzzword was "policy space," meaning that developing-country governments ought to keep some maneuvering room to shelter and nourish their producers rather than simply lowering their bound tariffs, because they knew best which of their industries and companies had the most potential to grow and prosper. In effect, this argument meant that the brakes should be applied to globalization, at least in the developing world.

One big drawback to this approach, of course, was that it offered a convenient cover for sheer protectionism—an intellectual excuse for policymakers who were simply carrying water for powerful special interests seeking to preserve control over their nation's domestic market. Another problem was that few developing countries had proven adept in the past at choosing which industries were most deserving of nurturing. In one particularly ill-starred venture, Brazil had used high tariffs during the 1970s as part of a plan, dubbed "Informatics," to build a domestic computer industry. The duties on foreign computers made them so expensive that Brazilian firms, forced to make do with poor-quality domestic ones, lagged in computerization, hobbling the entire economy.

Whatever the merits of their case, a potent coalition of developing countries was fending off demands from the rich countries for the round to include deep cuts in industrial tariffs. Calling itself the "NAMA-11," this group, whose leading members included Brazil, South Africa, Argentina, India, and Egypt, was insisting that developing countries should be allowed to apply a much laxer formula to their tariff cuts than rich countries would. They also wanted the tariff-cutting regime for manufactured goods to include loopholes, or "flexibilities," so that they could exclude some products from cuts or subject them to smaller cuts, in a manner similar to the planned system for agricultural tariffs.

Fueling this movement was another concern about China, one that was shared by a number of policymakers in rich countries and that the WTO appeared powerless to address.

| * |

Hunched over clattering machinery, the 170 workers at Shanghai Datong Automotive Industrial Company were churning out pistons for auto engines by the crateful in mid-2006, driven by surging demand from abroad. To hear managers at the Chinese firm tell it, their success overseas was due to efficiency and rock-bottom costs. "Our technology is good, our wages are low and materials are abundant," Jin Zhangfu, the plant's manufacturing supervisor, boasted to the *Washington Post*.

But in the American heartland towns where auto-parts makers were struggling to survive, an entirely different explanation—China's cheap currency—was proffered for the competitiveness of companies such as Shanghai Datong. Wes Smith, president of E&E Manufacturing Company of Plymouth, Michigan, a maker of fasteners and other auto components, blamed much of "the world of hurt" his company was suffering on Beijing's policy of keeping the value of the yuan tightly controlled at a level that, he said, gave Chinese manufacturers an unfair advantage. "It's not that we're competing against the so-called dollar-a-day wage," Smith protested. "It's that they subsidize their production with currency manipulation."

In recent decades most other major countries in the world have allowed their currencies to float in value on international markets. Not China, which used a different system that relied on strict controls over capital inflows and outflows. Starting in 1995 Beijing kept the yuan pegged at 8.28 per U.S. dollar, so even though other currencies began rising substantially against the greenback in 2002—including the euro, the British pound, the Japanese yen, and the Canadian and Australian dollars—the yuan's exchange rate against the dollar stayed the same. China announced in July 2005 that it would raise the value of the yuan by about 2 percent against the dollar and allow it to gradually move more in accord with supply and demand. But in the year after that, Beijing kept further appreciation to a minimum.

Criticism over China's currency policy, which had begun to flare in 2004, was reaching a new and potentially explosive stage in 2006 as Chinese manufacturers moved up the ladder from clothes, toys, and televisions to goods such as auto parts. Treasury Secretary Henry Paulson was pressuring Beijing to change its policy, members of Congress were threatening to impose punitive tariffs on Chinese goods, and U.S. manufacturers were calling for Washington to file a WTO case against Beijing (an idea that faded when the Office of the U.S. Trade Representative concluded that such a case was probably unwinnable). Although some economists viewed the matter as overblown, others contended that the yuan's exchange rate was so far out of line as to constitute a dangerous distortion in global trade. They cited the extraordinary increase in China's exports, which had roughly tripled from the 2002 level of about $325 billion, and the sixfold increase in the nation's current account surplus, the broadest measure of the gap between export and imports. These increases in turn were contributing to the growth in global trade imbalances—the swelling U.S. trade deficit and the mushrooming surpluses elsewhere—that were raising concerns, among some economists at least, about the stability of the world economy.

Chinese officials defended their currency regime as a legitimate choice for their still-developing nation. Limiting the amount of money flowing in and out of the country helped them keep the yuan steady and avoid the financial crises that had struck their Asian neighbors in the late 1990s, a feat for which Beijing drew international praise. The fixed-rate policy had also helped tame inflation during the 1990s. But by a very few years into the twenty-first century, the yuan was well below—by a margin of about 20 percent to 40 percent—the exchange rate that many economists considered appropriate. At that point, a major factor behind the policy was fear that appreciation of the yuan would make exports less competitive, threatening jobs. "Traditionally, China relies on exports for growth, and the government is very nervous about harming this," He Fan, an economist at the Chinese Academy of Social Sciences in Beijing, acknowledged in the *Post*. "There would be huge unemployment." To critics, Beijing was practicing beggar-thy-neighbor economics, exporting joblessness to the rest of the world.

What does all this have to do with the Doha Round? Nothing, and that is precisely the point. The talks didn't include the issue of China's currency, which surfaced well after the round was under way, even though it involved problems in the trading system that were arguably as serious, if not more so, than the other issues that *were* being negotiated.

As we shall see, the China currency issue would not be the only emerging problem in the trading system that would go unaddressed in the Doha talks. The negotiating agenda had been set in 2001, and revising it would require a whole new consensus among WTO members. So if the round were to resume following its suspension in July 2006, the existing, agreed-upon agenda would determine which issues were on the table and which were not.

That is what happened in late 2006. Lamy announced in November of that year that the talks were in a state of "soft re-launch." By that point, all hope had evaporated of completing the round before the expiration of Trade Promotion Authority. Still, there seemed to be a chance that WTO members might produce the detailed outline of a Doha package attractive enough to entice Congress into renewing the authority in some form, perhaps in time to finish the round sometime in late 2007 or 2008. Once again, therefore, the focus of negotiations was on forging a deal on modalities for cuts in tariffs and subsidies.

The good news was that WTO members were moving on from devoting almost all their energy to agriculture. The bad news was that they were turning their attention to NAMA, which would propel them to yet another embarrassment.

| * |

When two people intensely dislike each other but simply have to get along, they sometimes send emissaries in the hope of establishing some sort of functioning relationship. So it was with Susan Schwab and Peter Mandelson in the fall of 2006. Both understood the fact, so often articulated by their predecessors, that cooperation between their respective governments was necessary (even if it wasn't sufficient) to reach a WTO agreement. The European trade commissioner dispatched his chief of staff, Simon Fraser, to Washington to get together with Tim Keeler, Schwab's chief of staff, and discuss ways in which the two ministers could overcome the mutual distrust and animosity that had developed during the mid-2006 meetings in Geneva. One problem they had to surmount was a suspicion among the Americans that Mandelson didn't genuinely want a Doha deal and was concerned mainly with ensuring that Washington got most of the blame for the impasse. Thanks in part to the meetings between the chiefs of staff, those worries were assuaged. Schwab and her aides concluded that Mandelson really desired a pact, especially for legacy purposes, provided that the terms were reasonably acceptable from a European standpoint. His two appointments to the British cabinet, after all, had ended disastrously; it was only logical that he would want his term in Brussels to produce a major achievement.

So although direct contacts between Schwab and Mandelson remained limited, senior negotiators on both sides began a series of meetings aimed at resolving some of the issues that had caused such rancor in mid-2006. The ice between the two principals slowly began to melt as positive reports continued to filter back to them from their underlings about the informal understandings they were reaching in their meetings.

E.U. negotiators were able to offer the Americans more on access to European markets for products that Washington cared about, such as beef and poultry. This did not mean the Europeans had suddenly become willing to tear down trade barriers in ways that economists would applaud as a great boon for free markets and growth in developing countries. Rather, both Washington and Brussels were able to work out mutually satisfactory arrangements. These arrangements were called "dirty deals" by some in the WTO Secretariat, and with some justification. For every product that the European Union wanted to shelter from deep tariff cuts by using the sensitive products loophole, it was required to give *some* new market access for that product, in the form of an import quota—that is, a limited amount of tonnage that would be imported at a very low duty. U.S. negotiators got their E.U. counterparts to promise to expand these quotas sufficiently in products where American farmers and ranchers were especially competitive, so Washington could be content in the knowledge that U.S. agriculture exporters would do reasonably well in Europe. Inconsistent with the principles of Adam Smith though these "dirty deals" may have been, they helped solve a political problem for U.S. negotiators. (Similar deals were cut by other countries using the same mechanism.)

For their part, the Europeans were moderately pleased to learn from Joseph Glauber, the top U.S. agriculture negotiator, that Washington could lower the cap on its farm subsidies by at least a couple of billion dollars from the $19 billion that Schwab had offered previously. That reduction was partly because Glauber found a way for a substantial amount of U.S. crop insurance to be counted as "green box" subsidies rather than as "amber box" subsidies. Although this concession wouldn't entail any substantive change in U.S. farm programs, it meant that the United States could promise to cap its subsidies at a lower level than it had before, without triggering a political firestorm among U.S. farm groups.

Thanks largely to this progress in bridging the gaps between the United States and the European Union, the next act in the Doha Round drama was ready to unfold. To set the scene properly, it is necessary to conjure up an event that took place in the closing days of World War II, when the Third Reich lay in ruins and the Japanese Empire was reeling in retreat.

History buffs will recall that in Potsdam, Germany, the leaders of the "Big Three"—the United States, Great Britain, and the Soviet Union—met in July 1945 to make momentous decisions about the division and administration of the defeated Nazi state and the terms of surrender for Japan. This meeting among Harry Truman, Winston Churchill, and Joseph Stalin was held at the Cecilienhof Palace, which once housed Prussian royalty.

Truman, Churchill, Stalin: For those names, substitute Schwab, Mandelson, Amorim, and Nath. In the same Potsdam venue where the Big Three had met, the ministers representing the United States, the European Union, Brazil, and India in the Doha talks—the "G-4," as they called themselves—convened in June 2007. The informal discussions they had held among themselves had advanced to the stage where it appeared that they might be ready to cut the kind of deal they had failed to strike the year before. So they agreed to meet in the Cecilienhof, which is now a hotel-resort, and they invited their Japanese and Australian counterparts, who belonged to the G-6, to join them at the last stage of the five-day gathering.

Truman, Churchill, Stalin: Lucky for them that they never had to deal with the "NAMA coefficient."

| * |

The grounds of the Cecilienhof befit its status as a former palace. The building is designed in the style of an English Tudor country manor, with brick and oak timber-frame construction, carved chimneys, and courtyards, and it has lovely gardens and hiking trails for guests' enjoyment. Unfortunately, its accommodations tend to be rustic; the trade ministers from the G-4 and their top aides were dismayed to find themselves lodged in quarters that looked as if they had

undergone little modernization since the Truman era. Their rooms were sti-
flingly hot, and the air conditioning in their meeting room was noisy, so participants had to choose between being comfortable or being heard. In the room
housing one member of Schwab's Secret Service detail, the carpeting was so
musty that he couldn't bring himself to do his daily quota of push-ups.
Amorim's bathroom smelled bad.

The poor atmospherics only accentuated the substantive divisions between
participants, which, though different from before in terms of who was fighting
whom, were no less deep.

Amorim and Nath were thunderstruck to see how well Schwab and Mandelson seemed to be getting along. No longer was she hectoring him on European farm tariffs, and no longer was he giving her the third degree about
subsidies. Instead, they were jointly bearing down on the developing countries
concerning NAMA, and the meeting soon degenerated into a North-South confrontation, with the presence of China's ultracompetitive manufacturers keenly
felt even though no Chinese were in attendance.

Concerning tariff cuts on manufactured goods, Amorim said, "We cannot
even think of doing the numbers mentioned by the U.S. and the E.U.," because
that would risk "deindustrializing Brazil" in sectors such as autos and auto
parts, among others. Brazil needed to maintain its right to impose high tariffs on
manufactured goods so it would have "policy space for dealing with China,"
Amorim said, according to notes of the meeting.

Already, in fact, the Brazilian government was exercising its "policy space"
by hiking tariffs to stave off Chinese competition. Only a few weeks earlier, on
April 25, the Brazilian Finance Ministry had announced plans to raise duties
on apparel and footwear, from 20 percent all the way to the bound rate of 35
percent. This move had come in response to intense pressure from the country's
clothing and shoe manufacturers. They employed 1.6 million Brazilians and
were clamoring for relief from imports, which had more than doubled over the
preceding three years, with about half of those foreign goods coming from
China.

The number that Amorim could "not even think of doing," the one that
Schwab and Mandelson favored, was a NAMA coefficient of 18. The math involved needn't be a concern here. Suffice it to say that the lower the coefficient,
the deeper the tariff cuts; the higher the coefficient, the shallower the cuts; and
the coefficient is equal to the maximum tariff. A country with an 18 coefficient
could maintain bound tariffs no higher than 18 percent, for example. Amorim
said he could not accept a coefficient lower than 30. At that level, Brazil could
keep its highest bound tariffs at 30 percent.

Nath endorsed Amorim's stance and, indeed, took an even tougher position on the coefficient. "You want us to pay for someone else's ride," the Indian minister told Schwab and Mandelson, the implication being that by making concessions to appease the Americans and the Europeans, developing countries would be handing benefits to China.

The decrepit air conditioner in the meeting room was rumbling irritatingly on and off as Mandelson did his best to make clear how unreasonable the European Union thought the Brazilian and Indian position was. "We can't have movement in agricultural market access and [subsidies] if we don't deliver on NAMA," the European trade commissioner said, adding that the goal must be to reduce bound tariffs enough that they would end up below the applied levels then prevailing. Based on careful calculations, he said, applied tariffs of developing countries would be affected only if they adopted a NAMA coefficient of 20 or less; above that, "market access is insufficient."

Schwab backed up her newfound ally on the need for cuts in bound tariffs that would be deep enough to affect applied rates. If such a move were not forthcoming, she said, the negotiations would suffer an "overall downward spiral" in which the major parties retreat from the concessions they have offered in other areas, especially agriculture. Referring to Washington's stated willingness to lower its cap on farm subsidies to $17 billion, she warned: "If NAMA turns out to be low ambition, we would raise our [subsidy cap] to above 17."

Amorim responded to the Americans and Europeans with a mixture of conciliation and bluster. As he told Brazilian journalists later, he felt he was living through "Cancún II," in which the United States and the European Union had come to the meeting with a prearranged understanding aimed at minimizing the cuts they would have to make in farm subsidies and agricultural tariffs. He said that he was willing to try some "creative" approaches on NAMA if he got greater concessions from the rich nations on agriculture, but that those concessions would have to go much further than any he had yet seen, with Europe lowering its barriers more and the United States lowering its subsidies more.

"If we have to break up, let's do it," the Brazilian minister said defiantly. "We need bottom lines," on agricultural market access and subsidies. To that, Mandelson replied: "We can't go to our bottom lines if you can't go below a NAMA coefficient of 25." There was no way he would make such a tradeoff, Amorim retorted: "Last night you were talking in a range of $15.8 to $16 billion [as a cap on U.S. farm subsidies]. That would imply a coefficient of 30 for us."

No logical relationship exists, of course, between the amount of subsidies Washington might give to American farmers and the degree of protection needed by Brazilian manufacturers. But such is the nature of bargaining in the WTO, where each minister is obliged to score more wins than losses.

It is unnecessary to delve further into the back-and-forth of the meeting. The sorry tale can close with a brief account of a long odyssey—the travels of Warren Truss, Australia's trade minister, whose experience was emblematic of the Potsdam episode.

In the hope of joining the other ministers by the last phase of the five-day Potsdam session, Truss flew from Canberra to Sidney to Dubai to Frankfurt to Berlin. But as he got off the plane in the German capital on June 22, the meeting's third day, he was greeted by a downcast Australian diplomat bearing bad news: The meeting had already collapsed; the G-4 had just finished holding press conferences blaming each other.

And one more thing, the diplomat said apologetically: Truss's luggage had been lost at Frankfurt. The minister would not get his luggage back until a week after his return to Australia.

| * |

The death and resurrection cycle was now way out of whack. Three consecutive times, headlines blazing the words "failure" and "collapse" had followed high-profile meetings of ministers concerning the Doha Round. Not since 2004 had WTO members produced an accord that they could credibly trumpet as a significant advance, and even that one was looking problematic in hindsight.

No worries. For ten years, global trade had risen at almost 6 percent per annum. With or without a Doha Round, the world economy in June 2007 was doing just fine, and what could possibly disturb this state of bliss?

# 12 | EVEN THE LOOPHOLES HAVE GOT LOOPHOLES

AT FIRST, PASCAL LAMY DID NOT GET THE JOKE WHEN SUSAN SCHWAB gave him a copy of the film *Groundhog Day* during a meeting they had in Washington in the spring of 2008. Being a Frenchman, he was unfamiliar with the 1993 comedy about a man who finds himself living the same day—February 2, Groundhog Day—over and over again. Indeed, Lamy had not heard of the holiday, nor the corny celebration held in a Pennsylvania town that the main character repeatedly endures, in which crowds gather to witness a groundhog emerging from its burrow. But once the WTO director-general watched the film, he could see the humor.

What could be more like *Groundhog Day*, after all, than the Doha Round?

Just as the movie's main character has an overpowering sense of déjà vu when he wakes up in the morning and realizes that he will experience yet another February 2 almost identical to the one before, so it was for Schwab and her fellow trade ministers in the annual rituals they underwent concerning the Doha talks. Ever since 2003, each new year had dawned with exhortations to reach a breakthrough in the round. The process had acquired an almost monotonous sameness to it: Trade ministers would gather in early January at the World Economic Forum in Davos, Switzerland, usually for a luncheon, after which they would issue statements solemnly affirming their resolve to succeed that year in agreeing on modalities or at least something close thereto. The fact that they had failed the year before would be depicted as reason to redouble their efforts. In response to questions from skeptical reporters, the ministers would insist that the coming year would be different from previous ones.

Among observers of the Doha Round, the early months of 2008 certainly had a *Groundhog Day* feel to them. As usual, ministers met for lunch at Davos, and as usual, their rhetoric sounded hackneyed: "A make-or-break year." "Year of necessity." "The next two or three months are crucial." And as usual, the news media took note of the fact that similar phrases had been uttered in almost the same circumstances in prior years.

In some respects, prospects for the round appeared dimmer in 2008 than they had before, thanks mainly to political forces in the United States. Trade Promotion Authority had expired, with very little chance that Congress—now in Democratic hands—would renew it that year, because a presidential election was just months away. The election also meant that countries negotiating with Washington couldn't be certain that the next administration would be willing to accept whatever deal it inherited from the Bush team. That lack of clarity had a natural dampening impact on negotiators' willingness to make concessions for the sake of securing an accord. Who would want to incur the wrath of domestic interest groups, given the risk that there might be nothing positive to show for it? Furthermore, Congress was moving toward passing yet another expensive multiyear farm bill that, like the 2002 version, called into question Washington's political will to curb its agricultural subsidy programs.

Yet there were also reasons for optimism about the round's prospects in 2008. The Bush administration's lame-duck status meant that the White House would be especially eager to reach an agreement for the purposes of burnishing the president's legacy. White House aides were exerting considerable pressure on Schwab to aim for an accord, at least on modalities, and U.S. negotiators were not shy in telling their counterparts from other countries that there might never be a better time to cut a deal than in the months prior to the change in administration, because nobody could be sure who the new president would be, much less what sort of trade policy the new administration would adopt. Failure to produce an agreement in 2008 would mean that WTO members would have to take their chances with whoever won the White House; a golden opportunity would be forgone to deal with American interlocutors who were willing to show flexibility on some of the most contentious issues.

Moreover, an entirely new way of conducting the Doha negotiations had commenced in the weeks after the Potsdam meeting of June 2007. The initial results of this new approach were promising. Within just a few months of starting work on a modalities deal, negotiators were elatedly reporting that they were making progress—more, in fact, than had been achieved in most of the previous six years. Dared anyone hope that, after being stuck for so long, the round might be breaking out of *Groundhog Day* mode?

All this came against the backdrop of increasingly disconcerting tremors rattling the global economy. In the late summer and early fall of 2007, the giant subprime lender Countrywide Financial nearly fell into bankruptcy, hedge-fund woes hit a French bank, credit markets seized up, and Merrill Lynch announced startlingly high losses. A worldwide stock market plunge in January 2008 turned into a full-scale rout in March as the collapse of the investment bank Bear Stearns ended in the firm's being sold in a fire sale, with unprecedented intervention by the U.S. government.

What these events portended was unclear. But common sense suggested that it was a good time to bolster the fortifications of the global trading system.

| * |

Crawford Falconer is a career trade diplomat with auburn hair, a short graying beard, rectangular glasses, and an irreverent sense of humor. The last trait served him well in a task that Falconer, who was New Zealand's ambassador to the WTO, assumed in mid-2007—compiling a compromise agreement on agricultural trade aimed at securing consensus among WTO members. This was a challenge he took on as chairman of the Doha Round agriculture negotiations, and in the process of drafting a text intended to satisfy the myriad warring parties, he dispensed whimsical one-liners with aplomb.

"I've had to suffer writing it. So you're going to have to suffer reading it. There's no Classics Illustrated version, I'm afraid," Falconer told reporters at the Centre William Rappard on July 17, 2007, when he presented a forty-seven-page document filled with phrases like "product-specific AMS caps," "import duty commitments at 6-digits level," and "*de minimis* levels pursuant to Article 6.4(b)." Waxing philosophical about the difficulty of striking a balance between competing arguments over farm subsidies and tariffs, he quipped, "If I'm wrong, members will tell me I'm wrong. They'll tell me I'm wrong anyway, even if I'm right."

Falconer was a key player in what might be called "Doha Round 2.0." The issues were the same as before, but for a while at least, the talks were being taken away from the "Masters of the Universe"—the ministers from the most powerful WTO members such as the G-4 and the G-6. Now responsibility for achieving convergence on the big issues was passing to trade officials below the ministerial level in a number of WTO governments—people who were steeped in the technical details of the issues at stake and whose incremental moves would go largely ignored by the media. This was an approach that many in Geneva viewed as long overdue; they felt that Lamy had wasted considerable time by putting his faith in gatherings of a few ministers before the foundations of an agreement were in place. In the opinion of his critics, Lamy—for all his brilliance and grasp of the issues—was too enamored of the model he and Zoellick had used to achieve the 2004 framework. Ministers could not be expected to resolve their differences given the layer upon layer of complexity and the plethora of unresolved problems that were now involved, and Potsdam had convinced Lamy too that it was futile to pursue that modus operandi any longer. To be sure, talks among senior deputies and WTO ambassadors could go only so far; at some point, ministers would be needed to make political decisions about major sticking points. But in the meantime, the new mantra in Geneva, starting in the summer of 2007, was that if a deal were to be negotiated, there was no alternative to doing it issue by issue, for weeks at a time if necessary. As Falconer put it at his July 2007 news conference, "It will be dull, bureaucratic and bruising. But that's the only way that these kinds of negotiations ever get done. Slam dunk has been tried and failed. All that's left is a business-like grinding through."

With tongue in cheek, Falconer used the term "walks in the woods" to describe meetings he held with small numbers of representatives from WTO member countries to glean their views about various aspects of the agricultural deal. The term referred to a famous stroll taken in the early 1980s by negotiators from the United States and the Soviet Union who, while tramping through a forested area outside Geneva, struck the terms of an arms-control agreement. In Falconer's walks in the woods, the participants were neither walking nor in the woods; they were mostly sitting down in offices. But Falconer's "walks" were every bit as important for the proper execution of his task as the arms-controllers' hike had been for theirs. The New Zealander was *not* trying to write a text for the purpose of drafting the most economically sensible plan possible about agricultural trade. Rather, he was generating a text that would hopefully approach consensus on that issue, using a process that would make most WTO members feel as if their input had been taken into account.

The metaphors flew as WTO officials sought to explain how the new process improved upon the old. The frog was being cooked slowly in water that was getting progressively warmer, rather than being thrown onto a hot skillet from which he would jump. The house was being constructed with the scaffolding and walls going up first, so that ministers would be summoned only to place the roof on top. The football game was being run with a series of three-yard plays, instead of long "Hail Mary" passes.

Also centrally involved in this frog cooking, scaffolding erecting, and three-yard-play making was Donald Stephenson, the Canadian ambassador and chairman of the negotiations concerning the other big issue in the round—NAMA. Stephenson was much more straitlaced than Falconer, and whereas the New Zealander could claim decades' worth of expertise in trade, Stephenson had spent much of his career in Canadian Heritage, the government's cultural affairs department. But he made up for his lack of experience with a capacity for methodical work, rigorous logic, and patience for long meetings. He also took very seriously Canada's reputation in international diplomacy as an honest broker and bridge builder between rich and poor countries. Introducing his first text at the same July 2007 news conference where Falconer presented his, Stephenson explained, "This text has no standing. It is agreed by no one. . . . It is my best guess of where members might find consensus, based on, my guess would be, about 1,000 hours of listening to the members."

Lo and behold: As more and more "scaffolding" went up, a plausible version of the Doha Round began to take shape in much greater detail than before. From time to time, Falconer and Stephenson presented revised versions of their texts based on the discussions they had held with member-country officials in Geneva, and with each successive draft they filled in more of the gaps on issues that ministers had failed to resolve—some of which had been too complex for the Masters of the Universe. (One matter that took months to thrash out involved the method of calculating the consumption of sensitive products—whether, for example, sugar-consumption figures should include processed products like cookies and soda.) A few of the provisions in the texts had been decided beforehand, of course—notably the elimination of export subsidies on farm goods. But Doha Round 2.0 was making headway—dull, bureaucratic, and bruising though it may have been, just as Falconer had predicted.

It could hardly have been any more dull and bureaucratic, for instance, when Joe Glauber, the chief U.S. agriculture negotiator, quietly mentioned in a meeting chaired by Falconer on September 19, 2007, that the United States could accept "as a basis for negotiation" the range proposed in the text for a cap of $13 billion to $16.4 billion a year on U.S. subsidies that distort crop prices. Even though this sign of American flexibility was no ironclad commitment to curb subsidies—as always, it depended on concessions from other countries—it still represented forward movement. The figures in the range were markedly below the $17 billion that Sue Schwab had previously set forth as the lowest Washington could go.

Progress, however, had a price, as illustrated by Stephenson's comments at one of his news conferences. The normally even-tempered Canadian could not mask his exasperation, so frazzled had he become at "spending hundreds of soul-destroying hours in consultations with members." The problem, he said, was that trying to craft possible middle grounds was like "being asked to suck and blow at the same time."

Sucking and blowing, indeed. Not only was Stephenson's NAMA proposal cluttered with loopholes and exceptions, but those loopholes and exceptions had their own loopholes and exceptions. That was the only way, Stephenson had found, to respond to the conflicting clamor from WTO members over whether developing countries should be required to open their markets substantially for manufactured goods (as the rich countries wanted), or whether they should be allowed plenty of leeway to keep barriers high, for "policy space" and other reasons.

Stephenson started off with a compromise figure for the overall tariff-cutting formula that developing countries would adopt. His July 2007 text called for them to cut their duties using a coefficient of somewhere between 19 percent and 23 percent—that is, their maximum tariffs would fall somewhere in that range.

Then came the sucking part—the first layer of exceptions. Under Stephenson's plan, developing countries could exempt 5 percent of their tariffs on manufactured goods from any cuts. Or, if they preferred, they could cut 10 percent of those tariffs only half as much as they cut their other tariffs.*

If all that sounds complicated, it was nothing compared to the other layers of exceptions that Stephenson felt compelled to include. Countries belonging to certain regional trade agreements—South America's Mercosur trade bloc, for instance, and the Southern African Customs Union—argued that for technical reasons they would be at a disadvantage under Stephenson's plan, so they insisted on special rights to exempt even more tariffs from cuts. Other developing countries wanted, and got, special treatment for different reasons. Nations that had joined the WTO in the preceding few years—China and Taiwan were notable examples—pointed out that they had already been forced to cut their tariffs to low levels when they became members. On completely separate grounds, Bolivia's left-wing government argued that its tariffs should be kept off the chopping block because it was almost as poor as the WTO's least-developed countries, which were being spared from any requirement to reduce barriers.

The orgy of loophole creation in Stephenson's text inspired a bitter joke, whose humor was apparent only to those initiated in the mysteries of trade lingo. "Anyone reading this paper . . . would have to conclude that NAMA

---

*Those figures drew harsh denunciations from a number of developing countries, who demanded much broader flexibility to shelter their industries. So in later versions of his text, Stephenson allowed larger exemptions for countries that chose tougher tariff-cutting formulas and smaller exemptions for countries that chose less rigorous formulas.

stands for 'no additional market access,'" fumed Peter Allgeier, the U.S. ambassador to the WTO, at a meeting with his fellow negotiators on May 27, 2008.

Here was where the blowing part came in—the exceptions to the loopholes. The United States, with backing from other wealthy member nations, was pushing several proposals that would ensure access to at least *some* markets in big developing countries. Most important, Washington was demanding that the round include "sectoral" deals—special accords in which a handful of key countries would reduce tariffs to zero, or very close to zero, in individual sectors. The Americans were particularly keen to get such deals in chemicals, industrial machinery, and electrical equipment, and they argued that unless those deals included countries such as China, Brazil, and India, the whole Doha Round would offer negligible benefits to U.S. manufacturers. But the idea drew staunch resistance from developing nations, who noted that when it had arisen previously, an agreement had been reached that participation in sectoral deals would be strictly voluntary.

While all the sucking and blowing was continuing in Geneva, events were transpiring in the real world, far from the rarefied atmosphere of the Centre William Rappard, that completely changed some of the economics upon which the Doha Round had been premised.

| * |

In Egypt, rioters burned cars and smashed windows of buildings. In Haiti, at least five people were killed, and the injured filled hospitals after stone-throwing mobs took over streets, looted shops, and attacked passing vehicles. Ten thousand Bangladeshis went on a rampage in Dhaka, their country's capital. Citizens of Yemen torched police stations and set up roadblocks. In several Burkina Faso towns, protesters burned government buildings. Similar unrest erupted in Senegal, Mauritania, Cameroon, Côte d'Ivoire, and many other countries.

The grievances in all these episodes, which occurred in the early months of 2008, were the same—soaring food prices. The cost of rice, a staple food for about half the world's people, was more than double the 2007 level. Wheat prices had quadrupled since 2000, and that of corn had nearly tripled. Powering these price surges was the growing appetite of the rapidly expanding middle classes of Asia and Latin America, where demand had risen sharply not only for bread, tortillas, chapatis, and rice but also for meat and milk—products that require corn for feed. Other contributing factors included high oil prices, which drove up the cost of fertilizer, and America's ethanol program, which was diverting millions of tons of corn into the production of fuel for automobiles.

Thanks to the high cost of food, government policies were changing in ways that the Doha Round had never been able to achieve. Many countries were lowering tariffs on farm products—among them India, Indonesia, Turkey, and Peru, which slashed their duties on goods such as wheat, flour, soybeans, barley, and corn. The purpose of these moves was to provide some price relief to the poor, who devote an estimated 50 percent to 60 percent of their spending to food. In the United States, meanwhile, farm subsidies were declining—the U.S. total was just $8.5 billion in 2007—in accord with the way U.S. crop programs are supposed to work when prices are high. Of course, these changes were not binding, as they would be in a WTO agreement, so the governments in question could reverse them at any time. But the moves underscored how, in the round's seventh year, conditions were dramatically different from those of the first year. The old logic—that poor farmers desperately needed the higher prices they could earn in more open, subsidy-free world markets—seemed woefully out of date.

The new problem in food trade policy was the opposite of tariffs—it was export controls. To keep as much crops and other farm products as possible at home and available for domestic consumption, more than two dozen governments imposed restrictions on exports or taxed them heavily, and in some cases banned them altogether, with the affected items including rice, wheat, corn, beans, and beef. Argentina, which has long taxed the exports of its agricultural sector to help fill its government coffers, was one of the most aggressive practitioners of this approach. Others taking such steps were China, Egypt, India, Indonesia, Kazakhstan, Pakistan, Russia, Serbia, Ukraine, Vietnam, and Zambia. "Starve your neighbor policies" these were dubbed by Joachim von Braun, director-general of the International Food Policy Research Institute, because they exacerbated shortages elsewhere in the world and sent prices rocketing upward even faster.

The crisis sparked a fresh debate about trade and agriculture, reopening age-old questions about whether food is a special case that ought to be treated differently from other products in international commerce. "Food security" became the new rallying cry of free-trade skeptics. Where food was concerned, they argued, global markets plainly don't work, so governments need to take steps to ensure that their farmers can provide adequate supplies for their own people by protecting their agricultural sectors with tariffs or subsidies or both. At a theoretical level, this argument was economic know-nothingism of the lowest order; the best illustration of its idiocy is the failed economy of North Korea, which was based on the state philosophy of *juche,* or self-reliance. Given differences in rainfall, land arability, and other natural factors, it makes perfect sense for nations to specialize in the kinds of food they grow best and to trade those—or other goods and services—for the food they can't easily produce themselves. But at a time when some of the world's biggest breadbaskets were restricting exports to hoard their harvests for home consumption, free-market theorists were thrown on the defensive.

A grand bargain, in which all countries were to agree to abide by market principles, might have provided a sensible solution to the problem. As economists Nancy Birdsall and Arvind Subramanian proposed in April 2008, developing countries could pledge to eschew export restrictions, and rich countries could scrap biofuel subsidies, thereby assuring importers that reasonably plentiful supplies would be available on world markets. At the same time, food-importing countries could promise to fix their tariffs at permanently low levels, thereby assuring exporters of guaranteed open markets for their production.

But grand bargains of that nature were not what the Doha Round was about. The round had never focused on export quotas or taxes, which are permitted under WTO rules. Although a few countries that depend on foreign food, such as Japan, had often proposed international rules against export restrictions, their calls had gone nowhere, partly because of vehement opposition from the Argentines and a few other nations. The issue was not even mentioned in the agenda adopted in Doha in 2001, and in drafting his agriculture text, Falconer was able to shoehorn in only very weak provisions concerning the practice.

In addition to the food crisis, the economic ground was starting to shift under WTO negotiators' feet in other ways as well.

| * |

Time-wise, Lamy concluded, there was no more room for maneuver. The August holidays were looming, and after that, the U.S. presidential campaign would be in its most intensive phase. So on June 25, 2008, the director-general began spreading the word that ministers were being summoned to Geneva in a month's time, their aim being to strike a modalities deal the week of July 21. "With dark clouds on the economic horizon every day," he told WTO ambassadors, "we must shelter what we can now."

Dark clouds, indeed. Financial market sentiment, which had improved for a few weeks following the bailout of Bear Stearns, was souring anew as realization spread that the financial system was burdened with other, potentially bigger woes. The Dow Jones Industrial Average sank below 12,000 on June 20 amid fresh reports of troubles at bond-insurance firms and of one of the steepest monthly declines ever in U.S. home prices.

In calling for the ministerial meeting, Lamy admitted: "I know that this is not without its risks." That was abundantly clear from the mortifying number of false starts that had preceded his announcement. The director-general had originally hoped to call a meeting of ministers prior to the end of 2007, on the theory that holding such a gathering during the U.S. election year would be dicey. But that timing hadn't worked out. So in early 2008 the message switched: A ministerial would be convened as soon as mid-March, or "by April 12 at the latest," according to press reports from Geneva. When that attempt at scheduling also turned out to be premature, a new target date for a ministerial was set for the week of May 19. This too was overly optimistic. In mid-June Lamy was quoted as saying that if WTO members would "go like hell" toward convergence on some key issues, ministers could meet the first week of July. They did not.

The reason for the repeated delays was no secret: Too many issues remained unresolved in the negotiations being run by Falconer and Stephenson. Every time Lamy tried to set a deadline for ministers to meet, he got strong resistance, especially from Falconer, who kept warning the director-general that for all the progress that had been made, there were still too many problems in the texts—that is, too many items in square brackets signifying major disparities between member nations' positions. This was the case even though Lamy was taking every conceivable precaution to avoid extraneous issues that might complicate the effort to reach agreement on modalities in agriculture and NAMA. Requests by the Japanese and others for ministers to take up the antidumping issue were denied; it would be dealt with only after modalities had been done. Much the same went for numerous other issues that had to be settled before the round could be finalized. Countries interested in liberalizing trade in services, a subject of potentially vast importance, would have to settle for a discussion in which they would "signal" the amount of market opening they intended to put on the table in later stages of the round. Ministers' eyes would be kept on the modalities prize, because although resolving that question was still a far cry from completing the round, it would at least be a huge step toward the finish line.

Beyond the doubts about whether a deal would emerge from the July meeting, the more profound question was whether the terms would add up to much of a deal at all.

For those who tended to see the glass as half full—and Lamy was naturally the most forceful advocate of this view—the details contained in the texts could be used to make the case that the Doha Round would surpass even the Uruguay Round in ambition. In particular, there were now specific figures to flesh out the principle, first agreed in the 2004 framework, that the highest tariffs would be cut the most. In Falconer's text, rich countries would be required to reduce their steepest duties on farm products—the ones above 75 percent—by some-where between 66 percent and 73 percent. That was far deeper than anything contemplated in previous rounds. As for the NAMA text, a deal would cap the tariffs imposed by rich countries on manufactured goods at a maximum of 9 percent, which would significantly lower U.S. duties on goods such as clothing and shoes, though the reduction would be phased in over a decade.

But the greater specificity in the texts also gave ammunition to critics who saw Doha Lite in the making, because the loopholes and exceptions had also be-come more clearly defined. This was true not just of the NAMA plan devised by Stephenson, whose frustrations were noted previously, but of the agriculture proposal by Falconer. To take one of the most important examples, the New Zealander's proposal for the special products exemption would allow develop-ing countries to keep 10 percent to 18 percent of their agricultural tariffs from being cut much—the precise number of tariff lines would be negotiated at the ministerial—and to designate some of those as "super specials," for which tar-iffs would undergo no cut at all. The super specials would be up to 6 percent of a developing country's farm tariff lines; here too the exact number was subject to negotiation. This was no trivial matter, especially for the Americans, given their estimates that only a small number of tariff lines covered the vast bulk of the U.S. farm goods imported by many big developing countries.

As for rich countries, some of those with the most heavily protected farm sectors, such as Japan, Norway, Switzerland, and Iceland, would get consider-able flexibility to keep duties of over 100 percent on their sensitive products. This was a disappointment to reformers who had once dreamt that the round might put an end to all triple-digit tariffs.

In sum, faultfinders didn't have to search far for reasons to deride the pack-age that ministers were going to consider at the July 2008 meeting. It certainly didn't provide the sort of boost developing countries needed to make a signif-icant dent in poverty. It could fairly be accused of doing little to solve the food crisis. And with a few exceptions, it didn't even lower current barriers by much, especially not in the developing world. That was evident from a World Bank analysis that calculated how much the average tariff then being applied by coun-tries would fall on the goods they actually import. The average duties imposed by developing countries on agricultural products would barely budge, and on manufactured products, their average tariffs would decline less than a percent-age point. Rich countries' applied tariffs on farm goods would be lowered from an average of 15 percent to 11 percent—hardly a transformative change.

What great purpose, then, would be served by concluding an agreement in July? An analysis by Patrick Messerlin, an economics professor at the Institute of Political Studies in Paris, highlighted the most valuable element by far—"the real gold mine," as Messerlin put it.

The package would significantly constrain countries from going protectionist in the future, Messerlin asserted, because it would reduce bound tariffs, the legal maximums that countries can impose. The cuts in bound tariffs envisioned in the package might not be deep enough in many cases to affect applied rates. But the lower the bound rates are, the better, because, as Messerlin noted, in manufacturing in particular, "the current world trading regime . . . is a funambulist walking a tightrope above an abyss."

At any time, he pointed out, a number of sizable countries could jack up their barriers without violating WTO rules. In manufacturing, "average tariffs could surge . . . from 3.8 to 11 percent in Australia, from 6.6 to 10.2 percent in Korea, from 6.7 to 35.6 percent in Indonesia, from 12.5 to 30.8 percent in Brazil, or from 11.5 to 36.2 percent in India," Messerlin wrote. And that was just the average tariff rates; "increases are likely to be higher for those tariffs that remain high—up to 300 percent!—and hence much more devastating for concerned foreign exporters and domestic consumers." Other countries with large disparities between their bound and applied rates for manufactured goods included Argentina, Thailand, Malaysia, Pakistan, the Philippines, Nigeria, Egypt, and Bangladesh. The picture was similar in agriculture, Messerlin's analysis showed: India's average applied tariff for farm goods was 34.4 percent, but its average bound rate was 114.2 percent. The corresponding figures, respectively, for Indonesia were 8.6 percent and 47.0 percent; for South Africa, 9.2 percent and 40.8 percent; for Malaysia, 11.7 percent and 76.0 percent; for Pakistan, 15.8 percent and 95.6 percent.

This did not hold true in all economies. Several of the world's biggest ones— the United States, the European Union, Japan, Canada, and China—have bound rates that are very close to their applied levels. Still, by reducing the upper limit of potential tariffs in many countries around the world, the risk of a protectionist outbreak would be substantially diminished, according to Messerlin. "The benefits of binding," he contended, "stem from the elimination of the possibility" that emerging economies could raise their tariffs from an average 8 percent to 28 percent for industrial goods, and from 19 percent to 66 percent in agricultural goods.

It was Lamy who framed this argument most eloquently, highlighting the "insurance policy" value of a deal in speeches and op-eds. The insurance benefits were, to be sure, somewhere off in the future. Even if agreement were reached at the July ministerial, the reductions in bound tariffs would start to become effective only after the Doha Round was completed, not at the time of a modalities deal. And even after the finalization of the round, the tariff cuts would be phased in over several years.

All the more reason to move full steam ahead, in Lamy's view. In the days leading up to the ministers' meeting, financial indicators continued to worsen, as the Dow Jones dropped below 11,000, down about 22 percent from its peak, and federal regulators seized IndyMac Bancorp in one of the largest bank failures in U.S. history. The mortgage giants Fannie Mae and Freddie Mac fell into severe distress, prompting the Bush administration to rush out a rescue plan aimed at keeping them in business.

Perhaps if they had known how much worse things were going to get, the ministers who gathered in Geneva in July 2008 might have paid more heed to Messerlin's analysis and Lamy's entreaties. They were well versed in worries about the trading system; indeed, many voiced their unease. Such weighty concerns, however, will take ministers only so far when they have vital domestic interests at stake.

# 13 | LOSING IT

THURSDAY, JULY 24, 2008, WAS THE FOURTH DAY OF THE MINISTERIAL meeting that Pascal Lamy had called in the hope of finally reaching a breakthrough in the Doha Round before the election of a new U.S. president. The outcome was still uncertain, and fatigue was setting in. Late that evening, on the number 1 bus, which originates in front of the Centre William Rappard and winds through town to Geneva's central train station, I overheard a middle-aged man, who was wearing WTO credentials, speaking despondently into his mobile phone. "It's all going to collapse by the weekend," he lamented in a clipped British accent, seemingly oblivious to his fellow passengers. "I'm totally exhausted. We were up until 5:00 a.m. last night and then we went at it all day today. There just doesn't seem to be any chance it's going to come together."

In fact, he was half right, and the meeting was barely halfway through. There was considerable time to go, with many passions to be aroused, tempers to ignite, hopes to inflate, and spirits to crush.

On that Thursday, the WTO was still in the early stages of its longest-ever exercise in ministerial futility. Considering the modesty of the deal on the table, the number of days that would be spent fighting over its terms, and the perils that were then looming over the world economy, it is hard to imagine a starker illustration of the global trading system's troubled state than the events of late July 2008.

| \* |

Security always tightens around the Centre William Rappard during a ministerial meeting, and this one was no exception. Phalanxes of guards stood in the main entrance and doors, checking ID badges. The abundance of caution may have been understandable, given the mayhem that had plagued WTO meetings in the past. But in July 2008, protesters were nearly totally absent, one exception being a handful of campaigners from Oxfam dressed as rich WTO members who set up a "poker table" in a park and pretended to be "gambling with the future of the poor." Considering how much effort activists had thrown into keeping a round from being launched at Seattle and then into disrupting progress at Cancún and Hong Kong, it seemed odd that they would show so little interest at a time when the WTO's undertaking was reaching a potentially climactic point. In a Reuters news article, Oxfam spokeswoman Amy Barry explained, "The fact that these negotiations have been going on for so long has led to some dropping away of attention from the wider world."

By contrast with the activists, trade ministers were present in abundance, with about seventy of them responding to Lamy's summons. To manage the problem of making them feel as useful as possible, the director-general established three concentric circles.

The outer one consisted of the entire WTO membership and met briefly every day in the General Council chamber, with some countries represented by ministers and others by ambassadors. The second one, consisting of ministers representing thirty-five major powers and groups of allied nations, met in a large room on the third floor in the Centre William Rappard, and its gatherings were dubbed "the green room," meaning that it was ostensibly the main locus of decision-making. But during the first two days, the green room discussions produced little but reiteration of long-standing positions, as nearly all participants wanted to speak, and when they did, they used their precious allotted minutes mainly for point-scoring. So on the third day, the director-general announced the additional creation of a more manageable "G-7," with the promise that once this group had converged on a plan, the terms would have to be submitted to the green room and then to the full membership. The G-7's members included the usual suspects from the G-4—America's Susan Schwab, the European Union's Peter Mandelson, Brazil's Celso Amorim, India's Kamal Nath—and two new ministers from the other countries in the G-6, Australia's Simon Crean and Japan's Akira Amari.* The novelty in this inner circle, however, was the

---

*In addition to Amari, who was minister of economy, trade, and industry, Japanese agriculture minister Masatoshi Wakabayashi also attended G-7 meetings, in keeping with Japan's long-established custom of sending both its trade minister and its agriculture minister to such gatherings. This could be a source of irritation for others, because each minister usually required his or her own interpreter. But in fairness to the Japanese, the United States usually sent its agriculture secretary, and the European Union usually sent its agriculture commissioner. In July 2008, a U.S. undersecretary of agriculture, Mark Keenum, attended, as did Mariann Fischer Boel, the European agriculture commissioner.

participation of a minister whose country had never been in such elite company before—Chen Deming, head of China's Ministry of Commerce.

Chen was the first Chinese minister to take an active role at a WTO meeting. His predecessor, Bo Xilai, usually dispatched vice ministers to represent Beijing, which made it diplomatically impossible to include his country in small green rooms with others who held ministerial rank. Chen felt more confident in international forums; he spoke English fairly well and had experience working in coastal cities—notably Suzhou, of which he was mayor—where lots of foreign companies had located. He also held a doctorate in management and had trained in a Nanjing University program run jointly with Johns Hopkins University. Attendees of G-7 meetings were quickly impressed with his willingness to engage in give-and-take, especially compared with the more wooden Japanese. When Schwab used the term "elephant in the room" to describe the impact that China was having on the NAMA talks, Chen retorted a few minutes later: "If we are an elephant, maybe the U.S. is a dinosaur."

But repartee is no substitute for substantive progress, and the G-7 was just as deadlocked in its first sessions as the broader group was. Practically the only positive sign in the ministerial's early stages came from the Americans, in a public announcement on July 22 by Schwab offering to cap U.S. farm subsidies at $15 billion a year provided other major players responded with meaningful concessions of their own. U.S. officials portrayed this as a giant step, asserting that such a low ceiling on subsidies had been politically unthinkable to them two years earlier. The U.S. move generated only half-hearted applause, however. Although the proposed ceiling would keep subsidies from ever rising again to the bloated levels of years past, when they had exceeded $20 billion, it still meant that Washington could raise its spending from current levels. In any event, it did not prompt other G-7 members to budge from their positions.

So on the meeting's fifth day—Friday, July 25—Lamy was in a deep funk when he gathered his closest aides and advisers at their daily 8:00 a.m. meeting. To the surprise of some of those in attendance, who had grown accustomed to his upbeat exhortations, he sounded fatalistic, asking for suggestions about fundamental changes the WTO might adopt if the meeting were to end in failure. "Our chances for success are maybe 15 percent," he told the group, an estimate based on confessionals he had held with the G-7 ministers to ask each of them separately how far they were willing to move.

Only a daring stroke, he concluded, would raise the odds in a favorable direction. Although the director-generalship confers little formal power, Lamy was ready to offer his own proposal—a huge gamble, because when such steps flop, the director-general's credibility takes a big hit, reducing his ability to wield influence in the future.

As he explained to me later, "The image is like that of a midwife. The baby isn't coming, and the mother is screaming. At some point, you have to do a Caesarian. I thought it was the only way."

| * |

Later on that Friday, at 12:30 p.m., the G-7 ministers gathered in the director-general's conference room, sitting around the dark wood table with aides hovering behind them in seats along the wall. (Interpreters for the Chinese and Japanese were also present, as were several Secretariat officials.) Nath was wearing a *galabandh*, a closed-neck black suit; the others were in Western business attire. The seating arrangement included a couple of touches by Lamy's staff aimed at boosting, however slightly, the chances for overall harmony: Amorim and Nath, who had often sat next to each other in the past as a symbol of G-20 solidarity, were across from each other; Schwab was next to Nath instead. As all of them were painfully aware, ministers from a number of other countries who hadn't been invited into this inner sanctum were miffed at its exclusiveness. After five days, some of the outsiders were fuming over being made to sit around in Geneva with little to do.

One-page sheets of paper were distributed to each of the seven delegations. "This," Lamy told them, "is the moment of truth."

The paper was one he had drawn up that morning. Following his morose performance at his staff meeting, he had held a long brainstorming session with three ambassadors—New Zealand's Crawford Falconer and Canada's Don Stephenson, who knew in minute detail the positions of member countries on agriculture and NAMA by dint of their chairmanship of the respective negotiating committees, and Australia's Bruce Gosper, chairman of the General Council. They had produced a set of proposals that represented their best guess as to where compromise could be found within the ranges that had been spelled out in their texts, the idea being that it would stand or fall as a package, with a "balance of pain" distributing the gains and losses as fairly as possible among the main participants. It was written in the sparest trade jargon imaginable. There was no title; the first line read: "US OTDS 70% cut."

Six years, eight months, and eleven days had passed since the agreement in Doha on the declaration launching the round, and now it was all coming down to this. For trade ministers, their aides, and entourages, an unimaginably large number of air miles had been flown, hotel rooms occupied, restaurant meals consumed, and other costs incurred, with no deal yet even on modalities. Might the world's poor have been better off if, instead of spending all that money on negotiations for a development round, the funds had simply been disbursed in the form of aid? Perish such thoughts; the talks held at least some promise of improving the fairness of the trading system, and anyway, curing world poverty is not just a matter of handing out a few billion extra dollars. But the round had consumed so much of the time, energy, and political capital of the main participants that some of them were salivating for an agreement. Amorim was prominent among these, as was Mandelson, who was again fending off efforts by the French and other E.U. member states to force him into taking a harder line. To some extent this group included Schwab, because the legacy-conscious White House was leaning heavily on her to conclude a pact on reasonably acceptable terms.

On the other hand, as Lamy well knew, there were two ministers present for whom the cost of "no deal" was less than for the others, because of the antipathy and skepticism toward trade that was so pronounced within their nations' body politics. Schwab was one. The other was Nath, who harbored ambitions to become India's prime minister someday.

The ministers and their aides went into separate meeting rooms nearby to discuss the paper privately, and when they reconvened a little less than an hour later, each of them vented about points he or she didn't like. Mandelson griped that the figures would engender too paltry a reduction in barriers to manufactured goods in developing countries. (It never hurts, when you're anxious for a deal, to act as if you're feeling almost fleeced.) The Japanese said that crop-importing countries like theirs would have to be given greater ability to retain barriers on sensitive products. Others, including Chen and Amorim, complained that the proposed cap on U.S. farm subsidies was too high, though at $14.5 billion it was a bit lower than Washington's latest offer. Chen was also deeply concerned about the wording concerning proposals for sectoral negotiations aimed at slashing tariffs in specific industrial areas; he couldn't figure out whether the language required Beijing's involvement, which would be an unacceptable breach of the prior understanding that the talks would be purely voluntary.

Still, there were grounds for hope that the paper might work as the basis for a deal, because none of the ministers disavowed the paper outright—with one exception. "I reject everything," Nath said.

Nath's vehemence came as a surprise to some of the others. They all knew that India's prime minister, the scholarly economist Manmohan Singh, had spoken on the phone the day before with President Bush, so speculation was running high that New Delhi's position might soften a bit as a result. But Nath's response to Lamy's paper showed how misguided those expectations had been.

"I cannot place the livelihoods of hundreds of millions of people at risk," Nath said. "If the [Indian] government wants this, they'll have to find a new minister." Putting on his jacket, he rose to leave and headed for the door, prompting Lamy to practically leap out of his chair after him.

"Kamal, please stay and listen to the others," the director-general said, pointing out that the other ministers had been patiently awaiting Nath's engagement with them for some time. (Nath had come late to the ministerial, having been stuck in New Delhi for a critical vote in Parliament that threatened to bring down the government.) In response to similar pleas from the others, Nath returned to his seat, saying he was doing so "out of respect for my friend Pascal," but he said he would have nothing to add. "My silence will be my contribution," he concluded, and for the most part he sat impassively for the next couple of hours, showing his disregard for the proceedings by concentrating on his BlackBerry and excusing himself several times from the room to get food and to meet with outsiders.

His negativity drew an incredulous response from Schwab. "We're the ones going backwards. You've won!" she told the Indian minister, noting that under the terms of Lamy's proposal, developing countries' super specials—agricultural tariffs that would be exempt from any cut whatsoever—would be 5 percent of tariff lines, a number very close to New Delhi's demand.

It was other aspects of the paper that were the focus of Nath's ire—chief among them a line that read: "SSM for above bound rate trigger is 140 percent of base imports."

"SSM" is the acronym for the "special safeguard mechanism." As noted in Chapter 9, such a mechanism was one of India's demands, together with the loophole for special products. It is based on an idea that has long been an integral part of the trading rules for manufactured goods—that countries sometimes need to raise trade barriers for at least a while when a flood of imports threatens their industries, so that they have time to adjust. (The duties that Bush imposed on imported steel in 2002 were safeguard tariffs of this type.) Rich nations had gotten a special safeguard for their farm sectors some years earlier; developing nations were insisting that their agriculture should have similar rights. Suppose, for example, that foreign apples were to suddenly begin pouring into India's market, and India's apple growers were facing bankruptcy. An SSM would enable New Delhi to raise its tariff on apples above its 50 percent level for a limited period.

The problem was not that the SSM had been eliminated entirely from Lamy's paper. Even Schwab and her allies (the main one in the G-7 was Australia's Crean) were willing to concede that the mechanism should exist. Rather, the issue was what type of constraints ought to limit its use to ensure that it did not create new forms of protectionism. Taking again the apples example, India's 50 percent tariff on apples is equal to its bound rate, so raising the duty above that level would constitute the breaking of a commitment made by India in a previous global trade pact. A country would be allowed to take such a step, according to Lamy's paper, only when imports were truly surging—which the paper defined as a 40 percent increase over recent levels. This, Lamy knew, was the bare minimum that would be acceptable to the Americans and the Australians, who argued that without a highly restrictive rule, the SSM could be used to block trade that was growing normally.

But the paper's attempt at compromise on this issue was much too restrictive for Nath's taste. He was certain that he, and the Congress Party, would be pounded back home for agreeing to something that would be denounced as a sellout of farmers. Under Lamy's proposal, he argued, the SSM "cannot be operationalized," because India's ability to monitor its imports of individual products is so haphazard that by the time the government detected a 40 percent import surge, farmers would already be committing suicide en masse.

The drama intensified when Amorim, the gray-bearded, sixty-six-year-old elder statesman of the group, delivered his overall verdict on Lamy's paper: "As a package, I can swallow it," he said, to the shock of Nath, who couldn't believe that his erstwhile G-20 comrade in arms was failing to back him up. At last, the inherent contradictions in the Brazilian-Indian alliance were coming to the fore—the offensive interests in agriculture of Brazil, and the defensive interests in agriculture of India, which had been apparent for all to see when the G-20 was first formed in 2003. As far as Amorim was concerned, he was committing no breach of G-20 unity by backing Lamy's proposal; the grouping's main purpose had always been securing reductions in rich-country subsidies and trade barriers, and individual members were supposed to decide themselves whether or not they favored loopholes for developing countries such as special products and the SSM. Brazil's interests naturally lay on the side of greater market access, and Amorim wasn't about to oppose a package that could deliver substantial benefits to his nation's farm sector.

As it became clearer that Nath was the only G-7 participant who was firmly saying no, the big question racing through the minds of participants in the meeting was, what would Schwab do? She could let the meeting break down and insist that if Nath wasn't going to accept Lamy's paper, he should be forced to walk out so that India would take the blame for blowing up the round. Or she could announce that the United States was accepting the paper and hope that, eventually, a deal might emerge as pressure was brought to bear on the Indians. The latter course was risky, because it violated basic negotiating strategy; India would presumably pocket the concessions it had already received in the paper and demand more as the price of agreement.

In a striking testament to the intensity of the Bush administration's yen for a deal, Schwab told the G-7: "As a package, I can do this." At the same time, she added some crucial caveats—"potential deal breakers," she called them—because she knew that U.S. farmers and manufacturers would probably regard the Lamy paper, by itself, as insufficient in liberalizing foreign markets. In particular, China would have to agree to open up certain markets for farm and industrial goods, she said. But on the whole, she championed the Lamy paper as the only way forward, and she echoed Amorim in warning that it must remain intact as it underwent consideration by the wider group of ministers. "Pull one thread and it all unravels," she said. "We should be close enough on the basis of this paper to do this."

While all this was going on, gallows humor was the order of the day in the press room downstairs, where reporters from around the world were swapping bets about when the meeting would be officially declared a bust. The ennui was suddenly shattered in midafternoon, when WTO spokesman Keith Rockwell came in to report on the G-7 meeting. The scene was like a roomful of family members who have been awaiting word that their comatose relative has died, only to learn that the patient is conscious, alert, sitting up, and sipping a bowl of soup.

"There are some very encouraging signs of progress," Rockwell said. "There is a spirit of cooperation and they decided it's time to bring this to a wider group." Later that evening, after the thirty-five-minister green room had been briefed on the Lamy paper, Rockwell announced that it had received "overwhelming support" (though not from all participants, he acknowledged). And Schwab emerged from the meeting to tell reporters that, despite resistance from "a handful of large emerging markets" that threatened the round, "a clear majority of countries—both developed and developing—were able to endorse this package as a path forward to a potential successful outcome."

All this was true as far as it went. But the happy talk masked the tenuousness of the situation. A more accurate way of describing the state of play was that among the G-7, the six that weren't rejecting Lamy's package were agreeing merely to keep discussing it, and several of them had serious problems with it—including the Americans.

| * |

At 10:00 a.m. the next morning, a Saturday, representatives of American business and farm groups gathered in the lobby of the President Wilson, one of Geneva's premier hotels, together with a handful of congressional staffers. They sat in a large circle around a table while tourists, many of them wealthy Arab women in head scarves and burkas, strolled nearby and sat sipping tea. (Geneva's temperate summer weather is a big draw with Middle Easterners.) Among them were leaders and lobbyists from organizations whose support for trade agreements had always been enthusiastic and, at times, essential for passage in Congress—notably Bob Stallman, president of the American Farm Bureau, and Frank Vargo, vice president for international economic affairs at the National Association of Manufacturers. Although these private-sector representatives had not been allowed to enter the Centre William Rappard without going through a bothersome appointment procedure each time, they had stayed in very close touch with the U.S. negotiating team, thanks to e-mail, text messages, and frequent briefings at the hotel where the U.S. delegation was quartered. They had received copies of the Lamy paper at a briefing on Friday evening, a few hours after its presentation to the G-7.

They didn't like what they saw. "The best thing that could happen now," one farm lobbyist told the others, "would be for the thing to blow up."

Agriculture groups felt that the deal on the table simply wouldn't provide enough new market access for U.S. farm exports to compensate for the reduction in the cap on U.S. subsidies. They understood that the full impact of a final Doha accord would not be clear until WTO member countries had filled in the details of their tariff cuts for individual products, which would take at least six months. Still, the handwriting seemed to be on the wall: Although U.S. exporters would gain additional sales in high-income markets, such as the European Union, for beef, pork, and some other products, they wouldn't gain much, if anything, in the world's emerging markets, because the loopholes granted to developing countries were too large.

The Farm Bureau's Stallman lamented that U.S. hopes for market access in agriculture had been "continually whittled away" as the Doha talks had proceeded. The draft texts produced shortly before the meeting, he said, didn't promise enough, and "it's worse now" under the terms of the Lamy paper. Whereas in the past U.S. negotiators had vowed never to cross certain "red lines," the Lamy paper entailed just such an outcome, Stallman noted. In particular, it allowed developing countries to exempt a substantial number of their tariff lines from any cuts whatsoever, and it allowed them to use the SSM to raise tariffs above bound rates. Other representatives of commodity groups, especially the cotton and rice growers, were even more negative.

Agriculture was not the only problem; the National Association of Manufacturers' Vargo was almost equally downbeat. He estimated that under the formulas the trade ministers were considering, applied tariffs for industrial products would fall by an average of only about one-tenth in big markets like Brazil, and that even that would take about nine years to materialize.

The Lamy paper "offers the theoretical possibility of a successful outcome for U.S. manufacturers, but it's very unlikely," Vargo told the others at the President Wilson. The only hope, he said, "is to get market access from the sectorals"—the term for the proposed agreements to eliminate tariffs, or at least reduce them reasonably close to zero, in a few selected industries. And although Lamy's paper envisioned such agreements, it was far from clear in the language that big developing countries—China, in particular—would be required to participate in the sectoral deals that Washington wanted, namely, chemicals and machinery. "If there's no China on the list [of sectoral participants], there's no point," Vargo said. "We cannot support" the Lamy paper in that case.

"It was really sobering to hear the ag and NAM [National Association of Manufacturers] people say, 'Hmmm, this isn't worth the trouble,'" recalls one congressional staffer who attended the meeting. "How would you get that passed in Congress?"*

Pressure was now mounting from key lawmakers and their staffs to let the deal die. At a meeting with members of Schwab's team later that Saturday, the question was laid out bluntly by Hayden Milberg, an aide to Republican senator Saxby Chambliss of Georgia, the ranking member of the Senate Agriculture Committee: Because nobody in the private sector seemed to like the deal outlined in the Lamy paper, it wouldn't pass Congress, so would it be better for Schwab to walk away from the table here in Geneva or to accept a deal that

---

*Those with long memories might detect some U.S. chickens coming home to roost. The reasons for the complaints by the U.S. agriculture and manufacturers' groups about the lack of market access mainly concerned two loopholes that developing countries had won in previous meetings—the exemption for special products (which was agreed in the July 2004 framework deal) and the allowance for countries to opt out of sectoral accords (which was agreed at the 2005 Hong Kong ministerial). At both meetings, the United States had insisted on loopholes of its own to protect American special interests. These included the provision sheltering the U.S. countercyclical payment program from deep cuts and the provision giving Washington the ability to exempt its textile sector from eliminating tariffs on goods from very poor countries.

would face defeat on Capitol Hill? Wouldn't a negative vote in Congress be highly damaging for the WTO as an institution? A similar message was conveyed by phone the next day to Schwab directly, by Senator Max Baucus, a Democrat from Montana and chairman of the Senate Finance Committee, which has jurisdiction over trade legislation.

Schwab was keenly aware of the political difficulties the deal might face in Washington. One of her biggest concerns was the SSM, which could theoretically allow China to raise some of the tariffs it had cut when it joined the WTO. (The Chinese bound rate on soybeans, for instance, was 3 percent; by invoking the SSM to counter an import surge, Beijing could impose an 18 percent tariff, even if only for a limited period—the sort of scenario guaranteed to raise a tempest among farm-state lawmakers.) Still, her answer to these and other objections was, be patient. In meetings over the weekend with the private sector and conversations with the Hill, she noted the caveats she had raised in the G-7 meeting about "potential deal breakers," and she assured them that she was determined to get satisfaction from other nations on those issues before signing off on anything.

In fact, her subordinates were already hard at work trying to fix the deal, hoping to extract promises from the country whose market they cared about most.

| * |

China's mission to the WTO is conveniently located just down the road from the Centre William Rappard, in a recently built modern structure on Lake Geneva. There, on the Saturday and Sunday immediately following the presentation of Lamy's paper, Chinese officials met their U.S. counterparts, including the ambassador to the WTO, Peter Allgeier, and the chief agriculture negotiator, Joe Glauber.

Perhaps no other country on earth has as big a stake in the preservation of the multilateral system as does China, given its reliance on exports, and few countries if any stood to gain as much from the completion of the Doha Round, if World Bank estimates were to be believed. The Americans knew that Chinese policymakers would want to avoid, at almost any cost, being the main cause of a breakdown at a major WTO meeting. So they thought they might be able to persuade Beijing to make some concessions, on a bilateral basis, that would go beyond the requirements of the Lamy paper and thereby make the whole deal more attractive for U.S. industry and agriculture. But the U.S. negotiators also knew they would have a tough sell, because the Chinese have nursed grudges ever since the 1999 talks concerning their entry into the WTO;

officials in Beijing feel that the United States bullied them into accepting excessively stringent terms as the price of membership.

Tops on the list of U.S. concerns: cotton. Specifically, the U.S. team wanted China to effectively promise to buy more of the stuff from the United States. Recognizing that American cotton growers were facing the prospect of a severe reduction in subsidies in any conceivable Doha agreement, U.S. officials were hoping that if they could secure significant increases in export opportunities for the growers, they might be able to at least defuse the opposition of the National Cotton Council, a formidable power on Capitol Hill. That was where China came in, because with its vast clothing industry, it is the world's largest importer of cotton by far.

Accordingly, U.S. negotiators were anxious for Beijing to pledge that it would keep cotton off its list of special products that would be shielded from deep tariff cuts. By substantially reducing the 40 percent duty it imposes on most of the cotton it imports, China would presumably buy a lot more U.S. cotton than it does now, and the benefits for the world's poor would be significant, the Americans argued, because the move would also increase demand for African cotton.

Sorry, the Americans were told; China too has a political problem with cotton. Its cotton farmers, who number about 10 million, are mostly very poor and mostly live in the far western province of Xinjiang, a Muslim-dominated area that has become restive in recent years. Taking market-opening measures that might endanger those peoples' meager incomes could be foolhardy. So Beijing intended to exercise its right to choose cotton as one of its special products.

The Chinese also rejected American requests to promise that other crops, including wheat and corn, would be kept off Beijing's list of specials. And they were adamant that they would not participate in the "voluntary" sectoral deals for chemicals and machinery that the Americans wanted. China's chemical and machinery industries had already endured steep tariff cuts a few years earlier as part of the WTO membership deal, and Beijing had promised those industries that their barriers would not be lowered again.

Strike one, strike two, and strike three: The U.S. team had failed in its effort to improve the Lamy package by securing concessions from the Chinese. Conceivably the outcome would have been different if the Chinese had thought they would bear the sole responsibility for the meeting's collapse. But they knew, of course, that India was already taking a firm stance against the director-general's proposal.

Whatever was behind China's thinking, any hope of generating enthusiasm among U.S. farm and industry groups for the Lamy paper was now gone. Up until the weekend of July 26–27, the United States had acted as if it had been eager to cut a deal. From then on, during the remaining days of the ministerial, its behavior would change.

| * |

In fairness to Akira Amari, the Japanese trade minister, it must be said that his patience had been sorely tried before his rage boiled over in the middle of the night of Monday, July 28.

Amari, who was expecting a meeting of the G-7 to begin, had been kept cooling his heels outside the director-general's office for several hours while some of the other ministers—Schwab, Mandelson, Amorim, and Crean—were engaged in intensive discussions with Lamy. Incensed over his inability to get a straight answer to his questions about the meeting schedule even though it was past midnight, Amari leapt up when Lamy emerged from his office and, banging his briefcase for emphasis, began screaming in Japanese, as his interpreter did her utmost to convey not only his words but his wrath. Waving her arms and contorting her face at the startled director-general, the interpreter bellowed: "Mr. Lamy, I am a minister in the Japanese government with a very large portfolio, and it is intolerable that I have been made to wait this long!" The racket prompted curious people to poke their heads out of nearby doors; some could barely conceal their mirth over the interpreter's histrionics.

As that episode suggests, sleeplessness was taking a toll, and the scramble to find a compromise was turning disorderly, as the meeting—now in its eighth day—staggered on. A number of ministers who weren't in the G-7 had already headed home, leaving their ambassadors to represent them in case a deal materialized. The irritation of those participants who remained was in some cases compounded by the necessity of switching hotels; most had booked their lodging in the expectation that the meeting would last five days. Still, Lamy was desperately trying to stitch something together, with help from Mandelson and Amorim.

The main focus was to strike some deal on the SSM, on the theory that until that issue was settled, a consensus could not possibly be reached on other matters. Disagreements remained on a number of other key subjects, notably the reduction in developing-country barriers on manufactured products. Argentine officials, in particular, were objecting vociferously to the terms that the Lamy paper proposed on that issue, asserting that their nation's clothing and auto industries would be hurt; South Africa and Venezuela were also holding out. On still other tough issues, such as cotton subsidies, substantive negotiations had barely taken place. Although recognizing that these problems and others would be difficult to surmount, Lamy saw no choice but to direct the G-7's efforts into breaking the SSM logjam.

But the U.S. team's attitude had soured following the failure of their weekend effort to pry concessions from the Chinese, and Schwab took a decidedly jaundiced view of various SSM proposals as they were floated. One danger—which she was plainly anxious to avoid—was that the rest of the G-7 might unite behind a plan that was still seriously flawed from the U.S. standpoint; then Washington could be fingered as the main culprit for the breakdown in the talks. "I'm not getting fucking trapped into this, Pascal!" Schwab snarled at Lamy at one point, according to people who witnessed the exchange.

In a move that some insiders saw as a clear sign that the U.S. team had gone from a deal-making mode to a blame-avoidance one, American officials began blasting away not only at India but at China for undermining the talks. David Shark, the deputy in the U.S. mission to the WTO, delivered an unusually harsh statement in the General Council chamber on Monday morning asserting that the two countries "have thrown the entire Doha Round into the gravest jeopardy of its nearly seven year life" because India had "immediately rejected the [Lamy] package" and China had "walked away from it." The accusation against the Chinese—that they were reneging on their word—was repeated over and over by U.S. officials to the press. "China wanted a seat at the big kids' table," the *International Herald Tribune* quoted one anonymous member of the U.S. delegation as saying. "They got it, they agreed to the text, and now they are trying to walk that text back."

The Americans had legitimate reasons to be fed up with the Chinese, who had given nothing in response to the U.S. requests over the weekend despite Beijing's interest in having the meeting end successfully. Moreover, every time solutions were proposed for the impasse over the SSM, the Chinese—who are extremely sensitive to "discrimination" against them in international agreements—insisted on getting the same favorable terms as the Indians, which made it impossible to reach a compromise that might have satisfied the United States on that issue. But the claim that the Chinese "walked away" from Lamy's paper is disputed by nearly all neutral participants with whom I spoke. And the Americans had no moral standing to issue such condemnations; it was they who had touted the Lamy paper and then "walked away" from it by demanding Chinese concessions as part of the deal.

By Tuesday, July 29, the only sign of hope for the meeting was a box of cigars carried around by Jean-Luc Demarty, the European Union's chief agriculture negotiator, who was promising to pass out the stogies when a deal was finally struck. Demarty had been deputized to take one more stab at drafting an SSM compromise, and he did his best, using a complex two-tier structure, to find an approach that would meet the competing needs of the Americans, the Australians, the Indians, and the Chinese. But they all rejected it, and when Lamy implored them to try it again using different numbers, Schwab wouldn't.

"It's over," she told Lamy. "How do you want me to handle this so that there will be a soft landing?"

The word went forth in midafternoon from the Secretariat to WTO members' missions around Geneva, and soon a line of cars was slowly working its way down the U-shaped driveway of the Centre William Rappard to discharge ministers and ambassadors. The thirty-odd ministers who were green room invitees headed to their meeting first, to get the official word from a man who, up to that point, seemed one of the least likely on earth to lose his composure in a room full of people.

"The round has broken down," Lamy told them, and then he choked up. As his sadness permeated the room, the director-general halted to take a sip of water. Steadying himself, he said: "Differences on the SSM are irreconcilable. I have two recommendations: Please refrain from the blame game. The dust needs to settle. But we should be under no illusion. The system will be weakened."

Poignant words of regret also came from Amorim, who descended the steps in the lobby of the Centre William Rappard to address reporters, his weary expression reflecting the strain of the nine-day marathon. "We heard from several people that we should preserve what we have obtained," the Brazilian minister said, referring to the partial agreement on the Lamy paper's terms. "And I agree with that, but you know, it's not in our power; life goes on. You have the food crisis. You'll have other crises. Other preoccupations will look larger than they have been today."

| * |

With astounding swiftness, Amorim's prediction came true about the onset of "other crises" that would overshadow the failure of the WTO's July 2008 meeting. On September 7, the U.S. government announced that it was taking over Fannie Mae and Freddie Mac, which owned or guaranteed about half the U.S. mortgage market. A week later, Merrill Lynch escaped collapse only by selling itself to Bank of America, and Lehman Brothers was forced into bankruptcy; soon thereafter came a federal bailout of the insurance giant AIG and the federal seizure of the go-go bank Washington Mutual. Credit markets virtually ceased to function, and stock prices were in almost daily free fall, with the week of October 6–10 being the worst ever for the Dow Jones—a 22 percent drop, which brought the index 40 percent below its high a year earlier. As the turmoil spread to Europe and Asia, central banks there joined the U.S. Federal Reserve in emergency measures to ease the flow of credit, but the markets continued to reel from the constant drumbeat of shocking news.

The potential implications for the trading system dawned early on Fernando de Mateo, Mexico's ambassador to the WTO, who strode into the Council chamber on October 14 brandishing a large, grainy, black-and-white photo of two men.

"I said, 'Do you know who this is?'" de Mateo recalls. "I said, 'This is not a grandfather and uncle of mine. This is Senator Smoot, and Congressman Hawley, the real culprits of the Great Depression. Mr. Chairman, please put this picture on the front door. Ask the concierge not to let them into this building—and certainly not their spirits.'"

# 14 | IF ONLY THERE WERE
# A BETTER WAY

THE COMPLETE TERMINATION OF GLOBAL TRADE TALKS IS UNTHINKABLE.
Nothing of the sort has happened since the 1930s. Previous trade rounds had
very dark moments, and each of the rounds since the early 1960s has taken
longer than the one before. One way or another, the Doha Round will get done
eventually.

Those sentiments are articles of faith among many trade experts and Geneva
veterans, who have seen countless trade ministers and directors-general come
and go and whose experience has taught them that in the end, the self-interest
of the world's nations in preserving the multilateral trading system always pre-
vails. Perhaps they are right. But the risk that they will be proven wrong this
time looks uncomfortably high, especially as the global economy spirals downward and free-market ideology comes under unprecedented attack.

The financial crisis has made it all the more difficult for WTO members to
overcome the differences that sank the July 2008 meeting. Although the crisis
substantially raised the value of a deal that would put some constraints on protectionism, the political reality is that an economic slump is a lousy time to sell
a policy of trade liberalization. The rise in joblessness and bankruptcies and the
plunge in many crop prices have stiffened resistance to the idea of dismantling
trade barriers and farm subsidies. (Indeed, a collapse in dairy prices sparked a
"subsidy war" in mid-2009, with the United States reintroducing export subsidies on products such as milk powder and cheese in retaliation for the European Union offering aid earlier to its milk producers.)

How disheartening that after more than seven years, WTO members should
still be at such loggerheads over a deal that would do so little to change the

terms on which trade currently takes place. True, the Uruguay Round took eight years, but scant comfort should be taken from that fact. The Uruguay Round was sweeping in scope and impact; it will be difficult to credibly make the same claim for almost any conceivable Doha accord. Even if Doha negotiators manage to cobble together a pact in the next couple of years, the gap between the outcome and the initial aspirations will surely prompt questions about why so much time and effort were required and whether the WTO has any future as a negotiating forum.

Looking back at the events chronicled in this book, it is hard to find many encouraging signs that the WTO can do a lot better in the future. The failures—Cancún, the 2006 suspension of the round, the Potsdam meeting, and the nine days of July 2008—are only part of the reason for this dismal assessment. Even when ministers eked out progress, it was by the skin of their teeth. The July 2004 framework agreement depended on Bob Zoellick's virtually commandeering the meeting in the predawn hours at the end, after having stayed up several nights in a row. The Hong Kong ministerial was saved from turning into a fiasco when Celso Amorim's walkout was fortuitously impeded. Perhaps the July 2004 and Hong Kong meetings would have ended in agreements anyway. But these episodes underscore the pitfalls of trade rounds, which are "a terrible way to do business," as Patrick Low, the WTO's chief economist, put it at a Washington conference in the spring of 2009.

From the skimpiness of the advances made in the Doha Round, grim conclusions can be drawn, and not just in the realm of trade. The outcome in the talks to date is a symptom of what commentator David Brooks aptly calls "globosclerosis." Had WTO members achieved a creditable result, they would have provided some grounds for optimism that the world's big players are prepared to act in the collective global interest on other issues for which multilateralism offers by far the most sensible solution. These issues include climate change, nuclear nonproliferation, food shortages, terrorism, and energy security—and the financial crisis has lengthened the list considerably. A multilateral approach is essential to generating a balanced, sustainable economic recovery and to establishing a more effective international regulatory apparatus for preventing future crises.

Too bad the WTO could not emit a ray of hope about the chances for resolving those other tough challenges. There are much more compelling reasons, though, for fixing the shambles in the trading system. The world economy as we know it may survive—and even emerge stronger from—the crisis in financial globalization; the same cannot be said if the trading system too comes unglued.

| * |

Jennifer Hillman's office in the Centre William Rappard contains no pictures, crafts, flags, symbols, or other articles to indicate her U.S. citizenship. As one of the seven "justices" on the WTO's Appellate Body, she is expected to keep her workplace clear of anything that might be construed as suggesting a national bias. So although some artwork by her two school-age boys adorns her walls, and pictures of her family sit on her desk, she has refrained from displaying other mementos concerning her past affiliations, such as the photos she has of herself with Bill Clinton, in whose administration she served as a high-ranking trade policymaker in the mid-1990s.

This is one small way in which the Dispute Settlement System maintains its authority, Hillman explains—by scrupulously presenting its top judicial body as a neutral arbiter of international rules, untainted by political pressure. "The idea is to have objective judges," she says, adding that her six colleagues, who hail from Japan, Italy, Brazil, China, South Africa, and the Philippines, take the same approach with their offices. "I try to make sure that the appearance matches the fact that I'm not in any way, shape, or form advocating for, or on the side of, the United States."

But on the day I visited Hillman in Geneva, she was fretting about the durability of the institution's authority for reasons that went much deeper than office decor.

It was mid-December 2008, and despite the onset of the holiday season, an atmosphere of gloom and resignation was enveloping the Centre William Rappard. A few days earlier, on December 12, Pascal Lamy had announced that he was abandoning plans for one last ministerial in 2008. The director-general had hoped that once the U.S. election was over, WTO members might be able to reach an accord on modalities that the incoming Obama administration would feel obliged to accept—something close to the deal that had been on the table in July. With the economic crisis raging in full fury, he had traveled to New Delhi, Washington, and other capitals in an effort to convince policymakers that the merit of the July package was dramatically greater than before and that the need for progress in the Doha Round was more manifest than ever, now that protectionism was starting to appear in various forms throughout the world. At one point in early December, the word in Geneva was that ministers would be summoned; the leaders of the G-20 group of advanced and emerging countries endorsed the idea. But a series of conversations with the key players convinced Lamy that convening a parley would only lead to another crippling setback. The details of those talks need not be spelled out here, because the reasons were essentially the same as the ones that had led to the July debacle. India was still taking a hard line on the special safeguard mechanism, and the

Chinese were still balking at participating in sectoral talks in chemicals and ma-chinery. Most important, leading private-sector groups in the United States were still dissatisfied with the amount of new export opportunities they would get, and they had strong backing from powerful members of Congress, who publicly warned Bush administration trade negotiators against engaging in talks based on the terms of the July package.

Like others at the Centre William Rappard, Hillman lamented the lack of a deal because she believed that lowering bound tariffs would have provided helpful insurance against protectionism, and she was very concerned that the crisis would fuel pressures for a rise in trade barriers. But as an Appellate Body member, she could see more worrisome, longer-term implications for the system as a whole. In particular, she was focused on whether, in the future, she and her colleagues would be able to make their decisions stick. The failure to reach agreement in the Doha talks on even a relatively narrow agenda, she noted, meant that there was a serious imbalance between the WTO's very weak "ne-gotiating leg" and the trade body's dispute settlement side.

"This is not a situation that can continue for very long," Hillman told me. "The other parts of the WTO have to be as vibrant as the dispute settlement system. Otherwise, people just won't comply [with rulings] over the long haul."

To understand this reasoning, a little thought experiment is in order. Imag-ine a nation with a court system whose judges' opinions enjoy deep respect for their legal scholarship and impartiality, but whose legislature gets stuck in such endless political wrangling that the nation's laws grow increasingly outmoded. Suppose, for instance, this is a country in the early decades of the twentieth century, when automobiles were first traversing the roads, and the country's lawmakers are unable even to enact legislation governing car traffic. In this imaginary land, numerous statutes remain on the books governing transporta-tion on horseback—how fast a rider's steed may gallop through urban areas, where horses must be tethered, what responsibilities horse owners have for care of their animals, and the like—but the laws remain unclear regarding auto speed limits and traffic lights. What will happen to this country's judiciary? Eventually, its rulings will be treated with much less respect. People involved in auto acci-dents will bring cases to the courts for adjudication, and if judges refuse to issue rulings on the grounds that they have no legal basis for doing so, aggrieved par-ties in car crashes will presumably start taking the law into their own hands, based on the reasoning that the whole legal system is hopelessly behind the times. Alternatively, if the courts pluck up their courage and issue rulings, they will stand accused of usurping the role of the legislature. Either way, the chances for mass disobedience of court rulings will increase, as the public perception grows that judges are interpreting an obsolete body of law and as disrespect for court rulings in the field of auto traffic spreads to other areas.

For the multilateral trading system, the rule-making machinery managed to keep up reasonably well with changes in trade, technology, and policy during the latter part of the twentieth century. For example, in the Tokyo Round, negotiators dealt with problems involving subsidies and import licenses because a number of countries were using them to block foreign competition. And in the Uruguay Round, negotiators addressed the issue of intellectual property violations after it became a major source of complaint among some of America's most advanced industries. But now the WTO's rules are stuck in the mid-1990s, and the longer that continues, the greater the chances that countries will take measures damaging to its standing as the referee and arbiter of those rules.

The controversies over new issues that have arisen in recent years—currency manipulation and the food crisis prime among them—have already generated concern that time is passing the WTO's rulebook by. As noted in Chapter 1, climate change is another controversy requiring urgent attention by the WTO because of the potential for clashes between WTO rules and the green laws that countries are drafting, some of which include tariffs on carbon-heavy imports. Hillman is especially fearful that she and her colleagues will be forced to render a judgment on a case involving climate change before WTO members can agree on new rules.

"The perception is that the dispute settlement system has rendered decisions that are, at a basic level, fair and reasonable," she said. "And compliance, by and large, has been quite good. People are settling their trade disputes amicably. They're not starting trade wars, or literal wars, over disputes that they bring to the WTO. But not every issue ought to come to dispute settlement. And if the institution doesn't remain viable and relevant, then countries will quit either fully participating [in dispute settlement] or complying. So it is very important for all aspects of the WTO to be strong and functioning well."

Ernesto Zedillo, former president of Mexico and now a professor at Yale, has made a similar point using more colorful language: The "relevant question," he asserts, "will not be how can the WTO save the Doha Round, but, rather, how can the WTO be saved from the Doha Round?"

| * |

At almost every symposium or conference that is held these days on the global trading system, someone on the speakers' rostrum or in the audience will make the case that the Doha Round was a mistake from the outset. These critics typically argue that the Doha ministerial would never have succeeded but for the 9/11 attacks; some assert that big multilateral trade rounds should have ended with the Uruguay Round, and others contend that focusing the round on development was misplaced, having been based on an overblown sense of guilt over the impact of trade on the poor. This book has provided ample evidence for the contention that the round, despite its development focus, was largely the product of ambitious men with no small appetite for achievement—in particular Mike Moore, who wanted to make sure that his director-generalship would be remembered for more than Seattle, and Bob Zoellick, who reveled in showing up the Clintonites as unsteady stewards of U.S. leadership.

This does not mean, however, that the round was poorly conceived. Major inequities in the trading system needed correcting, especially those that adversely affected developing countries, and a round offered the only viable means for doing so. Although the idea of "re-branding" the WTO after Seattle may have been a bit crass, Moore was surely justified in his belief that a development focus was both an appropriate way forward for the organization and an opportunity for badly needed redemption. For getting the round launched, he and Zoellick—and Lamy as well—deserve to be commended, not condemned.

If there was a serious error committed at the time of Doha, it was hyping the round's antipoverty potential. The depiction of the round as a likely bonanza for the third world fed expectations in developing countries that nearly all the concessions would come from rich WTO members and that the South would surrender little or nothing. And when the updated World Bank estimates of 2005 showed the projected benefits as much smaller than before, the credibility of those urging an ambitious package of market-liberalizing measures was diminished.

It is in the events after the 2001 meeting that finger-pointers and blame-assigners can find the most targets of opportunity. *Murder on the Orient Express*, the Agatha Christie detective thriller in which all the suspects turn out to be guilty, has been frequently compared—with good reason—to the Doha Round. A variety of parties can be rightly accused of complicity in the round's afflictions.

The United States has much to answer for, starting with the 2002 farm bill, which got the round off inauspiciously by raising doubts about Washington's preparedness to limit subsidies. The same was true of U.S. insistence on sheltering its countercyclical payments program from deep cuts and of the insensitivity that Zoellick and his team showed on the cotton issue; those factors helped incite the developing-country backlash at Cancún. The decision to switch Rob Portman to a new job in 2006 sent a signal that the Bush administration saw little chance for progress in the Doha talks in the foreseeable future, and the move was understandably interpreted as evidence that the president's priorities lay elsewhere, no matter how much White House officials protested otherwise. Of all the people who might have turned things around after that, Susan Schwab was not the one. She was justified in feeling that she had been dealt a very poor hand, given the way the negotiations were structured after 2004, with all the loopholes obscuring the potential gains for American exporters. But her instinctive reluctance to challenge powerful domestic interests was hardly conducive to success.

As for the European Union, Lamy made his own contribution to the backlash at Cancún with his involvement in the U.S.-E.U. agriculture proposal and by his clinging to a tough position on the Singapore issues until the last minute. Under Peter Mandelson's commissionership, the hardball that the Europeans played in 2005 on the issue of agricultural market access stalled the round for at least a year. By strenuously resisting efforts to offer anything more than modest reductions in E.U. farm tariffs, the French and their allies in countries such as Ireland helped ensure that the round's accomplishments would be modest as well.

To hear many U.S. trade negotiators tell it, the overarching problem has been the reluctance of the big emerging markets—Brazil to some extent, India and China even more so—to assume global responsibilities in proportion to their economic heft and political clout. The gauntlet was thrown down to them at Cancún, when Zoellick derided them for not having an answer to his question about what they would offer in return for their demands of him. By banding together in the G-20, they were eventually able to advance coherent proposals and compromise to some extent. Their overall performance in the Doha Round, however, does not augur particularly well for their readiness to shoulder the burdens of great-power status. The Brazilians, Indians, and Chinese all too often sought to resist demands for market opening by proclaiming developing-world solidarity and draping themselves in the mantle of advocacy for the world's poor, even though they knew full well that the poorest WTO members would not have to lower barriers at all (thanks to the "round for free" arrangement). Paradoxically, one of the most helpful boosts that impoverished countries could receive would be a lowering of trade barriers by big emerging powers such as Brazil, India, and China, because the size of the markets in question have grown so large and have expanded so much faster than elsewhere in the world. In the July 2008 meeting, Brazil's Amorim finally broke out of the solidarity mode by supporting the director-general's package despite its rejection by India's Nath. But the Chinese, by refusing to be more forthcoming, gave the Indians cover;

perhaps if Nath had been isolated, he would have been forced to take a less re-calcitrant position.

China, more than any other country in the WTO, needs to take proper account of the long-run consequences that its negotiating positions may have for the trading system. A pointed question was posed to the country's top officials in the fall of 2008, when Schwab visited Beijing amid the eruption of the financial crisis. "I said to the Chinese, 'Imagine what might be happening to Chinese exports now if you were not in the WTO,'" Schwab recalls. Chinese leaders ought to ask themselves that question every day.

One more point concerning blame: The developing countries as a group, plus Asian powers like Japan, were responsible for foisting Supachai Panitch-pakdi on the WTO. As decent and smart as Supachai is, he was not cut out for the director-general's job, and that mismatch had consequences, notably at Cancún. Although the previous tradition of awarding the post only to Europeans deserved upending, Supachai's tenure at the WTO should serve as a warning about the foolishness of choosing leaders for important international institutions based on nationality.

But whatever the shortcomings of individual policymakers or shortsightedness on the part of individual governments or groups of countries, those factors merely exacerbated the more fundamental problems that brought the round to its current unhappy juncture. The WTO of today is operating in a vastly different political, economic, and diplomatic climate from the multilateral trading system of the past.

Gone are the Cold War circumstances that led the "English gentlemen's club" of rich powers to negotiate market-opening deals among themselves without expecting much in return from developing nations. In the club's place is a world of multipolarity, with all the globosclerotic tendencies that logically ensue. Gone too is the post-1989 flush of enthusiasm for capitalism. In its place is a pervasive sense of wariness, attributable largely, though not entirely, to the Chinese phenomenon, about the rapidity with which globalization giveth and taketh away. The 2008 financial crisis, of course, has only added to the ranks of the disenchanted.

So to return to the question posed in Chapter 1, about whether the WTO is capable of coping with the realities of the early twenty-first century, the answer is no—or perhaps more charitably, "not very well at all." That is especially unfortunate because, amid the global economic downturn, a healthy WTO has never been more important. How, then, can the WTO be saved from the Doha Round?

| * |

Put the round out of its misery.

No, harvest the organs.

No, stay the course and just get it done.

No, try doing smaller deals with "coalitions of the willing."

No, switch to negotiating bilateral pacts.

No, aim for a much bigger, more meaningful agreement on issues that really matter.

Those are capsule versions of the myriad proposals that are circulating in the aftermath of the July 2008 meeting about what to do with the Doha Round. The let-it-die school argues that the round has become such a hopeless cause that further efforts to revive it would only inflict further damage on the WTO. The organ-harvesters favor taking a couple of issues in the round on which there is little disagreement, such as trade facilitation, and finalizing accords that would show the WTO capable of generating at least some progress. The stay-the-course crowd subscribes to the view that the death and resurrection cycle will finally turn again and that the wait will be worthwhile.

The advocates of moving to bilateral arrangements contend that bilaterals are by far the fastest way to open markets further, and are perhaps the only practical way to do so. Those preferring to mobilize coalitions of the willing hope to duplicate the success of the deals that were negotiated on a plurilateral basis by the Clinton administration in the late 1990s, in information technology and other sectors. In these accords, groups of countries representing most of the commerce in certain areas (services, for instance) would jointly agree to liberalize in those areas whether or not the rest of the WTO membership did anything in return.

Finally, there is the expand-the-agenda argument, advanced in an important and provocative *Foreign Affairs* article that threw the Geneva trade community into a tizzy. The Doha negotiators, the article charged "have, Nero-like, spent too much time dwelling on minor issues while ignoring the burning questions."

The article's authors are economists Aaditya Mattoo of the World Bank and Arvind Subramanian of the Peterson Institute for International Economics. Citing the enormity of changes in the global economy since 2001, they urged a complete makeover of the subjects being negotiated, because "Doha distracts attention from other matters of greater significance." For instance, they wrote, "even as food prices soared and import barriers declined, the Doha talks continued to focus on traditional forms of agricultural protection, such as production subsidies, which have become less relevant." Accordingly, the round should shift, in their view, to dealing with both import and export barriers on agricultural products, as well as with biofuel policies. They also called for a multilateral

approach to deal with the "persistent and substantial undervaluation of major currencies," the Chinese yuan being the most obvious example. Concerning climate
change, the "growing talk" of using trade sanctions to enforce a greenhouse-gas-
emissions scheme was yet another challenge crying for attention.* They proposed
placing still other issues on the agenda, such as energy and financial regulation.

I have some ideas of my own about what to do. First, here are some overarching principles that I think ought to guide the debate, whatever specific approach is taken.

The most important goal is to ensure the survival of the rules-based trading
system. It is unwise to devote a lot of energy to opening markets more than they
already are; after eight rounds, global trade is already reasonably free. The focus
should be on keeping protectionism, and quasi-protectionism, from becoming
long-lasting features of the international economy, so that globalized trade can
help the world recover and prosper anew. It is worth recalling that one of the
most pernicious effects of protectionism in the 1930s was that it remained in
place for many years, hampering recovery and growth. A strong multilateral
trade body, with credible enforcement powers, is surely the best safeguard that
the world has against a protracted bout of protectionism. So in concrete terms,
the top priority of trade policy should be to shore up the WTO, for all the reasons stated throughout this book about the critical role the trade body plays in
fostering openness on a worldwide basis.

One step that would send a symbolic but powerful message of support for
multilateralism would be to declare a moratorium on all bilateral and regional
free-trade agreements and to agree that for the foreseeable future all trade negotiations—whether grand or limited in scope—will be conducted under the
auspices of the WTO. Another measure would be to remedy the flaws in the
dispute settlement system that put developing countries at a disadvantage. I'll
come back to these ideas later.

The boost the WTO most crucially needs is a way out of the Doha morass.

No question, Mattoo and Subramanian are right to scorn the round for missing the boat on big issues that have arisen since 2001. The round also deserves
disparagement for doing little on its initial objective of development. But aban-

---

*On climate change and some other issues, the WTO would have to work with other multi-
lateral bodies, Mattoo and Subramanian noted. The trade body's negotiations concerning the
legality of carbon tariffs would be subordinate to the environmental summit planned for
Copenhagen in late 2009, for example. Concerning currencies, the WTO would have to coordinate with the IMF, with the fund taking responsibility for assessing whether a currency is un-
dervalued and the WTO authorizing the imposition of sanctions against countries found to be
in violation of the rules.

doning the current focus of the talks would have a corrosive impact on confidence in the WTO, and it would go against the strong wishes of most developing-country members. Rather than ditching the present agenda, it makes more sense to capitalize on its virtues, limited though they may be.

The best way to impart new vitality to the round would be to recast it as an antiprotectionism exercise. The insurance benefits of reduced bound tariffs would at least help prevent long-term harm to world trade. Accordingly, the prospective deal should be narrowed down to something like the package of measures that was on the table at the July 2008 meeting. The other parts of the round—antidumping rules, fisheries subsidies, and so on—would have to be dealt with later, so that the stripped-down pact could be approved as speedily as possible. (If an agreement on opening up services markets could be struck quickly, it could help enhance the attractiveness of the overall accord; otherwise, it too should be deferred.)

Given the obstacles that prevented agreement in July 2008, the terms would obviously have to be altered somewhat. President Obama's trade representative, Ron Kirk, has floated an intriguing proposal, which is to move directly to negotiating tariff schedules for the thousands of products at stake, skipping the intermediate step of a modalities agreement. The idea is to give U.S. farm and industry groups a clearer idea than they have now of exactly what they will get in terms of new export opportunities, in the hope that at least some groups will become enthusiastic backers of the round.

Meanwhile, the far-reaching agenda proposed by Mattoo and Subramanian should not be left to molder. Even as negotiating continues on the antiprotectionism round, WTO members should start drawing up an agenda for a new round that would involve negotiations on the food crisis, on currencies, and on rules governing carbon tariffs, plus the leftover Doha issues and a few others.

Wait a minute—another round? Wasn't the WTO's chief economist quoted earlier in this chapter as saying that rounds are a terrible way to do business?

| * |

There has *got* to be a better way. That is one obvious lesson to be drawn from this book—from both its content and its length. Having now gained an appreciation of what was meant by my promise to tell a long saga of scrambling, floundering, and dysfunctionality, many readers will understandably conclude (or have their preexisting beliefs reinforced) that trade rounds belong in the dustbin of history along with other once-useful devices such as videocassette recorders and floppy disks.

Requiems have been held before for the idea of big trade rounds. After both the Tokyo and Uruguay rounds, fatigued trade negotiators, sounding like World War I veterans returning from the "war to end all wars," opined that never again should an enterprise of such complexity be undertaken. It would be soothing to believe that Doha will ring down the curtain on trade rounds once and for all and that the trading system can get by without them.

Be not soothed. Trade policymakers would be better advised to steel themselves for the inevitability of more rounds, because rounds offer the opportunity for countries to make tradeoffs among whole batches of issues that are often unrelated to each other. Cuts in farm subsidies can be traded for a lowering of tariffs on manufactured goods, for example, and the establishment of rules on intellectual property can be traded for the elimination of textile quotas. The Doha Round should certainly stand as a cautionary tale about the importance of looking before you launch. But when a variety of truly consequential steps must be taken in the multilateral trading system, the inconvenient truth is that a round is likely to be the only option.

Doha may well mark the end of an era for a particular type of round—those in which expanding the frontiers of free trade is a principal objective. The message emanating from many quarters during the Doha Round is that the world's appetite for further large dollops of globalization has approached its limit. This attitude doesn't apply to all countries by any means, and at some point down the road it may change for the world at large. But for now at least, the focus of the next trade round, and perhaps others in the future, should be on preserving, fortifying, and modernizing the multilateral system. Although additional liberalization may be a part of the mix, the main goal ought to be ensuring that the world continues to reap the tremendous benefits of this international public good.

Doha also probably marks the end of an era for another type of round—those in which nothing is agreed until all is agreed, *by everybody*. A number of reforms have been proposed to make WTO negotiations more efficient, though the challenge is coming up with reforms that don't cause more problems than they solve.

One oft-discussed idea, for example, is to end the tradition of requiring consensus and to switch to voting, on the theory that it's absurd to allow a single WTO member or small group of countries to hog-tie such an important institution. A pure majority-rule system would be rejected by the rich countries, of course, so some experts have proposed using weighted-voting rules, with the bigger economies having proportionately more say than smaller economies, as at the IMF and World Bank.

But the consensus principle has enormous value in instilling WTO rules with legitimacy, and it helps underpin the credibility of the dispute settlement system as well. Unlike the IMF and the World Bank, which lend money, the WTO makes rules to which all members are expected to adhere, including rules that often entail changing domestic laws and regulations. If the consensus principle were replaced by voting, a country that has been outvoted on a particular issue would have a much greater justification for thumbing its nose at a WTO tribunal decision on that issue, on the grounds that it had never consented to the rule in the first place.

Much more sensible is scrapping single undertakings and moving toward the coalition-of-the-willing approach. WTO members may well be able to strike some fruitful accords that would be endorsed by only those members that agreed to accept the obligations, with the understanding that the terms wouldn't be binding on others. This is by no means a new idea: Even before the late 1990s, when the Clinton administration negotiated its plurilateral deals on information technology and other sectors, a substantial part of the Tokyo Round consisted of these kinds of pacts. As will be recalled from Chapter 2, countries could choose à la carte style whether they wanted to accept certain Tokyo Round provisions or not. This approach has one big problem, which ended up giving the Tokyo Round a bad name: Nonparticipants can get a free ride, because they get all the benefits of the deal, thanks to the MFN rule, while shouldering none of the obligations. But as long as a "critical mass" of WTO members join in—that is, pretty much all the countries that matter regarding a particular issue—the free riders can just be ignored.

So in full recognition that rounds are indeed a terrible way to do business, I'm going to make the case that it's time to start launching another one—not a single undertaking this time—for the following reasons, starting with three from Mattoo and Subramanian's list:

> *Currencies*: China has set a noxious example by running its cheap-yuan policy for so long. (Although the yuan has appreciated about 20 percent since 2005, it's still arguably undervalued in mid-2009.) The world needs an effective multilateral approach for dealing with countries that use their currencies to subsidize their exports and penalize imports. A bilateral confrontation between Washington and Beijing over the issue would be bound to end badly, and in 2006 U.S. policymakers wisely backed away from escalating the dispute too far. But if China doesn't change its practices, or if other countries adopt similar approaches, trade wars or currency wars (that is, cycles of beggar-thy-neighbor currency devaluations)

would be all too plausible. It's high time to establish clear rules for deal-ing with this type of problem in a multilateral forum.

*Food:* It is outrageous that agricultural exporters like Argentina, which usu-ally agitate for trading partners to lower their farm-trade barriers, should withhold their production from world markets during periods of scarcity. By the time another big food crisis erupts, the world should have policies in place that would make it very costly for countries to impose starve-your-neighbor policies.

*Climate:* Jennifer Hillman and her colleagues on the Appellate Body should not be asked to make major judgments about global environmental policy by ruling on carbon tariffs in the absence of a negotiated agreement on the subject. (If this issue can be resolved on its own, before the completion of a round, so much the better.)

*Fairness in the courts:* Let's make the dispute settlement system really work for the small countries, and even for medium-sized countries challenging the superpowers. It will be recalled from Chapter 8 that Antigua and Brazil, having won judgments against the United States, couldn't get Washington to comply, and they argued persuasively that in their cases, punitive tariffs were an impractical method of retaliating against such an economically dominant adversary. WTO rules should be changed so that countries in these sorts of situations have the clear right to engage in vio-lations of intellectual property protections—not just by selling, say, copy-cat DVDs of Disney movies in their home markets, but by exporting those DVDs to the U.S. market (or the market of whichever country had been found guilty of violating WTO rules). No doubt Hollywood, along with the music, software, and pharmaceutical industries, would scream bloody murder. Sympathy for those industries should be tempered by considera-tion of what they have gained from the TRIPS rules. Given their stake in the system, they ought to make a contribution toward enhancing the cred-ibility of WTO dispute settlement.

And while we're at it, let's make dispute settlement retroactive, so that countries can be punished for violations of WTO rules that occur before a tribunal finds them guilty. The current arrangement makes it much too easy for WTO members to break the rules knowing that the worst that can happen is that they'll be required to stop at some point in the future.

*Murky protectionism:* This term refers to policies adopted by many coun-tries following the 2008 financial crisis that don't involve tariff-raising, and don't necessarily violate WTO rules, but do discriminate against for-eign goods and workers. "Buy local" requirements in government stimulus packages are one example; another is the political pressure that is being brought to bear on newly nationalized U.S. auto companies to refrain from outsourcing production abroad. Impossible though it may be to prevent such policies from going into effect now, rules that would restrict their imposition, and keep them from remaining in place for long periods of time, are essential.

Finally, if the nations of the world genuinely value the principles set forth in 1947 by Julio Lacarte and the other founding fathers of the multilateral trading system, there is one more thing they ought to do.

| * |

For all his moodiness, Bob Zoellick used to take great pleasure during his Bush administration years in the number of countries that were longing to sign free-trade agreements with the United States. How gratifying it was that so many trade ministers were making the pilgrimage to Zoellick's office and that so many heads of state were eagerly welcoming the U.S. trade representative on his trips abroad, in the hope that Washington might confer the status of free-trade partner on them. Naturally, Zoellick used the resultant leverage to the fullest, insisting that potential partners must adjust their policies to suit Washington's requirements, or he would find others that were keener to play in the competition for liberalization. His successors continued his policies, negotiating agreements with Oman, Peru, South Korea, Colombia, and Panama in addition to the ones that Zoellick had signed with Chile, Singapore, Australia, Morocco, Bahrain, and five Central American countries plus the Dominican Republic. The total haul for the Bush team was the completion of negotiations with sixteen countries.

This record has generated substantial support for the view among many American trade policymakers and specialists that the United States should pursue more bilateral accords. Thanks to the Bush-era deals, U.S. exporters now enjoy duty-free treatment, and U.S. multinationals benefit from various legal rights that exceed WTO rules, in all the sixteen countries except three (South Korea, Colombia, and Panama), whose pacts still await approval by Congress. Meanwhile, what have American firms gotten from negotiations at the WTO level during this period? Nothing, of course, and that leads inexorably to the conclusion that although it would be preferable to lower trade barriers globally, the dearth of progress in the Doha Round leaves the United States no choice but to seek market-opening opportunities elsewhere.

So goes the siren song of America's knee-jerk free traders, for whom any deal is attractive as long as barriers to U.S. goods, services, and capital are being lowered significantly in whichever country is negotiating with Washington. Mercantilist impulses all too often animate these supposed devotees of Adam Smith. They are obviously correct that agreements satisfactory to U.S. multinationals and agricultural producers are much easier to strike bilaterally than in the WTO. But the interests of the United States are poorly served in the process.

Even by mercantilist standards, the sixteen Bush pacts are small beer, given the dimensions of the $14.3 trillion U.S. economy. Consider the U.S.-Colombia deal, frequently touted by its boosters as a "no-brainer" because it would give U.S. exports the same duty-free access to Colombia's market that most Colombian goods already have in the U.S. market. Thoughtful free traders, as opposed to the knee-jerk variety, know that the case for the accord is not nearly as convincing as such propaganda would suggest. Sure, a few U.S. companies would increase sales in the Colombian market. But even if U.S. exports to Colombia doubled in a year—a totally implausible outcome—that would add less than .07 of 1 percent to the U.S. gross domestic product.

Looking at the broader picture, only about 11 percent of U.S. exports go to the sixteen countries involved in the Bush-era agreements. And that's just a sliver of the total economy; exports have accounted for only about 8 percent of U.S. gross domestic product in recent years.

U.S. interests, in both economic and security realms, are best served by supporting to the utmost a system that (1) promotes predictability and stability in commerce on a worldwide basis, (2) keeps protectionism and trade wars in check, and (3) gives developing countries the greatest possible opportunity to participate on reasonably fair terms in the global economy. Any initiatives inimical to that system—of which bilateral trade agreements are one—should be shunned.

When Zoellick applied his prodigious talent to launching the Doha Round in 2001 and to rescuing it in 2004, his self-interest in racking up achievements was consonant with the national interest. When he shifted his attention to bilaterals, I believe his self-interest conflicted with that of the nation. Bilaterals would be desirable if a convincing case could be made that, in accord with the competitive liberalization theory, they are building blocks to a multilateral agreement. But competitive liberalization, no matter how sincerely Zoellick believed in it, turned out to be an elaborate rationalization for a policy that simply didn't work. Worse yet was the host of cheap imitations that were spawned.

Estonia has a pact with Armenia. Taiwan has one with Guatemala. Those are just a couple of the head-scratchers on the list of bilateral and regional agreements currently in force. There's also the Trans-Pacific Economic Partnership, which erases trade barriers among Chile, New Zealand, Brunei, and Singapore. And let's not forget the EFTA-SACU agreement. That one links the European Free Trade Association (Iceland, Norway, Switzerland, and Liechtenstein) with the Southern African Customs Union (South Africa, Botswana, Lesotho, Swaziland, and Namibia).

Columbia professor Jagdish Bhagwati, the coiner of the term "spaghetti bowl," now has an even punchier image to illustrate his concern about bilateral deals. *Termites in the Trading System* is the name of a book he wrote in 2008—a title that conveys an apt analogy. At a time when the impasse in the Doha Round has already left the WTO enfeebled, the pervasiveness of bilateral and regional trade agreements risks a further rotting away of the WTO's standing. Viewed individually, these accords offer some benefits and do little damage; the problem is that collectively, they could end up sidelining and marginalizing the multilateral system.

Lamentations for the failed July 2008 ministerial were still reverberating when some of the WTO's most prominent members embarked on intensified campaigns to forge preferential trade agreements (and that is the proper term for them—*preferential* trade agreements," or PTAs). On August 28, 2008, India signed a PTA with ten Southeast Asian nations, and a separate deal was also finalized among those ten countries together with Australia and New Zealand. The Aussies didn't stop there; they agreed in principle to a PTA with South Korea and sought to accelerate their long-stalled negotiations with China. This was a turnabout for the new Australian prime minister, Kevin Rudd, who had previously been a stern critic of bilaterals; he once accused his predecessor of contributing to a "whittling away" of multilateralism by pursuing such accords. Meanwhile, Canada too was jumping more avidly than ever on the PTA bandwagon, as evinced by this editorial from the *Toronto Globe and Mail:*

It could be years before there is any attempt to breathe new life into the Doha Round. . . . The Canadians who participated in the Doha process, including Trade Minister Michael Fortier, say they will now turn to negotiating bilateral agreements with individual countries. That is a smart decision, and a first priority should be to get an agreement in place with the European Union. Canada has been a laggard in negotiating trade and investment deals with other countries and we need to catch up.

How much of a leap is it from such sentiments to a view that the WTO, as a forum for negotiating trade rules, is kaput? To be sure, neither Rudd nor Fortier, nor any of the other senior policymakers involved in the latest orgy of PTAs, was abandoning all hope of future multilateral agreements. But the more PTAs there are, the more likely it is that politicians will question why their nations should bother with multilateral negotiations or why they need the WTO at all. And from there, it is surely not a terribly long step to the point at which countries are disregarding the decisions of WTO panels.

The time has come to address the termite infestation, with a long moratorium, if not an outright ban, on new PTAs as a key element of a new WTO round. I'm not suggesting that existing PTAs should be repealed; even if that were legally practical it would be economically disruptive. Rather, the objective would be to keep the proliferation of PTAs from endangering the multilateral system any further. The Obama administration is ideally positioned to lead the way by declaring that it is renouncing the policies of the Bush team and will cease all bilateral and regional trade negotiations. It is far from certain that other countries would follow suit. But to reverse the dynamic that Zoellick helped propel forward, U.S. leadership would be essential and well worth trying.

Foreign policy must be taken into consideration, of course. As old State Department hands know, it's hard to resist appeals from countries to initiate talks on PTAs, because when a head of state visits Washington, often one of the only "deliverables" available for such trips is progress toward a bilateral trade deal. Furthermore, there is much to be said for securing congressional approval of the three pending bilateral agreements; Venezuelan president Hugo Chávez would be immensely pleased if the U.S.-Colombia accord were to go down in flames.

But that doesn't mean that Washington ought to pursue additional pacts for foreign policy reasons. Although some PTAs generate diplomatic benefits, others stir up anti-American tensions, because opponents of the agreements in the countries with whom Washington negotiates often raise accusations of U.S. bullying. Above all, aren't there a few foreign policy advantages to be reaped from the maintenance of a sturdy multilateral trading system?

So when foreign leaders come to Washington, their feelings shouldn't be hurt if the president politely explains that America has gone cold turkey on its PTA habit. And perhaps, after giving up PTAs, countries wishing to express mutual amity could try "friending" each other on Facebook instead.

| * |

In my book on the emerging market crises of the late 1990s, I wrote, "Unless steps are taken to make the system safer, future crises could be much more disastrous . . . boldness is warranted in shoring up the system's defenses before catastrophe strikes anew." In my book on the Argentine economic implosion of 2001–2002, I wrote, "It *could* happen here [in the United States]. Americans who give Argentina's story fair consideration and conclude otherwise are deluding themselves."

I relate this information not to brag, or to claim any special perspicacity, but in the hope of lending a dash of extra credibility to my concern about the risks that the trading system will follow the financial system into crisis. Others may have much better policy proposals than the ones presented above; the prospect of another trade round will make any sensible person quail. But the main point is that the system's problems cannot be allowed to fester. One way or another, the most favored nations must recommit themselves, in strong deeds as well as words, to multilateralism. If they don't, their misadventures may be just beginning.

# NOTES

Except where noted here, the information in this book was derived from interviews and from meeting notes that interviewees shared with the author. Some of the people interviewed were willing to be quoted by name, whereas others felt comfortable speaking candidly only if assured a cloak of anonymity—indeed, many were promised, in accord with "deep background" rules, that they would not be quoted even anonymously unless they granted permission to do so.

A list of interviewees follows. People interviewed on deep background were asked permission to be included on the list. Approximately forty people in addition to those listed below were interviewed. (That does not include the dozens of farmers, businesspeople, workers, and other individuals interviewed for the purpose of providing "real life" examples that illuminate trade issues.)

The job titles listed are in some cases current, but in general they refer to positions held by the individuals during the time period regarding which they were interviewed, so in some cases more than one job is listed, and a few people are listed under two different headings.

## WORLD TRADE ORGANIZATION
*Secretariat*

Michael Moore, Director-General

Supachai Panitchpakdi, Director-General

Pascal Lamy, Director-General (previously European Trade Commissioner)

Alejandro Jara, Deputy Director-General (previously Chilean Ambassador to WTO)

Valentine Rugwabiza, Deputy Director-General (previously Ambassador of Rwanda to WTO)

Harsha Singh, Deputy Director-General

Andrew Stoler, Deputy Director-General (previously Deputy Permanent Representative of United States to WTO)

Rufus Yerxa, Deputy Director-General (previously Deputy U.S. Trade Representative)

Arancha González, Head of Cabinet, Director-General's office (previously spokeswoman for European Trade Commissioner)

Patrick Low, Head of Cabinet, Director-General's office; Director, Economic Research and Statistics Division

Arif Hussain, Head of Cabinet, Director-General's office (GATT); Director, Accessions Division

Evan Rogerson, Head of Cabinet, Director-General's office; Director, Council and Trade Negotiations Committee Division
Keith Rockwell, Director, Information and External Relations Division
David Hartridge, Director, Trade in Services Division
Victor do Prado, Deputy Head of Cabinet, Director-General's office
Richard Eglin, Director, Trade and Finance Division
Chiedu Osakwe, Director, Doha Development Agenda Special Duties Division
Nusrat Nazeer, Deputy Director, Information and External Relations Division
John Hancock, Counsellor
Jean-Daniel Rey, Counsellor

*Appellate Body*
Julio Lacarte, Member of the Appellate Body; delegate to the 1947 U.N. Conference on Trade and Employment
Jennifer Hillman, Member of the Appellate Body

## UNITED STATES OF AMERICA
*Office of the U.S. Trade Representative*
Mickey Kantor, Trade Representative
Charlene Barshefsky, Trade Representative
Robert Zoellick, Trade Representative
Robert Portman, Trade Representative
Susan Schwab, Trade Representative
Richard Fisher, Deputy Trade Representative
Rufus Yerxa, Deputy Trade Representative (later Deputy Director-General of WTO)
Allen Johnson, Chief Agriculture Negotiator
Peter Allgeier, Deputy Trade Representative and Ambassador to WTO
John Veroneau, General Counsel; Deputy Trade Representative
Peter Scher, Special Trade Negotiator
Ira Shapiro, General Counsel
Joseph Glauber, Special Doha Agricultural Envoy; also Chief Economist, Department of Agriculture
Dorothy Dwoskin, Assistant U.S. Trade Representative for WTO and Multilateral Affairs
Matt Rohde, Assistant U.S. Trade Representative for WTO and Multilateral Affairs
Jason Hafemeister, Director of WTO Agriculture Negotiations
Matt Niemeyer, Assistant Trade Representative for Congressional Affairs
Jeffrey Bader, Assistant Trade Representative
Joseph Papovich, Assistant Trade Representative
M.B. Oglesby, Chief of Staff
Tim Keeler, Chief of Staff
Nao Matsukata, Director of Policy Planning
Sean Spicer, Assistant Trade Representative, Public and Media Affairs
Edward Gresser, Principal Policy Advisor
Andrew Stoler, Deputy Permanent Representative to WTO (later Deputy Director-General of WTO)
David Shark, Deputy Permanent Representative to WTO

*Other U.S. agencies*
William Daley, Secretary of Commerce
Stuart Eizenstat, Deputy Treasury Secretary; Undersecretary of State for Economic Affairs
Alan Larson, Undersecretary of State for Economic Affairs
Grant Aldonas, Undersecretary of Commerce for International Trade

J.B. Penn, Undersecretary of Agriculture
Allan Hubbard, Director of White House National Economic Council
Faryar Shirzad, Deputy Assistant to the President for International Economic Affairs
Karen Tramontano, Assistant to the President
Stephen Jacobs, Deputy Assistant Secretary of Commerce for Market Access and Compliance
Viji Rangaswami, House Ways and Means Committee Staff

*Officials responsible for security at Doha*
Maureen Quinn, Ambassador to Qatar
Doug Melvin, Director of Security, U.S. Trade Representative's office
Ed Winslow, Special Agent, Naval Criminal Investigative Service
Mark Russ, Special Agent, Naval Criminal Investigative Service

*City of Seattle**
Paul Schell, Mayor

## EUROPEAN UNION
*European Commission*
Pascal Lamy, Trade Commissioner (later Director-General, WTO)
Peter Mandelson, Trade Commissioner
Peter Carl, Director-General for Trade
Matthew Baldwin, Deputy Head of Cabinet for Trade Commissioner, Head of Unit for WTO
    Issues, Directorate-General for Trade
Roderick Abbott, Deputy Director-General for Trade
David Roberts, Deputy Director-General for Agriculture
João Pacheco, Head of WTO Unit, Directorate-General for Agriculture
Arancha González, Spokeswoman for the European Trade Commissioner (later Head of
    Cabinet, Director-General's office, WTO)
Anthony Gooch, Spokesman for the European Trade Commissioner

## FRANCE
Christine Lagarde, Trade Minister
Laurence Dubois-Destrizais, Deputy Assistant Secretary for Trade Policy and Investment,
    Ministry of Economy; Permanent Representative to WTO

## BRAZIL
Luiz Lampreia, Minister of External Relations
Celso Lafer, Minister of External Relations
Celso Amorim, Minister of External Relations
Roberto Azevedo, Undersecretary for Economic and Technological Affairs, Ministry of Ex-
    ternal Relations
José Graça Lima, Undersecretary-General for Integration, Economic and Trade Affairs, Min-
    istry of External Relations
Antonio Patriota, Deputy Permanent Representative to WTO; Chief of Staff to Minister of
    External Relations
Pedro de Camargo Neto, Secretary of Production and Trade, Ministry of Agriculture

---

*Concerning Seattle, Mayor Schell is the only individual from local government and local organizations
listed because he was the only such person interviewed by me. As described in the notes for Chapter 4,
I was able to obtain extensive transcripts of interviews with other local officials, law enforcement officers,
and demonstration leaders; those interviews were conducted in the months after the Seattle meeting
and I deemed them more illuminating than any interviewing I could conduct now.

### INDIA

Kamal Nath, Minister of Commerce and Industry
G.K. Pillai, Commerce Secretary
S.N. Menon, Commerce Secretary
Pronab Sen, Principal Adviser, Government Planning Commission
Srinivasan Narayanan, Ambassador to WTO
Ujal Singh Bhatia, Ambassador to WTO
Rajesh Aggarwal, Counselor, Indian Mission to the WTO

### CHINA

Sun Zhenyu, Ambassador to WTO

### JAPAN

Masakazu Toyoda, Vice Minister for International Affairs, Ministry of Economy, Trade and Industry
Shotaro Oshima, Ambassador to WTO, Chairman of General Council
Yoichi Suzuki, Deputy Permanent Representative to WTO

### AUSTRALIA

Tim Fischer, Trade Minister
Geoff Raby, Ambassador to WTO
David Spencer, Ambassador to WTO
Bruce Gosper, Ambassador to WTO, Chairman of General Council

### CANADA

Pierre Pettigrew, Minister for International Trade
Jim Peterson, Minister for International Trade
Sergio Marchi, Ambassador to WTO, Chairman of General Council
Don Stephenson, Ambassador to WTO, Chairman of NAMA negotiations

### ARGENTINA

Martín Redrado, Trade Secretary

### BENIN

Samuel Amehou, Ambassador to WTO

### CHILE

Alejandro Jara, Ambassador to WTO (later Deputy Director-General of WTO)

### COSTA RICA

Anabel González, Vice Trade Minister

### EGYPT

Youssef Boutros-Ghali, Minister of Foreign Trade

### HONG KONG, CHINA

Stuart Harbinson, Permanent Representative to WTO, Chairman of the General Council

### MEXICO

Fernando de Mateo, Ambassador to WTO

## NEW ZEALAND
Tim Groser, Ambassador to WTO, Chairman of Agriculture Negotiations
Crawford Falconer, Ambassador to WTO, Chairman of Agriculture Negotiations

## RWANDA
Valentine Rugwabiza, Ambassador to WTO (later Deputy Director-General of WTO)

## SINGAPORE
George Yeo, Minister for Trade and Industry

## SOUTH AFRICA
Alec Erwin, Ministry of Trade and Industry
Rob Davies, Deputy Minister for Trade and Industry
Xavier Carim, Deputy Director-General, Department of Trade and Industry; Ambassador
   to WTO

## TANZANIA
Ali Mchumo, Ambassador to WTO, Chairman of General Council

## ZAMBIA
Dipak Patel, Minister of Commerce, Trade and Industry

## NON-GOVERNMENTAL ORGANIZATIONS
Celine Charveriat, Oxfam
Nicholas Imboden, IDEAS Centre
Jamie Love, Consumer Project on Technology
Lori Wallach, Public Citizen's Global Trade Watch

## PRIVATE SECTOR
Thomas Bombelles, Merck
Geoffrey Gamble, DuPont
Shannon Herzfeld, Pharmaceutical Research and Manufacturers of America
Don Phillips, American Sugar Alliance
Frank Vargo, National Association of Manufacturers
Aracelia Vila, Schering-Plough

*Academics, economists, legal experts*
Antoine Bouet, International Food Policy Research Institute (U.S.)
Chad Bown, Brandeis University and the Brookings Institution (U.S.)
Jane Bradley, Georgetown University Law Center (U.S.)
Jean-Christophe Bureau, National Institute of Agronomy (France)
Rajesh Chadha, National Council of Applied Economic Research (India)
Ashok Gulati, International Food Policy Research Institute (India)
John Jackson, Georgetown University Law Center (U.S.)
Marcos Jank, Institute for International Trade Negotiations (Brazil)
Simon Lester, WorldTradeLaw.net (U.S.)
Will Martin, World Bank
Pratap Mehta, Center for Policy Research (India)
Patrick Messerlin, Sciences Po (France)
Andre Nassar, Institute for International Trade Negotiations (Brazil)
Amelia Porges, Sidley Austin (U.S.)

Amil Sharma, National Council of Applied Economic Research (India)
Jeffrey Schott, Peterson Institute for International Economics (U.S.)
John Weekes, Sidley Austin (Canada, based in Geneva)

## CHAPTER 1: PAGING MR. BLACK

2 Information concerning the Qatari government's depiction of the man who attacked the airbase, the number of people who traveled to Doha, and the medical teams and equipment sent by Japan and Taiwan comes from Helene Cooper, "Air Base Assault Fuels Fears About WTO," *Wall Street Journal*, November 8, 2001; "Navy Ships Move Toward WTO Meeting Site," Reuters News Service, November 9, 2001; and Paul Blustein, "WTO Leader Cautions Against 'Protectionism,'" *Washington Post*, November 10, 2001.

3 The *Financial Times* article reporting the importance of a trade round for "symbolic and psychological reasons" is Guy de Jonquieres, "A Round to Steady the Nerves," October 22, 2001.

3 Fed chairman Greenspan's testimony concerning the potential economic impact of a round came at his appearance on September 20, 2001, before the Senate Committee on Banking, Housing, and Urban Affairs and is cited on the WTO website at http://www.wto.org/trade_resources/quotes/new_round/new_round.htm.

3 Moore's speech is on the WTO's website at http://www.wto.org/english/news_e/spmm_e/spmm72_e.htm.

3 The Oxfam briefing paper is titled "Eight Broken Promises: Why the WTO Isn't Working for the World's Poor," published in October 2001, and is on the web at http://www.oxfam.org.uk/resources/policy/trade/downloads/bp09_8broken.rtf.

4 Pettigrew's op-ed, titled "How Trade Will Save the World," appeared in the *Globe and Mail*, October 11, 2001.

4 The *Chicago Tribune* editorial, titled "Trade—A Weapon Against Terror," was published November 9, 2001.

6 The Doha Declaration is on the WTO's website at http://www.wto.org/english/thewto_e/minist_e/min01_e/mindecl_e.htm.

6 The *Los Angeles Times* editorial, "Trade's Peacemaking Role," was published on November 15, 2001.

6 Bush's statement can be found in the *Weekly Compilation of Presidential Documents*, for the week of November 19, 2001.

9 Information regarding the protectionist and quasi-protectionist acts taken by G-20 countries after the November 15, 2008, summit comes from a report by Elisa Gamberoni and Richard Newfarmer, "Trade Protection: Incipient but Worrisome Trends," *World Bank, Trade Notes*, no. 37, March 2, 2009; a report by the WTO Secretariat, "Report to the TPRB from the Director-General on the Financial and Economic Crisis and Trade-Related Developments," March 26, 2009; and "The Nuts and Bolts Come Apart," *Economist*, March 26, 2009. Regarding Indonesia's changes in customs policy, information comes from John McBeth, "Self-Reliance the Current Refrain," *Straits Times*, December 20, 2008; and "Indonesia's Kadin Calls for Expansion of Import Restrictions," *Asia Pulse*, December 22, 2008.

11 The figure on the number of bilateral and regional trade agreements currently in operation comes from speaking points for remarks by Pascal Lamy, "Proliferation of Regional Trade Agreements 'Breeding Concern,'" September 10, 2007, on the WTO website at http://www.wto.org/english/news_e/sppl_e/sppl67_e.htm.

14 Zakaria's elucidation of the "rise of the rest" is made in his book *The Post-American World* (New York: W. W. Norton, 2008).

## CHAPTER 2: THE INTERGALACTIC TRADE ORGANIZATION

18  Information regarding the numbers of staff at the IMF, World Bank, and WTO is available on their respective websites, http://www.imf.org, http://www.world-bank.org, and http://www.wto.org.

18  Moore's quotation is from his book, *A World Without Walls: Freedom, Development, Free Trade and Global Governance* (New York: Cambridge University Press, 2003), p. 110.

21  The passage from Adam Smith, "the taylor does not attempt . . . ," comes from *An Inquiry into the Natural Causes of the Wealth of Nations*, vol. 1 (London: Methuen, 1922), p. 422. The passage "In the mercantile system . . ." comes from vol. 2, p. 159.

23  Information about Julio Lacarte's life comes from James Bacchus, *Trade and Freedom* (London: Cameron May, 2004), pp. 89–98.

23–24  Information about the Smoot-Hawley tariff and its impact comes from Douglas A. Irwin, "Multilateral and Bilateral Trade Policies in the World Trading System: A Historical Perspective," in *New Dimensions in Regional Integration*, ed. Jaime de Melo and Arvind Panagariya (New York: Cambridge University Press, 1993); Jeffry Frieden, *Global Capitalism: Its Fall and Rise in the Twentieth Century* (New York: W. W. Norton, 2006); William J. Bernstein, *A Splendid Exchange: How Trade Shaped the World* (New York: Atlantic Monthly Press, 2008); and Edward Gresser, *Freedom from Want: American Liberalism and the Global Economy* (Brooklyn, NY: Soft Skull Press, 2007).

25–30  Information about the creation of the GATT and the early rounds of the GATT system comes from Amrita Narlikar, *The World Trade Organization: A Very Short Introduction* (New York: Oxford University Press, 2005); I. M. Destler, *American Trade Politics* (Washington, DC: Institute for International Economics, 2005); Douglas A. Irwin, "Trade Liberalization: Cordell Hull and the Case for Optimism," Council on Foreign Relations working paper, July 31, 2008; Amelia Porges and Daniel M. Price, "The United States and the GATT/WTO System," chap. 80 in *The World Trade Organization: Legal, Economic and Political Analysis*, ed. P. Macrory, A. Appleton, and M. Plummer (New York: Springer, 2005); Joseph E. Stiglitz and Andrew Charlton, *Free Trade for All: How Trade Can Promote Development* (New York: Oxford University Press, 2006); Kent Jones, *Who's Afraid of the WTO?* (New York: Oxford University Press, 2004); and "The GATT Years: From Havana to Marrakesh," on the WTO website at http://www.wto.org/english/thewto_e/whatis_e/tif_e/fact4_e.htm.

29  The phrase "Don't obey, don't object," as an apt characterization of developing countries' behavior in the GATT, was originally coined by economist Richard Baldwin.

29  Lamy's speech is on the European Commission website at http://trade.ec .europa.eu/doclib/docs/2005/january/tradoc_121064.pdf.

29–30  Information about the troubles of the GATT system, especially its dispute settlement system, comes from Narlikar, *The World Trade Organization*; and Claude Barfield, *Free Trade, Sovereignty, Democracy: The Future of the World Trade Organization* (Washington, DC: American Enterprise Institute Press, 2001).

30  Thurow's statement "GATT is dead" was widely quoted, among other places in Edward Greenspon, "GATT Is Dead, Top Economist Tells Business, Political Leaders," *Globe and Mail*, January 28, 1989.

30–31  Tyson's book was *Who's Bashing Whom: Trade Conflict in High-Technology Industries* (Washington, DC: Institute for International Economics, 1992). The quotation describing the GATT as "largely irrelevant" is on p. 5, and the quotation calling for a policy that would "sometimes involve forceful unilateralism" is on p. 13.

31  John Jackson's book proposing the creation of the WTO is titled *Restructuring the GATT System* (New York: Royal Institute of International Affairs, Council on Foreign Relations Press, 1990). The quotation "at the risk . . . of appearing unrealistic . . ." is on p. 5. His article "The Crumbling Institutions of the Liberal Trade System"

was published in the *Journal of World Trade Law* 12, no. 13 (March–April 1978). The quotation from his book describing the GATT as a "weak framework" is on p. 4, and the quotation calling for the creation of an "institution which could be variously named . . ." is on p. 94.

31–36 Information on the Uruguay Round and on the eventual success of Jackson's WTO proposal comes from Ernest H. Preeg, *Traders in a Brave New World: The Uruguay Round and the Future of the International Trading System* (Chicago: University of Chicago Press, 1995); John Croome, *Reshaping the World Trading System: A History of the Uruguay Round* (Geneva: World Trade Organization, 1995); Will Martin and L. Alan Winters, eds., *The Uruguay Round and the Developing Countries* (New York: Cambridge University Press, 1996); Narlikar, *The World Trade Organization*; Barfield, *Free Trade, Sovereignty, Democracy*; Stiglitz and Charlton, *Free Trade for All*; Jeffrey J. Schott, *The Uruguay Round: An Assessment* (Washington, DC: Institute for International Economics, 1994); and Porges and Price, "The United States and the GATT/WTO System."

32–33 Information about the paradigm shift toward free markets in developing countries, including Brazil's, comes from Frieden, *Global Capitalism*, chap. 18. The figures for Argentina's tariff reductions (which did not include autos, clothing, or footwear) can be found in an IMF report, "Argentina: Recent Economic Developments," April 1998, on the IMF website, http://www.imf.org/external/pubs/ft/scr/1998/cr9838.pdf.

34–36 Details about the final stages of the Uruguay Round come from Larry Elliott and Edward Luce, "Trade Talks Cliff-Hanger Made for Hollywood," *Manchester Guardian Weekly*, December 19, 1993; "How the Talkers Finally Got to the Heart of the Matter," *Observer*, December 19, 1993; and Sarah Lambert, "Week of Fast Footwork, Beer and Skittles," *Independent*, December 15, 1993. The *New York Times* story reporting the establishment of the "MTO" was Keith Bradsher, "U.S. and Europe Clear the Way for a World Accord on Trade, Setting Aside Major Disputes," December 15, 1993.

36 The ceremony in which the new sign was installed at the Centre William Rappard can be seen on video on the WTO website at rtsp://rnd01sea.streamlogics.com/wto/gatttowto.rm.

36 Details about the festivities at the Summit of the Americas can be found in Judy Keen, "Mutuality, Milieu Add Magic in Miami," *USA Today*, December 12, 1994; and Jorge A. Banales, "Summit-Goers Find Trade in Parties," UPI, December 11, 1994.

36–37 Information about the Asia Pacific economic summit of 1994, and its implications, can be found in Paul Blustein, "Pact a Milestone in March of Capitalism," *Washington Post*, November 16, 1994.

38 Information on the Information Technology, Telecommunications, and Financial Services agreements can be found in Porges and Price, "The United States and the GATT/WTO System"; Anne Swardson and Paul Blustein, "Trade Group Reaches Phone Pact," *Washington Post*, February 16, 1997; and on the WTO website at http://www.wto.org/english/tratop_e/inftec_e/inftec_e.htm.

38–39 Information on China's WTO accession negotiations comes from Nicholas R. Lardy, *Integrating China into the Global Economy* (Washington, DC: Brookings Institution Press, 2002); Paul Blustein, "U.S. Tries to Placate China on WTO Talks," *Washington Post*, April 13, 1999; Blustein, "Clinton Scrambles to Appease Diverse Critics on China," *Washington Post*, April 15, 1999; David E. Sanger, "How U.S. and China Failed to Close Trade Deal," *New York Times*, April 10, 1999; Sanger, "At the Last Hour, Down to the Last Trick, and It Worked," *New York Times*, November 17, 1999; John F. Harris and Michael Laris, "'Roller-Coaster Ride' to an Off-Again, On-Again Trade Pact," *Washington Post*, November 16, 1999; and Helene Cooper, Bob Davis, and Ian Johnson, "To Brink and Back," *Wall Street Journal*, November 16, 1999.

## CHAPTER 3: THE WTO AND ITS DISCONTENTS

41 Don Lorentz's visit to Geneva in May 1998 was reported in Susan Gilmore and Alex Fryer, "WTO: Whose Idea Was This?" *Seattle Times*, November 26, 1999; and Kery Murakami, "Geneva Sounded WTO Warning That Went Unheeded in Seattle," *Seattle Post-Intelligencer*, March 10, 2000.

41 Details of the riots in Geneva can be found in "High Security for WTO Conference," Agence France-Presse, May 17, 1998; and Philip Waller, "Demonstrations Continue as World Leaders Help Mark Trade Birthday," AP News Service, May 19, 1998.

42 Martin Wolf's column, "Why Liberalization Won," was published in the *Financial Times*, May 18, 1998.

42–44 Information on the controversy over the environment in trade policy, including the "beef hormones" and "shrimp-turtle" cases, can be found in "Why Greens Should Love Trade," *Economist*, October 9, 1999; Destler, *American Trade Politics*; Barfield, *Free Trade, Sovereignty, Democracy*; Lori Wallach and Michelle Sforza, *Whose Trade Organization? Corporate Globalization and the Erosion of Democracy* (Washington, DC: Public Citizen Foundation, 1999); Francis Williams and Guy de Jonquieres, "WTO's Beef Rulings Give Europe Food for Thought," *Financial Times*, February 13, 1998; and Guy de Jonquieres, "One Man's Meat," *Financial Times*, April 15, 1998.

44–45 The *Chicago Tribune* article, by Merrill Goozner, was "Asian Labor: Wages of Shame," published November 6, 1994.

45–46 Alan Reuther was quoted in Paul Blustein, "Free Trade vs. Social Policy," *Washington Post*, September 19, 1997.

46 A detailed account of Clinton's efforts starting in 1997 to secure new authorization to negotiate trade agreements, and Congress's rejection of the legislation, can be found in Destler, *American Trade Politics*, chap. 10.

46 A transcript of Clinton's speech is available from *Federal Document Clearing House Political Transcripts*, May 18, 1998, available from LexisNexis®.

46 In summarizing the historical evidence against the race-to-the-bottom theory, I am indebted to the excellent discussion in Pietra Rivoli, *The Travels of a T-Shirt in the Global Economy: An Economist Examines the Markets, Power, and Politics of World Trade* (Hoboken, NJ: Wiley, 2005).

47 Kumar's comment can be found in Ranabir Ray Choudhury, "Neo-protectionist Policy Jeopardizing Labour Edge," *Business Line*, December 10, 1997.

47–48 The Uruguay Round documents, including the tariff schedules, can be found on the WTO website at http://www.wto.org/english/docs_e/legal_e/legal_e.htm.

48 The World Bank report concerning the costs incurred by developing countries is J. Michael Finger and Philip Schuler, "Implementation of Uruguay Round Commitments: The Development Challenge," World Bank Research working paper WPS2215, October 1999. It is part of a volume on the web at http://publications .worldbank.org/catalog/content-download?revision_id=1526187.

48 An account of the statement by Colombian ambassador Nestor Osorio can be found in Chakravarthi Raghavan, "Trade: Beginning the Long Haul to a New Round?" *SUNS (South-North Development Monitor*, published by the Third World Network), November 2, 1998.

49 The UNCTAD report is the "Trade and Development Report 1999," published on January 9, 1999, on the web at www.unctad.org/en/docs/tdr1999_en.pdf.

49–56 The distortions in global agricultural trade are comprehensively discussed in Kimberly Ann Elliott, *Delivering on Doha: Farm Trade and the Poor* (Washington, DC: Institute for International Economics, 2006); and Richard Newfarmer, ed., *Trade, Doha and Development: A Window into the Issues* (Washington, DC: World Bank, 2006).

50 Various estimates of the impact that cotton subsidies have had on world cotton prices are discussed in John Baffes, "Cotton and the Developing Countries: Implications for Development," in Newfarmer, *Trade, Doha and Development*; and Nicholas Minot and Lisa Daniels, "Impact of Global Cotton Markets on Rural Poverty in Benin," Markets and Structural Studies Division discussion paper 48, International Food Policy Research Institute, Washington, DC, November 2002.

52–53 Information on the Common Agricultural Policy, the political influence of European farmers, the role played by President Chirac, and the wealth of European subsidy recipients can be found in Elliott, *Delivering on Doha*; Jack Thurston, "Why Europe Deserves a Better Farm Policy," policy brief, Centre for European Reform, December 2, 2005; Martin Arnold, "French Farmers Dig In Against Subsidy Reform," *Financial Times*, December 8, 2005; Economic Intelligence Unit, "Backing a Wasteful Common Agricultural Policy," June 20, 2003, available on www.eiu.com; Roger Thurow and Geoff Winestock, "How an Addiction to Sugar Subsidies Hurts Development," *Wall Street Journal*, September 16, 2002; and Alan Beattie, "Sweetheart Deals," *Financial Times*, July 26, 2008. The leading campaigner for transparency in E.U. subsidy payments is farmsubsidy.org, whose data on subsidy recipients can be found on its website and whose findings have been reported in the following news stories: Heather Stewart, "Farming Giants Reap Most of EU's Benefits," *Observer*, March 11, 2007; Colin Coyle, "Revealed: The Irish Tycoons Milking EU Farm Payments," *Sunday Times* (London), May 3, 2009; and Stephen Castle and Doreen Carvajal, "Small Elite Reaps Millions in E.U. Farm Subsidies," *New York Times*, May 8, 2009. For an account of the sums collected by members of the British royal family, see David Hencke and Rob Evans, "Royal Farms Get £1m from Taxpayers," *Guardian*, March 23, 2005, and further information on the web at http://www.freedominfo.org/features/20050407.htm.

54 The series of articles about U.S. farm subsidies in the *Washington Post* was authored by Dan Morgan, Gilbert M. Gaul, and Sarah Cohen. Their article citing the case of John Phipps was "Federal Subsidies Turn Farms into Big Business," published on December 21, 2006.

54–56 Additional information about U.S. subsidies and the power of the American farm lobby can be found in Robert L. Thompson, "The U.S. Farm Bill and the Doha Negotiations: On Parallel Tracks or a Collision Course?" issues brief, International Food and Agricultural Trade Policy Council, September 2005; Elliott, *Delivering on Doha*; and Alan Beattie, "Pile-It-High Policies Likely to Win the Day," *Financial Times*, October 9, 2007.

55 The contrasting figures for average tariffs on manufactured goods versus those on agricultural goods comes from Kym Anderson, Harry de Gorter, and Will Martin, "Market Access Barriers in Agriculture and Options for Reform," in Newfarmer, *Trade, Doha and Development*.

55–56 The study by Dale E. Hathaway and Merlinda D. Ingco, titled "Agricultural Liberalization and the Uruguay Round," can be found in Martin and Winters, *The Uruguay Round and the Developing Countries*.

## CHAPTER 4: CLUELESS IN SEATTLE

Much of the information in this chapter concerning the Seattle demonstrations, the preparations by the activist groups, and the response by the city and the Seattle Police Department comes from several reports that were prepared in the aftermath of the meeting by the Seattle City Council, the city's police department, and the local branch of the American Civil Liberties Union. Also invaluable is the WTO History Project, a joint effort of several programs at the University of Washington; the project includes many interviews with leading activists, including

Michael Dolan, David Solnit, and others. Its material is on the web at http://depts.washington.edu/wtohist/index.htm.

The reports include the "Report of the WTO Accountability Review Committee, Seattle City Council," http://www.seattle.gov/wtocommittee/currentdocs.htm; Seattle Police Department, "The Seattle Police Department After Action Report, World Trade Organization Ministerial Conference/Seattle, Washington/November 29–December 3, 1999," April 4, 2000, www.seattle.gov/Police/Publications/WTO/WTO_AAR.pdf; American Civil Liberties Union of Washington, "Out of Control: Seattle's Flawed Response to Protests Against the World Trade Organization," June 2000, http://aclu-wa.org/library_files/WTO%20Report%20Web.pdf; R. M. McCarthy and Associates in conjunction with Robert J. Louden, "An Independent Review of the 1999 World Trade Organization Conference Disruptions in Seattle, Washington," April 2000, http://www.seattle.gov/wtocommittee/WTOpreliminaryReport.pdf; and Patrick F. Gillham and Gary T. Marx, "Complexity and Irony in Policing and Protesting: The World Trade Organization in Seattle," *Social Justice* 27, no. 2 (2000): 212.

57 The account of the Globalize This! Action Camp is drawn from Helene Cooper, "These Recruits Train for a Trade Mission of a Different Sort," *Wall Street Journal*, September 20, 1999; and David Postman, "Protesting Is Their Trade; World Trade Is Their Target," *Seattle Times*, September 20, 1999.

58 Information about Wallach can be found in Bob Davis, "Free-Trade Foe, Stymied on IMF, Shifts to Other Fights," *Wall Street Journal*, April 6, 1998; and Moisés Naím, "Lori's War," *Foreign Policy*, Spring 2000.

58–59 The full title of the book published by Wallach in 1999, which was coauthored with Michelle Sforza, is *Whose Trade Organization? Corporate Globalization and the Erosion of Democracy*. A later edition, titled *Whose Trade Organization? A Comprehensive Guide to the World Trade Organization*, was coauthored with Patrick Woodall and was published by New Press in 2004. In the first edition, the quotation "favors huge multinational companies . . ." is on p. 3; the quotation "global commerce takes precedence over everything . . ." is on p. 7; the quotations "effectively eviscerate[s] the Precautionary Principle . . ." and "Governments rely on this principle" are on p. 54; and the quotation "the effect is to constrain the power . . ." is on p. 58.

59 The article about Michael Dolan is Steven Pearlstein, "Protest's Architect 'Gratified'; D.C.-Based Activist Brought Diverse Groups Together," *Washington Post*, December 2, 1999.

59–60 Information about Dolan's interactions with the unions and the Direct Action Network comes from interviews conducted by the WTO History Project at the University of Washington.

60 The Direct Action Network Internet message of September 6, 1999, "Tens of thousands of people will converge on Seattle . . ." can be found in the report by the ACLU of Washington, "Out of Control," p. 27.

60–64 Information about the Moore/Supachai race comes from Frances Williams, "Race Hots Up to Lead World Trade Body," *Financial Times*, January 21, 1999; Daniel Pruzin, "Race Tightens for Top WTO Spot as Poll Shows Diminished Support for Panitchpakdi," *International Trade Reporter* (Bureau of National Affairs), March 3, 1999; Pruzin, "WTO Again Fails to Pick New Chief," *International Trade Reporter*, April 21, 1999; Williams, "Stalemate in Vote for WTO Leader," *Financial Times*, May 1, 1999; Williams, "Warning of WTO Paralysis over Leadership Battle," *Financial Times*, May 3, 1999; Bhushan Bahree, "WTO Deadlock on New Chief Proves Costly," *Wall Street Journal*, May 4, 1999; Frances Williams and Guy de Jonquieres, "Trading Blows," *Financial Times*, May 7, 1999; and Paul Blustein, "WTO Meets Today to Discuss Plan to End Leadership Struggle," *Washington Post*, July 15, 1999.

61–62  Information about Michael Moore comes from his book *A World Without Walls*; "The Human Face of Globalization," *Economist*, August 28, 1999; and Guy de Jonquieres, "Trading Places," *Financial Times*, September 3, 1999.

62  Moore's quotation "that is not the Kiwi way" is cited in Ted Bardacke and Frances Williams, "WTO Snub Angers Thais," *Financial Times*, May 6, 1999.

62  The New Zealand article worrying that Moore would be "a cause for national embarrassment" is Warren Berryman, "Why Was $920K Spent Finding Mike Moore a Job?" *Independent* (New Zealand), April 21, 1999.

63  The quotation from Mchumo at the General Council meeting is cited in Daniel Pruzin, "Stalemate over New Leader Continues with Council Meeting's Postponement," *International Trade Reporter*, May 5, 1999.

63–64  Surin's account of his conversation with Albright is Surin Pitsuwan, "Dr. Supachai's Long and Winding Road to Geneva," *Bangkok Post*, August 25, 2002.

65  The State Department memo urging the proposal of a "Clinton Round" can be found in the papers of Stuart Eizenstat, who was undersecretary of state for economic, business, and agricultural affairs at the time the memo was written. I am grateful to Mr. Eizenstat for facilitating my access to his papers, which are on file at the Library of Congress.

65  Information about the various proposed names for the round can be found in Bob Davis and Helene Cooper, "Round and Round They Go, to Name New Trade Talks," *Wall Street Journal*, November 29, 1999.

65–66  An explanation of the rationale for the Singapore issues can be found in two articles published in the *Economist*, "All Free Traders Now?" December 7, 1996, and "Tequila Sunset in Cancún," September 17, 2003. An explanation of the argument against them can be found in Martin Khor, "Present Problems and Future Shape of the WTO and the Multilateral Trading System," Third World Network briefing paper 2, September 2001.

66–67  Information about Barshefsky can be found in Bob Davis and Jacob Schlesinger, "War of Words," *Wall Street Journal*, February 9, 1994; Elsa Walsh, "The Negotiator," *New Yorker*, March 18, 1996; David E. Sanger, "Tough Talker for a Delicate Job," *New York Times*, May 16, 1996; Ronald Brownstein, "Master Deal Maker Faces Test at Home," *Los Angeles Times*, July 26, 1997; and Mark Suzman, "The First Lady of Trade," *Financial Times*, November 27, 1999.

67–68  Information about the views of developing countries opposed to a round in 1999 can be found in Frances Williams, "WTO Members Square Up for New Round of Discord," *Financial Times*, July 30, 1999; and Elizabeth Olson, "Anger on Agenda for World Trade Meeting," *New York Times*, October 14, 1999.

67  Ambassador Mounir Zahran's statement was reported in Chakravarthi Raghavan, "Trade: Beginning the Long Haul to a New Round?" *SUNS*, November 2, 1998.

68  The draft text with the myriad square brackets can be found on the website of the International Centre for Trade and Sustainable Development, http://ictsd.net/downloads/2008/04/declaration3.pdf.

69  Barshefsky's comment that "failure is not an option" can be found in John F. Harris, "White House Optimistic on WTO Summit," *Washington Post*, November 25, 1999.

69–70  Paxton's quotations and recollections come from an interview conducted by the Seattle City Council's Accountability Review Committee.

70  Joiner's words at the city council meeting were cited in "Report of the WTO Accountability Review Committee, Seattle City Council."

70  The November 17, 1999, FBI report, titled "Threat Update: World Trade Organization Ministerial Meeting, Seattle, Washington, November 30–December 3, 1999," was prepared by the bureau's Counterterrorism Threat Assessment and Warning

Unit. It is one of the documents available as part of the Accountability Review Committee's report.

71 The "Schell mail" is quoted in Norm Stamper, *Breaking Rank: A Top Cop's Exposé of the Dark Side of American Policing* (New York: Nation Books, 2006), p. 331.

71 Vivian Phillips's quotation comes from Stephen H. Dunphy, "We're Ready for Anything, Officials Say," *Seattle Times*, November 10, 1999.

71 Stamper's quotation "we didn't have *nearly* enough cops" comes from his book *Breaking Rank*, p. 341.

71–74 The police department's acknowledgment appears in "The Seattle Police Department After Action Report, World Trade Organization Ministerial Conference / Seattle, Washington / November 29–December 3, 1999." In addition to the reports by the city council, the police department, the ACLU, and others cited above, information about the events of November 30 comes from Rick Anderson, "Violence Works," *Seattle Weekly*, December 1, 1999; Knute Berger, "Not-So-Nice Seattle," *Seattle Weekly*, December 1, 1999; Mike Carter, David Postman, Steve Miletich, Susan Gilmore, and James V. Grimaldi, "Unrest Even at the Top During Riots," *Seattle Times*, December 16, 1999; Timothy Egan, "Black Masks Lead to Pointed Fingers in Seattle," *New York Times*, December 2, 1999; and John Burgess and Steven Pearlstein, "Protests Delay WTO Opening," *Washington Post*, December 1, 1999.

72 The graffito "Fuck WTO Bitches" was reported in Rick Anderson, "Violence Works," *Seattle Weekly*, December 1, 1999.

73 The *Seattle Times* report that "with each gassing, protesters get more defiant" is in an article by Alex Tizon titled "Countdown to Chaos in Seattle," December 5, 1999.

73 Steve Williamson's quotation comes from an interview conducted for the WTO History Project.

74 The description of Reichert as "apoplectic . . ." comes from Stamper's book, *Breaking Rank*, p. 344.

74 The quotation by the Dominican Republic's ambassador comes from Evelyn Iritani, "Poor Nations Defy, Derail WTO 'Club,'" *Los Angeles Times*, December 5, 1999.

75 Barshefsky's apology to the delegates and her explanation of how the meeting was to proceed can be found on the WTO's website at http://www.wto.org/english/thewto_e/minist_e/min99_e/english/about_e/resum01_e.htm.

75–76 The December 1, 1999, *Seattle Post-Intelligencer* article quoting Clinton's remarks about labor standards was written by Michael Paulson and titled "Clinton Says He Will Support Trade Sanctions for Worker Abuse."

76 Lamy's account of Barshefsky's reaction to the *Post-Intelligencer* article is reported in his book *L'Europe en première ligne* (Paris: Seuil, 2002), pp. 57–58.

76–77 Clinton's luncheon remarks are reported in David E. Sanger, "President Chides World Trade Body in Stormy Seattle," *New York Times*, December 2, 1999, as are Mayor Schell's defense of his law enforcement strategy.

77 In addition to the various reports cited above, events in the Seattle streets on December 1, 1999, are reported in Mark Suzman, "Seattle Police Clamp Down on Protesters with Mass Arrests," *Financial Times*, December 2, 1999; and Rene Sanchez, "Extensive Security Planning Fails Text," *Washington Post*, December 2, 1999.

77 The *Seattle Times* article reporting the anger of merchants, "Shoppers Barred in Retail Core; Downtown Loss Is $4 million," was written by Robert T. Nelson, Gordon Black, and Lisa Pemberton-Butler and published on December 3, 1999.

77–78 An account of the progress, and lack thereof, of the various negotiating groups can be found in the December 3, 1999, edition of the *Bridges Daily Update*. The *Daily Update* is an invaluable compendium of events published during WTO ministerials by the International Centre for Trade and Sustainable Development, a Geneva-based NGO website is http://ictsd.net/.

78 Barshefsky's comment about reserving "the right to use a more exclusive process" is reported in "Charlene Barshefsky Announces Procedure for Drafting Declaration," *Inside U.S. Trade*, December 2, 1999.

78–79 The statements issued by the delegates from Africa, the Caribbean, and Latin America are reported in "Seattle and the Smaller Countries," *Business Line*, December 14, 1999; and "WTO Impasse Opens Opportunities and Dangers for Africa," *Africa News*, January 23, 2000.

79–81 Information on the events of December 3, 1999, can be found in John Burgess, "Green Room's Closed Doors Couldn't Hide Disagreements," *Washington Post*, December 5, 1999; Hal Bernton, "Conference on Trade Concludes in Seattle," *Oregonian*, December 4, 1999; Daniel Pruzin and Gary G. Yerkey, "Trade Officials Made Headway Before Talks Stalled in Seattle," *International Trade Reporter*, December 9, 1999; and Lamy, *L'Europe en première ligne*, pp. 64–68.

79–80 The joking remark to Pettigrew about being "the orchestra conductor on board the *Titanic*," and the explanation for the Seattle failure offered by Barshefsky and other Clinton administration officials—that the European Union backed away from an agreement on agriculture—can be found in Robert G. Kaiser and John Burgess, "A Seattle Primer: How Not to Hold WTO Talks," *Washington Post*, December 12, 1999.

81 Barshefky's comment at the closing session, that "it would be best to take a time out," can be found on the WTO website at http://www.wto.org/english/thewto_e/minist_e/min99_e/english/about_e/resum03_e.htm.

81 Lamy's assertion that the WTO is a "medieval" institution can be found in Steven Pearlstein, "WTO Negotiators' Reach Far Exceeded Grasp of Complexities," *Washington Post*, December 5, 1999.

82 Moore's assertion that he "could see how the deal would be done" can be found in his book *A World Without Walls*, p. 112.

## CHAPTER 5: "THERE ARE ONLY A-PLUSES"

83–84 An account of the WTO's choice of Doha, including Keith Rockwell's quotation and the protests citing the State Department report about Qatar, can be found in Paul Blustein, "A Quiet Round in Qatar?" *Washington Post*, January 30, 2001.

84–85 Moore's speeches are on the WTO website at http://www.wto.org/english/news_e/spmm_e/spmm_e.htm. Evidence for his support of a development round prior to Seattle can be found in Guy de Jonquieres, "Free Trade Under Fire," *Financial Times*, October 11, 1999.

85–86 The study coauthored by Dollar and Kraay is "Trade, Growth and Poverty," World Bank Policy Research working paper 2615, June 2001.

85–88 The intellectual battle between Dollar and Rodrik is reported in Paul Blustein, "Cause, Effect and the Wealth of Nations," *Washington Post*, November 4, 2001.

87–88 The monograph in which Rodrik argued that "the benefits of trade openness are now greatly oversold" is *The Global Governance of Trade as if Development Really Mattered* (n.p.: U.N. Development Programme, October 2001).

88–89 The *Washington Post* article asserting that Zoellick's résumé "might be mistaken for a parody of overachievement" is Steven Pearlstein, "Bush Selection Zoellick Is a Free-Trader on a Mission," January 13, 2001. Information about Zoellick can also be found in Joseph Kahn, "A Tested Negotiator for Trade," *New York Times*, January 12, 2001.

89 Zoellick's *Foreign Affairs* article, published in the January–February 2000 issue, was titled "A Republican Foreign Policy."

89–90 Zoellick's testimony was delivered March 7, 2001, before the House Ways and Means Committee. It can be found in a transcript prepared by *Federal Document Clearing House*, available from LexisNexis®.

91 Zoellick's comments about the Russians came at his appearance before the National Press Club with Pascal Lamy on July 17, 2001. They can be found in a transcript prepared by Federal News Service.

92–94 Information about Lamy can be found in Guy de Jonquieres, "Liberal with a Social Mission," *Financial Times*, October 21, 1999; "Pascal Lamy," *Economist*, July 7, 2001; and his Wikipedia biography, on the web at http://en.wikipedia.org/wiki/Pascal_Lamy.

93–94 Information about the ties between Zoellick and Lamy can be found in Paul Blustein, "Trade's Friendly Warriors," *Washington Post*, May 28, 2002.

94 Zoellick's comment "How much more food can Americans eat?" can be found in Jerry Hagstrom, "Bush to Meet with Ag Leaders on Trade Authority Plans," *CongressDaily* (National Journal Group), June 18, 2001, available from LexisNexis®. His comment about "the biggest payoff for agriculture" came in a press briefing delivered on June 18, 2001, a transcript of which was prepared by *Federal Document Clearing House*, available from LexisNexis®.

95 Lamy's position on the precautionary principle is cited in "EU Paper on Precaution Seeks to Allay Fears of Protectionism," *Inside U.S. Trade*, July 27, 2001.

95 The *Washington Post* op-ed that Zoellick and Lamy jointly wrote, "In the Next Round," was published on July 17, 2001.

95 The comments by Zoellick and Lamy at the National Press Club on July 17, 2001, can be found in a transcript prepared by Federal News Service.

96 The comments made at the Reality Check can be found in "No Progress on Doha Agenda at WTO's 'Reality Check,'" *Bridges Weekly Trade News Digest*, July 31, 2001; C. Rammanohar Reddy, "No Consensus Yet on New WTO Round," *Hindu*, August 1, 2001; Jean-Louis de la Vaissiere, "Opinions Divided on Trade Round Ahead of Doha WTO Meeting," Agence France-Presse, July 31, 2001; and Elizabeth Olson, "Discord Mars WTO's Prospects," *New York Times*, July 31, 2001.

96 Simba's comment can be found in "LDCs Say 'Not Ready' for New Round," *Bridges Weekly Trade Digest*, July 31, 2001.

97 Moore's quotation that a second failure "would certainly condemn us to a long period of irrelevance" can be found in Frances Williams, "WTO Head Tells Members to 'Get Real,'" *Financial Times*, July 31, 2001.

97 Zoellick's September 20, 2001, op-ed in the *Washington Post* was titled "Countering Terror with Trade."

98 Zoellick's October 30, 2001, speech was delivered to the Council on Foreign Relations in Washington. A transcript was prepared by Federal News Service.

98–99 Some of the academic studies projecting a large economic impact from a successful round are cited in Guy de Jonquieres, "Dealing in Doha," *Financial Times*, November 6, 2001. The World Bank study, titled "Global Economic Prospects and the Developing Countries 2002," was published in late 2001, and the quotation about "The average poor person selling goods into globalized markets . . ." is on p. xii. It can be found on the web at http://www-wds.worldbank.org/external/default/WDSContentServer/IW3P/IB/2002/02/16/000094946_0202020411334/Rendered/PDF/multi0page.pdf.

99 Zoellick's first public hint that the Doha meeting might have to be moved can be found in Gary G. Yerkey, "USTR Says 'Security' Primary Concern in Planning for WTO Discussions in Qatar," *WTO Reporter* (Bureau of National Affairs), September 26, 2001.

100 Zoellick's comment that the ministerial should be held "in one location or the other" can be found in "Qatar Ups Political Ante in Fight to Host Next WTO Ministerial," *Inside U.S. Trade*, October 19, 2001. The Qatari diplomatic démarches were quoted in the same article.

100–101 Information about the protests delivered by developing-country ambassadors at the October 31, 2001, General Council meeting and the responses by Moore and Harbinson can be found in Fatoumata Jawara and Aileen Kwa, *Behind the Scenes at the WTO: The Real World of International Trade Negotiations* (London and New York: Zed Books, in association with Focus on the Global South, Bangkok, 2004), pp. 70–72.

101–103 The draft text prepared by Stuart Harbinson is available on the website of the International Centre for Trade and Sustainable Development, at http://ictsd.net/news/wto/archive/doha/resources-documents/.

102 Trojan's complaints about the environmental portion of the Harbinson text can be found in Daniel Pruzin, "WTO Chair Defends Draft Declaration Against Developing Countries' Criticisms," *WTO Reporter*, November 1, 2001.

104 Information about the South African program that was providing treatment to Vuyani Jacobs can be found in "Fighting Back," *Economist*, May 11, 2002.

104–107 Information and analysis about the intellectual property rights issue, the TRIPS, and the battle over the issue in South Africa can be found in Keith E. Maskus, *Intellectual Property Rights in the Global Economy* (Washington, DC: Institute for International Economics, 2000); Narlikar, *The World Trade Organization*; Helene Cooper, Rachel Zimmerman, and Laurie McGinley, "AIDS Epidemic Traps Firms in a Vise," *Wall Street Journal*, March 2, 2001; and Wallach and Woodall, *Whose Trade Organization?*

106–107 Zoellick's announcement on the Bush administration's TRIPS policy can be found in Donald G. McNeil Jr., "Bush Keeps Clinton Policy on Poor Lands' Need for AIDS Drugs," *New York Times*, February 22, 2001.

107 Bale's use of the term "nutty" to describe the developing countries' TRIPS proposal can be found in Daniel Pruzin, "Global Drug Industry Association Blasts 'Nutty' WTO Text on TRIPS, Public Health," *WTO Reporter*, November 2, 2001.

## CHAPTER 6: REMOVING THE STAIN

110 Moore's speech to the inaugural session at Doha is on the WTO website at http://www.wto.org/english/news_e/news01_e/min01_dgstat_inaugural_session_e.htm.

111 An account of the episode in which the exchange between Moore and Kamal was accidentally overheard can be found in Jawara and Kwa, *Behind the Scenes at the WTO*, pp. 91–92.

111 The article describing Maran as looking like a "comical villain" is Sanjaya Baru, "I'm Back with Many Trophies from the Battlefront: Murasoli Maran," *Financial Express*, November 19, 2001.

111–112 Information about India's relationship with the global trading system can be found in Edward Luce, *In Spite of the Gods: The Strange Rise of Modern India* (New York: Doubleday, 2007); T. N. Srinivasan and Suresh D. Tendulkar, *Reintegrating India with the World Economy* (Washington, DC: Institute for International Economics, 2003); and "Trade Policies in South Asia: An Overview," World Bank report no. 29949, September 7, 2004.

113 Maran's reference to the WTO as a "necessary evil" can be found in Harkaksh Singh Nanda, "India, Down on Doha Draft Declaration, Threatens to Leave WTO to Protest Agenda," *WTO Reporter*, November 5, 2001. His assertion that the United States wants to "strike while the iron is hot" can be found in Daniel Pruzin, "Indian Commerce Minister Maran Takes Hard Stance in WTO Talks on New Round," *WTO Reporter*, November 11, 2001.

114–115 A comprehensive history of U.S. antidumping laws can be found in Destler, *American Trade Politics*. An account of the De Cecco case and analysis of foreign complaints against U.S. antidumping laws can be found in Paul Blustein, "Italy Loses the Pasta Wars," *Washington Post*, July 31, 1996. A further account of the way U.S. antidumping laws are allegedly abused can be found in Blustein, "Free Trade's Muddy Waters,"

*Washington Post*, July 13, 2003, and an accompanying sidebar published on the same day, "When the U.S. Thinks Goods Were 'Dumped,' He Steps Up."

115 The figures showing the number of antidumping cases filed against the United States and China were reported in Gary G. Yerkey and Daniel Pruzin, "Accord Possible on Dumping, Subsidies at Doha WTO Talks; U.S. Shows Flexibility," *WTO Reporter*, November 13, 2001.

116–117 The final version of the provision on the antidumping issue that was eventually approved by the WTO membership can be found in the Doha Declaration, paragraph 28, on the WTO website at http://www.wto.org/english/thewto_e/minist_e/min01_e/mindecl_e.htm.

117 Klinefelter's comment "There will be political consequences" comes from notes I took of a conversation he had with me in Doha.

117 The *Bridges Daily Update* assertion that the U.S. position on the antidumping issue reflected a "major shift" comes from the November 13, 2001, edition.

118–120 The options under consideration concerning TRIPS at the Doha meeting are available at the website of the International Centre for Trade and Sustainable Development at http://ictsd.net/news/wto/archive/doha/resources-documents/. The final version that was eventually approved by the WTO membership can be found on the WTO website at http://www.wto.org/english/thewto_e/minist_e/min01_e/mindecl_trips_e.htm.

121 The quotation from Teixeira was reported in Geoff Winestock and Helene Cooper, "Activists Outmaneuver Drug Makers at WTO," *Wall Street Journal*, November 14, 2001.

121 The quotation from Love was reported in Paul Blustein, "Getting WTO's Attention," *Washington Post*, November 16, 2001.

121 The quotation from Bale was reported in Paul Blustein, "WTO Agreement Appears Near," *Washington Post*, November 13, 2001.

121 The claims by pharmaceutical firms that the TRIPS declaration had little practical import were reported in Gardiner Harris and Rachel Zimmerman, "Drug Makers Say WTO Setback Will Not Have Significant Impact," *Wall Street Journal*, November 15, 2001.

123 The conversation between Moore and Kamal about closing the Doha airport is recounted in Moore's book *A World Without Walls*, p. 123.

123 Information about the dispute over the waiver for the African, Caribbean, and Pacific countries can be found in *Bridges Daily Update*, November 13 and 14, 2001, issues.

124–127 An illuminating account of the all-night green room meeting is provided in Lamy, *L'Europe en première ligne*. The quotation about Lamy's note to E.U. ministers, "This is still taking a long time . . . ," is on pp. 155–156. The quotation that "the hour of truth" had arrived for him is on p. 157, and the quotation "Let's not say, 'Europe is the problem'" is on p. 158. The quotations from Moore, "Well, Ladies and Gentlemen . . . ," and Kamal, "Bravo . . . ," are on p. 161, as is Lamy's recollection of thinking that "the optimism was without doubt a bit forced." The account of the alarmed expression on the face of his aide Matthew Baldwin is on p. 163.

124–127 The final versions of the provisions on the Singapore issues, the environment, and agriculture that were eventually approved by the WTO membership can be found in the Doha Declaration, available on the WTO website at http://www.wto.org/english/thewto_e/minist_e/min01_e/mindecl_e.htm.

127 Maran's quotations, "[they] thought they could exhaust me" and "My heart is okay," come from Sanjaya Baru, "I'm Back with Many Trophies from the Battlefront," *Financial Express*, November 19, 2001.

130 Kamal's statement closing the meeting comes from the WTO website at http://www.wto.org/english/thewto_e/minist_e/min01_e/min01_chair_speaking_e.htm.

130 Information about the Indian delegation's stony silence comes from Sanjaya Baru, "I'm Back with Many Trophies from the Battlefront," *Financial Express*, November 19, 2001.

130 Zoellick's quotation about removing the "stain" of Seattle was widely reported in, among others, Paul Blustein, "142 Nations Reach Pact on Trade Negotiations," *Washington Post*, November 15, 2001.

## CHAPTER 7: THE UPRISING OF THE REST

131, 133 The quotations from Zoellick about the 2005 deadline and the feeling that he gets from battlefields can be found in Paul Blustein, "Trade's Friendly Warriors," *Washington Post*, May 28, 2002.

134 Information about the steel tariffs and the ensuing transatlantic dispute can be found in Paul Blustein, "Trade Partners Trading Threats; EU, Japan Plan Retaliation for U.S. Tariffs," *Washington Post*, April 27, 2002; and Blustein, "WTO Rejects Steel Tariffs; U.S. Says Decision Will Be Appealed," *Washington Post*, March 27, 2003.

134 Information about the farm bill, including Truss's comment that the bill sent an "appalling signal," can be found in Paul Blustein and Dan Morgan, "Showdown on Subsidies," *Washington Post*, May 2, 2002; Paul Blustein, "U.S. Farm Bill Finds Few Fans Abroad," *Washington Post*, May 5, 2002; Dan Morgan, "Farm Revolution Stops at Subsidies; Efficiency Fails to Stem Flow of Federal Cash," *Washington Post*, October 3, 2004.

134 Information about Zoellick's early proposals on agriculture and manufactured goods can be found in Daniel Pruzin and Gary Yerkey, "U.S. Proposes Five-Year Timetable for Elimination of Agriculture Subsidies," *WTO Reporter*, June 5, 2002; and Paul Blustein, "U.S. Urges Abolition of Tariffs," *Washington Post*, November 27, 2002.

135–136 A comprehensive history and explanation of fast track and trade promotion authority legislation can be found in Destler, *American Trade Politics*.

137 An account of the 215–214 vote in the House, including Zoellick's quotation that the deal with DeMint was "necessary to achieve a larger good," can be found in Juliet Eilperin, "Trade Bill Passes House by One Vote; Bush Closer to Obtaining More Negotiating Power," *Washington Post*, December 7, 2001.

137–140 The quotations from participants at the Montreal mini-ministerial, starting with Zoellick's attack on the Japanese and including the discussion about plans for the United States and the European Union to present a joint proposal on agriculture, come from notes of the meeting furnished by a confidential source.

138 Information about the stalemate in the Doha Round in 2003, including the rejection of Harbinson's agriculture text, can be found in Daniel Pruzin, "WTO Members Blast Harbinson Ag Text; Draft to Serve as 'Catalyst' for Future Talks," *WTO Reporter*, February 19, 2003; Pruzin, "Gloomy Harbinson Says WTO Deadline on Agriculture Modalities to be Missed," *WTO Reporter*, March 31, 2003; and "The Doha Squabble," *Economist*, March 29, 2003.

139 Information about the European Union's reform of the CAP, including Fischler's claim that "we have done our homework," can be found in Tobias Buck, Guy de Jonquieres, and Frances Williams, "Fischler's Surprise for Europe's Farmers," *Financial Times*, June 27, 2003; Elliott, *Delivering on Doha*; Charlotte Denny, "CAP Deal Looks More Horlicks Than Radical," *Guardian*, June 30, 2003; "More Fudge than Breakthrough," *Economist*, June 28, 2003; Robert Uhlig, "A Bloated Beast That Spawned Beef Mountains and Wine Lakes," *Daily Telegraph*, June 27, 2003; "Sacred Cows," *Times* (London), June 27, 2003; and "Drops on Parched Soil," *Economist*, July 5, 2003.

140–144 Information about the U.S.-E.U. agriculture paper can be found in "U.S., EU Framework Sees Partial Elimination of Export Subsidies," *Inside U.S. Trade*, August 15, 2003; and Guy de Jonquieres, "US-EU Farm Proposal Leaves WTO Members in a Dilemma," *Financial Times*, August 15, 2003.

143 The figure on the size of the average Indian farm was furnished by Ashok Gulati, one of the country's premier agricultural economists.

143 Information about Brazil's rapidly growing prowess in agriculture can be found in Larry Rohter, "South America Seeks to Fill the World's Table," *New York Times*, December 12, 2004; and Simon Romero, "Brazil's Spreading Exports Worry Minnesota Farmers," *New York Times*, June 22, 2004.

144 Information about the 2003 agreement on TRIPS can be found in Edward Luce and Frances Williams, "WTO Deal on Cheap Drugs Ends Months of Wrangling," *Financial Times*, August 28, 2003; and Frances Williams, "Drugs Accord Fails to Heal Rifts in WTO," *Financial Times*, August 29, 2003.

144 Information about the planning for Cancún, including Supachai's playing down of expectations for the meeting, can be found in John Authers and Guy de Jonquieres, "With the Priorities of Member Nations Conflicting Sharply, Agreement May Prove Elusive at Next Week's Ministerial Meeting," *Financial Times*, September 4, 2003.

145 The full title of the 2002 Oxfam report is "Cultivating Poverty: The Impact of US Cotton Subsidies on Africa," Oxfam briefing paper 30.

145 The *Wall Street Journal* article about cotton is Roger Thurow and Scott Kilman, "U.S. Subsidies Create Cotton Glut That Hurts Foreign Cotton Farms," June 26, 2002.

146 Compaore's speech is on the WTO website at http://www.wto.org/english/news_e/ news03_e/tnc_10june03_e.htm.

147 The G-20's demands can be found in the *Bridges Daily Update*, September 11, 2003.

148–149 Information about Amorim can be found in Carolyn Whelan, "Brazil's Top Diplomat Fills Out the Plot Line," *International Herald Tribune*, December 4, 2004; and Tom Holland, "G-20's Double Act Takes Up the Cudgels for Farming Reform," *South China Morning Post*, December 17, 2005.

150 Erwin's quotation about the "historic moment" can be found in Guy de Jonquieres and Frances Williams, "Third World Alliance Hits at Trade Rules," *Financial Times*, September 11, 2003.

150–151 Supachai's comments about cotton on the ministerial's first day are cited in Kate Millar, "African Cotton Producers Demand End of Subsidies by Rich Countries," Agence France-Presse, September 10, 2003; and *Bridges Daily Update*, September 11, 2003.

151–152 Detailed information about the U.S. proposal on cotton and how it fared can be found in the *Bridges Daily Update* editions of September 11, 12, 13, and 14, 2003. The quotation from the African delegate, "Now the WTO is against us," was reported in the September 14 edition.

153 Jaitley's speech to the plenary session can be found on the WTO website, at www.wto.org/english/theWTO_e/minist_e/min03_e/statements_e/st7.pdf.

153 Quotations by participants in the green room at Cancún come from notes furnished by confidential sources.

153–155 Information about the scene at the end of the Cancún meeting can be found in Kevin Sullivan, "Rich-Poor Rift Triggers Collapse of Trade Talks," *Washington Post*, September 15, 2003; Guy de Jonquieres and Frances Williams, "Investment Row Causes WTO Talks to Collapse," *Financial Times*, September 15, 2003; and "The WTO Under Fire," *Economist*, September 20, 2003.

156 Zoellick's angry news conference statement can be found in Sullivan's piece in the *Post.*

156 Lamy's op-ed describing the WTO as "neolithic" is "Post-Cancún Primer," *Wall Street Journal*, September 23, 2003.

## CHAPTER 8: JEWELS AND PIRATES

157–158 The quotations from Christopher Ward come from a confidential transcript of his remarks in the WTO case DS267, *Subsidies on Upland Cotton*.

158–159  A wealth of information and analysis about the dispute settlement system can be found in Merit Janow, Victoria Donaldson, and Alan Yanovich, eds., *The WTO: Governance, Dispute Settlement and Developing Countries* (Huntington, NY: Juris Publishing, 2008). Jackson's quotation, that the WTO has "clearly the most powerful dispute settlement system . . . ," can be found on p. 388 of that volume. Further information can be found in Narlikar, *The World Trade Organization*; Barfield, *Free Trade, Sovereignty, Democracy*; Robert Z. Lawrence, "The United States and the WTO Dispute Settlement System," Council on Foreign Relations, Council Special Report no. 25, March 2007; Chad Bown, *Self-Reinforcing Trade: Developing Countries and WTO Dispute Settlement* (Washington, DC: Brookings Institution Press, forthcoming); and Scott Miller, "EU-U.S. Dispute Puts WTO Court in the Spotlight," *Wall Street Journal*, June 1, 2005.

159  Information about the European Union's threats during the steel dispute to impose punitive tariffs on politically sensitive U.S. goods can be found in Paul Blustein, "EU Lists Possible Targets for New Tariffs," *Washington Post*, April 20, 2002; and Mike Allen, "President to Drop Tariffs on Steel," *Washington Post*, December 1, 2003.

159  WTO members have brought a total of 388 complaints from the time of the organization's founding in 1995 until 2008, and only in about 10 cases has the dispute reached the stage at which the WTO has authorized retaliation, according to Bown in his forthcoming book, *Self-Reinforcing Trade*. However, another analysis of 79 cases that reached the stage of a final decision presents a somewhat less encouraging set of statistics. According to this analysis, by Washington attorneys Gary Horlick and Judith Coleman, 53 of these cases (67.1 percent) resulted in "more-or-less full compliance," 19 cases (24.1 percent) resulted in "gestures at compliance/partial compliance," and 7 cases (8.9 percent) resulted in "unabashed noncompliance." This analysis, "A Comment on Compliance with WTO Dispute Settlement Decisions," can be found in Janow, Donaldson, and Yanovich, *The WTO: Governance, Dispute Settlement and Developing Countries*, pp. 771–776.

160  Information about U.S. victories in dispute settlement cases can be found in "World Trade Organization: U.S. Experience to Date in Dispute Settlement System," U.S. General Accounting Office, briefing report to the chairman, Committee on Ways and Means, House of Representatives, June 2000; and Mark Drajem, "China Must Revamp Auto Component Tax Rules, WTO Says," Bloomberg News, July 18, 2008.

160–162  Information about the *Upland Cotton* case comes from Ray A. Goldberg, Robert Lawrence, and Katie Milligan, "Brazil's WTO Cotton Case: Negotiation Through Litigation," Harvard Business School, case no. N9–905–405, November 1, 2004, available on the website of the Peterson Institute for International Economics at http://www.petersoninstitute.org/publications/chapters_preview/3632/05iie3632.pdf; "Unpicking Cotton Subsidies," *Economist*, April 30, 2004; and Paul Blustein, "U.S. Farmers Get a Lesson in Global Trade," *Washington Post*, April 28, 2004.

161–162  Information about Daniel Sumner's involvement in the cotton case comes from Paul Blustein, "In U.S., Cotton Cries Betrayal," *Washington Post*, May 12, 2004.

162  Senator Conrad's quotation can be found in Elizabeth Becker, "Lawmakers Voice Doom and Gloom on WTO Ruling," *New York Times*, April 27.

162–163  Bacchus's memoir is *Trade and Freedom*. His quotation "We do not wear robes. We do not wear wigs . . ." can be found on p. 24, and his quotation "hour after hour, day after day . . ." can be found on p. 39.

163  Information about the first opening of a WTO panel proceeding to the public, and the controversy surrounding transparency in the dispute settlement system, can be found in Susan Esserman and Robert Howse, "The Creative Evolution of World Trade," *Financial Times*, August 23, 2005.

165 Horlick's quotation, "Prudence, diplomacy and client confidentiality . . . ," can be found on p. 826 of Janow, Donaldson, and Yanovich, *The WTO: Governance, Dispute Settlement and Developing Countries.*

165 The data showing that developing countries filed a majority of WTO cases in 2001–2006 can be found in Lawrence, "The United States and the WTO Dispute Settlement System." The degree to which Brazil, India, and other big developing countries dominate that list can be found in Bown, *Self-Reinforcing Trade.*

165–169 Information about the *Gambling* case is heavily drawn from Paul Blustein, "Against All Odds: Antigua Besting U.S. in Internet Gambling Case at WTO," *Washington Post*, August 4, 2006.

166 Reno's statement "You can't go offshore and hide . . ." can be found in a transcript of the "Weekly U.S. Justice Department Media Availability," March 5, 1998, compiled by Federal News Service.

169–171 Information about the later stages of the *Gambling* and *Upland Cotton* cases can be found in Daniel Pruzin, "Antigua Allowed to Impose $21 Million Annually as Sanctions on U.S. in Gambling Dispute," *WTO Reporter*, December 24, 2007; "WTO to Determine Worth of Gambling Concession," *Bridges*, February 2008; William Triplett, "Antigua Threatens to Allow Piracy," *Variety*, March 18, 2008; "Cotton Dispute Ends in Comprehensive Victory for Brazil," *Bridges*, August 2008; "U.S., Brazil Spar over Level of Trade Retaliation, in WTO Cotton Case," *Inside U.S. Trade*, January 9, 2009; "Brazil Argues for Expansive Retaliation Rights in WTO Cotton Case," *Inside U.S. Trade*, January 30, 2009; and "Brazil Warns of Dire Consequences if Granted Small Award in Cotton Case," *Inside U.S. Trade*, March 13, 2009. Azevedo's full statement at the March 3, 2009, hearing can be found on the website of the Brazilian Ministry of External Relations at http://www2.mre.gov.br/cgc/DS267_Arb_22.6_7.10_Brazil's_Oral_Statement_as_delivered.pdf.

172 Information about Costa Rica's complaint involving U.S. underwear quotas can be found on the WTO's website at http://www.wto.org/english/res_e/booksp_e/casestudies_e/case12_e.htm.

## CHAPTER 9: HIS HOLINESS, POPE BOB

174 Zoellick's September 22, 2003, op-ed in the *Financial Times* was titled "Free Trade: America Will Not Wait."

174–178 The earliest and most influential advocate of competitive liberalization was C. Fred Bergsten, director of the Peterson Institute for International Economics. One of his first writings on the subject was "Competitive Liberalization and Global Free Trade: A Vision for the Early 21st Century," Institute for International Economics working paper 96–15, 1996. Other information about bilateral and regional agreements and about Zoellick's competitive liberalization strategy comes from Daniel Drezner, *U.S. Trade Strategy: Free vs. Fair* (New York: Council on Foreign Relations Press, 2006); Destler, *American Trade Politics*; Mark Thirwell, *The New Terms of Trade* (Alexandria, New South Wales, Australia: Lowy Institute, Longueville Media, 2006); Jagdish Bhagwati, *Termites in the Trading System: How Preferential Agreements Undermine Free Trade* (New York: Oxford University Press, 2008); Michael M. Phillips, "Trade Aide Plays Latin America, Asia Off Each Other to Win Pacts," *Wall Street Journal*, June 5, 2001; Guy de Jonquieres, "Governments' Willingness to Use Trade Pacts to Cement Diplomatic Ties and Forge Alliances Risks Slowing the Momentum Behind Multilateral Trade Talks," *Financial Times*, November 19, 2002; Guy de Jonquieres and Victor Mallet, "Failure at Cancún Prompts Flurry of Trade Deals in Asia," *Financial Times*, October 16, 2003; and Paul Blustein, "Lowered Expectations," *Washington Post*, April 23, 2004. Zoellick made the case for his strategy in numerous speeches and appearances before congressional committees, many of which can be found on the website of the U.S. Trade Representative, http://www.ustr.gov. One example is his testimony on March 5, 2003, at http://ustr.gov/assets/Document_Library/USTR_Testimony/2003/asset_upload_file96_4330.pdf.

176–177 Bhagwati and Garnaut's op-ed opposing the U.S.-Australian agreement was "Say No to This Free Trade Deal," *Australian*, July 11, 2003.

177 Hatakeyama's quotation "we have started to become surrounded" can be found in James Brooke, "Ready for WTO Talks, and Ready to Deal," *New York Times*, November 9, 2001.

178–180 Information about the Miami meeting on the Free Trade Area of the Americas comes from Simon Romero, "Trade Talks in Miami End Early," *New York Times*, November 21, 2003; "Business Derides Miami Declaration for Creating Weak FTAA," *Inside U.S. Trade*, November 21, 2003; Paul Blustein, "Free Trade Area of Americas May Be Limited," *Washington Post*, November 19, 2003; and "New Doubts About Bush Trade Agenda," *Washington Post*, November 22, 2003.

180–181 The *Financial Times* story reporting Zoellick's letter was Edward Alden and Lionel Barber, "US Tries to Reactivate Failed Talks over Trade," January 12, 2004. Zoellick's letter was carried in full by *Inside U.S. Trade*, accompanying its story, "Zoellick Letter Shows No Concessions but Some Flexibility," January 16, 2004.

182 Zoellick's remarks in Singapore come from a transcript of his remarks on the website of the Office of the U.S. Trade Representative at http://ustr.gov/assets/Document_Library/Transcripts/2004/February/asset_upload_file211_5403.pdf.

183–184 Information about the May 14, 2004, announcement that a meeting would be held in Geneva in July, including Lamy's "volcano" quotation, can be found in Guy de Jonquieres, "Hopes Rising for Restart of Doha World Trade Talks," *Financial Times*, May 15, 2004. Fischler's quotation about export subsidies can be found in Paul Blustein, "EU Offers to End Farm Subsidies," *Washington Post*, May 11, 2004. Further information about the European Union's concessions, including the figures on export subsidies, can be found in Paul Meller, "France Splits with Europe over Farm Subsidy Plan," *New York Times*, May 11, 2004. Additional information, including Boutros-Ghali's quotation about the "round for free" proposal, can be found in Daniel Pruzin, "EU 'Round for Free' Proposal for Poorest Countries Gets Cool Reception," *WTO Reporter*, May 14, 2004.

185–186 Information about Nath comes from his book *India's Century* (New York: McGraw-Hill, 2008); Priya Sahgal and Rohit Saran, "Kamal's Trademark," *India Today*, September 26, 2004; Priya Sahgal, "Cabinet Showcases," *India Today*, April 25, 2004; Yogesh Vajpeyi, "Saheb Keeps Seat Warm with Heart, Helicopter," *Indian Express*, August 27, 1999; Kenneth J. Cooper, "Indian Politicking in Name Only; Tainted by Scandal, Ex-Official Stumps for Wife's Substitute Candidacy," *Washington Post*, April 27, 1996; and Peter Wonacott, "A Voice for Developing Nations," *Wall Street Journal*, December 5, 2005. Nath's quotation "Next time can you bring a picture of an American farmer?" is from Priya Saghal, "Cabinet Showcase," *India Today*, April 25, 2005. His quotation "I had had little exposure . . ." is on pp. 14–15 of *India's Century*. The quotation from Indira Gandhi, "This is my third son . . . ," can be found in Sahgal and Saran, "Kamal's Trademark."

187–190 Information about India's agricultural tariffs for staple crops can be found in "India: Re-energizing the Agricultural Sector to Sustain Growth and Reduce Poverty," World Bank report no. 27889-IN, July 30, 2004. Additional information about India's anti-poverty policies comes from Luce, *In Spite of the Gods*; Srinivasan and Tendulkar, *Reintegrating India with the World Economy*; and "Trade Policies in South Asia: An Overview," World Bank report no. 29949; see also "Domestic Agricultural Market Reforms and Border Trade Liberalization: The Case of India," National Council for

Applied Economic Research, New Delhi, 2006. Amartya Sen's lamentation about "friendly fire" comes from his book *The Argumentative Indian: Writings on Indian History, Culture and Identity* (New York: Picador, 2005); his quotation "The overall effect of high food prices . . ." is on p. 215.

190   The NASSCOM study, conducted by Credit Rating and Information Services of India Ltd. (CRISIL), a leading Indian research firm, was authored by Subir Gokarn, Dharmakirti Joshi, Vidya Mahambare, Pooja Mirchandani, Manoj Mohta, and Kumar Subramaniam and is titled "The Rising Tide: Employment and Output Linkages of IT-ITES," February 2007, available on the web at http://www.nasscom.in/upload/51269/NASSCOM_CRISIL.pdf.

191   Supachai's op-ed in the *International Herald Tribune* was titled "A Chance to Salvage a Doha Trade Deal," and was published July 27, 2004.

191   Information about the repeated delays that ministers and others endured as the Five Interested Parties met in July 2004 can be found in Daniel Pruzin, "WTO Framework Text Delayed as AG Chair Warns That Text Is 'Substantially Revised,'" *WTO Reporter*, July 28, 2004; and Paul Blustein, "Five Powers Agree at WTO on Farm Talks," *Washington Post*, July 30, 2004. Wasescha's complaint can be found in Guy de Jonquieres and Frances Williams, "Five Powers Agree Doha Negotiating Position," *Financial Times*, July 30, 2004. Nakagawa's complaint can be found in "WTO General Council Head to Present Amended Draft Accord Thurs.," Japan Economic Newswire, July 29, 2004.

193–196   The text that was submitted to the green room, as well as the final text that was agreed, can be found on the WTO website at http://www.wto.org/english/tratop_e/dda_e/dda_package_july04_e.htm.

195–197   Quotations from participants in the green room come from notes of the meeting that were furnished by confidential sources.

197   The quotations by Zoellick and Lamy at their press conferences can be found in Paul Blustein, "Accord Reached on Global Trade," *Washington Post*, August 1, 2004.

## CHAPTER 10: ONE CHICKEN McNUGGET

199   The *Wall Street Journal* article citing analysts' fears about the future of U.S.-European trade relations was Scott Miller, "Trading on a Friendship for EU-U.S. Commerce," October 18, 2004.

200–201   The headlines "Love Triangle Ended Spin Agency Contract" and "'Exotic' Party Animal Stands Out from Dull Cabinet Pack" appeared in the *Times* (London) on January 27, 2001, and December 23, 1998, respectively. Information about Mandelson comes from "Evil Genius of the Labour Party: Peter Mandelson," *Independent*, July 1, 1989, in which the statement "He wheedles journalists, cajoles them . . ." can be found, as well as the following: a series of articles by Donald Macintyre published in the *Independent* during the week of April 19, 1999, excerpting a biography of Mandelson that Macintyre wrote; Macintyre, "The Mandelson Loan: Exotic in Both His Plumage and Connections," *Independent*, December 23, 1998; Colin Brown, "'Fixers' in the Shadow of the Red Rose," *Independent*, October 4, 1990; Peter Lennon, "Guarding the Good Name of the Rose," *Guardian*, October 2, 1989; Patrick Wintour, "The Rise of the Red Rinse Conference—How Peter Mandelson and His Aides Have Subdued the Firebrands for the Cameras," *Guardian*, October 6, 1990; Wintour, "This Time There Will Be No Comeback," *Guardian*, January 25, 2001; Geoffrey Levy, "It's a Long Way from Stoneybroke Cottage," *Daily Mail*, December 23, 1998; and T. R. Reid, "As Scandal Brews, Two British Officials Quit," *Washington Post*, December 24, 1998.

201–202   Information about the hostile phone call between Mandelson and Zoellick, including their quotations, can be found in Edward Alden, Daniel Dombey, and Raphael Minder, "Zoellick Blasts Mandelson 'Spin' on Aircraft Subsidy Dispute," *Financial Times*,

April 6, 2005; and Paul Meller, "Accusations Fly in EU-U.S. Dispute," *International Herald Tribune*, April 7, 2005.

202–203 Information about Portman comes from Elizabeth Auster, "Ready for Prime Time," *Cleveland Plain Dealer*, March 20, 2005; and Auster, "Portman Steers GOP on Bipartisan Course," *Cleveland Plain Dealer*, January 29, 2001. Additional information, including his words when his nomination was announced, can be found in Paul Blustein, "Rep. Portman Named Next U.S. Trade Representative," *Washington Post*, March 18, 2005. The *New York Times* profile citing Portman's lack of detractors is David E. Rosenbaum, "Bush Loyalist's New Role Is 'Facilitator' in House," February 16, 2003.

204 Bush's speech to the United Nations in which he proposed to end all subsidies can be found in the *Weekly Compilation of Presidential Documents*, for the week of September 19, 2005.

205 Johanns's statement to the Senate Agriculture Committee can be found in "Johanns Signals U.S. Subsidies Must Change in New Farm Bill," *Inside U.S. Trade*, September 23, 2005.

205 Portman's statement "Our ambitious initiative demonstrates a seriousness of purpose . . ." can be found in "U.S. Offers Plan on Agriculture for Hong Kong Trade Talks," States News Service, October 10, 2005.

205–207 Analyses of the U.S. proposal of October 10, 2005, including the assertion by Oxfam that the proposal was "smoke and mirrors," can be found in "America Tries to Get Things Moving," *Economist*, October 12, 2005; and Daniel Pruzin, "U.S. Unveils Ag Subsidy Proposal for WTO, Would Cut U.S. Amber Box Support by 60%," *WTO Reporter*, October 12, 2005. Charveriat's and Vaile's quotations can both be found in Pruzin's article.

208 The attacks on the European Union by Vaile, Portman, and Charveriat after the October 20, 2005, meeting of the Five Interested Parties can be found in Paul Blustein, "Nations Blame EU for Stalling Trade Talks," *Washington Post*, October 21, 2005.

208 Portman's statement that the E.U. position on sensitive products would create "a big enough hole to drive a truck through" can be found in Paul Blustein, "Dispute over Farm Subsidies Stalls Global Trade Negotiations," *Washington Post*, October 16, 2005.

209 Chirac's threat that "France reserves the right not to approve" a Doha deal can be found in "Chirac: France Reserves Right to Block Deal," Associated Press, October 27, 2005.

209–210 The remarks by participants in the videoconference come from notes furnished by a confidential source.

210 The "one Chicken McNugget" argument comes from a briefing paper titled "Implications of EU Agriculture Market Access Position" that was distributed to reporters, including the author, by the Office of the U.S. Trade Representative.

210–211 Information about Lamy's election as director-general and the contrast with the Moore/Supachai fight comes from Elizabeth Becker, "French Economist to Lead World Trade Organization," *New York Times*, May 14, 2005.

211 The remarks of participants at the November 9, 2005, meeting come from notes furnished by a confidential source.

211 Portman's statement "We have not given up . . ." can be found in Daniel Pruzin, "Talks on WTO Ministerial in Disarray as EU, G20 Members Clash over Ag, NAMA," *WTO Reporter*, November 10, 2005.

211 Mandelson's lamentation about the lowering of expectations for Hong Kong can be found in Paul Blustein, "Hope Fades for a Pact Easing Trade Barriers," *Washington Post*, November 10, 2005.

212 For my account regarding Finta Danish Dairies, I am indebted to my colleague Alan Beattie of the *Financial Times*, whose marvelous article "Dipak and the Goliaths," published December 9, 2005, discussed some of the company's problems in exporting its milk.

213–214 The new World Bank estimates were published in Thomas W. Hertel and L. Alan Winters, eds., *Poverty and the WTO: Impacts of the Doha Development Agenda* (Washington, DC: Palgrave Macmillan and the World Bank, 2006), in which the statements "there are more losses than gains" (p. 36) and "the liberalization targets . . . have to be quite ambitious" (p. 3) can also be found; and Newfarmer, *Trade, Doha and Development*, in which the statement "these numbers are significantly lower . . ." (p. 59) can also be found. The estimates released at the time of the Doha meeting, as previously noted, were in a report published in 2001 titled "Global Economic Prospects and the Developing Countries 2002." The estimates concerning Zambia can be found in the Hertel and Winters volume, in a chapter by Jorge F. Balat and Guido G. Porto, "The WTO Doha Round, Cotton Sector Dynamics, and Poverty Trends in Zambia."

214 The full title of Frank Ackerman's paper is "The Shrinking Gains from Trade: A Critical Assessment of Doha Round Projections," Global Development and Environment Institute working paper 05–01, October 2005.

215–217 The bank's view about the correct interpretation of its studies, including the quotations by Newfarmer and Winters to reporters, can be found in Paul Blustein, "World Bank Reconsiders Trade's Benefits to Poor," *Washington Post*, October 17, 2005.

216 The statement "exempting even two percent of tariff lines could eviscerate the round" is from Newfarmer, *Trade, Doha and Development*, p. 43.

217 Mandelson's exhortation to officials from developing countries can be found in "EU Seeks Alliance with Poor Countries to Preserve High Ag Tariffs," *Inside U.S. Trade*, December 2, 2005.

218 The *Bridges Daily Update* report about the diminution of complaints about inclusiveness and transparency was published in the December 14, 2005, issue.

219 The isolation of the European Union and Switzerland on the issue of export subsidies was reported by *Bridges Daily Update* in the December 15, 2005, issue.

219 Information about the riots on the final night in Hong Kong can be found in Philip P. Pan and Paul Blustein, "Stormy Times at Trade Talks," *Washington Post*, December 18, 2005.

221 Guy de Jonquieres's memorable lead came in his article, "Tentative Steps Forward Seen as Better Than None at All," *Financial Times*, December 19, 2005.

221 The Hong Kong ministerial text can be found on the WTO website at http://www.wto.org/english/thewto_e/minist_e/min05_e/final_text_e.htm.

## CHAPTER 11: WHEN PETER MET SUSAN

224 Lamy's warning against postponing a deal on modalities until later in 2006 can be found in Daniel Pruzin, "WTO's Lamy Stresses April Deadline's Important, Says Delay Is 'Recipe for Disaster,'" *WTO Reporter*, March 29, 2006.

225 Bush's statement "Now she will use her experience . . ." can be found in the *Weekly Compilation of Presidential Documents* for the week of April 24, 2006.

225 Grassley's statement that Portman's departure was "bad news" for the Doha talks can be found in Gary G. Yerkey, "President Nominates Schwab as New USTR to Replace Portman, Who Will Move to OMB," *WTO Reporter*, April 19, 2006.

225 Mandelson's statement, "We will, of course, manage without him . . ." can be found in Paul Blustein, "Hopes for Trade Talks Dim After Personnel Switch," *Washington Post*, April 19, 2006.

225–227 Information on Schwab comes from Bruce Stokes, "Employing Tough Talk, Schwab Builds Consensus on Trade," *National Journal*, August 31, 1985; Eric Pianin, "Enforcer Behind the Trade Bill; Economist Schwab Wants the U.S. to Get Tough and Get Reciprocity," *Washington Post*, July 24, 1987; Paul Blustein, "Dealt a Difficult Hand, Trade Official Presses On," *Washington Post*, June 13, 2006; Evan Clark, "Bush Trade Chief

Schwab: Persistent, Persuasive and Pragmatic," *WWD* (*Women's Wear Daily*), July 21, 2006; Nina Easton, "Can This Woman Save Free Trade?" *Fortune*, September 26, 2007, where her comments about her efforts to save her late husband can be found; and Susan C. Schwab, "Diplomacy over Drama," as told to Patricia R. Olsen, *New York Times*, September 28, 2008, where her comments about him after his death can be found.

227–228 Schwab's comment that Doha Lite "would waste a once-in-a-lifetime opportunity" can be found in Paul Blustein, "Dealt a Difficult Hand, Trade Official Presses On," *Washington Post*, June 13, 2006.

228 Grassley's admonition that he would reject a "Plan B . . . minimalist approach" came at Schwab's Senate confirmation hearing on May 16, 2006. A transcript of the hearing was prepared by Federal News Service.

228 Information about the farm groups' letter can be found in "Lamy Sets June Meeting, Ag Groups Warn Against More U.S. Concessions," *Inside U.S. Trade*, June 2, 2006. A copy of the letter accompanied the article.

229–231 The comments of participants in the G-6 meeting come from notes furnished by confidential sources.

231 Lamy's comments at the postmeeting press conference, "There has been no progress, and therefore we are in a crisis . . ." can be found in Paul Blustein, "Trade Ministers Give Up on Compromise," *Washington Post*, July 2, 2006.

231 Schwab's comment "Isn't that what leadership is all about?" can be found in Paul Blustein, "Trade Deal Looks More Like a Distant Dream," *Washington Post*, July 4, 2006.

232 The St. Petersburg G-8 communiqué on trade is on the web at http://en.g8russia.ru/docs/16.html.

232–234 The remarks of participants at the July 23 G-6 meeting come from notes furnished by confidential sources.

234 Lamy's comment that "there are no winners . . ." can be found in Alan Beattie, "WTO Faces an Uncertain Future as Its Negotiating System Seizes Up," *Financial Times*, July 25, 2006.

234 Schwab's remark about Mandelson, that "he didn't want to talk," can be found in Paul Blustein, "U.S. Not Giving Up on Failed WTO Negotiations," *Washington Post*, July 27, 2006.

235–238 The story about Danubia Rodriguez is drawn largely from Paul Blustein, "Banking on Openness and Proximity to U.S.," *Washington Post*, November 17, 2004, and an accompanying article, by Paul Blustein and Peter S. Goodman, "A New Pattern Is Cut for Global Textile Trade; China Likely to Dominate as Quotas Expire," *Washington Post*, November 17, 2004.

237 Additional information about developing countries' manufacturing sectors' sufferings from Chinese competition, including the job losses in Turkey's textile sector, can be found in Helen Murphy, Christopher Swann, and Mark Drajem, "China's Power Erodes Free-Trade Support in Developing Nations," Bloomberg News, April 2, 2007.

239–241 Information about China's alleged currency manipulation, including details about Shanghai Datong and E&E Manufacturing, comes from Paul Blustein and Peter S. Goodman, "China's Export Engine; International Competitors Crying Foul over Cheap Currency," *Washington Post*, September 13, 2006.

241 Information about Lamy's "soft re-launch" of the round can be found in Daniel Pruzin, "WTO Chief Lamy Announces 'Soft' Restart to Doha Round Talks," *WTO Reporter*, November 17, 2006.

244–245 The remarks of participants in the Potsdam G-4 meeting come from notes furnished by a confidential source.

244 Information about Brazil's hike in tariffs on apparel and footwear, and the reasons for it, can be found in U.S. Department of Agriculture GAIN (Global Agriculture Information Network) report BR7621, on the web at http://www.fas.usda.gov/gainfiles/

200705/146281089.pdf; and Hong Kong Trade Development Council, "Business Alert-US," issue 10, May 10, 2007, on the web at http://info.hktdc.com/alert/us0710g.htm.

245 Amorim's comments to Brazilian journalists after the Potsdam meeting can be found in "Brazil's Amorim Accuses US, EU of Making Prior Agreement," *Valor Econômico*, June 22, 2007 (translated from Portuguese).

246 Figures on growth in global trade since 1998 can be found on the WTO website at http://www.wto.org/english/news_e/pres09_e/pr554_e.htm.

## CHAPTER 12: EVEN THE LOOPHOLES HAVE GOT LOOPHOLES

248 Quotations from ministers at the World Economic Forum meeting in early 2008 can be found in Sean O'Grady, "Mandelson in Call to Rescue World Trade Talks," *Independent*, January 28, 2008; and Patrick Baert, "WTO Ministers Hope for April Breakthrough," Agence France-Presse, January 26, 2008.

249 Falconer's comments at his July 17, 2007, press conference can be found on the WTO website at http://www.wto.org/english/news_e/news07_e/news07_e.htm. His text can be found at http://www.wto.org/english/tratop_e/agric_e/chair_texts07_e.htm.

251 Stephenson's quotations from the July 17, 2007, press conference can also be found on the WTO website at http://www.wto.org/english/news_e/news07_e/news07_e.htm.

251–253 Information about the evolution of the agriculture text can be found on the WTO website at http://www.wto.org/english/tratop_e/agric_e/negoti_e.htm, and information about the evolution of the NAMA texts can be found at http://www.wto.org/english/tratop_e/markacc_e/markacc_chair_texts07_e.htm. Further information about both texts, and the reaction to them, can be found in the following articles in *WTO Reporter*, all authored by Daniel Pruzin: "WTO Chairmen Issue Draft Ag, NAMA Texts Outlining Tough Concessions Needed in Doha," July 18, 2007; "U.S. Criticizes Draft NAMA Text, Refutes Developing Nations' Arguments on Tariffs," July 26, 2007; "WTO Ag, NAMA Chairs Issue Revised Negotiating Texts with Few Surprises," February 11, 2008; "U.S. Business Groups Say Sectorals Key to Doha Round Industrial Tariffs Deal," April 17, 2008; "WTO Agriculture, NAMA Chairmen Issue Revised Draft Texts, New NAMA Coefficients," May 20, 2008; and "Doha Chairs Issue Final Revised Draft Texts on NAMA and Agriculture with Few Changes," July 11, 2008.

251 Glauber's statement that the U.S. could accept the subsidy figures in Falconer's text "as a basis for negotiation" can be found in Daniel Pruzin, "Trade Officials Welcome U.S. Signal of Flexibility on Farm Tariff Reductions," *WTO Reporter*, September 20, 2007.

251–252 Stephenson's "suck and blow at the same time" comment can be found in Daniel Pruzin, "Chair Admits 'Desperation' with NAMA Talks, Pins Hope on Progress in Agriculture," *WTO Reporter*, May 21, 2008.

252–253 Allgeier's comment about "no additional market access" can be found in "Longstanding Differences Resurface in Talks on NAMA Text," *Bridges Weekly Trade News Digest*, May 28, 2008.

253–255 Information on the food crisis and the implications for trade policy can be found in Matthew Benjamin and Mark Drajem, "Global Import Barriers Fall as Food Prices Trump Doha," Bloomberg News, April 14, 2008; "High Food Prices Leave Developing Countries Struggling to Cope," *Bridges Weekly Trade News Digest*, April 23, 2008; Alan Beattie, "Making Hay," *Financial Times*, May 14, 2008; "The Doha Dilemma," *Economist*, May 29, 2008; "The Right Time to Chop," *Economist*, May 1, 2008; Keith Bradsher and Andrew Martin, "Hoarding Nations Drive Food Costs Ever Higher," *New York Times*, June 30, 2008; and Joachim von Braun, "Rising World Food Prices: How to Address the Problem," *Bridges*, May 2008.

254 The figure on U.S. farm subsidy spending in 2007 can be found in "U.S. Notifies Overall Agriculture Subsidies Below Doha Round Limits," *Inside U.S. Trade*, February 6, 2009.

254 Von Braun's coinage of the term "starve your neighbor policies" is cited in Jo Chandler, "The Changing Face of Hunger," *The Age* (Melbourne, Australia), April 19, 2008.

255 Birdsall and Subramanian's proposal can be found on the website of the Center for Global Development at http://blogs.cgdev.org/globaldevelopment/2008/04/trade-policy-for-a-new-deal-on.php.

255 Lamy's comments "With dark clouds on the economic horizon every day" and "I know that this is not without its risks" can be found on the WTO website at http://www.wto.org/english/news_e/news08_e/tnc_dg_stat_june08_e.htm.

256 Information about the repeated postponements in ministerials comes from Daniel Pruzin, "Lamy Admits No Chance of Doha Breakthrough Before End of Year," *WTO Reporter*, November 23, 2007; Pruzin, "WTO Members Set for Ministerial Meeting on Doha by Mid-April, Despite Misgivings," *WTO Reporter*, February 14, 2008; Gary G. Yerkey, "Ministerial Being Planned for Week of May 19 to Advance WTO Trade Talks," *WTO Reporter*, April 8, 2008; and Pruzin, "WTO Chief Lamy Says Ministerial 'Premature' as Members Prepare for Critical NAMA Week," *WTO Reporter*, June 16, 2008.

257 The World Bank analysis of the July deal is Will Martin and Additya Mattoo, "The Doha Development Agenda: What's on the Table?" World Bank Policy Research working paper 4672, July 2008.

257–258 Messerlin's analysis is titled "Walking a Tightrope: World Trade in Manufacturing and the Benefits of Binding," policy brief, German Marshall Fund of the United States, June 2008, on the web at http://www.gmfus.org//doc/GMF_Messerlin-Brief_NAMA_Final.pdf.

258 One of Lamy's op-eds citing the "insurance" value of a deal is "Striking a Deal at Trade Talks Would Create Needed Momentum," *Edmonton (Alberta) Journal*, July 4, 2008.

## CHAPTER 13: LOSING IT

262 The Oxfam "gambling" stunt is described in Alan Beattie, "Ministers Go Shopping to Escape Doha Tedium," *Financial Times*, July 26, 2008.

262 Amy Barry's comment can be found in Laura MacInnis, "WTO Protesters Absent During Geneva Talks," Reuters News Service, July 24, 2008.

263–275 Remarks made by participants in private meetings, starting with Chen's joke "If we are an elephant, maybe the U.S. is a dinosaur" and including all the comments made in WTO Secretariat meetings, G-7 meetings, the meeting of American lobbyists, and the green room, come from notes of the meetings furnished by confidential sources. The only exceptions, which were recounted in interviews by sources who recalled the incidents vividly, were Amari's outburst, "Mr. Lamy, I am a minister in the Japanese government . . . ," and Schwab's, "I'm not getting fucking trapped into this, Pascal!"

268 Rockwell's comments to the press on July 25, 2008, concerning "some very encouraging signs of progress" and "overwhelming support" for the Lamy paper come from my own notes of his remarks. Schwab's comments to the press concerning the "handful of large emerging markets" can be found in Daniel Pruzin, "Key WTO Members Close in on Doha Breakthrough, but India, Argentina Raise Objections in Talks," *WTO Reporter*, July 28, 2008.

274 Shark's statement in the General Council was circulated to journalists at the meeting, including me.

274 The anonymous comment about China wanting "a seat at the big kids' table" can be found in Stephen Castle, "Bananas a Stumbling Block as World Trade Talks Edge Toward Resolution," *International Herald Tribune*, July 28, 2008.

275 Amorim's comments to the press were witnessed by me, and I am grateful to his office for sending me a verbatim transcript.

## CHAPTER 14: IF ONLY THERE WERE A BETTER WAY

277 Information about the "subsidy war" in dairy products comes from Josh Gordon, "U.S. 'Kick in Guts' to Dairy Farmers," *The Age* (Australia), May 24, 2009; and Brian Scheid, "U.S. Revival of Dairy Subsidies Sparks Global Outrage, but Effect Minimal," *Inside U.S. Trade*, May 29, 2009.

278 Patrick Low's comment that trade rounds are "a terrible way to do business" came at a March 25, 2009, conference titled The Next Frontier: Rethinking the Global Trading System, at the House of Sweden in Washington, attended by the author.

278 David Brooks's reference to "globosclerosis" came in a column he authored titled "Missing Dean Acheson" in the *New York Times* on August 1, 2008.

279–280 Information about Lamy's failed effort to convene a ministerial meeting in December 2008 can be found in "Lamy Leaning Towards Calling Mid-December Mini-Ministerial," *Bridges Weekly Trade Digest*, December 3, 2008; Jamie Strawbridge, "Hopes for Doha Ministerial Fade as Lamy Consultations Stall," *Inside U.S. Trade*, December 12, 2008; "Planned WTO Mini-Ministerial Postponed as Prospects for Doha Deal Diminish," *Bridges Weekly Trade Digest*, December 10, 2008; Alan Beattie and Frances Williams, "WTO Chief Drops Plans to Press Ministers for Outline Doha Deal," *Financial Times,* December 13, 2008; and Daniel Pruzin, "WTO's Lamy Calls Off Doha Ministerial; Deal Up to Obama Team, U.S. Official Says," *WTO Reporter*, December 15, 2008.

281 Zedillo's quotation, that the relevant question is "how can the WTO be saved from the Doha Round?" can be found in his article, "Save the WTO from the Doha Round," *Forbes*, May 9, 2007.

285 The various proposals concerning what to do about the Doha Round come from discussions at conferences held in Washington and attended by the author during the spring of 2009. An example of the coalition-of-the-willing argument is Charlene Barshefsky, "Trading Up to Global Recovery," *Washington Post*, March 10, 2009.

285–286 Mattoo and Subramanian's *Foreign Affairs* article, titled "From Doha to the Next Bretton Woods," appeared in the January–February 2009 issue.

287 Information about Kirk's proposal to skip the modalities step can be found in "Kirk's Geneva Visit Signals U.S. Engagement on Doha," *Bridges Weekly Trade Digest*, May 13, 2009.

288 Information about previous instances in which trade experts thought future rounds unlikely can be found in Ernest H. Preeg, *Traders in a Brave New World*, p. 27. For a compelling presentation of the argument that Doha will be the last major round, see Daniel K. Tarullo, "The End of the Big Trade Deal," *International Economy*, Summer 2006.

288 Two major commissions in recent years have examined proposals for reforming the WTO's negotiation process (as well as other issues) and have made recommendations. One, chaired by former WTO director-general Peter Sutherland, issued a report that is formally titled *Report of the Consultative Board to the Director-General Supachai Panitchpakdi on the Future of the WTO: Addressing Institutional Challenges in the New Millennium* (Geneva: WTO, 2004). The second, known as the Warwick commission and chaired by former Canadian trade minister Pierre Pettigrew, issued a report formally titled "The Multilateral Trade Regime: Which Way Forward?" (Coventry: University of Warwick, 2007).

291 Information on the bilateral and regional trade agreements negotiated by the United States can be found on the website of the Office of the U.S. Trade Representative at http://ustr.gov/Trade_Agreements/Section_Index.html.

292 The calculation of the percentage of U.S. exports going to countries with whom the Bush administration struck bilateral and regional trade agreements was performed by the author using data from the website of the Bureau of Economic Analysis, U.S.

Department of Commerce. The data on U.S. exports to individual countries can be found at http://bea.gov/newsreleases/international/trade/2008/pdf/trad1308.pdf.

293 A wealth of information about bilateral and regional agreements around the world can be found on the websites http://bilaterals.org and http://ptas.mcgill.ca, as well as on the WTO's website at http://rtais.wto.org/UI/PublicMaintainRTAHome.aspx.

293 Bhagwati's book is *Termites in the Trading System: How Preferential Agreements Undermine Free Trade* (New York: Oxford University Press, 2008).

293 Information about the spate of bilateral negotiations following the July 2008 meeting can be found in "A Second-Best Choice" and "After Doha," *Economist*, September 4, 2008; Patricia Kowsmann and P. R. Venkat, "Asia Seeks Its Own Trade Deals as Global Talks Stall," *Wall Street Journal*, August 29, 2008; and Bernard K. Gordon, "Bilateral Trade-Off," *Wall Street Journal Asia*, September 5, 2008.

293 Rudd's quotation alleging the "whittling away" of multilateralism by his predecessor's government can be found in Dennis Shanahan and Patricia Karvelas, "Labor to Pursue Bilateral FTAs," *The Australian*, August 13, 2008.

293 The *Globe and Mail* editorial, titled "Seeking a Trade Deal," was published on July 31, 2008.

295 The quotation ". . . future crises could be much more disastrous" can be found in Paul Blustein, *The Chastening: Inside the Crisis That Rocked the Global Financial System and Humbled the IMF* (New York: PublicAffairs, 2001), p. 10; and the quotation "boldness is warranted . . ." can be found on page 388. The quotation "It *could* happen here . . ." can be found in Blustein, *And the Money Came Rolling In (And Out): Wall Street, the IMF, and the Bankrupting of Argentina* (New York: PublicAffairs, 2005), p. 234.

# INDEX

Abbott, Roderick, 75
Ackerman, Frank, 214
ACT UP (AIDS Coalition to Unleash Power), 120
Adenauer, Konrad, 23
Afghanistan, 1, 99
AFL-CIO, 59
African Group, 13, 79, 124
African Growth and Opportunity Act, 178, 212–213, 217
Aggarwal, Rajesh, 143
Agriculture. See Doha Round: and agriculture; Duties: and agriculture; European Union (E.U.): and agriculture; Exports: and agriculture; General Agreement on Tariffs and Trade (GATT): and agriculture and textiles; Imports: and agriculture; Lamy, Pascal: and agriculture; Poverty: and agriculture; Protectionism: and agriculture; Quotas: and agriculture; Tariffs: and agriculture; Trade: and agriculture; Trade barriers: and agriculture; World Trade Organization (WTO): and agriculture; Zoellick, Robert: and agriculture; particular countries
AIDS, 103–104, 105–107, 119–121
AIG, 275
Al-Jazeera, 83
Al Qaeda, 1, 99
Albright, Madeleine, 63–64, 73, 74
Aldonas, Grant, 113, 115, 116, 117, 176
Allgeier, Peter, 253, 271
Amari, Akira, 262, 273
Amehou, Samuel, 146, 194
American Airlines plane crash (2001), 5
American Farm Bureau Federation, 54–55, 269
Amorim, Celso, 13
  and Five Interested Parties, 184, 209
  and Free Trade Area of the Americas, 180
  and G-4 meeting (2007), 243, 244, 245
  and G-6 meetings (2006), 230, 231, 234
  and meeting in Brazil (2006), 223
  and WTO meeting in Doha, Qatar (2001), 119, 120
  and WTO ministerial in Cancún, Mexico (2003), 148–149
  and WTO ministerial in Geneva, Switzerland (2008), 262, 264, 265, 267, 268, 273, 275, 283
  and WTO ministerial in Hong Kong (2005), 211, 220, 278
  and Zoellick phone call (2004), 182
Anarchists, 72
Angola, 212
Anthrax, 1, 2, 99
Antidumping
  and Doha Round, 224, 287
  duties, 34, 68, 114
  laws, 27, 114–117
  and WTO meeting in Doha, Qatar (2001), 102, 113–117, 121, 122, 125, 132
  and WTO meeting in Seattle, Washington (1999), 75, 79, 115
  and WTO ministerial in Geneva, Switzerland (2008), 256
Antigua and Barbuda, 165–170, 171, 290
Argentina, 7, 174, 182, 231, 295
  and agriculture, 143, 254, 255, 290
  and antidumping laws, 115
  and dispute settlement, 165
  and Free Trade Area of the Americas, 179

327

Argentina (*continued*)
  and manufactured goods, 239, 258, 273
  and protectionism, 9
  and tariffs, 33, 39, 86
  and trade, 86, 214
  and Uruguay Round, 48
  and WTO meeting in Geneva, Switzerland
    (2004), 196
Armenia, 293
Art and Revolution, 59
Asia Pacific Economic Cooperation forum,
  36–37
Association of Southeast Asian Nations, 174
Australia
  and agriculture, 132, 134, 183, 206, 208, 209
  and bilateral and regional deals, 175,
    176–177, 291, 293
  and Five Interested Parties, 183, 184, 191,
    192, 208, 209, 229
  and G-4 meeting (2007), 243, 246
  and manufactured goods, 258
  and WTO meeting in Geneva, Switzerland
    (2004), 191, 192
  and WTO meeting in Seattle, Washington
    (1999), 68
  and WTO ministerial in Cancún, Mexico
    (2003), 154
  and WTO ministerial in Geneva,
    Switzerland (2008), 262, 264, 267, 275
  and WTO's inner circle of power, 13
Azevedo, Roberto, 170–171
AZT, 104

Bacchus, James, 162–163
Bader, Jeffrey, 2, 92, 130
Bahrain, 175, 291
Bailouts, 9, 10, 255, 275
Baker, James, 88, 89, 91
Baldwin, Matthew, 127
Bale, Harvey, 107, 121
Bananarchy Movement, 72
Bangladesh, 86, 214, 221, 253, 258
Bank of America, 275
Banks, 10, 19, 39, 93, 114, 164, 166, 249,
  259, 275, 276
Barry, Amy, 262
Barshefsky, Charlene, 13, 94
  background of, 66–67
  and China, 39
  and WTO meeting in Seattle, Washington
    (1999), 66, 68, 69, 73, 74, 75, 76, 77, 78,
    79, 80, 81

Baucus, Max, 271
Bear Stearns, 249, 255
Beef, 22, 43, 52, 56, 58, 95, 187, 206, 208,
  209, 226, 242, 254, 269
Belgium, 52
Benedito de Assis, Jorge, 50–51
Benin, 145, 146, 150, 194, 219
Bhagwati, Jagdish, 176–177, 293
Bilateral and regional trade agreements. *See*
  Trade: bilateral and regional deals
Bin Khalifa al-Thani, Sheik Hamad, 83
Bin Laden, Osama, 98
Birdsall, Nancy, 255
Blair, Tony, 200, 201
Blumenfeld, Bob, 167
Bo Xilai, 263
Bolivia, 180, 252
Bolten, Joshua, 224–225
Bombelles, Thomas, 119
Botswana, 18, 153, 154, 293
Boutros-Ghali, Youssef, 112, 154, 184
Braun, Joachim von, 254
Brazil, 81, 174, 211
  and agriculture, 50–51, 132, 142–143, 148,
    149, 157–158, 160–162, 170–171, 181,
    187, 205, 209, 230, 231, 267
  and AIDS drugs, 104, 106, 107, 119
  and dispute settlement, 165, 167, 169,
    170–171, 279, 290
  and Five Interested Parties, 183, 184, 191,
    192, 208, 209, 229
  and Free Trade Area of the Americas,
    179–180
  and G-4 meeting (2007), 243, 244, 245,
    246
  and GATT, 29, 149
  increasing influence of, 15
  and manufactured goods, 239, 244, 253,
    258, 270
  meeting in Rio de Janeiro (2006), 223
  as party to Doha Round's problems, 283
  and tariffs, 33, 39, 171, 211, 290
  and trade, 214, 217
  and WTO meeting in Doha, Qatar (2001),
    96, 107, 119, 120, 121, 126
  and WTO meeting in Geneva, Switzerland
    (2004), 191, 192
  and WTO ministerial in Cancún, Mexico
    (2003), 147, 148, 149–150, 174
  and WTO ministerial in Geneva,
    Switzerland (2008), 262, 267, 270,
    275

and WTO ministerial in Hong Kong (2005), 220
and WTO's inner circle of power, 13
*Bridges Daily Update* (newspaper), 117, 152, 218
Brittan, Sir Leon, 33–34, 35, 65, 67, 76, 94
Brooks, David, 278
Brunei, 293
Bulgaria, 175
Burkina Faso, 145, 146, 150, 167, 253
Burma, 86
Bush, George H. W., 88, 91, 161, 202, 226
Bush, George W., 131, 202, 265
  and agriculture, 134, 135, 145, 204
  and AIDS drugs, 106
  and Doha Round, 182, 225
  and Hubbard, 204
  and Portman, 202, 225, 227, 282–283
  and Schwab, 225
  and trade, 6, 10, 91, 134, 173, 177, 178–179, 204, 248, 266, 291
  and WTO meeting in Doha, Qatar (2001), 100
  and Zoellick, 88, 89, 91–92
Business representatives, 109

Camargo Neto, Pedro de, 160–161
Cameron, Don, 161–162
Cameroon, 217, 253
Camilo, Federico Cuello, 74
Canada, 4, 61, 79, 128, 227, 264
  and agriculture, 195–196
  and beef, 43
  and bilateral and regional deals, 174, 179, 293
  and dispute settlement, 160
  and Doha Round, 250–251
  and GATT, 29, 182
  and Messerlin analysis, 258
  and NAFTA, 36, 176
  and Quad, 13, 29, 182, 183
  and Smoot-Hawley, 24
  U.S. free-trade agreement with (1988), 30
  and WTO meeting in Geneva, Switzerland (2004), 195–196, 197
  and WTO's inner circle of power, 13
Canadian Wheat Board, 195, 197
Cancún, Mexico. *See* World Trade Organization (WTO): ministerial in Cancún, Mexico (2003)
Carl, Peter, 141
Carroll, Curtis, 226–227

Central American Free Trade Agreement, 238
Chad, 146, 150
Chambliss, Saxby, 270
Chandrasekhar, K. M., 142–143
Charles, Prince, 53, 200
Charveriat, Celine, 198, 206, 208
Chávez, Hugo, 294
Chen Deming, 263, 265
Cheney, Richard, 2, 100
*Chicago Tribune* (newspaper), 4, 44
Chile
  and bilateral and regional deals, 174, 175, 177, 179, 291, 293
  and dispute settlement, 165
  and living standards, 42
  and WTO meeting in Doha, Qatar (2001), 115, 116, 117
China, 5, 92, 182, 189
  and agriculture, 143, 187, 254, 272
  and Asia Pacific Economic Cooperation forum, 37
  and bilateral and regional deals, 177, 293
  and climate change, 11–12
  and currency, 239–241, 286, 289
  and dispute settlement, 160, 279
  and dumping complaints, 115
  emerging market in, 206
  as export powerhouse, 15, 236, 240
  fear of, 15
  and joining WTO, 38–39, 216, 271–272
  and living standards, 42
  and manufactured goods, 214, 236, 237, 238, 239–241, 244, 245, 252, 253, 270, 272, 279–280
  and Messerlin analysis, 258
  as party to Doha Round's problems, 283–284
  and tariffs, 39, 216, 271
  and trade, 84, 86, 87, 196, 214, 216, 217, 271–272, 284
  and workers, 45, 46
  and WTO meeting in Geneva, Switzerland (2004), 196
  and WTO ministerial in Geneva, Switzerland (2008), 263, 264, 265, 268, 270, 271–272, 274, 275
  and WTO's inner circle of power, 13
  *See also* Exports: Chinese
Chirac, Jacques, 53, 207, 209
Christie, Agatha, 282
Chrysler, 9

Churchill, Winston, 221, 243
CIA, 108
Civil War, U.S., 133
Climate change, 11–12, 14, 131–132, 278, 281, 286, 290
Clinton, William J. "Bill," 30, 279
  and Barshefsky, 67
  and films, 35
  and NAFTA, 64, 89
  and Summit of the Americas and Asia Pacific Economic Cooperation forum, 36
  trade record of, 64, 175
  and WTO meeting in Geneva (1998), 41, 46
  and WTO meeting in Seattle, Washington (1999), 41, 57, 64, 65, 74, 75–76, 77, 79
Clinton Round, 64, 65
Cohen, Jay, 165–167, 168
Cold War, 26, 85, 284
Cole, U.S.S., bombing (2000), 5
Colombia, 175, 180, 227, 291, 292, 294
Combest, Larry, 134
Commerce Department, U.S., 114–115, 116, 226
Common Agricultural Policy (CAP), 52, 139, 208, 210
Compaore, Blaise, 146
Conrad, Kent, 162
Costa Rica, 77, 172, 175, 179
Cotton, 26–27, 46, 48, 112
  and Brazil, 157–158, 160–162, 170–171, 181
  Upland case, 158, 160–162, 163, 165, 167, 169, 170–171
  U.S. farmers of, 50, 145, 151, 152, 157–158, 181, 205, 237, 272 (see also Cotton: Upland case)
  and western African countries, 145–147, 150–152
  and WTO meeting in Geneva, Switzerland (2004), 191, 194, 198
  and WTO ministerial in Cancún, Mexico (2003), 154, 155, 156, 282
  and WTO ministerial in Geneva, Switzerland (2008), 270, 272, 273
  and WTO ministerial in Hong Kong (2005), 219
  and Zambia, 49, 50, 214
Cotton Four, 151, 152
Countrywide Financial, 249
Crean, Simon, 262, 267, 273
Credit Lyonnais, 93

Cretin, Olivier, 51–52, 53
Crosbie, John, 31
Cross-retaliation, 169–170, 171
Cuba, 23, 25
Currency manipulation, 240, 281, 289–290

Da Silva, Luiz Inácio Lula, 149–150, 179
Danforth, John, 226
De Cecco pasta, 114, 115
De Mateo, Fernando, 276
Delors, Jacques, 93
Demarty, Jean-Luc, 274–275
DeMint, Jim, 137
Democratic Republic of the Congo, 212
Denmark, 53
Derbez, Luis Ernesto, 120, 140, 150, 151, 153, 154, 155
Development. See World Trade Organization (WTO): and development
Development Round, 64, 65, 88, 96, 130, 156, 213, 265
Dillon, Douglas, 65
Direct Action Network (DAN), 59–60, 70, 72
"Dirty deals," 242
Doctors Without Borders, 104, 120
Doha, Qatar. See World Trade Organization (WTO): meeting in Doha, Qatar (2001)
Doha Declaration, 131, 132, 142
Doha Development Agenda, 6, 129, 181, 182, 196, 211, 216
Doha Round
  and acrimony, 8, 14
  and agriculture, 134–135, 138, 139, 140, 142, 145, 146, 148, 151, 152, 160, 171, 186–187, 190, 192, 193, 194, 195, 204–205, 207, 209, 210, 215, 217, 224, 228, 232–234, 235, 249, 250, 251, 254, 255, 256, 257, 269, 272, 283, 285
  ambition of, 256–257
  and Bush administration's lame-duck status, 248
  and China, 15, 241, 271
  and congressional vote, 229
  deadline for completing, 131, 199
  disillusionment over, 11
  and Doha Lite, 207, 215, 227, 257
  downward spiral of, 203
  and export subsidies, 184
  and food prices, 254, 255
  and Foreign Affairs article, 285–286
  in future, 277, 278, 281, 285, 286–287, 288

and G-4 meeting (2007), 243, 246
and globalization, 15
and *Groundhog Day,* 247–248
and individual failings, 14
Lamy report on, 18
in late 2008, 279–280
launching of, 6, 12, 183, 292
loss of momentum in, 138, 173, 204, 211
and Mandelson, 242
and manufactured goods, 235, 238, 244,
  252, 253, 257 (*see also* NAMA)
and meeting in Brazil (2006), 223
and Messerlin analysis, 258–259
as mistake, 281–282
and modalities, 132–133, 138, 193, 198,
  203–204, 211, 221, 224, 228–229, 232,
  241, 247, 248, 255, 256, 259, 265, 279,
  287
parties complicit in its afflictions, 282–284
and poverty, 215, 282
and protectionism, 10, 279, 287
rationale for, 7
re-launch of, 241
and Schwab, 225, 227–228
and slashing tariffs, 216
suspension and impasse in, 234–235, 278,
  280, 291, 293
2.0, 249–253
and World War II event, 243
and WTO meeting in Geneva, Switzerland
  (2004), 183, 190–192, 193, 197, 198
and WTO ministerial in Geneva,
  Switzerland (2008), 261, 264–265, 268,
  269, 274
and WTO ministerial in Hong Kong
  (2005), 218, 221, 222
and Zambia, 213
and Zoellick letter (2004), 180–182
Doha Work Programme, 153
Dolan, Michael, 59–60, 73
Dollar, David, 85–87, 88
Dolphins, 43–44, 58
Dominican Republic, 67, 74, 175, 291
Doux (French company), 53
Dunkel, Arthur, 28, 32
Duties
  and agriculture, 55, 56, 139–140, 187, 188,
    193, 205, 206, 208, 210, 233, 254, 257,
    267, 272
  and bilateral and regional deals, 177, 291,
    292
  and dispute resolution, 159

and E.U. market, 123
on exports from poorest countries,
  132–133, 221
and GATT, 27
and Kantor and Brittan's negotiations in
  Geneva (1993), 34
and manufactured goods, 238, 239, 244,
  252, 257
and national treatment, 25
and Smoot-Hawley, 23–24
and Uruguay Round, 47–48, 49
*See also* Antidumping: duties

Economic stimulus (2009), 9
*Economist* (magazine), 235
Ecuador, 123, 180
EFTA-SACU agreement, 293
Eggs, 24
Egypt, 67, 81, 112, 154, 184
  and food prices, 253, 254
  and GATT, 27
  increasing influence of, 15
  and manufactured goods, 239, 258
  and WTO Appellate Body, 163
El Salvador, 175, 237
Elizabeth, Queen, 53
Environment. *See* European Union (E.U.):
  and environment; Trade: and
  environment; World Trade Organization
  (WTO): and environment
Environmentalists, 58, 59, 110
Erwin, Alec, 126, 140, 150
Estonia, 293
European Commission, 33, 93
European Community, 27, 29, 93
European Free Trade Association, 293
European Union (E.U.), 63, 133
  and agriculture, 52, 53, 78, 79, 80–81, 102,
    122, 123, 126, 132, 134, 139–140,
    141–144, 148, 156, 162, 181, 187, 203,
    205, 207–210, 218, 219, 230, 233, 234,
    242–243, 245, 283
  and beef, 43, 95, 187, 242
  and bilateral and regional deals, 174, 176,
    178, 179, 293
  and dispute settlement, 160, 162, 168
  and duties, 123
  and environment, 95, 96, 102, 122, 125
  and export subsidies, 184, 218, 219, 220,
    277
  and Five Interested Parties, 183, 191, 192,
    208, 209, 229

European Union (E.U.) (*continued*)
and G-4 meeting (2007), 243, 244, 245
and GATT, 29, 182
and genetically engineered crops, 10
and import quotas, 242
and Lamy, 94, 95, 211
and Messerlin analysis, 258
as party to Doha Round's problems, 283
and power in WTO, 13, 20, 147
and Quad, 13, 29, 182, 183
and Singapore issues, 94–95, 153, 156, 184
and steel, 134, 159, 168
and transatlantic conference call (2003), 141
and TRIPS, 107, 118
and Uruguay Round, 48
and WTO meeting in Doha, Qatar (2001),
    122, 123, 124, 125, 127, 130
and WTO meeting in Geneva, Switzerland
    (2004), 191, 192, 196
and WTO meeting in Seattle, Washington
    (1999), 75, 78, 79, 80–81
and WTO mini-ministerial in Montreal
    (2003), 139, 140
and WTO ministerial in Cancún, Mexico
    (2003), 147, 148, 153, 155, 156
and WTO ministerial in Geneva,
    Switzerland (2008), 262, 265, 269, 274
and WTO ministerial in Hong Kong
    (2005), 218, 219, 220
and Zambia, 212–213
Evans, Donald, 176
Exports
and agriculture, 32, 54, 55, 68, 78, 94, 102,
    122, 126, 142, 143, 144, 145, 148, 151,
    181, 183, 187, 193, 195, 196, 206, 210,
    214, 218, 230–231, 233, 242, 251, 254,
    255, 269, 272, 277, 285, 290
Antiguan, 170
Argentine, 179, 196, 214, 254, 290
Brazilian, 143, 214, 217
Chinese, 38–39, 214, 217, 236, 237,
    239–241, 271, 284
and currency, 289
and GATT, 26, 29
and globalization, 86
growth of, 42
Honduran, 235
Indian, 112
Japanese, 30, 138
Korean, 87
and manufactured goods, 235, 239–241,
    258

Mexican, 216
from poorest countries, 132–133, 221
and restraints, 30, 34
and sensitive and special products
    loopholes, 227, 230, 242
and subsidies, 26, 33, 55, 87, 102, 122,
    126, 142, 144, 148, 161, 181, 184, 193,
    195, 196, 218–220, 221, 222, 228, 231,
    233, 251, 269, 277
and Trade Act (1988), 30
and trade theory and WTO course, 20–21,
    22
and Uruguay Round, 48, 49
U.S., 24, 159, 160, 171, 176, 210, 226, 227,
    228, 233, 242, 269, 280, 283, 287, 291,
    292
and Zambia, 212–213, 221

Falconer, Crawford, 249–250, 251, 255, 256,
    257, 264
Fannie Mae, 93, 259, 275
FBI, 70
Federal Reserve, U.S., 3, 24, 276
Financial crisis, 7, 8, 277, 278, 284, 290, 295
*Financial Times* (newspaper), 3, 42, 174, 181,
    205, 206, 221
Finta Danish Dairies, 212, 221
Fischler, Franz, 126, 139, 184
Fisher, Richard, 81
Five Interested Parties, 13, 183, 184, 185,
    186, 187, 211
and G-6 meeting (2006), 229
and Mandelson, 208, 209
and WTO meeting in Geneva, Switzerland
    (2004), 191, 192, 193
Fleet Antiterrorism Security Teams (FAST),
    4–5
Flynn, Val, 121
Food Corporation of India, 189
Food crisis, 14, 253–255, 257, 275, 278, 281,
    285, 287, 290
Food safety, 19, 43, 58, 59, 125, 139
*Foreign Affairs* (journal), 89, 285
Fortier, Michael, 293, 294
*Fortune* (magazine), 226
France, 182
and agriculture, 51–53, 122, 126, 139, 145,
    207, 208–209
and car manufacturers, 9
and Doha Round, 184, 283
and Lamy, 93, 211
and trade blocs, 24

and WTO meeting in Doha, Qatar (2001), 122

and WTO ministerial in Hong Kong (2005), 222

Fraser, Simon, 242

Freddie Mac, 259, 275

Free Trade. *See* Free-trade agreements; Trade: benefits of; Trade: skepticism of benefits of free; United States: and free trade; World Bank: and trade: completely free

Free-trade agreements, 11, 30, 36–37, 90, 174–178, 179, 180, 227, 286, 288, 291

*See also* particular free-trade agreements

Free Trade Area of the Americas, 90, 175, 178–180, 182

G-4, 13, 243–246, 249, 262

G-6, 13, 229–231, 232–234, 243, 249, 262

G-7, 13, 89, 93, 262, 263, 264, 267, 268, 269, 271, 273, 274

G-8, 232

G-20, 13, 183, 208, 279
  formation and momentum of, 143, 144
  2008 summit of, 9
  and U.S. farm subsidies, 229–230, 231
  and WTO ministerial in Cancún, Mexico (2003), 147–150, 156, 182, 283
  and WTO ministerial in Geneva, Switzerland (2008), 264, 267
  and WTO ministerial in Hong Kong (2005), 220

G-33, 13, 230

G-77, 27, 112, 147

G-90, 153

Gamble, Geoffrey, 109–110

*Gambling* case, 165–170, 171

Gandhi, Indira, 23, 185–186

Gandhi, Sanjay, 186

Gap (company), 44

Garnaut, Ross, 176–177

General Agreement on Tariffs and Trade (GATT), 37, 78, 116, 149, 205, 210
  and agriculture and textiles, 27, 33
  and consensus, 26, 30
  death of, 30–31, 36
  and dispute settlement, 29–30, 159, 164, 172
  and dolphins, 44
  and free-trade agreements, 176
  goals of, 25–26
  and "Greta Garbo policy" of developing countries, 27–28
  and import restrictions, 26–27
  and Jackson, 31
  and Kantor and Brittan's negotiations in Geneva (1993), 34
  and Quad, 29, 182
  Secretariat, 25, 28–29, 31
  signing of (1948), 25
  and tariffs, 26, 27, 29, 30, 33
  and Trade Act (1988), 30
  U.S. and European dominance of, 29, 140

General Motors, 9

Germany, 24, 89, 163, 231, 243
  *See also* Potsdam, Germany

Gettysburg, Battle of, 133

Gilmartin, Raymond, 119

Glauber, Joseph, 151, 242–243, 251, 271

Global Trade Watch, 58, 214

Global warming, 125
  *See also* Climate change

Globalization
  anti, 1, 10, 44, 85
  backlash to, 39
  and bilateral and regional deals, 176
  and dispute settlement, 162
  and economic growth, 86
  and *Economist* magazine, 235
  financial side of, 7, 278
  giving and taking by, 284
  irregularity of, 7
  and labor and environment, 45
  and limits, 15, 288
  and living standards, 12
  and manufactured goods, 235, 236, 238
  protesters, 1, 10, 44
  and Singapore issues, 65
  and trade, 7, 86, 87
  and WTO meeting in Doha, Qatar (2001), 3, 4
  and WTO's creation, 36, 38

Globalize This! Action Camp, 57, 70

Globosclerosis, 278, 284

González, Anabel, 77

González, Arancha, 155

Gorbachev, Mikhail, 91

Gore, Albert, 64, 76, 106, 202

Gosper, Bruce, 264

Gramm, Phil, 91

*Grapes of Wrath* (movie), 149

Grassley, Charles, 225, 228

Great Britain, 46, 243

Great Depression, 8, 23, 24, 276

Greece, 53

Green rooms, 28–29, 75, 78, 79, 122, 124–127, 138, 150, 153–155, 192, 194, 195, 197, 218, 219–220, 228–229, 262, 263, 268, 275
Greencore, 52
Greenhouse gases, 11, 286
Greens and green movement, 42, 47, 56, 82, 95, 96, 125
Greenspan, Alan, 3
Groser, Tim, 192–193, 194, 196, 197
Groundhog Day (movie), 247, 248
Guatemala, 45, 175, 293
Guevara, Che, 23
Gulati, Ashok, 190

Hafemeister, Jason, 92, 135
Haiti, 87, 253
Harbinson, Stuart, 101, 102, 103, 113, 115, 116, 122, 126, 127, 138
Hatakeyama, Noboru, 177
Hathaway, Dale, 55, 56
Hayes, Rita, 62
He Fan, 241
Herzfeld, Shannon, 117–118, 120
Hillman, Jennifer, 279–280, 281, 290
Hiranuma, Takeo, 117, 128
HIV/AIDS, 104, 105, 107, 119, 120
Holmer, Alan, 120
Home loans and prices, 7, 255
Honduras, 123, 175, 235–238
Hong Kong, 32, 42, 46, 101
   See also World Trade Organization (WTO): ministerial in Hong Kong (2005)
Hood, Kenneth, 145
Hoover, Herbert, 23
Horlick, Gary, 165
Hubbard, Allan, 204
Hungary, 48, 86
Hussein, Arif, 28
Huwart, François, 122

Iceland, 174, 257, 293
Imboden, Nicholas, 144–145, 146, 151
Import substitution, 27, 33, 238
Imports
   and agriculture, 50, 53, 54, 139–140, 141, 187, 188, 198, 214, 230, 231, 255, 257, 272, 285
   and antidumping laws, 114
   and Brazil, 244
   carbon-heavy, 281

   and China, 39, 238, 244, 272
   and creating multilateral institution, 25, 34
   and currency, 289
   and drugs, 106
   and GATT, 26–27, 31
   and globalization, 86
   and India, 112
   and liquor, 168
   from low-income countries, 215, 221
   and manufactured goods, 238, 244, 257, 266
   and national treatment, 25
   and production standards, 44
   and quotas, 242
   and rice, 34, 37, 220
   and safety, 59
   and South Korea, 87
   and SSM, 266, 267, 271
   and steel, 134, 159, 266
   and Tokyo Round, 281
   and trade theory and WTO course, 20–21, 22
   and Uruguay Round, 47–48
Independent (newspaper), 200
India, 13, 44, 67, 182, 212, 279
   and agriculture, 112, 142–143, 148, 149, 186–190, 194, 230, 233, 254, 258, 266, 267
   and antidumping laws, 115
   and bilateral and regional deals, 177, 293
   and dispute settlement, 165
   emerging market in, 206
   and Five Interested Parties, 183, 185, 186, 187, 191, 192, 208, 209, 229
   and G-4 meeting (2007), 243, 245
   and GATT, 27, 29
   increasing influence of, 15
   and information technology, 189–190
   and manufactured goods, 239, 253, 258
   as party to Doha Round's problems, 283–284
   and protectionism, 9, 112
   and tariffs, 39, 86, 111–112, 211, 215
   and trade, 86, 111–112
   and workers, 47
   and WTO meeting in Doha, Qatar (2001), 6, 96, 102, 103, 111–113, 127–129, 130, 152
   and WTO meeting in Geneva, Switzerland (2004), 191, 192, 194, 196
   and WTO ministerial in Cancún, Mexico (2003), 147, 148, 149, 153

and WTO ministerial in Geneva, Switzerland (2008), 262, 265–268, 272, 274, 275, 283
and WTO ministerial in Hong Kong (2005), 219
and WTO's inner circle of power, 13
India's Century (Nath), 186
Indonesia, 36, 39, 174
  and agriculture, 187, 254, 258
  and Asian financial crisis, 136
  and GATT, 27
  and living standards, 42
  and manufactured goods, 258
  and protectionism, 9
  and workers, 44–45
IndyMac Bancorp, 259
Information technology, 38, 189–190, 285, 289
Information Technology Agreement, 38
Ingco, Merlinda, 55, 56
Intellectual property rights
  and AIDS drugs, 106–107, 119, 121
  and Antigua, 169–170
  and bilateral and regional deals, 175, 179
  and developing countries, 88, 104–105, 107, 119
  and foreigners, 105
  and future trade rounds, 288, 290
  and TRIPS, 104, 105, 106, 118–121, 290
  and Uruguay Round, 31, 48, 104, 118, 170, 281
  and WTO, 19, 32, 37, 42, 104, 105, 118–121
International Federation of Pharmaceutical Manufacturers & Associations, 107, 121
International Food Policy Research Institute, 254
International Herald Tribune (newspaper), 191, 274
International Labor Organization, 47
International Monetary Fund (IMF), 18–19, 23, 288, 289
International Trade Organization (ITO), 25, 32
Iraq War, 132
Ireland, 53, 283
Israel, 174
Italy, 52, 114, 279
Ivanov, Sergei, 91

Jackson, John, 31, 33, 35, 158
Jacobs, Stephen, 116

Jacobs, Vuyani, 103–104
Jaitley, Arun, 148, 153
Jamaica, 187
Japan, 49, 107, 179, 182, 220, 226
  and agriculture, 53, 54, 65, 68, 132, 138, 140, 187, 205, 255, 257, 265
  and Asia Pacific Economic Cooperation forum, 37
  and bilateral deals, 177
  and exports, 30, 138
  and foreign technology, 105
  and G-4 meeting (2007), 243
  and G-6 meeting (2006), 229
  and GATT, 26, 29, 30, 182
  industrial juggernaut of, 30
  and liquor taxes, 160
  and Messerlin analysis, 258
  as party to Doha Round's problems, 284
  and Quad, 13, 29, 182, 183
  and rice, 34, 187
  and Singapore issues, 184
  and trade blocs, 24
  and workers, 46
  and World War II, 243
  and WTO Appellate Body, 163, 279
  and WTO meeting in Doha, Qatar (2001), 2, 115, 116, 117, 128
  and WTO meeting in Geneva, Switzerland (2004), 191, 196
  and WTO meeting in Seattle, Washington (1999), 68
  and WTO mini-ministerial in Montreal (2003), 137–138, 140
  and WTO ministerial in Cancún, Mexico (2003), 153
  and WTO ministerial in Geneva, Switzerland (2008), 256, 262, 264, 265, 273
  and WTO's inner circle of power, 13
Japan External Trade Organization, 177
Jara, Alejandro, 116
Jin Zhangfu, 239
Johanns, Mike, 205, 230, 233
Johnson, Allen, 141, 144, 175, 196
Joiner, Ed, 70
Jonquieres, Guy de, 221
Jordan, 175

Kamal, Yousef Hussain, 13, 100, 103, 111, 123, 124, 126, 127, 128, 129, 130
Kantor, Mickey, 33–34, 35
Kaunda, Kenneth, 27

Kawaguchi, Yoriko, 137
Kazakhstan, 254
Keeler, Tim, 242
Kennedy, John F., 26, 65
Kennedy Round, 26
Kenny G, 36
Kenya, 123, 128, 182
*Killer Angels* (book), 133
Kirk, Ron, 287
Klinefelter, Bill, 117
Kraay, Aart, 86
Kumar, Veerendra, 47
Kyoto Protocol, 125

Labor unions, 56, 96, 137, 200
  and race to the bottom, 45–46, 47
  and steel, 134
  and WTO meeting in Seattle, Washington
    (1999), 58, 59, 60, 73, 74, 76
Lacarte, Julio, 23, 24–25, 32, 291
Lafer, Celso, 13, 120, 126
Lampreia, Luiz, 81
Lamy, Pascal, 13
  and agriculture, 94, 139, 140, 143, 193,
    195
  background of, 92–93
  brilliance of, 14
  and Civil War, 133
  and Doha Round, 131, 184, 199, 224, 234,
    241, 247, 249–250, 256, 279, 282, 283
  election as WTO director-general,
    210–211
  and environment, 95
  and Five Interested Parties, 184, 185
  and G-6 meetings (2006), 229, 231,
    232–234
  and GATT, 29
  leaves job as European trade
    commissioner, 199–200, 201–202
  and Messerlin analysis, 258–259
  and Singapore issues, 94–95, 153, 154,
    184, 283
  Spartan diet of, 93–94
  and steel, 134
  and WTO General Council meeting
    (2006), 18
  and WTO green room meeting (2006),
    228–229, 231
  and WTO meeting in Doha, Qatar (2001),
    95, 121–122, 124–125, 126, 127, 130
  and WTO meeting in Geneva, Switzerland
    (2004), 183–184, 193, 195, 196, 197–198

  and WTO meeting in Seattle, Washington
    (1999), 76, 79, 81
  and WTO mini-ministerial in Montreal
    (2003), 139, 140, 141
  and WTO ministerial in Cancún, Mexico
    (2003), 153–154, 155, 156, 283
  and WTO ministerial in Geneva,
    Switzerland (2008), 255, 256, 259, 261,
    262, 263–264, 265, 266, 267, 268, 269,
    270, 271, 272, 273, 274, 275
  and WTO ministerial in Hong Kong
    (2005), 211, 218, 219, 220–221
  and Zoellick, 92–95, 124–125, 199
Larson, Alan, 119, 120
LeaMond, Nancy, 69
Least Developed Country Group, 124
Lehman Brothers, 275
Lesbian Avengers, 72
Lesotho, 293
Liechtenstein, 293
Like Minded Group, 13, 67, 82, 96, 98,
  101
Locke, Gary, 73, 74
Lorentz, Don, 41
*Los Angeles Times*, 6
Love, James, 121
Low, Patrick, 100, 278
Luxembourg, 52

Malaysia, 44, 67
  and bilateral and regional deals, 174, 177
  and living standards, 42
  and tariffs, 258
  and trade, 86
  and WTO meeting in Doha, Qatar (2001),
    96, 98, 102
  and WTO ministerial in Cancún, Mexico
    (2003), 154
Mali, 145, 146, 150, 151
Mandela, Nelson, 105
Mandelson, Peter
  and agriculture, 207–210, 217, 219
  background and private life of, 200–201
  and Doha Round, 242, 283
  and G-4 meeting (2007), 243, 244, 245
  and G-6 meetings (2006), 229–230, 233
  and meeting in Brazil (2006), 223
  and Portman, 225
  replaces Lamy, 200, 201
  and Schwab, 232, 234, 241–242
  and WTO ministerial in Geneva,
    Switzerland (2008), 262, 265, 273

and WTO ministerial in Hong Kong
(2005), 211, 219, 220, 222
and Zoellick, 201–202
Manufactured goods. *See* Doha Round: and
manufactured goods; Trade: and
manufactured goods; particular
countries
Maran, Murasoli, 111–113, 127–129
Mattoo, Aaditya, 285, 286, 287, 289
Mauritania, 253
Mauritius, 211
Mchumo, Ali, 62, 63
Melvin, Doug, 108, 130
Mendel, Mark, 167
Mercantilism, 21, 22, 26, 205, 228, 292
Mercês Almeida, João das, 51
Merck & Company, 119
Mercosur, 174, 252
Merrill Lynch, 249, 275
Messerlin, Patrick, 257–258, 259
Mexico, 30, 174, 276, 281
and NAFTA, 36, 176, 177, 216
and trade, 86, 214, 216, 217
and Uruguay Round, 48
and WTO meeting in Doha, Qatar (2001),
96, 120
and WTO mini-ministerial in Montreal
(2003), 140
and WTO ministerial in Cancún, Mexico
(2003), 150, 153
Milberg, Hayden, 270
Millennium Round, 64, 65
Mohamed, Amina, 123
Moore, Mike, 13
ambition of, 282
and development, 82, 84–85, 88, 282
and Supachai, 144, 150
and WTO election battle, 61–64, 69
and WTO meeting in Doha, Qatar (2001),
3, 6, 84, 100, 101, 103, 110, 111, 122–
123, 124, 125, 126, 127, 128, 129, 213
and WTO meeting in Seattle, Washington
(1999), 69, 75, 79–80, 81
and WTO Reality Check meeting (2001),
96, 97
and WTO Secretariat meeting (2000), 81–82
and WTO's decision-making, 18
Morocco, 61, 175, 176, 291
Most favored nation (MFN) treatment
and creation of multilateral institution, 25
and GATT, 26
and WTO, 11, 19, 38, 158, 174, 178, 289

Mozambique, 212, 217
Multilateral Trade Organization (MTO), 32,
36
*Murder on the Orient Express* (Christie), 282

Nader, Ralph, 58, 121
Nakagawa, Shoichi, 191, 220, 229, 234
NAMA (Non-agricultural market access),
238–239, 241, 243, 244, 245, 251, 252,
256, 257, 263, 264
Namibia, 293
Narayanan, Srinivasan, 129
Nasser, Gamal Abdel, 27
Nath, Kamal, 13, 185–188, 190, 191, 209,
219, 220, 230, 231, 233, 234, 243, 244,
245, 262, 264, 265–268, 283–284
National Association of Manufacturers, 269,
270
National Association of Software and Service
Companies (NASSCOM), 190
National Center for Food and Agricultural
Policy, 55
National Cotton Council, 272
National Economic Council, 204
National Press Club, 95
National treatment, 25, 26, 168
Naval Criminal Investigative Service (NCIS),
4, 5
Nehru, Jawaharlal, 27, 112
Netherlands, 52, 61
*New York Times,* 36, 177, 202, 227
New Zealand, 61–62, 85, 157, 192
and bilateral and regional deals, 177, 293
and Falconer, 249, 250, 251, 257, 264
and WTO Appellate Body, 163
Newfarmer, Richard, 215
Nicaragua, 175, 237
Niemeyer, Matt, 89, 92, 175
Nigeria, 258
Nkate, Jacob, 153, 154, 155
Non-Aligned Movement, 27, 37
Nongovernmental organizations (NGOs), 145
and WTO meeting in Doha, Qatar (2001),
2, 84, 99, 108, 110, 121
and WTO ministerial in Cancún, Mexico
(2003), 154, 156
North American Free Trade Agreement
(NAFTA), 11, 136, 174, 176, 216
and Clinton, 64, 89
and Free Trade Area of the Americas, 179
and North American products, 177
and Summit of the Americas, 36

North Korea, 254
Norway, 53, 174, 257, 293
Nuclear nonproliferation, 278
Nyambe, Joseph, 49, 50

Obama, Barack, 9–10, 279, 287, 294
Office of Management and Budget,
    224–225
Office of the U.S. Trade Representative, 1,
    32, 64, 167, 240
  and Hubbard, 204
  and Jackson, 31
  location of, 97
  and Melvin, 108
  and Portman, 203
  and Schwab, 226
  and Trade Promotion Authority, 136
  and Zoellick, 89, 173, 175
Oglesby, M. B., Jr., 97
O'Leary, Michael, 53
Oman, 291
O'Reilly, Sir Anthony, 53
Oshima, Shotaro, 191
Osorio, Nestor, 48
Oxfam, 3, 145, 198, 206, 208, 262

Pakistan, 44, 67, 77, 182
  and agriculture, 187, 254, 258
  and manufactured goods, 258
  and trade, 6, 86
  and WTO meeting in Doha, Qatar (2001),
    98
Panama, 123, 180, 291
Papovich, Joseph, 2
Paraguay, 174
Parbhoo, Brush, 212
Parbhoo, Ron, 212
Patel, Dipak, 154
Patents and copyrights, 19, 34, 48, 67,
    104–106, 118
Paulson, Henry, 224, 240
Paxton, Kathy, 70
Pérez del Castillo, Carlos, 140
Peru, 18, 175, 180, 227, 254, 291
Peterson, Jim, 195–196, 197
Pettigrew, Pierre, 4, 79, 128
Pfizer Corporation, 119
Pharmaceutical Research and Manufacturers
    of America (PhRMA), 117–118, 119, 120
Philippines, 86, 123, 163, 174, 258, 279
Phillips, Vivian, 71
Phipps, John, 54

Poland, 175
Portman, Rob, 13
  and agriculture, 203, 204–205, 206, 208,
    209, 210, 217
  background of, 202–203
  becomes U.S. trade representative, 202,
    203
  and Bushes, 202, 225, 227
  and meeting in Brazil (2006), 223–224
  and mercantilism, 228
  and Schwab, 226, 227, 229
  selected to head Office of Management
    and Budget, 224–225, 282–283
  and WTO ministerial in Hong Kong
    (2005), 211, 219, 220
Potsdam, Germany
  and G-4 meeting (2007), 243–246, 248,
    250, 278
  and World War II, 243
Poverty, 149
  and agriculture, 49–50, 145, 146, 189
  and trade, 3, 4, 6, 8, 14, 82, 84, 86, 95, 97,
    98, 213–215, 216, 217, 282
  See also World Trade Organization
    (WTO): and poverty
Powell, Colin, 182
Precautionary principle, 59, 95
Preeg, Ernest, 15
Preferential trade agreements (PTAs),
    293–294
Protectionism, 89, 136, 222, 280
  and agriculture, 49–56, 135, 144–145, 188,
    190, 257, 285
  and antidumping laws, 114
  and bilateral and regional deals, 175
  checking, 286, 292
  and Doha talks, 10, 279, 287
  and financial market crash, 8, 277
  and G-20, 9
  and G-77, 112
  and GATT, 30
  and Greens, 82, 96, 125
  and manufactured goods, 239
  and Messerlin analysis, 258
  murky, 290–291
  in 1930s, 7, 23, 24, 286
  and Obama, 9–10
  quasi, 9, 286
  and Schwab, 226
  and SSM, 267
  and workers, 45, 76
  and WTO, 10, 12, 32

*See also* Duties; Quotas; Tariffs; Trade barriers
Public Citizen, 58, 214
Puente, Tito, 36

Quad, 13, 29, 182–183
Quotas
  and agriculture, 51, 54
  and China, 39
  defined, 20
  and G-77, 112
  and GATT, 27, 33
  import, 242
  and India, 112
  and poorest countries, 221
  and textiles, 34, 237–238, 288
  and underwear, 172
  and Uruguay Round, 48

Rafidah Aziz, 153–154
Raging Grannies, 57
Rainforest Action Network, 57
Reagan, Ronald, 30, 88
Reality Check meeting (2001), 96–97
Redrado, Martín, 179–180, 196
Reichert, Dave, 74
Reno, Janet, 73, 166
Reuther, Alan, 45
Rey, Jean-Daniel, 21, 22
Robbins, B. J., 236–237
Rockwell, Keith, 83, 121, 268
Rodriguez, Danubia, 235–237
Rodrik, Dani, 86–88, 238
Rogerson, Evan, 85
Romania, 175
Ross, Dennis, 5
Ruckus Society, 57, 59, 83
Rudd, Kevin, 293, 294
Ruggiero, Renato, 60, 63
Russia, 9, 32, 91, 232, 254

Salon International de l'Agriculture, 53
Sangare, Mody, 145
Sara Lee Branded Apparel, 236
Saunders, Sir Ronald, 167
Schell, Paul, 71, 74, 77, 80
Schwab, Susan, 13
  background and personal life of, 225–227
  becomes U.S. trade representative, 225, 227, 229
  and Doha Round, 225, 227–228, 243, 247, 248, 251, 283

  and G-4 meeting (2007), 243, 244, 245
  and G-6 meetings (2006), 229, 230, 231–232, 233, 234
  and Mandelson, 232, 234, 241–242
  visit to China of (2008), 284
  and WTO ministerial in Geneva, Switzerland (2008), 262, 263, 264, 265, 266, 267, 268, 270–271, 273, 274, 275
Seattle, Washington. *See* World Trade Organization (WTO): meeting in Seattle, Washington (1999)
*Seattle Post-Intelligencer* (newspaper), 75, 76
Seattle Round, 64, 65
*Seattle Times* (newspaper), 73, 77
Secret Service, 70, 74, 97, 244
Sectoral deals, 253, 270, 272, 280
Seixas Corrêa, Luiz Felipe de, 142–143
Sen, Amartya, 189
Senegal, 253
"Sensitive products," 187, 198, 208, 210, 216, 227, 230, 233, 242, 251, 257, 265
September 11, 2001, terrorist attacks, 1, 3, 4, 12, 97–99, 108, 113, 128, 131, 282
Serbia, 254
Serra, José, 120
Shark, David, 274
Shirzad, Faryar, 88
Short, Clare, 65
Sidley Austin (law firm), 160, 167
Simba, Iddi, 96
Singapore, 2, 33, 78, 81, 147, 155
  and bilateral and regional deals, 174, 175, 177, 291, 293
  and living standards, 42
  as possible alternative meeting site to Doha, Qatar, 99–100
  WTO meeting in (1996), 65, 99
  WTO meeting in (2001), 100
  Zoellick stop in (2004), 182
Singapore issues, 65–66, 67, 68, 75, 79, 94–95, 96, 102, 122, 124, 125, 126, 127, 128, 129, 152–153, 153–155, 156, 184, 283
Singapore-Jordan free-trade agreement, 11
Singh, Arjan, 188, 189
Singh, Manmohan, 265
Smith, Adam, 20–21, 242, 292
Smith, Wes, 239–240
Smoot-Hawley Tariff Act, 7, 23–24, 276
Smoot-Hawleyism, 10
Solnit, David, 59–60

South Africa, 81, 126, 150, 182, 212, 293
  and agriculture, 140, 143, 258
  and AIDS, 103–104, 105–107
  and antidumping laws, 115
  and dispute settlement, 279
  increasing influence of, 15
  and manufactured goods, 239, 273
South Korea, 32
  and agriculture, 53, 132, 187, 219–220
  and Asia Pacific Economic Cooperation
    forum, 37
  and Asian financial crisis, 136
  and bilateral deals, 177, 291, 293
  and foreign technology, 105
  and living standards, 42
  and manufactured goods, 258
  and rice, 34, 187, 220
  and Singapore issues, 155, 184
  and trade, 84, 87, 88
  and workers, 46
  and WTO meeting in Doha, Qatar (2001),
    115, 116, 117
Southern African Customs Union, 252, 293
Soviet Union, 25, 27, 112, 243, 250
"Special products" (staple foods), 187–188,
  191, 198, 216, 227, 230, 233, 257, 266,
  267, 272
Sri Lanka, 18, 45
SSM (special safeguard mechanism),
  266–267, 270, 271, 273–274, 275, 279
Stalin, Joseph, 243
Stallman, Bob, 269–270
Stamper, Norm, 71, 74, 77
STARC Naked, 72
Steel, 10, 134, 135, 137, 159, 164, 168, 266
Stephenson, Donald, 250–252, 256, 257,
  264
Stock market decline, 249, 255, 259, 276
Stoler, Andrew, 62, 63, 64, 80, 123, 126
Subramanian, Arvind, 255, 285, 286, 287,
  289
Subsidies on Upland Cotton case, 158,
  160–162, 163, 165, 167, 169, 170–171
Sukarno, 27
Summit of the Americas, 36–37
Sumner, Daniel, 161–162
Sun Tzu, 182
Supachai Panitchpakdi, 13, 61, 62–64, 69,
  199
  and Doha Round, 180, 211, 284
  and WTO meeting in Geneva, Switzerland
    (2004), 191, 192

and WTO ministerial in Cancún, Mexico
  (2003), 144, 150–151, 152, 153, 284
Surin Pitsuwan, 63–64
Sutherland, Peter, 33, 35
Suzuki, Yoichi, 116
Swaziland, 293
Switzerland, 53, 107, 118, 144–145, 182,
  187, 196, 219, 247, 257, 293

Taiwan, 2, 32, 37, 42, 46, 252, 293
Tanzania, 62, 67, 96
Tariffs, 9, 43, 99, 104
  and agriculture, 51, 52, 54, 55–56, 132,
    134, 140, 143, 183, 186–188, 193, 196,
    198, 204, 205, 206, 208, 209–210, 216,
    217, 230, 231, 233, 239, 245, 249, 254,
    255, 257, 258, 266, 267, 269, 270, 271,
    272, 283
  and Antigua, 169–170, 290
  and Argentina, 33, 39
  and bilateral and regional deals, 174, 175,
    178
  binding, 25, 206, 258
  and Brazil, 33, 39, 171, 211, 290
  and China, 39, 216, 271
  and course on WTO, 20, 22
  and creating multilateral institution, 25
  cuts in, 8, 15, 26, 33, 39, 42, 47, 55–56, 86,
    132, 134, 140, 143, 175, 186–187, 188,
    193, 196, 198, 204, 205, 206, 208,
    209–210, 213, 215, 216, 217, 224, 227,
    230, 233, 238, 239, 241, 242, 244, 245,
    252, 253, 256–257, 258–259, 269, 272,
    280, 287, 288
  defined, 20
  and environment, greenhouse gases, and
    carbon, 11–12, 125, 281, 287, 290
  and G-77, 112
  and GATT, 26, 27, 29, 30, 33
  and India, 39, 86, 111–112, 211, 215
  and information technology, 38
  and Kantor and Brittan's negotiations in
    Geneva (1993), 34
  and manufactured and industrial goods,
    197, 211, 216, 238, 239, 244, 245,
    252, 253, 257, 258, 265, 266, 270,
    272, 288
  and Messerlin analysis, 258
  and most favored nation treatment, 25
  and poorest countries, 221
  and Smoot-Hawley, 7, 23–24
  and steel, 10, 134, 135, 137, 159, 164

and Uruguay Round, 47–48, 49, 170
and Zambia, 213
Teamsters, 59
Teixeira, Paulo, 121
Telecommunications, 19, 38, 39, 226
*Termites in the Trading System* (Bhagwati), 293
Terrorism, 278
  and impoverished countries, 12
  and trade, 97–98
  war against, 134
  and WTO meeting in Doha, Qatar (2001), 1–2, 4–5, 6, 98, 99, 100, 107, 108, 110, 123
  *See also* September 11, 2001, terrorist attacks
Textiles. *See* General Agreement on Tariffs and Trade (GATT): and agriculture and textiles; World Trade Organization (WTO): and textiles
Thailand, 44, 61, 86, 123, 143
  and AIDS drugs, 106
  and bilateral and regional deals, 174, 175, 177
  and dispute settlement, 165
  and living standards, 42
  and manufactured goods, 258
Third World Network, 120
Thurow, Lester, 30
Tokyo Round, 3, 26, 34, 65, 136, 281, 288, 289
*Toronto Globe and Mail* (newspaper), 293
Trade
  and agriculture, 4, 6, 49–56, 65, 68, 78, 79, 94, 102, 122, 126, 132, 134–135, 139, 141–144, 145–147, 148, 149, 150–152, 156, 157–158, 160–162, 171, 173, 177, 187, 193–194, 196, 204–210, 216, 217, 222, 229–231, 232–234, 242–243, 245, 249, 250, 254–255, 258, 269–270
  aid for, 217, 221
  annual percentage rise in, 246
  benefits of, 7, 20–21, 42, 84, 85–86, 87, 98, 136, 203, 213–214, 215, 216, 217, 288
  bilateral and regional deals, 11, 90, 174–180, 181, 198, 252, 285, 286, 291, 292, 293, 294
  blocs, 11, 24, 177, 252
  and "concentric circle" system, 182, 192
  and Congress, 91, 135–137, 176, 224, 248, 269
  and crisis, 8, 295

disputes, 11, 12, 14, 25, 37, 94, 157–172, 279, 280–281, 289, 292
  and environment, 42–43, 44, 45, 46, 47, 58, 136, 137
  facilitation, 65, 66, 95, 127, 153, 154, 184, 285
  and fast track, 135, 136
  future of rounds, 287–291, 294, 295
  and GATT, 26, 30, 31, 33
  and globalization, 7, 86, 87
  and Great Depression, 24
  importance of survival of rules-based system, 286
  and manufactured goods, 21, 26, 27, 29, 34, 52, 55, 102, 132, 214, 216, 224, 235–241, 244, 245, 252, 253, 257, 258, 265, 266, 268, 270, 273
  and poverty, 3, 4, 6, 8, 14, 82, 84, 86, 95, 97, 98, 213–215, 216, 217, 282
  preferences, 216
  and "rise of the rest," 14–15
  skepticism of benefits of free, 86–88, 214, 215–216, 265
  and "spaghetti bowl," 177–178, 180, 293
  and spilled blood in negotiations, 195
  and terrorism, 97–98
  U.N. conference on (1947–1948), 23
  and workers, 45–47, 62, 75–76, 77–78, 82, 136, 137
  *See also* Bush, George W.: and trade; Trade barriers; United States: and free trade; World Trade Organization (WTO); Zoellick, Robert: desire for trade deals; particular trade agreements
Trade Act (1988), 30
Trade barriers, 11, 136
  and agriculture, 51, 52, 54, 94, 139, 141, 205, 206, 230, 242, 267, 285, 290
  and bilateral and regional deals, 174, 176, 291, 292, 293
  costs of, 20
  and financial market crash, 8, 9, 277
  lowering, 15, 22, 31, 42, 207, 228, 245, 252, 283, 290, 291, 292
  lowering: and developing countries, 33, 85, 87, 88, 98–99, 141–142, 205, 206, 217, 238, 242, 257, 265, 273
  lowering: and GATT, 26, 28
  lowering: and World Bank research, 215, 216, 217, 230
  and manufactured goods, 252, 265, 266
  and Messerlin analysis, 258

Trade barriers (*continued*)
most common, 20
and NAFTA, 36
and poverty, 215
pressures for rise in, 280
and Smoot-Hawley, 23, 24
and Uruguay Round, 49
*See also* Protectionism; specific types of
trade barriers
Trade Promotion Authority legislation,
135–137, 224, 229, 235, 241, 248
Trade-Related Aspects of Intellectual
Property Rights (TRIPS), 104, 105, 106,
107, 118–121, 122, 128, 129, 144, 290
*Traders in a Brave New World* (Preeg), 15
Trans-Pacific Economic Partnership, 293
Trilateral Commission, 10
Trojan, Carlo, 102
Truman, Harry, 243, 244
Truss, Warren, 134, 246
Turkey, 114, 238, 254
Turtles, sea, 43–44, 58, 72
Tyson, Laura D'Andrea, 30–31

Ukraine, 254
United Auto Workers, 45
United Farm Workers, 59
United Kingdom, 24
United Nations, 10, 149, 204
Conference on Trade and Development
(1999), 49
Conference on Trade and Employment
(1947–1948), 23, 25
United States
and agriculture, 53–55, 65, 68, 78, 79, 94,
102, 134–135, 137, 139–140, 141–144,
145, 146, 148, 151–152, 156, 157–158,
160–162, 170–171, 173, 181, 185, 187,
190, 194, 195, 203, 204–210, 228,
229–231, 233, 234, 242–243, 245, 248,
251, 254, 257, 263, 265, 268, 269–270,
272, 277, 282, 283, 287
and China, 38–39
and climate change, 131–132
and dispute settlement, 157–158, 160–162,
165–171, 172, 279, 290
and dumping complaints, 115
and environment, 125
and Five Interested Parties, 183, 191, 192,
208, 209, 229
and free trade, 10, 90, 91, 134, 174, 175,
176–177, 178–180, 204, 226, 228, 291, 292
and GATT, 26–27, 29, 30, 182
and manufactured goods, 9, 26, 27, 29, 45,
239, 240, 244, 253, 257, 268, 269, 270,
291
as party to Doha Round's problems,
282–283
and power in WTO, 13, 18, 19, 20, 147
and Quad, 13, 29, 182, 183
size of economy of, 292
trade deficit of, 30, 136, 240
and WTO's creation, 32
*See also* Exports: U.S.
United Steelworkers, 117
Uruguay, 23, 163, 174, 211
Uruguay Round, 3, 15, 33, 65, 89, 102, 109,
256, 282, 288
adjustments, 75
and agriculture, 55–56, 81, 140, 209
and Clinton, 64
congressional approval of, 136
and developing countries, 67, 68
and dispute settlement, 37
and intellectual property rights, 31, 48,
104, 118, 170, 281
and Kantor and Brittan's negotiations in
Geneva (1993), 34, 35
launching of, 31
length of, 278
ratification of, 37
and services, 167
text of, 47–49
and textiles, 237
and WTO meeting in Doha, Qatar (2001),
96, 129
and WTO's creation, 31, 32

Vaile, Mark, 154, 184, 206, 208, 209
Vajpayee, Atal Bihari, 128
Valenti, Jack, 35
Vargo, Frank, 269, 270
Veneman, Ann, 151
Venezuela, 273, 294
Veroneau, John, 90, 167
Vietnam, 46, 85, 254
Vietnam War, 31, 66
Villepin, Dominique de, 207, 222

*Wall Street Journal*, 121, 145, 199
Wallach, Lori, 58–59, 214
Ward, Christopher, 157–158, 163
Wasescha, Luzius, 191
Washington Mutual, 275

*Washington Post,* 54, 59, 88, 95, 97, 121, 239, 241
Wasserman, Lew, 35
*The Wealth of Nations* (Smith), 20–21
West Germany, 52
*Whose Trade Organization?* (Wallach), 58–59
Williamson, Steve, 73
Winslow, Ed, 5
Winters, Alan, 215
Wolf, Martin, 42
Workers
  and antisweatshop movement, 45
  and Indonesia, 44–45
  and trade, 45–47, 62
  and WTO meeting in Seattle, Washington (1999), 68, 75–76, 77–78, 82
  *See also* Labor unions
World Bank, 14, 285
  and agriculture, 55, 151, 188, 213, 214, 230
  analysis of tariffs on imported goods, 257
  bureaucracy of, 18
  creation of, 23
  and Doha Round, 15, 215, 271, 282
  and Dollar, 85, 86, 87, 88
  and Honduras, 235
  and power, 18–19
  and trade, 4, 87, 98–99, 213
  and trade: completely free, 213–217
  and TRIPS, 104
  and Uruguay Round, 48
  and weighted voting, 288–289
World Economic Forum, 247–248
World Trade Organization (WTO)
  and agriculture, 55, 65, 68, 75, 78, 79, 80–81, 94, 102, 122, 124–125, 126, 132, 134–135, 138, 139–140, 141–144, 146, 147, 150–152, 155, 156, 157–158, 160–162, 183, 191, 192, 193–194, 195–196, 198, 204–210, 217, 218–220, 241, 242–243, 245, 249, 250, 251, 263, 265, 266, 267, 269–270, 272
  Appellate Body, 37, 159, 162, 163–164, 168, 279, 280, 290
  and "boxes," 142, 148, 205, 206, 243
  China's joining, 38–39, 216, 271–272
  and climate change, 11–12, 14, 281, 286, 290
  compared to GATT, 37
  and competition, 65, 66, 67, 95, 102, 127, 153, 154, 184

and consensus, 4, 13, 15, 18, 19, 21, 22, 62, 63, 75, 78–79, 101, 103, 113, 128–129, 138, 152, 288–289
courses on, 19–22
creation of, 16, 31–36
critics of, 10, 42, 56, 57–60, 103, 164, 214
and development, 4, 6, 18, 82, 84–85, 95, 96, 101, 110, 129–130, 153, 156, 181, 182, 213, 265, 282, 286
and dispute settlement, 11, 31, 32, 37, 103, 157–172, 279, 280–281, 286, 289, 290
and Doha Round (*see* Doha Round)
and environment, 42–43, 43–44, 58, 59, 78, 82, 95, 102, 124, 125–126, 290
and food safety, 19, 43, 58, 59, 125
Friends of the Chair, 75
in future, 278, 280, 281, 284–285, 286, 287, 288–291, 294
General Council meetings, 17–18, 67, 96–97, 100–101, 123, 146, 197, 274
Geneva headquarters, 2, 17–18, 19, 167, 210
and government procurement, 65, 66, 69, 95, 127, 153, 154, 184
importance for stability of global economy and as central rule-setter for international trade, 10, 11, 12, 286
inner circle of power, 13
and investment, 65–66, 67, 95, 96, 102, 126, 127, 153, 184
and manufactured goods (*see* Doha Round: and manufactured goods; Trade: and manufactured goods)
meeting in Doha, Qatar (2001), 1–6, 8, 10, 12, 13, 58, 83–84, 95, 96, 98, 99–103, 104, 107–108, 109–130, 131, 132, 138, 144, 152, 180, 213
meeting in Geneva, Switzerland (2004), 12, 182, 183–184, 190–198, 278
meeting in Potsdam, Germany (2007), 13, 243–246, 248, 250, 278
meeting in Seattle, Washington (1999), 1, 4, 12, 41, 56, 57–60, 64–82, 83, 84, 89, 95, 101, 110, 115, 122, 130, 180, 282
meeting in Singapore (1996), 65, 99
meeting of world leaders in Geneva, Switzerland (1998), 41, 42, 43, 70
as member-driven, 18
mini-ministerial in Montreal (2003), 137–141

World Trade Organization (WTO)
(*continued*)
ministerial in Cancún, Mexico (2003), 12,
133, 138, 144, 147–156, 162, 173, 174,
180, 181, 182, 191, 197, 198, 278, 282,
283, 284
ministerial in Geneva, Switzerland (2008),
13, 255–259, 261–275, 277, 278, 279,
283, 287, 293
ministerial in Hong Kong (2005), 12–13,
203–204, 208, 210, 211, 213, 217–222,
223, 224, 227, 278
and multinational corporations, 42, 58, 96,
291
and negotiations, 3, 14, 21–22, 28, 61, 69,
102, 103, 156, 288
and nondiscrimination, 37
number of member countries, 11
and point-scoring, 218, 262
and poverty, 3, 4, 8, 14, 58, 82, 84, 97,
213–214, 215, 216, 257, 265, 282
power of, 18–19, 159
rancor over election battle in, 60–64, 79
and "rise of the rest," 14–15
and rule waivers, 123
Secretariat, 18, 81, 85, 128, 150, 163, 192,
210, 218, 242, 264, 275
and services, 19, 32, 37, 38, 81, 102, 132,
167, 168, 175, 215, 224, 256, 285, 287
and textiles, 22, 33, 34, 48, 67, 159, 171,
221, 236, 237–238
tribunals, 10, 11, 19, 39, 43, 59, 157, 164,
171, 205, 289, 290
and workers, 46, 47, 68, 75–76, 77–78, 79,
82, 96
World War I, 288
World War II, 3, 11, 23, 46, 243

Yemen, 253
Yeo, George, 78, 81, 99, 147, 155
Yerxa, Rufus, 32

Zahran, Mounir, 67
Zakaria, Fareed, 14
Zambia, 154
and agriculture, 49, 51, 214, 254
and GATT, 27
and trade, 212–213, 214, 221

Zedillo, Ernesto, 281
Zhu Rongji, 38–39
Zimbabwe, 103, 212
Zoellick, Robert, 13, 225, 229
and agriculture, 94, 134, 135, 139, 143,
181, 183, 194, 195–196, 228
and AIDS drugs, 106–107
background and selection as U.S. trade
representative, 88–89, 92–93
becomes deputy secretary of state, 202
brilliance of, 14
and Civil War, 133
compared to Portman, 203
and Congress, 90–91
desire for trade deals, 89–90, 91,
173–174, 175–176, 178, 180, 181, 291,
292, 294
and dispute settlement, 167
and Doha Round, 131, 180–182, 190, 199,
228, 250, 282, 292
and Five Interested Parties, 183, 184, 185
and Free Trade Area of the Americas,
179–180
and Lamy, 92–95, 124–125, 199
and Mandelson, 201–202
and presidential debate preparation, 202
and Quad, 183
relations with Bush, 91–92
and resuming WTO negotiations (2004),
182
round-the-world trip of (2004), 182
and September 11, 97–98
and steel, 134, 135
and subordinates, 92
and Trade Promotion Authority, 135, 137
work habits of, 90
and WTO meeting in Doha, Qatar (2001),
1, 4, 5–6, 95, 99, 100, 102, 113, 115, 116,
117, 119, 120, 121, 124–125, 127, 130,
213
and WTO meeting in Geneva, Switzerland
(2004), 182, 183, 190, 191, 194, 195–196,
197, 278
and WTO mini-ministerial in Montreal
(2003), 137–138, 139, 140, 141
and WTO ministerial in Cancún, Mexico
(2003), 147–148, 151–152, 154, 155–156,
173, 174, 283

*Credit: The Brookings Institution*

Paul Blustein has written about economic issues for more than thirty years, most recently as journalist in residence in the Global Economy and Development Program at the Brookings Institution. For most of his career he reported for *The Washington Post* and *The Wall Street Journal*. A graduate of the University of Wisconsin and Oxford University, where he was a Rhodes Scholar, he has won several prizes for his work, including business journalism's most prestigious, the Gerald Loeb Award.

PublicAffairs is a publishing house founded in 1997. It is a tribute to the standards, values, and flair of three persons who have served as mentors to countless reporters, writers, editors, and book people of all kinds, including me.

I.F. STONE, proprietor of *I. F. Stone's Weekly*, combined a commitment to the First Amendment with entrepreneurial zeal and reporting skill and became one of the great independent journalists in American history. At the age of eighty, Izzy published *The Trial of Socrates*, which was a national bestseller. He wrote the book after he taught himself ancient Greek.

BENJAMIN C. BRADLEE was for nearly thirty years the charismatic editorial leader of *The Washington Post*. It was Ben who gave the *Post* the range and courage to pursue such historic issues as Watergate. He supported his reporters with a tenacity that made them fearless and it is no accident that so many became authors of influential, best-selling books.

ROBERT L. BERNSTEIN, the chief executive of Random House for more than a quarter century, guided one of the nation's premier publishing houses. Bob was personally responsible for many books of political dissent and argument that challenged tyranny around the globe. He is also the founder and longtime chair of Human Rights Watch, one of the most respected human rights organizations in the world.

· · ·

For fifty years, the banner of Public Affairs Press was carried by its owner Morris B. Schnapper, who published Gandhi, Nasser, Toynbee, Truman, and about 1,500 other authors. In 1983, Schnapper was described by *The Washington Post* as "a redoubtable gadfly." His legacy will endure in the books to come.

Peter Osnos, *Founder and Editor-at-Large*